THE BOOK ®

D0519177

Austin Montego
Service and Repair Manual

John S Mead

(1066-272-5Y10)

Models covered

Austin (Rover) Montego 1.3 & 1.6 litre models with petrol engines
Saloon and Estate, including special/limited editions
1275 cc & 1598 cc

Does not cover 2.0 litre petrol or Diesel engine models

WITHDRAWN

Printed by **J H Haynes & Co Ltd, Sparkford, Nr Yeovil, Somerset BA22 7JJ, England**

Haynes Publishing
Sparkford, Nr Yeovil, Somerset BA22 7JJ, England

Haynes North America, Inc
861 Lawrence Drive, Newbury Park, California 91320, USA

Editions Haynes S.A.
Tour Aurore - La Défense 2, 18 Place des Reflets,
92975 PARIS LA DEFENSE Cedex, France

Haynes Publishing Nordiska AB
Box 1504, 751 45 UPPSALA, Sweden

* 000136041 *

Contents

Contents

Introduction to the Austin Montego

Introduced in Spring 1984, the Montego has many design features of its sister car the Maestro, both being conceived and developed as members of a fully integrated range of medium-sector vehicles.

1.3 litre versions are powered by the proven A+ series overhead valve engine used in the Metro and Maestro range. The 1.6 litre S series engine is an all-new belt-driven overhead camshaft unit, used for the first time in Montego models. Also available is a 2.0 litre version which is the subject of a separate publication.

All models are available with 4- or 5-speed manual gearboxes with a fully automatic transmission being offered as an option on 1.6 litre versions.

The Montego range features the now almost universal medium saloon configuration of front-wheel-drive, independent front/semi-independent rear suspension and servo-assisted self-adjusting brakes to give precise roadholding and smooth ride characteristics.

A computer-controlled engine management system, together with 12 000 mile service intervals, make this a very economical and attractive package which should prove highly successful in a very competitive sector of the market.

Note: *Frequent oil and filter changes are good for the engine. We recommend changing the oil at the mileage specified in Routine maintenance.*

BL and BL Cars Limited are now known as the Rover Group (previously Austin Rover Group). All instances in which we recommend owners seek the advice of a BL dealer should now, of course, be taken to mean seek the advice of a Rover Group dealer.

Acknowledgements

Thanks are due to Champion Spark Plug who supplied the illustrations showing spark plug conditions. Thanks are also due to BL Cars Limited for the supply of technical information and to Unipart for their assistance. Sykes-Pickavant Limited provided some of the workshop tools. Special thanks are due to all those people at Sparkford who helped in the production of this manual.

We take great pride in the accuracy of information given in this manual, but vehicle manufacturers make alterations and design changes during the production run of a particular vehicle of which they do not inform us. No liability can be accepted by the authors or publishers for loss, damage or injury caused by any errors in, or omissions from, the information given.

1.6 litre Austin Montego

Working on your car can be dangerous. This page shows just some of the potential risks and hazards, with the aim of creating a safety-conscious attitude.

General hazards

Scalding

• Don't remove the radiator or expansion tank cap while the engine is hot.
• Engine oil, automatic transmission fluid or power steering fluid may also be dangerously hot if the engine has recently been running.

Burning

• Beware of burns from the exhaust system and from any part of the engine. Brake discs and drums can also be extremely hot immediately after use.

Crushing

• When working under or near a raised vehicle, always supplement the jack with axle stands, or use drive-on ramps. *Never venture under a car which is only supported by a jack.*
• Take care if loosening or tightening high-torque nuts when the vehicle is on stands. Initial loosening and final tightening should be done with the wheels on the ground.

Fire

• Fuel is highly flammable; fuel vapour is explosive.
• Don't let fuel spill onto a hot engine.
• Do not smoke or allow naked lights (including pilot lights) anywhere near a vehicle being worked on. Also beware of creating sparks (electrically or by use of tools).
• Fuel vapour is heavier than air, so don't work on the fuel system with the vehicle over an inspection pit.
• Another cause of fire is an electrical overload or short-circuit. Take care when repairing or modifying the vehicle wiring.
• Keep a fire extinguisher handy, of a type suitable for use on fuel and electrical fires.

Electric shock

• Ignition HT voltage can be dangerous, especially to people with heart problems or a pacemaker. Don't work on or near the ignition system with the engine running or the ignition switched on.

• Mains voltage is also dangerous. Make sure that any mains-operated equipment is correctly earthed. Mains power points should be protected by a residual current device (RCD) circuit breaker.

Fume or gas intoxication

• Exhaust fumes are poisonous; they often contain carbon monoxide, which is rapidly fatal if inhaled. Never run the engine in a confined space such as a garage with the doors shut.
• Fuel vapour is also poisonous, as are the vapours from some cleaning solvents and paint thinners.

Poisonous or irritant substances

• Avoid skin contact with battery acid and with any fuel, fluid or lubricant, especially antifreeze, brake hydraulic fluid and Diesel fuel. Don't syphon them by mouth. If such a substance is swallowed or gets into the eyes, seek medical advice.
• Prolonged contact with used engine oil can cause skin cancer. Wear gloves or use a barrier cream if necessary. Change out of oil-soaked clothes and do not keep oily rags in your pocket.
• Air conditioning refrigerant forms a poisonous gas if exposed to a naked flame (including a cigarette). It can also cause skin burns on contact.

Asbestos

• Asbestos dust can cause cancer if inhaled or swallowed. Asbestos may be found in gaskets and in brake and clutch linings. When dealing with such components it is safest to assume that they contain asbestos.

Special hazards

Hydrofluoric acid

• This extremely corrosive acid is formed when certain types of synthetic rubber, found in some O-rings, oil seals, fuel hoses etc, are exposed to temperatures above 400°C. The rubber changes into a charred or sticky substance containing the acid. *Once formed, the acid remains dangerous for years. If it gets onto the skin, it may be necessary to amputate the limb concerned.*
• When dealing with a vehicle which has suffered a fire, or with components salvaged from such a vehicle, wear protective gloves and discard them after use.

The battery

• Batteries contain sulphuric acid, which attacks clothing, eyes and skin. Take care when topping-up or carrying the battery.
• The hydrogen gas given off by the battery is highly explosive. Never cause a spark or allow a naked light nearby. Be careful when connecting and disconnecting battery chargers or jump leads.

Air bags

• Air bags can cause injury if they go off accidentally. Take care when removing the steering wheel and/or facia. Special storage instructions may apply.

Diesel injection equipment

• Diesel injection pumps supply fuel at very high pressure. Take care when working on the fuel injectors and fuel pipes.

⚠ *Warning: Never expose the hands, face or any other part of the body to injector spray; the fuel can penetrate the skin with potentially fatal results.*

Remember...

DO

• Do use eye protection when using power tools, and when working under the vehicle.

• Do wear gloves or use barrier cream to protect your hands when necessary.

• Do get someone to check periodically that all is well when working alone on the vehicle.

• Do keep loose clothing and long hair well out of the way of moving mechanical parts.

• Do remove rings, wristwatch etc, before working on the vehicle – especially the electrical system.

• Do ensure that any lifting or jacking equipment has a safe working load rating adequate for the job.

DON'T

• Don't attempt to lift a heavy component which may be beyond your capability – get assistance.

• Don't rush to finish a job, or take unverified short cuts.

• Don't use ill-fitting tools which may slip and cause injury.

• Don't leave tools or parts lying around where someone can trip over them. Mop up oil and fuel spills at once.

• Don't allow children or pets to play in or near a vehicle being worked on.

For information applicable to later models, see Supplement at end of manual

Dimensions

Turning circle (between kerbs):
  Saloon .... 34 ft 4 in (10.46 m)
  Estate .... 34 ft 6 m (10.52 m)
Wheelbase .... 101.5 in (2578 mm)
Overall length .... 176 in (4470 mm)
Overall width (excluding mirrors) .... 67.3 m (1710 mm)
Overall height:
  Saloon .... 55.2 in (1402 mm)
  Estate .. .. 57.0 in (1445 mm)
Ground clearance (nominal) .... 6.5 in (165 mm)
Track:
  Front .... 57.7 in (1465 mm)
  Rear .... 56.7 in (1439 mm)

Weights

Kerb weight:	Saloon	Estate
1.3	2140 lb (970 kg)	
1.6	2170 lb (985 kg)	2315 lb (1050 kg)
1.6 L	2250 lb (1020 kg)	2370 lb (1075 kg)
1.6 HL	2260 lb (1025 kg)	2395 lb (1085 kg)
1.6 L automatic	2290 lb (1040 kg)	2410 lb (1095 kg)
1.6 HL automatic	2300 lb (1045 kg)	2435 lb (1105 kg)
Maximum roof rack weight (distributed)	155 lb (70 kg)	as Saloon
Towing hitch downward load	75 to 100 lb (35 to 45 kg)	as Saloon

Capacities

Engine oil (refill with filter change):
  1.3 litre models .... 5 pt (2.8 litres)
  1.6 litre models .... 6.75 pt (3.8 litres)
Manual gearbox refill:
  4-speed .... 2.75 pt (1.6 litres)
  5-speed .... 3.5 pt (2.0 litres)
Automatic transmission:
  Drain and refill .... 4 pt (2.3 litres)
  Total capacity .... 10.5 pt (6.0 litres)
  Final drive unit .... 1.25 pt (0.71 litres)
Cooling system:
  1.3 litre models .... 11.6 pt (6.6 litres)
  1.6 litre models .... 15.0 pt (8.5 litres)
Fuel tank .... 11.0 gal (50 litres)
Fuel octane rating (all models) .... 97 RON (4-star)

Jump starting

HAYNES HiNT

Jump starting will get you out of trouble, but you must correct whatever made the battery go flat in the first place. There are three possibilities:

1 *The battery has been drained by repeated attempts to start, or by leaving the lights on.*

2 *The charging system is not working properly (alternator drivebelt slack or broken, alternator wiring fault or alternator itself faulty).*

3 *The battery itself is at fault (electrolyte low, or battery worn out).*

When jump-starting a car using a booster battery, observe the following precautions:

✔ Before connecting the booster battery, make sure that the ignition is switched off.

✔ Ensure that all electrical equipment (lights, heater, wipers, etc) is switched off.

✔ Make sure that the booster battery is the same voltage as the discharged one in the vehicle.

✔ If the battery is being jump-started from the battery in another vehicle, the two vehcles MUST NOT TOUCH each other.

✔ Make sure that the transmission is in neutral (or PARK, in the case of automatic transmission).

1 Connect one end of the red jump lead to the positive (+) terminal of the flat battery

2 Connect the other end of the red lead to the positive (+) terminal of the booster battery.

3 Connect one end of the black jump lead to the negative (-) terminal of the booster battery

4 Connect the other end of the black jump lead to a bolt or bracket on the engine block, well away from the battery, on the vehicle to be started.

5 Make sure that the jump leads will not come into contact with the fan, drive-belts or other moving parts of the engine.

6 Start the engine using the booster battery, then with the engine running at idle speed, disconnect the jump leads in the reverse order of connection.

Identifying leaks

Puddles on the garage floor or drive, or obvious wetness under the bonnet or underneath the car, suggest a leak that needs investigating. It can sometimes be difficult to decide where the leak is coming from, especially if the engine bay is very dirty already. Leaking oil or fluid can also be blown rearwards by the passage of air under the car, giving a false impression of where the problem lies.

 Warning: Most automotive oils and fluids are poisonous. Wash them off skin, and change out of contaminated clothing, without delay.

 The smell of a fluid leaking from the car may provide a clue to what's leaking. Some fluids are distinctively coloured. It may help to clean the car carefully and to park it over some clean paper overnight as an aid to locating the source of the leak.
Remember that some leaks may only occur while the engine is running.

Sump oil

Engine oil may leak from the drain plug...

Oil from filter

...or from the base of the oil filter.

Gearbox oil

Gearbox oil can leak from the seals at the inboard ends of the driveshafts.

Antifreeze

Leaking antifreeze often leaves a crystalline deposit like this.

Brake fluid

A leak occurring at a wheel is almost certainly brake fluid.

Power steering fluid

Power steering fluid may leak from the pipe connectors on the steering rack.

Jacking, towing and wheel changing

To change a roadwheel, remove the spare wheel and tool kit from the well in the rear compartment. Apply the handbrake and chock the wheel diagonally opposite the one to be changed. Make sure that the car is located on firm level ground. Lever off the wheel trim (photo) and slightly loosen the wheel nuts with the spanner provided. Position the jack under the nearest jacking point to the wheel being removed. Using the handle provided, raise the jack until the wheel is free of the ground. Unscrew the wheel nuts and remove the wheel.

Fit the spare wheel on the studs, then fit and tighten the wheel nuts with their tapered ends towards the wheel. Lower the jack, then finally tighten the wheel nuts and refit the wheel. Remove the chock, and refit the wheel and tool kit in the rear compartment.

When jacking up the car with a trolley jack, position the head of the jack under the jacking bracket/towing hook in the centre of the front crossmember (position 1 in the illustration) (photo) to raise both front wheels.

To raise both rear wheels, position the jack head under the rear jacking bracket towing hook (position 2 in the illustration) (photo).

To raise one side of the car at the front or rear, place the jack head between the front or rear jacking points. In all cases make sure the handbrake is firmly applied and the wheels chocked before raising the car. Always position axle stands or suitable supports under a structural member, such as a chassis member or crossmember, to support the car securely when it is raised.

The car may be towed, or tow another vehicle, using the front or rear jacking bracket/towing hooks.

If automatic transmission is fitted the vehicle should only be towed at slow speed for a short distance. If a greater distance must be covered or if there is the possibility of any fault in the transmission, the car must be towed with the front wheels lifted.

Wheel changing
1 Jacking point locations 3 Locating hole in jacking point
2 Peg on jack head

Jacking bracket/towing hook locations
1 Front   2 Rear

Use the tool provided, or a screwdriver, to lever off the wheel trim

Front jacking bracket/towing hook

Rear jacking bracket/towing hook

Tyre condition and pressure

It is very important that tyres are in good condition, and at the correct pressure - having a tyre failure at any speed is highly dangerous. Tyre wear is influenced by driving style - harsh braking and acceleration, or fast cornering, will all produce more rapid tyre wear. As a general rule, the front tyres wear out faster than the rears. Interchanging the tyres from front to rear ("rotating" the tyres) may result in more even wear. However, if this is completely effective, you may have the expense of replacing all four tyres at once! Remove any nails or stones embedded in the tread before they penetrate the tyre to cause deflation. If removal of a nail does reveal that

the tyre has been punctured, refit the nail so that its point of penetration is marked. Then immediately change the wheel, and have the tyre repaired by a tyre dealer.

Regularly check the tyres for damage in the form of cuts or bulges, especially in the sidewalls. Periodically remove the wheels, and clean any dirt or mud from the inside and outside surfaces. Examine the wheel rims for signs of rusting, corrosion or other damage. Light alloy wheels are easily damaged by "kerbing" whilst parking; steel wheels may also become dented or buckled. A new wheel is very often the only way to overcome severe damage.

New tyres should be balanced when they are fitted, but it may become necessary to re-balance them as they wear, or if the balance weights fitted to the wheel rim should fall off. Unbalanced tyres will wear more quickly, as will the steering and suspension components. Wheel imbalance is normally signified by vibration, particularly at a certain speed (typically around 50 mph). If this vibration is felt only through the steering, then it is likely that just the front wheels need balancing. If, however, the vibration is felt through the whole car, the rear wheels could be out of balance. Wheel balancing should be carried out by a tyre dealer or garage.

1 Tread Depth - visual check
The original tyres have tread wear safety bands (B), which will appear when the tread depth reaches approximately 1.6 mm. The band positions are indicated by a triangular mark on the tyre sidewall (A).

2 Tread Depth - manual check
Alternatively, tread wear can be monitored with a simple, inexpensive device known as a tread depth indicator gauge.

3 Tyre Pressure Check
Check the tyre pressures regularly with the tyres cold. Do not adjust the tyre pressures immediately after the vehicle has been used, or an inaccurate setting will result.

Tyre tread wear patterns

Shoulder Wear

Underinflation (wear on both sides)
Under-inflation will cause overheating of the tyre, because the tyre will flex too much, and the tread will not sit correctly on the road surface. This will cause a loss of grip and excessive wear, not to mention the danger of sudden tyre failure due to heat build-up.
Check and adjust pressures
Incorrect wheel camber (wear on one side)
Repair or renew suspension parts
Hard cornering
Reduce speed!

Centre Wear

Overinflation
Over-inflation will cause rapid wear of the centre part of the tyre tread, coupled with reduced grip, harsher ride, and the danger of shock damage occurring in the tyre casing.
Check and adjust pressures

If you sometimes have to inflate your car's tyres to the higher pressures specified for maximum load or sustained high speed, don't forget to reduce the pressures to normal afterwards.

Uneven Wear

Front tyres may wear unevenly as a result of wheel misalignment. Most tyre dealers and garages can check and adjust the wheel alignment (or "tracking") for a modest charge.
Incorrect camber or castor
Repair or renew suspension parts
Malfunctioning suspension
Repair or renew suspension parts
Unbalanced wheel
Balance tyres
Incorrect toe setting
Adjust front wheel alignment
Note: *The feathered edge of the tread which typifies toe wear is best checked by feel.*

Maintenance is essential for ensuring safety, and desirable for the purpose of getting the best in terms of performance and economy from your car. Over the years the need for periodic lubrication has been greatly reduced, if not totally eliminated. This has unfortunately tended to lead some owners to think that, because no such action is required, the items either no longer exist, or will last forever. This is certainly not the case; it is essential to carry out regular visual examination as comprehensively as possible in order to spot any possible defects at an early stage before they develop into major expensive repairs.

The following service schedules are a list of the maintenance requirements and the intervals at which they should be carried out, based on the schedule recommended by the manufacturers. Where applicable these procedures are covered in greater detail throughout this manual, near the beginning of each Chapter.

Every 250 miles (400 km) or weekly – whichever occurs first

☐ Check the engine oil level and top up, if necessary
☐ Check the coolant level and top up, if necessary
☐ Check the brake fluid level and top up, if necessary
☐ Check the operation of all interior and exterior lights, wipers and washers
☐ Check and, if necessary, top up the washer reservoir, adding a screen wash
☐ Check the tyre pressures
☐ Visually examine the tyres for wear or damage

Oil filler and dipstick details

A 3 litre models   B 1.6 litre models   1 Dipstick   2 Oil breather/filler cap

Check the engine oil level on the dipstick and top up if necessary

**Rear underbody view
(1.6 litre model)**

1 Exhaust intermediate silencer
2 Handbrake cable adjuster
3 Handbrake cable connectors
4 Exhaust rear silencer
5 Rear jacking bracket/towing hook
6 Rear suspension strut lower mounting
7 Rear axle mounting pivot bolt
8 Rear brake hose
9 Rear axle transverse member
10 Fuel tank rear mounting bolts
11 Fuel tank front mounting bolts
12 Rear jacking point

Every 6 000 miles (10 000 km) or 6 months – whichever occurs first

Note: *Frequent oil and filter changes are good for the engine. We recommend changing the oil at the mileage specified here, or at least twice a year if the mileage covered is less*

☐ Renew the engine oil and filter

Every 12 000 miles (20 000 km) or 12 months – whichever occurs first

☐ Check and, if necessary, adjust the valve clearances on 1.3 litre models

☐ Visually check the engine for oil leaks and for the security and condition of all related components and attachments

☐ Check the coolant hoses, hose clips and visible joint gaskets for leaks and any signs of corrosion or deterioration

☐ Check the condition of the alternator drivebelt and renew if worn.

☐ Adjust the belt tension.

☐ Visually check the fuel pipes and hoses for security, chafing, leaks and corrosion

☐ Check the fuel tank for leaks and any signs of damage or corrosion

☐ Top up the carburettor piston damper

☐ Check the operation of the accelerator and linkage

☐ Check and, if necessary, adjust the carburettor slow running characteristics

☐ Check the exhaust system for corrosion, leaks and security

☐ Inspect the fuel evaporative control (EVAP) system components for condition and security.

☐ Renew the spark plugs

☐ Clean the distributor cap, coil tower and HT leads, and check for tracking

☐ Check the operation of the clutch and clutch pedal

☐ Visually check for oil leaks around the gearbox joint faces and oil seals

☐ Check and, if necessary, top up the gearbox oil

☐ Lubricate the gearchange linkage

☐ Visually check for oil leaks around the automatic transmission joint faces and oil seals

☐ Check and, if necessary, top up the automatic transmission fluid

☐ Check and, if necessary top up the final drive gear oil

☐ Check the driveshaft constant velocity joints for wear or damage and check the rubber gaiters for condition

☐ Check visually all brake pipes, hoses and unions for corrosion, chafing, leakage and security

☐ Check the operation of the brake warning indicators

☐ Check the brake servo vacuum hose for condition and security

☐ Check the operation of the hand and footbrake

☐ Check the front brake pads for wear, and the discs for condition

☐ Check the rear brake shoes for wear, and the drums for condition

☐ Check the condition and security of all accessible wiring connectors, harnesses and retaining clips

☐ Check the operation of all electrical equipment and accessories (lights, indicators, horn, wipers, etc)

☐ Clean the battery terminals and smear with petroleum jelly

☐ Have the headlamp alignment checked and, if necessary, adjusted

☐ Check the front and rear suspension struts for fluid leaks

☐ Check the condition and security of the steering gear, steering and suspension joints, and rubber gaiters

☐ Check the front wheel toe setting

☐ Inspect the roadwheels for damage

☐ Check the tightness of the wheel nuts

☐ Check the power-assisted steering reservoir fluid level

☐ Carefully inspect the paintwork for damage and the bodywork for corrosion

☐ Check the condition of the underseal

☐ Oil all hinges, door locks and the bonnet release mechanism with a few drops of light oil (not the steering lock)

☐ Check the operation of all instruments and electrical equipment

☐ Check the operation of the seat belts

☐ Check for any abnormalities in the steering, suspension, handling or road feel

☐ Check the performance of the engine, clutch and transmission

☐ Check the operation and performance of the braking system

Every 24 000 miles (40 000 km) or 24 months – whichever occurs first

☐ Renew the engine oil filler cap on 1.3 litre models
☐ Clean the engine breather filter on 1.6 litre models
☐ Check and, if necessary, adjust the valve clearances on 1.6 litre engines
☐ Flush the cooling system and renew the antifreeze solution
☐ Renew the alternator drivebelt
☐ Renew the air cleaner element
☐ Check and adjust the carburettor idle speed and mixture settings
☐ Check and, if necessary, adjust the ignition timing on 1.3 litre models
☐ Lubricate the distributor centrifugal advance mechanism on 1.3 litre models
☐ Drain the transmission fluid, clean the oil strainer and refill with fresh fluid
☐ Check the operation of the parking pawl
☐ Renew the brake fluid

Every 36 000 miles (60 000 km) or 36 months – whichever occurs first

☐ Renew the flexible rubber hoses and the rubber seals in the calipers, wheel cylinders and master cylinder
☐ Renew the air filter in the servo unit

Every 48 000 miles (80 000 km) or 4 years – whichever occurs first

☐ Renew the timing belt on 1.6 litre engines

OIL CARE FOLLOW THE CODE

OIL BANK LINE
0800 66 33 66

Note: It is antisocial and illegal to dump oil down the drain. To find the location of your local oil recycling bank, call this number free.

Top up the brake fluid at the master cylinder reservoir

Sump drain plug location on 1.3 litre models . . .

. . . and 1.6 litre models

Oil filter location on 1.3 litre models

Top up the carburettor piston damper with engine oil

Gearbox filler plug location (5-speed gearbox)

Engine and under-bonnet component locations (1.6 litre models)

1 Cooling system expansion tank
2 Cooling system filler cap
3 Brake master cylinder
4 Oil filter
5 Master cylinder reservoir filler cap
6 Clutch cable self-adjusting mechanism
7 Carburettor
8 Main vacuum line
9 Air cleaner plenum chamber
10 Ignition coil
11 Distributor
12 Air cleaner
13 Braking system twin GP valve
14 Ignition system electronic control unit (ECU)
15 Battery negative terminal
16 Fusible links
17 Battery positive terminal
18 Oil filler/ breather cap
19 Water outlet elbow
20 Oil dipstick
21 Alternator
22 Front body panel

Front underbody view (1.6 litre models)

1 Brake caliper
2 Gearbox filler/level plug
3 Steering tie-rod outer balljoint
4 Suspension lower arm rear mounting
5 Gearbox drain plug

6 Driveshaft inner constant velocity joint
7 Suspension crossmember
8 Engine oil drain plug
9 Anti-roll bar clamp

10 Front jacking point
11 Access panel
12 Front snubber cup
13 Front jacking bracket/towing hook

1.3 litre models

1.6 litre models

Component or system	Lubricant type/specification
1 Engine*	Multigrade engine oil, viscosity SAE 10W/40
2 Manual gearbox:	
Models up to 1989	Hypoid gear oil, viscosity SAE 80 EP
1.6 five-speed models, 1989-on*	Multigrade engine oil, viscosity SAE 10W/40
3 Distributor – 1.3 only	Multigrade engine oil, viscosity SAE 10W/40
4 Final drive (automatic transmission)	Hypoid gear oil, viscosity SAE 90EP
5 Carburettor piston damper	Multigrade engine oil, viscosity SAE 10W/40
6 Brake fluid reservoir	Hydraulic fluid to FMVSS 116 DOT 4 or SAE J1703C
7 Automatic transmission	Dexron IID type ATF
8 Power steering	Dexron IID type ATF

*Note: *Austin Rover specify a 10W/40 oil to meet warranty requirements for models produced after August 1983.*

Chapter 1 Engine

For modifications, and information applicable to later models, see Supplement at end of manual

Contents

Degrees of difficulty

Easy, suitable for novice with little experience	Fairly easy, suitable for beginner with some experience	Fairly difficult, suitable for competent DIY mechanic	Difficult, suitable for experienced DIY mechanic	Very difficult, suitable for expert DIY or professional

Specifications

Part A: 1.3 litre engine

General

Type	Four-cylinder in-line, overhead valve (12H - 'A+'- series)
Bore	2.780 in (70.61 mm)
Stroke	3.200 in (81.28 mm)
Capacity	1275 cc (77.8 cu in)
Firing order	1-3-4-2 (No 1 cylinder at crankshaft pulley end)
Compression ratio	9.75 : 1

Crankshaft

Main journal diameter	2.0012 to 2.0017 in (50.83 to 50.84 mm)
Main bearing running clearance	0.0003 to 0.0030 in (0.008 to 0.076 mm)
Main journal minimum regrind diameter	1.9811 in (50.32 mm)
Crankpin journal diameter	1.7497 to 1.7504 in (44.44 to 44.46 mm)
Crankpin running clearance	0.0015 to 0.0032 in (0.0381 to 0.0813 mm)
Crankpin minimum regrind diameter	1.7297 in (43.93 mm)
Crankshaft endfloat	0.002 to 0.003 in (0.051 to 0.076 mm)

Connecting rods

Length between centres	5.750 in (146.05 mm)

Pistons

Skirt clearance in cylinder:	
Top	0.0029 to 0.0045 in (0.074 to 0.114 mm)
Bottom	0.0009 to 0.0025 in (0.023 to 0.064 mm)
Oversizes available	0.020 in (0.51 mm)

Piston rings

Clearance in groove (compression rings)	0.0015 to 0.0035 in (0.038 to 0.089 mm)
Fitted end gap:	
Top compression	0.010 to 0.017 in (0.25 to 0.43 mm)
Second compression	0.008 to 0.013 in (0.20 to 0.33 mm)
Oil control	0.015 to 0.041 in (0.38 to 1.04 mm)

Gudgeon pins

Diameter	0.8123 to 0.8125 in (20.63 to 20.64 mm)
Clearance in piston	Hand push fit at 68°F (20°C)
Interference fit in connecting rod	0.0008 to 0.0015 in (0.02 to 0.04 mm)

Valves

Seat angle	45°
Head diameter:	
Inlet	1.307 to 1.312 in (33.20 to 33.32 mm)
Exhaust	1.1515 to 1.1565 in (29.25 to 29.38 mm)
Stem diameter:	
Inlet	0.2793 to 0.2798 in (7.094 to 7.107 mm)
Exhaust	0.2788 to 0.2793 in (7.082 to 7.094 mm)
Clearance in guide:	
Inlet	0.0015 to 0.0025 in (0.038 to 0.064 mm)
Exhaust	0.002 to 0.003 in (0.051 to 0.076 mm)
Valve guides:	
Length	1.687 in (42.85 mm)
Outside diameter	0.470 to 0.471 in (11.94 to 11.96 mm)
Inside diameter	0.2813 to 0.2818 in (7.145 to 7.158 mm)
Fitted height above head	0.540 in (13.72 mm)
Valve springs:	
Free length	1.95 in (49.53 mm)
Valve timing (at valve clearance of 0.021 in/0.53 mm):	
Inlet opens	20° BTDC
Inlet closes	52° ABDC
Exhaust opens	55° BBDC
Exhaust closes	17° ATDC
Valve clearances (cold)	0.014 in 10.36 mm)

Camshaft

Journal diameter:	
Front	1.6655 to 1.6660 in (42.304 to 42.316 mm)
Centre	1.62275 to 1.62325 in (41.218 to 41.231 mm)
Rears	1.37275 to 1.3735 in (34.868 to 34.887 mm)
Running clearance in bearings	0.001 to 0.00225 in (0.025 to 0.057 mm)
Endfloat	0.003 to 0.007 in (0.076 to 0.178 mm)
Valve lift	0.318 in (8.08 mm)
Cam followers outside diameter	0.812 in (20.62 mm)

Lubrication system

Oil type/specification*	Multigrade engine oil, viscosity SAE 10W/40
Oil filter	Champion B101 with oil cooler or D102 without oil cooler
Oil pump:	
Type	Bi-rotor
Outer rotor endfloat	0.005 in (0.127 mm)
Inner rotor endfloat	0.005 in (0.127 mm)
Outer rotor-to-body clearance	0.010 in (0.254 mm)
Rotor lobe clearance	0.006 in (0.152 mm)
System pressure:	
Idling	15 lbf/in^2 (1.0 bar)
Running	60 lbf/in^2 (4.1 bar)
Warning light switch operating pressure	6 to 10 lbf/in^2 (0.4 to 0.7 bar)
Pressure relief valve operating pressure	60 lbf/in^2 (4.1 bar)
Pressure relief valve spring free length	2.86 in (72.64 mm)

Note: *Austin Rover specify a 10W/40 oil to meet warranty requirements for models produced after August 1983.*

Torque wrench settings

	lbf ft	Nm
Camshaft locating plate bolts	8	11
Camshaft retaining nut	65	88
Connecting rod big-end cap nuts	30	41
Crankshaft pulley bolt	105	142
Cylinder head nuts	55	75
Front plate to main bearing cap	5	7
Front plate to cylinder block	16	22
Gearbox adaptor plate bolts	18	24
Main bearing cap bolts	65	88
Oil pressure switch	18	24
Oil pump retaining bolts	8	11
Oil pressure relief valve cap nut	45	61
Oil separator bolts	16	22
Rocker cover bolts	3	4
Rocker shaft pedestal nuts	24	33
Sump drain plug	28	38
Sump retaining bolts	8	11
Timing cover to front plate:		
1/4 in bolts	5	7
5/16 in bolts	12	16
Vacuum hose banjo union bolt	37	50
Left-hand engine mounting bracket to body	18	24
Left-hand engine mounting-to-bracket retaining bolts	18	24
Left-hand engine mounting through-bolt	34	46
Left-hand engine mounting to gearbox	30	41
Right-hand engine mounting support strap bolts	18	24
Right-hand engine mounting bracket-to-engine side bolts	18	24
Right-hand engine mounting bracket top and bottom bolts	30	41
Right-hand engine mounting through-bolt	34	46
Tie-rod bracket bolts	34	46
Tie-rod to engine bracket	67	91
Tie-rod to crossmember	34	46

Part B: 1.6 litre engine

General

Type	Four-cylinder in-line, overhead camshaft (16H - 'S' series)
Bore	3.000 in (76.20 mm)
Stroke	3.443 in (87.38 mm)
Capacity	1598 cc (97.5 cu in)
Firing order	1-3-4-2 (No 1 cylinder at crankshaft pulley end)
Compression ratio	9.6 : 1

Crankshaft

Main journal diameter	2.2515 to 2.2520 in (57.19 to 57.20 mm)
Main bearing running clearance	0.002 to 0.0035 in (0.05 to 0.09 mm)
Main journal minimum regrind diameter	2.2115 in (56.17 mm)
Crankpin journal diameter	1.8759 to 1.8765 in (47.65 to 47.66 mm)
Crankpin running clearance	0.0015 to 0.003 in (0.04 to 0.08 mm)
Crankpin minimum regrind diameter	1.8359 in (46.63 mm)
Endfloat	0.004 to 0.007 in (0.10 to 0.18 mm)

Connecting rods

Length between centres	5.830 in (148.08 mm)

Pistons

Skirt clearance in cylinder:

Top	0.0028 to 0.0044 in (0.07 to 0.11 mm)
Bottom	0.001 to 0.002 in (0.03 to 0.05 mm)
Oversizes available	0.020 in (0.51 mm)

Piston rings

Clearance in grooves	0.0015 to 0.0035 in (0.04 to 0.09 mm)

Fitted gap:

Compression	0.012 to 0.022 in (0.30 to 0.56 mm)
Oil control rails	0.015 to 0.045 in (0.38 to 1.14 mm)

Gudgeon pins

Diameter	0.8123 to 0.8125 in (20.63 to 20.64 mm)
Clearance in piston	Hand push fit at 68°F (20°C)
Interference fit in connecting rod	0.0008 to 0.0015 in (0.02 to 0.04 mm)

Camshaft

Journal diameter:

Front	1.9355 to 1.9365 in (49.16 to 49.19 mm)
Centre	1.9668 to 1.9678 in (49.96 to 49.98 mm)
Rear	1.998 to 1.999 in (50.75 to 50.77 mm)
Running clearance in bearings	0.001 to 0.0023 in (0.025 to 0.058 mm)
Endfloat	0.002 to 0.007 in (0.05 to 0.18 mm)

Valve lift:

Inlet	0.342 to 0.344 in (8.69 to 8.74 mm)
Exhaust	0.338 to 0.340 in (8.58 to 8.64 mm)

Tappets

Adjustment	Selective shims
Outside diameter	1.1865 in (30.14 mm)
Adjustment shim number:	**Corresponding thickness**
97 to 49	0.097 in (2.46 mm) to 0.149 in (3.78 mm), in 0.002 in (0.05 mm) steps

Valves

Seat angle	45.25°

Head diameter:

Inlet	1.500 in (38.1 mm)
Exhaust	1.218 in (30.9 mm)

Stem diameter (standard):

Inlet	0.3115 to 0.3120 in (7.91 to 7.92 mm)
Exhaust	0.3109 to 0.3114 in (7.90 to 7.91 mm)
Stem diameter (oversize)	0.3331 to 0.3336 in (8.46 to 8.47 mm)
Stem-to-guide clearance	0.0015 in (0.038 mm)
Valve spring free length	1.810 in (45.97 mm)

Valve timing (at tappet clearance of 0.021 in/0.53 mm):

Inlet opens	17° BTDC
Inlet closes	59° ABDC
Exhaust opens	57° BBDC
Exhaust closes	19° ATDC

Tappet clearances (cold):

Inlet	0.014 to 0.015 in (0.36 to 0.38 mm)
Exhaust	0.017 to 0.018 in (0.43 to 0.46 mm)
Adjust only if less than	0.012 in (0.30 mm)

Valve sequence (from front of head):

Inlet	2,3,6,7
Exhaust	1,4,5,8

Timing belt

Tensioning method	Torque wrench engaged with hole in tensioner bracket
Tension:	
Used belt	10 lbf ft (14 Nm)
New belt	15 lbf ft (20 Nm)

Cylinder head

Height:	
New	3.312 to 3.322 in (84.12 to 84.38 mm)
Minimum	3.302 in (83.87 mm)
Maximum clearance under straight-edge across surface	0.002 in (0.05 mm)

Lubrication system

Oil type/specification*	Multigrade engine oil, viscosity SAE 10W/40
Oil filter	Champion C104
Oil pump:	
Type	Bi-rotor
Outer rotor endfloat	0.001 to 0.003 in (0.03 to 0.08 mm)
Outer rotor-to-body clearance	0.007 to 0.011 in (0.18 to 0.27 mm)
Rotor lobe clearance	0.001 to 0.006 in (0.025 to 0.15 mm)
System pressure:	
Running	55 lbf/in^2 (3.8 bar)
Idling	10 lbf/in^2 (0.7 bar)
Pressure relief valve spring free length	2.47 in (62.7 mm)
Warning light switch operating pressure	6 to 10 lbf/in^2 (0.4 to 0.7 bar)

*Note: Austin Rover specify a 10W/40 oil to meet warranty requirements for models produced after August 1983.

Torque wrench settings

	lbf ft	Nm
Timing belt tensioner bolts	18	24
Camshaft carrier bolts	18	24
Camshaft carrier cover bolts	6	8
Camshaft sprocket bolt	41	56
Connecting rod big-end cap nuts	34	46
Crankshaft pulley bolt	34	46
Cylinder head bolts (lightly oiled):		
Stage 1	30	40
Stage 2	60	80
Stage 3	Tighten by a further quarter-turn (90°)	Tighten by a further quarter-turn (90°)
Gearbox adaptor plate:		
M8 bolts	18	24
M 10 bolts	34	46
M12 bolts	67	91
Knock sensor	9	12
Main bearing cap bolts	67	91
Oil pump-to-cylinder block bolts	19	26
Oil pressure switch	18	24
Sump drain plug	18	24
Sump bolts	6	8
Vacuum hose banjo union bolt	37	50
Left-hand engine mounting to gearbox	34	46
Left-hand mounting body bracket to body	30	41
Left-hand mounting through-bolt	67	91
Right-hand engine mounting to cylinder block and head	34	46
Right-hand mounting support plate-to-body bolts	30	40
Right-hand mounting body bracket to body	34	46
Right-hand mounting through-bolt	67	91
Rear engine mounting support bracket to crossmember	34	46
Rear mounting to support bracket	18	24
Rear mounting to gearbox casing	34	46
Front snubber bracket to engine	38	52
Snubber cup bolts	30	40

1

Part A: 1.3 litre engine

1 General description

The engine is of four-cylinder, in-line overhead valve type, mounted transversely at the front of the car.

The crankshaft is supported in three shell-type main bearings. Thrust washers are fitted at the centre main bearing to control crankshaft endfloat.

The connecting rods are attached to the crankshaft by horizontally split shell-type big-end bearings, and to the pistons by interference fit gudgeon pins. The aluminium alloy pistons are of the slipper type and are fitted with three piston rings; two compression rings and a three piece oil control ring.

The camshaft is chain driven from the crankshaft and operates the rocker arms via pushrods. The inlet and exhaust valves are each closed by a single valve spring and operate in guides pressed into the cylinder head. The valves are actuated directly by the rocker arms.

Engine lubrication is by an eccentric rotor type oil pump. The pump is mounted on the gearbox end of the cylinder block and is driven by the camshaft, as are the distributor and fuel pump.

2 Maintenance and inspection

1 At the intervals given in Routine Maintenance at the beginning of this manual, carry out the following service operations on the engine.
2 Visually inspect the engine joint faces, gaskets and seals for any sign of oil or water leaks. Pay particular attention to the areas around the rocker cover, cylinder head, timing cover and sump joint faces. Rectify any leaks by referring to the appropriate Sections of this Chapter.

Fig. 1.1 Exploded view of the 1.3 litre engine main components (Sec 1)

1 Dipstick	10 Oil separator	19 Oil pick-up pipe and strainer	28 Cylinder block
2 Temperature gauge sensor	11 Crankshaft oil seal	20 Sump	29 Oil filter
3 Spark plug	12 Manifold gasket	21 Main bearing cap	30 Oil pressure relief valve
4 Thermostat housing cover	13 Inlet manifold	22 Timing cover oil seal	31 Cylinder head gasket
5 Oil filler cap	14 Exhaust manifold	23 Timing cover	32 Thermostat and housing
6 Rocker cover	15 Hot air box	24 Crankshaft pulley	33 Oil pump cover plate
7 Gasket	16 Gearbox adaptor plate & gasket	25 Drivebelt	34 Fuel pump and insulating block
8 Cylinder head	17 Drain plug	26 Water pump and gasket	35 Front support bracket
9 Oil pressure switch	18 Sump gasket and oil seals	27 Engine front plate and gasket	36 Rear support bracket

3 Place a suitable container beneath the oil drain plug on the right-hand side of the sump. Unscrew the plug using spanner or socket and allow the oil to drain. Inspect the condition of the drain plug sealing washer and renew it, if necessary. Refit and tighten the plug after draining.

4 Move the bowl to the rear of the engine, under the oil filter.

5 Using a strap wrench, or filter removal tool, slacken the filter and then unscrew it from the engine and discard.

6 Wipe the mating face on the cylinder block with a rag and then lubricate the seal of a new filter using clean engine oil.

7 Screw the filter into position and tighten it by hand only, do not use any tools.

8 Refill the engine, using the correct grade of oil, through the filler neck on the rocker cover. Fill until the level reaches the MAX mark on the dipstick.

9 With the engine running, check for leaks around the filter seal.

10 Adjust the valve clearances using the procedure described in Section 44.

11 At less frequent intervals (see Routine Maintenance) renew the oil filler cap on the rocker cover.

3 Major operations possible with the engine in the car

The following operations can be carried out without having to remove the engine from the car:
(a) Removal and refitting of the cylinder head
(b) Removal and refitting of the timing cover, chain and gears
(c) Removal and refitting of the sump
(d) Removal and refitting of the piston and connecting rod assemblies (after removal of the cylinder head)
(e) Renewal of the engine mountings

4 Major operations requiring engine removal

The following operations can only be carried out after removal of the engine from the car:
(a) Removal and refitting of the camshaft
(b) Removal and refitting of the oil pump
(c) Removal and refitting of the crankshaft and main bearings
(d) Removal and refitting of the tappets (cam followers)

5 Methods of engine removal

The engine and gearbox assembly can be lifted from the car as a complete unit, as

Fig. 1.2 Exploded view of the 1.3 litre engine internal components (Sec 1)

1 Valve rocker
2 Rocker shaft pedestal
3 Rocker shaft spring
4 Rocker shaft
5 Rocker shaft locating screw and lockplate
6 Piston rings and piston
7 Distributor driveshaft
8 Oil pump
9 Camshaft
10 Crankshaft
11 Main bearing shells
12 Crankshaft thrust washers
13 Big-end bearing shells
14 Connecting rod and cap
15 Crankshaft sprocket packing shims
16 Crankshaft sprocket
17 Crankshaft oil thrower
18 Camshaft locating plate
19 Chain tensioner
20 Timing chain
21 Camshaft sprocket
22 Tappet
23 Valve guide
24 Exhaust valve
25 Gudgeon pin
26 Valve spring, cap and collets
27 Rocker adjusting screw
28 Push-rod
29 Inlet valve
30 Valve stem oil seal

described in the following Section, or the gearbox may first be removed, as described in Chapter 6. It is not possible, due to the limited working clearances, to remove the engine leaving the gearbox in position.

6 Engine and gearbox assembly - removal

1 Remove the bonnet, as described in Chapter 12, and the battery, as described in Chapter 10.
2 Undo and remove the bolts securing the battery tray to the body and remove the tray.
3 Drain the cooling system, as described in Chapter 2.
4 Remove the air cleaner, as described in Chapter 3.
5 Slacken the retaining clips and detach the radiator top hose from the thermostat housing, the bottom hose from the water pump and the two heater hoses from the inlet manifold.
6 Slacken the clips and detach the supply hose from the base of the expansion tank, and the overflow hose from the thermostat housing.

7 Undo and remove the retaining bolts, noting their different lengths, and lift off the expansion tank.
8 Detach the main vacuum pipe from the banjo union on the inlet manifold and disconnect the pipes at the connector.
9 Undo and remove the bolt securing the heater hose clip to the cylinder head and position the heater hose and vacuum pipe clear of the engine.
10 Disconnect the electrical wiring multi-plugs from the carburettor.
11 Spring back the clip and disconnect the wiring multi-plug from the alternator.
12 Disconnect the distributor wiring multi-plug from the ignition amplifier wiring connector.
13 Note the position of the wiring connections at the starter motor solenoid and disconnect the wires.
14 Note the positions of the oil pressure switch and water temperature gauge wires and disconnect them from their sensors. Detach the reversing lamp switch wires from the gearbox.
15 Undo and remove the bolt securing the wiring harness clip to the gearbox, and release the clips securing the harness to the rocker cover brackets. Check that all the

wiring has been disconnected and move the harness clear of the engine.

16 Pull the HT leads off the spark plugs and detach the HT lead from the coil and rubber boot. Spring back the clips and remove the distributor cap and leads.

17 Undo and remove the banjo union retaining bolt at the inlet manifold and lift off the union, noting the arrangement of the copper washers.

18 Slacken the retaining screw and remove the accelerator cable from the linkage connector and from the carburettor bracket.

19 Undo and remove the bolt securing the speedometer cable to the gearbox. Withdraw the cable, squarely and without twisting, from the gearbox.

20 Refer to Chapter 5 and detach the clutch cable from the operating lever and gearbox bracket.

21 Remove the retaining clip and slide the gearchange rod out of the selector shaft lever. Disconnect the rear selector rod from the relay lever on the gearbox by prising off the balljoint with a screwdriver.

22 Detach the fuel inlet pipe from the fuel pump and plug the pipe after removal.

23 Jack up the front of the car and support it securely on axle stands.

24 From underneath the car, undo and remove the nuts securing the exhaust front pipe to the manifold. Remove the hot air box as necessary to provide access. Release the pipe-to-manifold flange joint and recover the gasket.

25 Undo and remove the nut and through-bolt securing the engine tie-rod and stay to the engine bracket.

26 Undo and remove the two nuts and bolts securing the tie-rod bracket to the engine and withdraw the bracket from the engine and tie-rod.

27 Mark the relationship of the driveshaft inner constant velocity joints to the differential drive flanges.

28 Lift off the protective caps and unscrew the joint-to-drive flange retaining bolts using an Allen key.

29 Undo and remove the screws securing the left-hand access panel under the wheel arch and lift out the panel.

30 Remove the axle stands and lower the car to the ground.

31 Position a jack under the gearbox and just take the weight of the engine and gearbox assembly on the jack.

32 Undo and remove the nuts and bolts securing the left-hand engine mounting to the body and gearbox bracket and remove the mounting. Note the location of the engine earth strap.

33 Undo and remove the two bolts securing the right-hand engine mounting support strap to the body and the two bolts securing the strap to the body mounting bracket. Lift off the strap.

34 Attach a suitable hoist to the engine using chains or rope slings, or by attaching the

chains or ropes to sturdy brackets bolted to the engine and gearbox.

35 Make a final check that everything attaching the engine and gearbox to the car has been disconnected and that all detached components are well clear.

36 Lift the engine and gearbox slightly and, as soon as sufficient clearance exists, release the driveshaft inner joints from the drive flanges. Support or tie up the driveshafts to avoid straining the outer joints.

37 Continue lifting the engine and gearbox assembly and. when it has been raised sufficiently, draw the hoist forward or push the car backwards and lower the engine and gearbox to the ground.

7 Engine - separation from gearbox

1 With the engine and gearbox removed from the car, undo and remove the two starter motor retaining bolts using an Allen key and suitable spanner. Lift off the starter motor.

2 Support the engine and gearbox and remove the bolts securing the stiffener plates to the engine and gearbox. Remove the stiffener plates.

3 Undo and remove the bolts securing the gearbox to the adaptor plate, noting the different lengths and their locations.

4 Withdraw the gearbox from the engine after releasing the dowels. Draw the gearbox off squarely and do not allow the weight of the gearbox to hang unsupported on the gearbox shaft.

8 Engine dismantling - general

1 If possible, mount the engine on a stand for the dismantling procedure, but failing this support it in an upright position with blocks of wood placed under each side of the sump or crankcase.

2 Drain the oil into a suitable container before cleaning the engine or major dismantling.

3 Cleanliness is most important, and if the engine is dirty it should be cleaned with paraffin or a suitable solvent while keeping it in an upright position.

4 Avoid working with the engine directly on a concrete floor, as grit presents a real source of trouble.

5 As parts are removed, clean them in a paraffin bath. However, do not immerse parts with internal oilways in paraffin as it is difficult to remove, usually requiring a high pressure hose. Clean oilways with nylon pipe cleaners.

6 It is advisable to have suitable containers to hold small items, as this will help when

reassembling the engine and also prevent possible losses.

7 Always obtain complete sets of gaskets when the engine is being dismantled, but retain the old gaskets with a view to using them as a pattern to make a replacement if a new one is not available.

8 When possible, refit nuts, bolts and washers in their location after being removed, as this helps to protect the threads and will also be helpful when reassembling the engine.

Retain unserviceable components, including gaskets, in order to compare them with the new parts supplied.

9 Ancillary components - removal

With the engine separated from the gearbox the externally mounted ancillary components, as given in the following list, can be removed. The removal sequence need not necessarily follow the order given:

Inlet and exhaust manifolds and carburettor (Chapter 3)
Fuel pump (Chapter 3)
Alternator (Chapter 10)
Spark plugs (Chapter 4)
Distributor (Chapter 4)
Water pump (Chapter 2)
Thermostat housing and thermostat (Chapter 2)
Oil filter (Section 2 of this Chapter)
Dipstick
Engine right-hand mounting (Section 29 of this Chapter)
Clutch and flywheel (Chapter 5)

10 Cylinder head - removal

Note: *If the engine is still in the car, first carry out the following operations with reference to the relevant Sections and Chapters of this manual:*

(a) Disconnect the battery negative lead
(b) Drain the cooling system
(c) Remove the inlet and exhaust manifold, complete with carburettor
(d) Disconnect the cooling system top hose, heater hose, and expansion tank hose from the thermostat housing
(e) Remove the HT leads and spark plugs
(f) Disconnect the lead from the coolant temperature thermistor
(g) Release the engine mounting bracket on the thermostat housing
(h) Remove the bolt securing the heater hose clip to the cylinder head

10.1A Remove the rocker cover washer and seal

10.1B Lift off the rocker cover and gasket

10.5 Withdraw the pushrods, keeping them in order

1 Unscrew the two rocker cover retaining bolts and lift off the wiring harness support brackets. Collect the washers and lift off the rocker cover and gasket (photos).

2 Unscrew the rocker shaft pedestal small nuts and remove the washers. Note the lockwasher fitted to the second pedestal from the front.

3 Unscrew the cylinder head nuts half a turn at a time in the reverse order to that shown in Fig. 1.11, and then remove the nuts.

4 Lift the rocker shaft and pedestals from the studs.

5 Shake the pushrods free from the tappets (cam followers), then withdraw them from the cylinder head keeping them in strict order to ensure correct refitting (photo).

6 Lift the cylinder head from the block. If it is stuck, tap it free with a wooden mallet. *Do not insert a lever into the gasket joint - you may damage the mating surfaces.*

7 Remove the cylinder head gasket from the cylinder block.

11 Cylinder head - dismantling

1 Using a valve spring compressor, compress each valve spring in turn until the split collets can be removed (photo). Release the compressor and remove the cup and spring.

> **HAYNES HiNT**
> *If the cups are difficult to release, do not continue to tighten the compressor, but gently tap the top of the tool with a hammer. Always make sure that the compressor is held firmly over the cup.*

2 Remove the oil seals from the inlet valve guides (photo). A small seal may also be fitted at the bottom of the collet groove on the valve stems.

3 Remove each valve from the combustion chambers keeping them in their order of removal, together with the respective valve springs and cups (photos). Identify each valve according to the cylinder, remembering that No 1 cylinder is at the thermostat end of the cylinder head.

12 Timing cover, chain and gears - removal

Note: *If the engine is still in the car, carry out the following operations with reference to the relevant Sections and Chapters of this manual:*
(a) Disconnect the battery negative lead
(b) Remove the drivebelt and the water pump pulley
(c) Remove the access panel from the right-hand wheel arch

1 Disconnect the crankcase ventilation hose from the oil separator on the timing cover and release the fuel pipe clips from the timing cover studs.

2 Using a spanner or socket on the crankshaft pulley bolt, rotate the engine until No 4 piston is at top-dead-centre on the compression stroke. This will align the timing gear marks.

3 Undo and remove the crankshaft pulley bolt after releasing the lockwasher. If the engine is removed, lock the crankshaft using a bar or stout screwdriver across two bolts fitted to the crankshaft rear boss. If the engine is in the car, engage top gear and apply the handbrake.

11.1 With the valve spring compressed, lift out the split collets

11.2 Remove the valve stem oil seals

11.3A Remove the valves . . .

11.3B . . . and keep the components together

1

12.5 Remove the timing cover

12.6 Note the fitted position of the oil thrower

12.7 Remove the camshaft gear retaining nut and lockwasher

4 Lever the pulley and damper off the front of the crankshaft.

5 Unbolt and remove the timing cover, and remove the gasket (photo).

6 Remove the oil thrower, noting which way round it is fitted (photo).

7 Flatten the lockwasher, then unscrew the camshaft gear retaining nut (photo). Use a screwdriver through one of the gear holes to restrain the gear. Remove the lockwasher.

8 Check that the alignment marks on the timing gears are facing each other, then unbolt and remove the chain tensioner.

9 Using two levers, ease the two gears and chain from the camshaft and crankshaft.

10 Remove the gears from the chain, but identify the outer face of the chain so that it can be refitted in its original position.

13 Sump - removal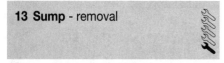

Note: *If the engine is still in the car carry out the following operations with reference to the relevant Sections and Chapters of this manual:*
(a) Disconnect the battery negative lead
(b) Drain the engine oil
(c) Unbolt and remove the engine tie-rod

1 Undo and remove the bolts securing the sump to the crankcase and withdraw the sump. If it is initially stuck, give it a tap with a

hide or plastic mallet to break the seal. Remove the gaskets and the end seals.

2 To remove the oil pick-up pipe and strainer, unscrew the bolt securing the support bracket to the main bearing cap. Undo the pipe union nut and withdraw the pipe and strainer.

14 Gearbox adaptor plate - removal

1 Remove the engine and gearbox, as described in Section 6, separate the gearbox and remove the clutch assembly. as described in Chapter 5.

2 Remove the sump, as described in the previous Section.

3 Undo and remove the bolts securing the adaptor plate to the engine, noting the location of the three long screws.

4 Withdraw the adaptor plate and recover the gasket.

15 Oil pump - removal

1 Remove the gearbox adaptor plate, as described in the previous Section.

2 Bend back the locktabs and unscrew the bolts securing the oil pump to the cylinder block.

3 Withdraw the oil pump and recover the gasket.

16 Camshaft and tappets - removal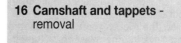

1 Remove the engine and gearbox, as described in Section 6, then separate the gearbox from the engine, as described in Section 7.

2 Remove the fuel pump, as described in Chapter 3, and the distributor, as described in Chapter 4.

3 Remove the timing cover chain and gears, as described in Section 12, and the sump, as described in Section 13.

4 Remove the rocker cover, rocker shaft and the pushrods.

5 Screw a long 5/16 in bolt into the centre of the distributor driveshaft and withdraw the shaft from its location in the cylinder block (photo).

6 Undo and remove the three bolts securing the camshaft locating plate to the front of the cylinder block and lift off the plate (photo).

7 Turn the engine on its side to prevent the tappets fouling the camshaft as it is withdrawn.

8 Turn the camshaft through one complete turn to move all the tappets away from the cam lobes and then withdraw the camshaft from the cylinder block (photo). Take care not

16.5 Use a bolt to remove the distributor driveshaft

16.6 Remove the camshaft locating plate

16.8 Withdraw the camshaft from the front of the engine

16.9 Remove the tappets from their bores

17.3 Remove the connecting rod cap and bearing shell

Recover the thrust washers from the centre main bearing cap.
9 Lift the crankshaft from the crankcase and remove the remaining centre bearing thrust washers.
10 Extract the bearing shells from the crankcase recesses and the caps, and identify them for location (photo).

to damage the three camshaft bearings as the cam lobes pass through them.
9 Withdraw each of the eight tappets through the crankcase (photo) and keep them in strict order as they must be refitted in their original locations unless they are to be renewed.

17 Pistons and connecting rods - removal

Note: *If the engine is still in the car, carry out the following operations with reference to the relevant Sections and Chapters of this manual:*
(a) Remove the sump and oil pick-up pipe
(b) Remove the cylinder head (this is not necessary if only the big-end bearings are to be removed)
1 Check the big-end caps for identification marks. If necessary, use a centre-punch on the caps and connecting rods to identify them; mark them on the camshaft side to ensure correct refitting.
2 Turn the crankshaft so that No 1 crankpin is at its lowest point. Using a suitable socket, undo and remove the nuts securing the connecting rod cap to the rod.
3 Withdraw the cap complete with the bearing shell (photo).
4 Using the handle of a hammer, tap the piston and connecting rod from the bore and withdraw it from the top of the cylinder block.
5 Loosely refit the cap to the connecting rod.
6 Repeat the procedure given in paragraphs

1 to 5 on No 4 piston and connecting rod, then turn the crankshaft through half a turn and repeat the procedure on No 2 and No 3 pistons.

18 Crankshaft and main bearings - removal

1 Remove the engine and gearbox from the car, as described in Section 6, and separate the gearbox, as described in Section 7.
2 Remove the timing cover gears and chain, as described in Section 12.
3 Remove the gearbox adaptor plate, as described in Section 14.
4 Follow the procedure for removing the pistons and connecting rods described in Section 17, but it is not necessary to completely withdraw them from the cylinder block.
5 Unbolt the front plate from the engine, and remove the gasket (photo). Invert the engine.
6 Check the main bearing caps for identification marks, and if necessary use a centre-punch to identify them.
7 Before removing the crankshaft, check that the endfloat is within the specified limits by inserting a feeler blade between the centre crankshaft web and the thrust washers (photo). This will indicate whether new thrust washers are required or not.
8 Unscrew the bolts and remove the main bearing caps, complete with bearing shells.

19 Crankcase ventilation system - description

The crankcase ventilation system consists of hoses from the crankcase area linked and connected to a port on the carburettor.
One hose is attached to an oil separator bolted to the gearbox adaptor plate and the other is attached to an oil separator on the timing cover.
Periodically the hoses should be examined for security and condition. Cleaning them will not normally be necessary except when the engine is well worn and sludge has accumulated.

20 Examination and renovation - general

With the engine completely stripped, clean all the components and examine them for wear. Each part should be checked and, where necessary, renewed or renovated as described in the following Sections. Renew main and big-end shell bearings as a matter of course, unless you know that they have had little wear and are in perfect condition.

21 Oil pump - examination

1 Remove the retaining screw(s) and withdraw the cover (photo).
2 Lift the two rotors from the pump body.
3 Clean the components with paraffin and wipe dry.

18.5 Engine front plate removal

18.7 Check the crankshaft endfloat with feeler gauges

18.10 Remove the main bearing shells

21.1 Remove the screw and lift off the oil pump cover

21.5A Checking the oil pump inner rotor endfloat . . .

21.5B . . . and outer rotor endfloat . . .

4 Refit the rotors to the pump body, making sure that the chamfer on the outer rotor enters the body first.
5 Using a feeler blade, and where necessary a straight-edge, check that the rotor clearances are as given in the Specifications (photos). If any clearance is outside that specified, or if damage is evident on any component, renew the complete oil pump.
6 If the oil pump is serviceable, refit the cover and tighten the retaining screw. Operate the pump in clean engine oil to prime it.

22 Crankshaft and main bearings - examination and renovation

1 Examine the bearing surfaces of the crankshaft for scratches or scoring and, using a micrometer, check each journal and

Fig. 1.3 Oil pump rotor lobe clearance checking point (Sec 21)

crankpin for ovality. Where this is found to be in excess of 0.001 in (0.0254 mm) the crankshaft will have to be reground and undersize bearings fitted.
2 Crankshaft regrinding should be carried out by a suitable engineering works, who will normally supply the matching undersize main and big-end shell bearings.
3 If the crankshaft endfloat is more than the maximum specified amount, new thrust washers should be fitted to the centre main bearing; these are usually supplied, together with the main and big-end bearings, with a reground crankshaft.

23 Cylinder block and crankcase - examination and renovation

1 The cylinder bores must be examined for taper, ovality, scoring and scratches. Start by examining the top of the bores: if these are worn, a slight ridge will be found which marks the top of the piston ring travel. If the wear is excessive, the engine will have had a high oil consumption rate accompanied by blue smoke from the exhaust.
2 If available, use an inside dial gauge to measure the bore diameter just below the ridge and compare it with the diameter at the bottom of the bore, which is not subject to wear. If the difference is more than 0.006 in (0.152 mm), the cylinders will normally require

boring with new oversize pistons fitted.
3 Provided the cylinder bore wear does not exceed 0.008 in (0.203 mm), however, special oil control rings and pistons can be fitted to restore compression and stop the engine burning oil.
4 If new pistons are being fitted to old bores, it is essential to roughen the bore walls slightly with fine glasspaper to enable the new piston rings to bed in properly.
5 Thoroughly examine the crankcase and cylinder block for cracks and damage, and use a piece of wire to probe all oilways and waterways to ensure they are unobstructed.
6 Check the tappet bores for wear and scoring; if excessive, they can be reamed and oversize tappets fitted.
7 Unscrew the oil pressure relief valve cap and remove the valve and spring. Check the valve seating for excessive wear and check that the spring free length is as specified. Renew the valve and spring as necessary, and refit them to the cylinder block.

24 Pistons and connecting rods - examination and renovation

1 Examine the pistons for ovality, scoring and scratches. Check the connecting rods for wear and damage (photo).
2 If the pistons or connecting rods are to be renewed it is recommended that this work is

21.5D . . . and rotor lobe clearance . . .

21.5C . . . outer rotor clearance . . .

24.1 Piston and connecting rod components

carried out by a BL garage, who will have the necessary tooling to extract the gudgeon pins from the connecting rods.

3 If new rings are to be fitted to the original pistons, expand the old rings over the top of the pistons. The use of two or three old feeler blades will be helpful in preventing the rings from dropping into empty grooves (photo). Note that the oil control ring is in three sections.

4 Before fitting the new rings to the piston, insert them into the cylinder bore and use a feeler gauge to check that the end gaps are within the specified limits.

5 After fitting the rings, check the compression rings for groove clearances using a feeler blade (photo). Make sure that the word 'Top', where marked on the compression rings, is toward the top of the piston. Arrange the compression ring gaps at 90 degrees to each other on the camshaft side of the piston.

25 Camshaft and tappets - examination

1 Examine the camshaft bearing surfaces, cam lobes and skew gear for wear. If excessive, renew the shaft.

2 Check the locating plate for wear, and renew it if necessary.

3 Check the camshaft bearings for wear and if necessary remove them with a suitable diameter length of tubing. Fit the new prefinished bearings with their oil holes aligned with the oilways in the cylinder block.

4 Examine the tappets for wear, and renew them if necessary.

26 Timing cover, chain and gears - examination

1 Examine all the teeth on the camshaft and crankshaft sprockets. If these are hooked in appearance, renew the sprockets.

2 Examine the chain tensioner for wear, and renew it if necessary.

3 Examine the timing chain for wear. If it has

24.3 Piston ring removal

been in operation for a considerable time, or if when held horizontally (rollers vertical) it takes on a deeply bowed appearance, renew it.

4 Check the timing cover for damage, and renew it if necessary. It is good practice to renew the timing cover oil seal whenever the timing cover is removed. To do this, drive out the old seal with a suitable drift, and install the new seal using a block of wood to make sure that it enters squarely (photo).

27 Gearbox adaptor plate - examination and renovation

1 The oil seal in the gearbox adaptor plate should be renewed as a matter of course if the engine is being overhauled.

2 Remove the old seal by prising or drifting it out of its location (photo).

3 Lubricate a new seal in engine oil and place it in position on the adaptor plate, with its sealing lip towards the engine (photo).

4 Using a block of wood and a hammer, drive the seal into its location until it is flush with the adaptor plate face.

28 Cylinder head - decarbonising, valve grinding and renovation

1 The operation will normally only be required at comparatively high mileages. However, if persistent pinking occurs and performance

24.5 Checking the piston ring-to-groove clearance

has deteriorated even though the engine adjustments are correct, decarbonising and valve grinding may be required.

2 With the cylinder head removed, use a scraper to remove the carbon from the combustion chambers and ports. Remove all traces of gasket from the cylinder head surface, then wash it thoroughly with paraffin.

3 Use a straight-edge and feeler blade to check that the cylinder head surface is not distorted. If it is, it must be resurfaced by a suitably equipped engineering works.

4 If the engine is still in the car, clean the piston crowns and cylinder bore upper edges, but make sure that no carbon drops between the pistons and bores. To do this, locate two of the pistons at the top of their bores and seal off the remaining bores with paper and masking tape.

> **HAYNES HiNT** *Press a little grease between the two pistons and their bores to collect any carbon dust, this can be wiped away when the piston is lowered.*

To prevent carbon build-up, polish the piston crown with metal polish, but remove all traces of polish afterwards.

5 Examine the heads of the valves for pitting and burning, especially the exhaust valve heads. Renew any valve which is badly burnt. Examine the valve seats at the same time. If the pitting is very slight, it can be removed by

26.4 Fitting the timing cover oil seal

27.2 Removing the crankshaft rear oil seal in the adaptor plate

27.3 Fit the crankshaft rear oil seal with its sealing lip towards the engine

Fig. 1.4 Valve guide fitted height dimension 'A' (Sec 28)

Arrow indicates direction of both removal and refitting

grinding the valve heads and seats together with coarse, then fine, grinding paste.

6 Where excessive pitting has occurred, the valve seats must be recut or renewed by a suitably equipped engineering works.

7 Valve grinding is carried out as follows. Place the cylinder head upside down on a bench with a block of wood at each end to give clearance for the valve stems.

8 Smear a trace of coarse carborundum paste on the seat face and press a suction grinding tool onto the valve head. With a semi-rotary action grind the valve head to its seat, lifting the valve occasionally to redistribute the grinding paste. When a dull matt even surface is produced on both the valve seat and the valve, wipe off the paste and repeat the process with fine carborundum paste. A light spring placed under the valve head will greatly ease this operation. When a smooth unbroken ring of light grey matt finish is produced on both the valve and the seat, the grinding operation is complete.

9 Scrape away all carbon from the valve head and stem, and clean away all traces of grinding compound. Clean the valves and seats with a paraffin-soaked rag, then wipe with a clean rag.

10 If the valve guides are worn, indicated by a side-to-side motion of the valve, new guides must be fitted. To do this, use a suitable mandrel to press the worn guides downwards and out through the combustion chamber. Press the new guides into the cylinder head in

Fig. 1.5 Rocker shaft components (Sec 28)

the same direction until they are at the specified fitted height.

11 If the original valve springs have been in use for 20 000 miles (32 000 km) or more, renew them. Where fitted, the inlet valve oil seals should also be renewed whenever the cylinder head is dismantled.

12 Examine the pushrods and rocker shaft assembly for wear, and renew them as necessary. Dismantling and reassembly of the rocker components is straightforward if reference is made to Figs. 1.2 and 1.5.

29 Engine mountings - removal and refitting

Left-hand mounting

1 Place a jack beneath the gearbox, with a block of wood between the jack head and the gearbox. Raise the jack and just take the weight of the gearbox.

2 Undo and remove the through-bolt securing the engine mounting to the gearbox bracket. Lift off the upper rebound washer, lower the jack slightly and slide out the lower rebound washer.

3 Undo and remove the two bolts and withdraw the mounting from the body bracket.

4 Refitting is the reverse sequence to removal.

Right-hand mounting

5 Jack up the front of the car so that the front wheels are just clear of the ground and support it securely on axle stands.

6 Undo and remove the securing screws and withdraw the access panel from under the right-hand wheel arch.

7 Undo and remove the bolts securing the

Fig. 1.6 Left-hand engine mounting details (Sec 29)

1 Engine mounting-to-body bracket	3 Through-bolt
	4 Mounting
2 Gearbox mounting bracket	5 Rebound washers
	6 Earth cable

cooling system expansion tank to the body and move the tank to one side.

8 Position a jack beneath the right-hand side of the sump with a block of wood placed between the jack head and sump. Raise the jack and just take the weight of the engine.

9 Slacken the mounting centre through-bolt, undo and remove the bolts securing the support strap to the body and body mounting bracket. Lift off the support strap.

10 Undo and remove the bolts securing the mounting and brackets to the engine and withdraw the mounting assembly.

11 To refit the mounting assembly, first position it with the spacer offset towards the top, and place the reinforced buffer plate on one side, engaging the top location hole on the mounting.

12 Place the support straps on the mounting, refit the through-bolt and refit the assembly to the mounting bracket and buffer plates.

13 Place this assembly on the body mounting bracket and refit the retaining bolts, but do not tighten at this stage.

14 Refit the bolts securing the mounting assembly to the engine and tighten fully. Tighten the through-bolt.

15 Refer to Fig. 1.7 and move the support straps as necessary to give the specified clearances, then tighten the support strap retaining bolts.

16 Refit the access panel, remove the axle stands and lower the car to the ground.

Fig. 1.7 Right-hand engine mounting details (Sec 29)

1 *Buffer plates*
2 *Support strap*
3 *Body mounting bracket*
4 *Buffer plate restraint bracket*
5 *Engine mounting bracket*
6 *Mounting through-bolt*
A = 0.16 to 0.20 in (4.0 to 5.0 mm)
B = Gap to be parallel over full length

30.2 Tie-rod-to-engine and crossmember bracket through-bolts (arrowed)

30.3 Tie-rod engine support bracket retaining bolts (arrowed)

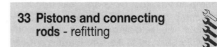

32.3A Installing the centre main bearing thrust washers

30 Engine tie-rod - removal and refitting

1 Jack up the front of the car and support it securely on axle stands.
2 Undo and remove the through-bolts securing the tie-rod to the engine support bracket (photo) and the crossmember bracket. Withdraw the tie-rod from its location.
3 If necessary the tie-rod engine support bracket can be removed after unscrewing the two nuts and bolts securing the bracket to the engine (photo).
4 Refitting is the reverse sequence to removal.

31 Engine reassembly - general

1 To ensure maximum life with minimum trouble from a rebuilt engine, not only must everything be correctly assembled, but it must also be spotlessly clean. All oilways must be clear, and locking washers and spring washers must be fitted where indicated. Oil all bearings and other working surfaces thoroughly with engine oil during assembly.
2 Before assembly begins, renew any bolts or studs with damaged threads.

3 Gather together a torque wrench, oil can, clean rags and a set of engine gaskets and oil seals, together with a new oil filter.

32 Crankshaft and main bearings - refitting

1 Clean the backs of the bearing shells and the bearing recesses in both the cylinder block and main bearing caps.
2 Press the main bearing shells into the cylinder block and caps and oil them liberally.
3 Using a little grease, stick the thrust washers to each side of the centre main bearings with their oilways facing away from the bearing (photo). Similarly fit the thrust washers to the centre main bearing cap (photo).
4 Lower the crankshaft into position, then fit the main bearing caps in their previously noted locations.
5 Insert and evenly tighten the main bearing cap bolts to the specified torque (photo). Check that the crankshaft rotates freely, then check that the endfloat is within the specified limits by inserting a feeler blade between the centre crankshaft web and the thrust washers.
6 Smear the front plate gasket with sealing compound and locate it on the front of the cylinder block. Fit the engine front plate and tighten the two lower retaining bolts.

7 With the engine upright, refit the timing cover, chain and gears, as described in Section 38.
8 Refit the pistons and connecting rods as described in Section 33.

33 Pistons and connecting rods - refitting

1 Clean the backs of the bearing shells and the recesses in the connecting rods and big-end caps.
2 Press the big-end bearing shells into the connecting rods and caps in their correct position and oil them liberally.
3 Fit a ring compressor to No 1 piston, then insert the piston and connecting rod into No 1 cylinder. With No 1 crankpin at its lowest point, drive the piston carefully into the cylinder with the wooden handle of a hammer, and at the same time guide the connecting rod onto the crankpin. Make sure that the 'Front' mark on the piston crown is facing the timing chain end of the engine, and that the connecting rod offset is as shown in Fig. 1.8.
4 Fit the big-end bearing cap in its previously noted position, then tighten the nuts evenly to the specified torque.
5 Check that the crankshaft turns freely.

32.3B Installing the centre main bearing cap and thrust washers

32.5 Tightening the main bearing bolts with a torque wrench

Fig. 1.8 Connecting rod offset positioning – arrowed (Sec 33)

6 Repeat the procedure given in paragraphs 3 to 5 for No 4 piston and connecting rod, then turn the crankshaft through half a turn and repeat the procedure on No 2 and No 3 pistons.
7 Refit the gearbox adaptor plate, as described in Section 36.
8 Refit the sump, as described in Section 37.
9 Refit the cylinder head, as described in Section 39.
10 Attach the gearbox to the engine (Section 41) and then refit the engine and gearbox assembly, as described in Section 42.

34 Oil pump - refitting

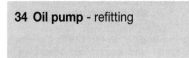

Note: *Prime the pump with clean engine oil before fitting*
1 Make sure that the mating faces of the oil pump and cylinder block are clean then fit the oil pump, together with a new gasket, and tighten the retaining bolts evenly to the specified torque. Make sure that the cut-outs in the gasket are correctly aligned with the pump, and, if the camshaft is already in position, make sure that the pump spindle engages the slot in the camshaft.
2 Bend the lockwashers to lock the bolts.
3 If the engine and gearbox were removed purposely to remove the oil pump, refit the gearbox adaptor plate, with reference to Section 36, and attach the gearbox. Refit the engine and gearbox, as described in Section 42.

35 Camshaft and tappets - refitting

1 Lubricate the tappets (cam followers) with engine oil and insert them into their bores. If the original tappets are being refitted, insert them in their original locations.
2 Oil the camshaft bearings and carefully insert the camshaft from the timing chain end

of the cylinder block. Make sure that the oil pump spindle engages the slot in the camshaft.
3 Fit the locating plate to the front plate and tighten the bolts evenly.
4 Temporarily refit the camshaft sprocket then, using a dial gauge, vernier calipers or feeler blade and bridging piece, check that the camshaft endfloat is within the specified limits. If not, renew the locating plate.
5 With the engine upright, refit the timing cover, chain and gears, as described in Section 38.
6 Turn the engine until No 1 piston is at top-dead-centre (TDC) on the compression stroke. If the cylinder head is not yet fitted, use two pushrods to determine the point when No 4 cylinder valves are rocking - in this position No 1 piston is at TDC compression.
7 Using the 5/16 in bolt used for removal, insert the distributor driveshaft into the cylinder block with the slot in the vertical position and the larger offset segment towards the crankshaft pulley end of the engine (see Fig. 1.9). As the driveshaft engages the skew gear on the camshaft, it will turn anti-clockwise so that the slot is in the horizontal position. Remove the bolt.
8 Refit the distributor (Chapter 4) and the fuel pump (Chapter 3).
9 Refit the pushrods and rocker shaft and adjust the valve clearances, as described in Section 44. Refit the rocker cover.
10 Attach the gearbox to the engine (Section 41) and refit the engine and gearbox, as described in Section 42.

36 Gearbox adaptor plate - refitting

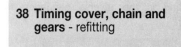

1 Ensure that the mating faces are perfectly clean and place a new gasket in position on the cylinder block.
2 Lubricate the crankshaft oil seal with engine oil and refit the adaptor plate to the cylinder block.
3 Refit the retaining bolts and tighten them evenly to the specified torque.
4 Refit the sump, as described in Section 37.
5 Refit the clutch assembly, as described in

Chapter 5, attach the gearbox to the engine (Section 41) and refit the engine and gearbox as described in Section 42.

37 Sump - refitting

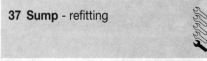

1 If the oil pick-up pipe and strainer were removed, refit the pipe to the crankcase and engage the union nut.
2 Refit and tighten the bolt securing the support bracket to the main bearing cap and then tighten the union nut.
3 Ensure that the sump and crankcase mating faces are clean and free from all traces of old gasket.
4 Apply jointing compound to both sides of the new side gaskets and position them on the sump.
5 Locate the new end seals in the sump recesses so that when they are pushed fully into place, an equal amount of gasket at each side protrudes above the sump face.
6 Refit the sump to the crankcase and secure with the retaining bolts. Tighten the bolts in a diagonal sequence to the specified torque in two or three stages.
7 If the engine is in the car, refit the tie-rod, as described in Section 30, fill the engine with oil and reconnect the battery.

38 Timing cover, chain and gears - refitting

1 Locate the timing gears on the crankshaft and camshaft without the chain, and check their alignment using a straight-edge.
2 Remove the gears, and if necessary extract the Woodruff key and fit shims to the crankshaft to obtain the alignment (photo). Refit the key.
3 Turn the crankshaft so that the Woodruff key is at top-dead-centre, and turn the camshaft so that the key is at 2 o'clock. In this position No 4 cylinder is at TDC compression.
4 Loop the timing chain over the two gears so that the timing marks are facing each other on the centre line (see Fig. 1.10).

Fig. 1.9 Distributor driveshaft fitting procedure (Sec 35)

1 Initial fitting position   2 Fitted position

38.2 Crankshaft gear shim location (arrowed)

Fig. 1.10 Timing gear alignment marks (arrowed) and centre line (Sec 38)

38.6A Tightening the camshaft gear retaining nut

38.6B Camshaft gear retaining nut locked and timing marks aligned

38.7 Fitting the timing chain tensioner

5 Locate the two gears on the crankshaft and camshaft and press them firmly home. Using a straight-edge check that the timing marks are still on the centre line.

6 Fit the camshaft gear retaining nut and lockwasher, and tighten the nut while using a screwdriver through one of the gear holes to restrain the gear (photo). Bend the lockwasher to lock the nut (photo).

7 Fit the chain tensioner and tighten the bolts, while keeping firm thumb pressure against the top of the bracket to provide the preload (photo).

8 Locate the oil thrower on the crankshaft with the side marked F facing outwards.

9 Stick the timing cover gasket to the front plate, then fit the timing cover and retain it with two upper bolts inserted loosely.

10 Oil the timing cover oil seal, then temporarily fit the crankshaft pulley to centralise the timing cover. Insert and tighten evenly the upper retaining bolts, then remove the pulley and fit the lower bolts.

11 Fit the crankshaft pulley on the crankshaft followed by the lockwasher and bolt. Tighten the bolt to the specified torque (photo) and bend over the lockwasher tab. Adopt the same procedure as used during removal to lock the crankshaft as the bolt is tightened (Sec 12).

12 Connect the crankcase ventilation hose to the oil separator and attach the fuel pipe clips to the timing cover studs.

13 If the engine is in the car, refit the access panel to the wheel arch, refit the water pump pulley and drivebelt, with reference to Chapter 2, and reconnect the battery.

39 Cylinder head - reassembly and refitting

1 Fit the valves in their original sequence or, if new valves have been obtained, in the seat to which they have been ground.

2 Oil the valve stems liberally and fit the oil seals to the inlet valve guides and collet grooves, where applicable.

3 Working on one valve, fit the spring and cup, then compress the spring with the compressor and insert the split collets. Release the compressor and remove it.

4 Repeat the procedure given in paragraph 3 on the remaining valves. Tap the end of each valve stem with a non-metallic mallet to settle the collets.

5 Make sure that the faces of the cylinder head and block are perfectly clean, then fit the new gasket over the studs with the words TOP and FRONT correctly positioned. FRONT being the crankshaft pulley end of the engine.

Fig . 1.11 Cylinder head nut tightening sequence (Sec 39)

Do not use jointing compound.

6 Lower the cylinder head over the studs and onto the gasket.

7 Insert the pushrods in their original locations, then lower the rocker shaft and pedestals over the studs, at the same time guiding the adjusting screws into the pushrods (photo).

8 Locate the coil and bracket on the stud furthest from the crankshaft pulley, and fit the rocker shaft lockwasher to the second pedestal from the front (crankshaft pulley end).

9 Fit the cylinder head nuts and tighten them to half the specified torque in the order shown in Fig. 1.11 (photo). After several minutes, tighten the nuts to the final torque, again in the order recommended.

10 Fit the rocker shaft pedestal washers and nuts and tighten them evenly to the specified torque (photo).

38.11 Tightening the crankshaft pulley bolt

39.7 Fit the rocker shaft assembly over the cylinder head studs

39.9 Tightening the cylinder head . . .

39.10. . . and rocker pedestal nuts using a torque wrench

11 Adjust the valve clearances, as described in Section 44.

12 Fit the rocker cover with a new gasket, place the wiring harness support brackets in position and refit the rocker cover retaining bolts and washers. Tighten the bolts to the specified torque.

13 If the engine is in the car, reverse the introductory procedure given in Section 10, and refill the cooling system, with reference to Chapter 2.

14 Drive the car for five to ten miles then allow the engine to cool, and remove the rocker cover. Working in the order shown in Fig. 1.11, slacken half a turn, then immediately tighten each cylinder head nut to the specified torque. Readjust the valve clearances then refit the rocker cover.

40 Ancillary components - refitting

Refer to Section 9 and refit the listed components with reference to the Chapters indicated.

41 Engine - attachment to gearbox

Refer to Section 7 and attach the gearbox to the engine using the reverse of the removal procedure. Tighten the retaining bolts to the specified torque.

42 Engine and gearbox assembly - refitting

Refer to Section 6 and refit the engine and gearbox using the reverse of the removal procedure, noting the following additional points:

(a) Align the marks on the driveshaft joints and drive flanges made during removal
(b) Adjust the accelerator cable, as described in Chapter 3, and the clutch cable, as described in Chapter 5
(c) Refill the engine with oil
(d) Refill the cooling system, as described in Chapter 2

43 Engine - adjustments after major overhaul

1 With the engine and gearbox refitted to the car, make a final check to ensure that everything has been reconnected and that no rags or tools have been left in the engine compartment.

2 Make sure that the oil and water levels are topped up and then start the engine; this may take a little longer than usual as the fuel pump and carburettor float chamber may be empty.

3 As soon as the engine starts, watch for the oil pressure light to go out and check for any oil, fuel or water leaks. Don't be alarmed if there are some odd smells and smoke from parts getting hot and burning off oil deposits.

4 Drive the car until normal operating temperature is reached and then allow it to cool. Re-torque the cylinder head nuts, as described in Section 39, and adjust the valve clearances, as described in Section 44.

5 If new pistons, ring or crankshaft bearings have been fitted, the engine must be run-in for the first 500 miles (800 km). Do not exceed 45 mph (72 kph), operate the engine at full throttle or allow it to labour in any gear.

44 Valve clearances - adjustment

1 The valve clearances must be adjusted with the engine cold.

44.4 Valve clearance adjustment

2 Remove the rocker cover and gasket.

3 Turn the engine with a spanner on the crankshaft pulley bolt until No 8 valve (No 4 cylinder exhaust) is fully open.

4 Insert a feeler blade of the correct thickness between the rocker arm and valve stem of No 1 valve (No 1 cylinder exhaust). If the blade is not a firm sliding fit, loosen the locknut on the rocker arm with a ring spanner and turn the adjusting screw with a screwdriver (photo). Tighten the locknut whilst holding the adjusting screw stationary, then recheck the adjustment.

5 Repeat the procedure given in paragraphs 3 and 4 on the remaining valves using the 'rule of nine' method as given below:

Valve open	Adjust valve
8 exhaust	1 exhaust
6 inlet	3 inlet
4 exhaust	5 exhaust
7 inlet	2 inlet
1 exhaust	8 exhaust
3 inlet	6 inlet
5 exhaust	4 exhaust
2 inlet	7 inlet

6 Check the rocker cover gasket for damage, and renew it if necessary. Refit the rocker cover and gasket with the filler cap towards the crankshaft pulley end of the engine. Tighten the nuts to the specified torque.

Part B: 1.6 litre engine

45 General description

The engine is of four-cylinder, in-line overhead camshaft type, mounted transversely at the front of the car.

The crankshaft is supported in five shell-type main bearings. Thrust washers are fitted to the centre main bearing in the crankcase to control crankshaft endfloat.

The connecting rods are attached to the crankshaft by horizontally split shell-type big-end bearings, and to the pistons by interference fit gudgeon pins. The aluminium alloy pistons are of the slipper type and have their gudgeon pins offset to the thrust side to reduce piston slap. Two compression rings and a three-piece oil control ring are fitted to each piston.

The overhead camshaft is mounted in a carrier attached to the cylinder head and is driven via a toothed belt by the crankshaft. The camshaft operates the valves through inverted bucket type tappets which are also housed in the camshaft carrier. Tappet adjustment is by shims fitted between the valve stems and the tappet buckets.

The inlet and exhaust valves are mounted at an angle in the cylinder head and are each closed by a single valve spring.

The oil pump, pressure relief valve and full-flow oil filter are located in a housing attached to the front of the cylinder block. The rotor type oil pump is driven directly by the crankshaft.

The distributor rotor is driven directly by the camshaft whereas the fuel pump is operated by an eccentric camshaft lobe. The toothed timing belt also drives the water pump and a separate drivebelt is used for the alternator, driven by a sprocket on the crankshaft.

Fig. 1.12 Exploded view of the 1.6 litre engine main components (Sec 45)

1 Inlet manifold
2 Inlet manifold induction
   temperature sensor
3 Fuel pump
4 Insulating block
5 Camshaft carrier front cover
6 Camshaft carrier rear cover
7 Cover gaskets
8 Camshaft carrier
9 Water outlet elbow
10 Thermostat
11 Coolant temperature thermistor
12 Thermostat housing

13 Oil filler cap
14 Oil filler tube
15 Water inlet elbow
16 Spark plug
17 Crankshaft rear oil seal
18 Dipstick tube
19 Dipstick
20 Gearbox adaptor plate
21 Crankshaft sensor
22 Knock sensor
23 Main bearing cap
24 Sump gasket
25 Sump

26 Oil separator
27 Main bearing shells
28 Water pump
29 Oil pressure relief valve
30 Oil pump and housing
31 Oil pick-up tube
32 Crankshaft front oil seal
33 Alternator drivebelt
34 Crankshaft pulley
35 Oil pressure switch and
   adaptor
36 Timing belt lower cover

37 Timing belt upper cover
38 Oil filter
39 Timing belt tensioner
40 Cylinder block
41 Manifold gasket
42 Cylinder head gasket
43 Cylinder head
44 Camshaft carrier O-ring seal
45 Inlet manifold support struts
46 Exhaust manifold
47 Inlet manifold induction heater
48 Hot air box

Fig. 1.13 Exploded view of the 1.6 litre engine internal components (Sec 45)

1 Timing belt
2 Camshaft sprocket
3 Camshaft oil seals
4 Camshaft locating plate
5 Camshaft
6 Gudgeon pin
7 Piston and piston rings
8 Connecting rod and cap

9 Big-end bearing shells
10 Crankshaft
11 Main bearing shells
12 Woodruff key
13 Guide plate
14 Crankshaft sprocket
15 Crankshaft pulley
16 Pulley retaining bolt and
     washer

17 Timing belt tensioner
18 Tappet bucket and
     shim
19 Inlet valve components
20 Exhaust valve
21 Piston and connecting rod
     assembly
22 Crankshaft thrust
     washers

46 Maintenance and inspection

1 At the intervals given in Routine Maintenance at the beginning of this manual, carry out the following service operations on the engine.
2 Visually inspect the engine joint faces, gaskets and seals for any sign of oil or water leaks. Pay particular attention to the areas around the camshaft cover, cylinder head, crankshaft front oil seal and sump joint faces. Rectify any leaks by referring to the appropriate Sections of this Chapter.
3 Place a suitable container beneath the oil drain plug located on the rear facing side of the sump. Unscrew the plug using a spanner or socket and allow the oil to drain. Inspect the condition of the drain plug sealing washer, and renew it if necessary. Refit and tighten the plug after draining.
4 Move the bowl to the right-hand side of the engine under the oil filter.

5 Using a strap wrench or filter removal tool, slacken the filter and unscrew it from the engine and discard.
6 Wipe the filter mating face on the sump with a rag and then lubricate the seal of a new filter using clean engine oil.
7 Screw the filter into position and tighten it by hand only, do not use any tools.
8 Refill the engine using the correct grade of oil through the filler on the front of the engine. Fill until the level reaches the MAX mark on the dipstick - 0.5 litres will raise the level from MIN to MAX.
9 With the engine running, check for leaks around the filter seal.
10 At less frequent intervals (see Routine Maintenance), check and if necessary, adjust the tappet clearances, as described in Section 86.
11 At the same interval clean the filter gauze in the oil filler cap using paraffin or a suitable solvent and dry using compressed air.
12 When specified, renew the timing belt using the procedure given in Sections 55 and 85.

47 Major operations possible with the engine in the car

The following operations can be carried out without having to remove the engine from the car:
(a) Removal, refitting and adjustment of the timing belt and tensioner
(b) Removal and refitting of the camshaft and tappets
(c) Removal and refitting of the cylinder head
(d) Removal and refitting of the sump
(e) Removal and refitting of the big-end bearings
(f) Removal and refitting of the piston and connecting rod assemblies
(g) Removal and refitting of the oil pump
(h) Removal and refitting of the gearbox adaptor plate (after removal of the gearbox or automatic transmission)
(i) Removal and refitting of the engine mountings

48 Major operations requiring engine removal

Strictly speaking it is only necessary to remove the engine if the crankshaft or main bearings require attention. However, due to the possibility of dirt entry, and to allow greater working access, it is preferable to remove the engine if working on the piston and connecting rod assemblies, or when carrying out any major engine overhaul or repair.

49 Methods of engine removal

The engine, complete with gearbox or automatic transmission, is removed by lifting it upwards and out of the engine compartment as a complete assembly. The gearbox or automatic transmission is then separated from the engine after removal. Due to the limited working clearances it is not possible to remove the engine on its own.

50 Engine - removal with manual gearbox

1 Remove the bonnet, as described in Chapter 12, and the battery, as described in Chapter 10.
2 Undo and remove the bolts securing the battery tray to the body and take out the tray. Note the arrangement of earth wires on the front retaining bolt (photos).
3 Drain the cooling system, as described in Chapter 2.
4 Remove the air cleaner assembly and the plenum chamber, as described in Chapter 3.

50.2A Earth wire arrangement on battery tray front retaining bolt

50.2B Remove the battery tray

50.5 Disconnect the reversing lamp switch wires (arrowed)

5 Slide back the protective cover, then disconnect the two reversing lamp wires at the gearbox switch (photo).
6 Undo the nut and bolt securing the earth strap and cable retaining clip to the gearbox casing (photo).
7 Make a note of the wiring connections at the starter motor solenoid and disconnect the wires.
8 Disconnect the crankshaft sensor wiring plug (photo) then, using a spanner and suitable Allen key, undo the two starter motor retaining bolts. Remove the starter, crankshaft sensor bracket and engine front snubber.
9 Disconnect the wiring plug at the knock sensor on the front face of the cylinder block (photo).
10 Spring back the clip and disconnect the wiring plug at the rear of the alternator.
11 Disconnect the wiring plug from the coolant temperature thermistor in the thermostat housing.
12 Disconnect the inlet manifold induction heater lead at the wiring connector and the two wires at the inlet manifold induction temperature sensor.
13 Disconnect the wire at the oil pressure switch adjacent to the crankshaft pulley (photo).
14 Disconnect the wiring plug at the carburettor stepping motor and the two leads at the fuel shut-off valve solenoid (photos).
15 Release the retaining clip and remove the fuel inlet hose from the fuel pump (photo). Plug the hose after removal.

50.6 Remove the earth strap and cable clip retaining bolt (arrowed)

50.8 Disconnect the crankshaft sensor wiring plug . . .

50.9 . . . and knock sensor wiring plug

50.13 Disconnect the oil pressure switch wire

50.14A Disconnect the wiring at the carburettor stepping motor . . .

50.14B . . . and fuel shut-off valve solenoid

50.15 Remove the fuel inlet hose from the pump

1

50.16 Detach the float chamber vent hose (A) and crankcase breather hose (B)

50.18 Detach the two ignition vacuum advance hose connectors (arrowed)

50.19 Remove the banjo union bolt and washers from the inlet manifold

50.20A Slip the accelerator cable end (arrowed) out of the throttle lever . . .

50.20B . . . unscrew the lower accelerator cable locknut (arrowed) and remove the cable

16 Pull the float chamber vent hose off the carburettor outlet and remove the hose and pipe from the engine (photo).

17 Detach the crankcase breather hoses at the carburettor, oil filler cap and oil separator, then remove the hose assembly.

18 Disconnect the two ignition vacuum advance hose connectors at the carburettor (photo).

19 Disconnect the vacuum hose from the inlet manifold banjo union, undo the union bolt and recover the two washers (photo). Place the servo vacuum hose to one side.

20 Open the throttle linkage by hand and slip the accelerator cable end out of the slot on the throttle lever (photo). Slacken the outer cable locknuts, unscrew the lower locknut fully and release the cable from the support bracket (photo). Place the cable to one side.

21 Slacken the retaining clips and disconnect the heater hoses at the inlet manifold.

22 Slacken the retaining clips and disconnect the heater hose and radiator bottom hose from the water inlet elbow (photo), followed by the expansion tank hose, radiator top hose and heater hose from the water outlet elbow and thermostat housing (photos).

23 Refer to Chapter 5 and detach the clutch cable from the operating lever and gearbox bracket.

24 Undo and remove the bolt securing the speedometer cable to the gearbox. Withdraw the cable and pinion assembly and place them aside (photo).

50.22A Disconnect the hoses at the water inlet elbow . . .

50.22B . . . water outlet elbow . . .

50.22C . . . and thermostat housing

50.24 Remove the speedometer cable and pinion assembly

50.25A Extract the retaining clip and release the gearchange rod . . .

50.25B . . . then prise the selector rod balljoint socket (arrowed) off the relay lever

50.29 Undo and remove the rear mounting-to-crossmember nuts (arrowed)

50.33 Remove the right-hand mounting support bracket

25 Remove the retaining clip and slide the gearchange rod out of the selector shaft lever (photo). Disconnect the rear selector rod from the relay lever on the gearbox by prising off the balljoint socket with a screwdriver (photo).

26 Jack up the front of the car and support it securely on axle stands.

27 From underneath the car, undo the nuts securing the exhaust front pipes to the manifold. Separate the joint flange and recover the gasket.

28 Mark the relationship of the driveshaft inner constant velocity joints to the differential drive flanges. Lift off the protective caps and unscrew the joint-to-drive flange retaining bolts using a suitable Allen key.

29 Undo the two nuts securing the rear engine mounting to the front crossmember (photo).

30 Undo the retaining screws and remove the left-hand and right-hand access panels from under the wheel arches.

31 Remove the axle stands and lower the car to the ground.

32 Attach a suitable hoist to the engine using chains or rope slings, or by attaching the chains or ropes to sturdy brackets bolted to the engine and gearbox. Raise the hoist to just take the weight of the engine.

33 Undo the screw securing the expansion tank to the support bracket and the two bolts securing the bracket to the body. Withdraw the bracket (photo).

34 From under the right-hand wheel arch, undo the two bolts securing the right-hand engine mounting to the body, noting the distance spacer on each bolt (photo).

35 Undo the bolts securing the right-hand engine mounting to the engine and remove the complete mounting assembly (photo).

36 Undo the two bolts securing the left-hand engine mounting to the gearbox, and the through-bolt and nut securing the mounting to the body bracket. Remove the mounting (photo).

37 Undo the three bolts securing the left-hand engine mounting bracket to the body

and remove the bracket (photo).

38 Make a final check that everything attaching the engine and gearbox to the car has been disconnected and that all detached components are well clear.

39 Lift the engine and gearbox slightly and, as soon as sufficient clearance exists, release the driveshaft inner joints from the drive flanges. Support or tie up the driveshafts to avoid straining the outer joints.

40 Continue raising the engine and gearbox assembly (photo), and, when it has been raised sufficiently, draw the hoist forward or push the car backwards and lower the engine and gearbox to the ground.

1

50.34 Undo the right-hand mounting-to-body bolts from under the wheel arch

50.35 Remove the right-hand mounting from the engine

50.36 Remove the left-hand mounting from the gearbox and body bracket . . .

50.37 . . . then undo the three bolts and remove the body bracket

50.40 Removing the engine and gearbox from the car

52.1 Gearbox-to-adaptor plate bolt, nut and support strut arrangement

52.2 Removing the gearbox from the engine

54.1A Lift off the timing belt upper cover . . .

51 Engine - removal with automatic transmission

1 Remove the bonnet, as described in Chapter 12, and the battery, as described in Chapter 10.
2 Undo and remove the bolts securing the battery tray to the body and take out the tray.
3 Drain the cooling system, as described in Chapter 2.
4 Remove the air cleaner assembly and the plenum chamber, as described in Chapter 3.
5 Make a note of the wiring connections at the starter motor solenoid and disconnect the wires.
6 Disconnect the crankshaft sensor wiring plug then, using a spanner and suitable Allen key, undo the two starter motor retaining bolts.
7 Remove the starter motor, crankshaft sensor bracket and the engine front snubber bracket.
8 Undo the nut and release the selector cable trunnion from the selector lever on the transmission.
9 Slip the kickdown cable end out of its operating lever on the transmission. Release the clevis pin and disconnect the other end of the kickdown cable from the carburettor linkage and support bracket.
10 Undo the retaining bolts securing the selector cable and kickdown cable support bracket to the transmission. Move the bracket and cables clear of the engine and transmission.
11 Disconnect the speedometer cable from its attachment on the transmission.
12 Refer to Section 50 and carry out the operations described in paragraphs 9 to 22 inclusive.
13 Jack up the front of the car and support it securely on axle stands.
14 From underneath the car, undo the nuts securing the exhaust front pipes to the manifold. Separate the joint flange and recover the gasket.
15 Mark the relationship of the driveshaft inner constant velocity joints to the differential drive flanges. Lift off the protective caps and unscrew the joint-to-drive flange retaining bolts using a suitable Allen key.

16 Undo the nuts securing the rear engine/transmission mounting to the crossmember.
17 Undo the retaining screws and remove the left-hand and right-hand access panels from under the wheel arches.
18 Remove the axle stands and lower the car to the ground.
19 Attach a suitable hoist to the engine using chains or rope slings, or by attaching chains or ropes to sturdy brackets bolted to the engine and transmission. Raise the hoist to just take the weight of the engine.
20 Undo the screw securing the expansion tank to the support bracket and the two bolts securing the bracket to the body. Withdraw the bracket.
21 From under the right-hand wheel arch, undo the two bolts securing the right-hand engine mounting to the body, noting the distance spacer on each bolt.
22 Undo the bolts securing the right-hand mounting to the engine and remove the mounting.
23 Undo the bolt securing the left-hand mounting to the transmission and body then remove the complete mounting assembly.
24 Make a final check that everything attaching the engine and transmission to the car has been disconnected and that all attached components are well clear.
25 Lift the engine and transmission slightly and, as soon as sufficient clearance exists, release the driveshaft inner joints from the drive flanges. Support or tie up the driveshafts to avoid straining the outer joints.
26 Continue raising the engine and transmission assembly and, when it has been raised sufficiently, draw the hoist forward or push the car backwards and lower the engine and transmission to the ground.

52 Engine - separation from manual gearbox or automatic transmission

Manual gearbox

1 With the engine and gearbox removed from the car, support the two units and undo all the

bolts securing the gearbox to the engine adaptor plate. Note the locations of the different lengths of bolts and also the arrangement of retaining nut and captive nut on the bolt that secures the inlet manifold support strut (photo).
2 When all the bolts have been removed, ease the gearbox off its locating dowels and withdraw it squarely from the engine (photo). Do not allow the weight of the gearbox to hang unsupported on the gearbox shaft.

Automatic transmission

3 Turn the crankshaft as necessary until each of the torque converter retaining bolts becomes accessible through the starter motor aperture. Undo the bolts using a socket and extension bar.
4 Undo the bolts securing the transmission to the engine adaptor plate, noting the different bolt lengths and the arrangement of support brackets, where applicable.
5 Ease the transmission off the adaptor plate dowels and withdraw it from the engine, ensuring that the torque converter remains on the transmission shaft.

53 Engine dismantling - general

Refer to Section 8.

54 Ancillary components - removal

1 If the engine has been removed from the car for major overhaul or repair the externally-mounted ancillary components, as given in the following list, should first be removed. Removal is straightforward, but where necessary reference should be made to the relevant Chapters of this manual as indicated. The removal sequence need not necessarily follow the order given:
Alternator (Chapter 10)
Timing belt covers - photos
Fuel pump (Chapter 3)

54.1B . . . then undo the screws (arrowed) and remove the lower cover

54.1C Remove the distributor cap and HT leads . . .

54.1D . . . followed by the rotor arm and shield

54.1E Undo the bolts (arrowed) and remove the alternator mounting bracket

54.1F Unscrew the knock sensor

54.1G Remove the crankshaft sensor

Distributor cap and rotor arm (Chapter 4) - photos
Oil filler tube
Thermostat, housing and water inlet elbow (Chapter 2)
Alternator mounting bracket - photo
Knock sensor - photo
Crankshaft sensor (Chapter 4) - photo
Spark plugs (Chapter 4)
Inlet and exhaust manifolds and carburettor (Chapter 3)
Clutch and flywheel assembly (Chapter 5)
Water pump (Chapter 2) - after removal of the timing belt
Oil filter (Section 46 of this Chapter)
Dipstick

55 Timing belt - removal

1 Jack up the front of the car and support it on axle stands.
2 Remove the right-hand front roadwheel and the access panel under the wheel arch.
3 Disconnect the battery negative terminal.
4 Slacken the alternator pivot mounting bolt and the adjustment arm bolts. Move the alternator towards the engine and remove the drivebelt from the pulleys (photo).
5 Lift off the timing belt upper cover then undo the screws and remove the lower cover (photos).

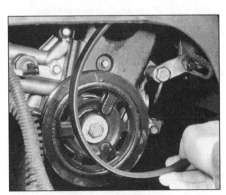

55.4 Remove the alternator drivebelt

55.5A Remove the timing belt upper. . .

55.5B . . . and lower covers

55.6A Align the dimple on the camshaft sprocket with the notch on the carrier . . .

55.6B . . . and the notch on the crankshaft pulley with the mark on the oil pump housing

55.7 Slacken the two tensioner retaining bolts (arrowed)

55.8 Remove the timing belt from the sprockets

6 Using a socket or spanner on the crankshaft pulley bolt, turn the engine over until the dimple on the rear face of the camshaft sprocket is aligned with the notch on the camshaft carrier (photo). Check also that the notch on the crankshaft pulley is aligned with the timing mark on the oil pump housing (photo).
7 Slacken the two timing belt tensioner retaining bolts and move the tensioner away from the engine (photo).
8 Slip the timing belt off the three sprockets and remove it from the engine (photo).
9 Store the belt on its edge while off the engine.

 HAYNES HiNT *If the original belt is to be re-used, mark it with chalk to indicate of its direction of rotation and also its outer facing edge.*

56 Cylinder head removal - engine in car

1 Refer to Section 55 and remove the timing belt.
2 Drain the cooling system, as described in Chapter 2.
3 Remove the air cleaner and plenum chamber, as described in Chapter 3.

4 Remove the alternator, as described in Chapter 10.
5 Undo the three bolts securing the alternator mounting bracket to the cylinder head and block, then remove the bracket (photo).
6 Disconnect the fuel inlet hose at the carburettor and plug the hose after removal.
7 Undo the two bolts securing the fuel pump to the cam cover. Withdraw the pump, insulating block and gaskets, and place it to one side with hoses still attached (photo).
8 Disconnect the vacuum hose from the inlet manifold banjo union, undo the union bolt and recover the two copper washers. Place the servo vacuum hose to one side.
9 Undo the small bolt and release the oil dipstick tube from the camshaft cover.
10 Slacken the retaining clips and disconnect

the expansion tank hose, radiator top hose and heater hose from the water outlet elbow and thermostat housing (photo).
11 Slacken the retaining clips and disconnect the heater hose and radiator bottom hose from the water inlet elbow (photo).
12 Slacken the retaining clips and disconnect the heater hoses at the inlet manifold.
13 Disconnect the wiring plug at the carburettor stepping motor and the two wires at the fuel shut-off valve solenoid.
14 Open the throttle linkage by hand and slip the accelerator cable end out of the slot on the throttle lever. Slacken the outer cable locknuts, unscrew the inner cable locknut and release the cable from the support bracket. Place the cable to one side.
15 On vehicles equipped with automatic

56.5 Undo the bolts (arrowed) and remove the alternator mounting bracket

56.7 Remove the pump with the hoses still attached

56.10 Disconnect the hoses at the water outlet elbow and thermostat housing . . .

56.11 . . . and at the water inlet elbow

56.16 Disconnect the vacuum hoses at the carburettor connectors

56.17 Disconnect the induction temperature sensor leads at the manifold

56.18 Disconnect the coolant temperature thermistor wiring plug

56.19 Undo the manifold support strut retaining bolts

transmission, remove the clevis pin securing the kickdown cable to the throttle lever and remove the cable from the support bracket.

16 Disconnect the two ignition vacuum advance hose connectors at the carburettor (photo).

17 Disconnect the inlet manifold induction heater lead at the wiring connector and the two wires at the inlet manifold induction temperature sensor (photo).

18 Disconnect the wiring plug from the coolant temperature thermistor in the thermostat housing (photo).

19 Undo the two bolts securing the support struts to the inlet manifold (photo).

20 Undo the nuts securing the exhaust front pipes to the manifold. Separate the joint flange and recover the gasket.

21 Undo the two bolts securing the oil filler tube to the adaptor plate and remove the tube and gasket.

22 Disconnect the spark plug HT leads from the plugs then undo the two distributor cap retaining screws. Remove the cap and leads and place them to one side.

23 Place a suitable jack beneath the right-hand side of the engine with a block of wood between the jack head and the sump. Raise the jack and just take the weight of the engine.

24 Undo the bolts securing the right-hand engine mounting to the cylinder head. Slacken

the mounting through-bolt and swivel the mounting as far away from the cylinder head as possible.

25 Gradually slacken the cylinder head retaining bolts, half a turn at a time, in the reverse order to that shown in Fig. 1.18. When all the bolts have been slackened, remove them from their locations noting where the bolts having upper thread extensions are fitted.

26 Lift the cylinder head and manifold assembly from the engine (photo). If it is stuck, tap it free with a soft-faced mallet, do not attempt to prise it free using a lever between the head and cylinder block, or the mating faces may be damaged.

27 Remove the cylinder head gasket from the cylinder block.

57 Cylinder head removal - engine on bench

The procedure for removing the cylinder head with the engine on the bench is similar to that for removal when the engine is in the car with the exception of disconnecting the controls and services. Refer to Section 56 and follow the procedure given as applicable.

58 Camshaft and tappets - removal

Note: *If the engine is in the car, carry out the following operations with reference to the relevant Sections and Chapters of this manual:*
(a) Disconnect the battery negative terminal
(b) Remove the air cleaner
(c) Remove the timing belt
(d) Remove the fuel pump
(e) Remove the distributor cap, rotor arm and shield

1 Undo the retaining bolts and lift off the two camshaft carrier covers (photo). Note the position of the cable and hose clips on the cover bolts.

2 Using a suitable socket, or spanner, undo the camshaft sprocket retaining bolt. Engage a stout screwdriver or bar through the sprocket holes and in contact with the carrier to prevent the camshaft turning. Remove the sprocket retaining bolt and washer then withdraw the sprocket from the camshaft. Carefully ease it off using two levers if it is tight.

3 Using pliers, withdraw the camshaft locating plate from the carrier (photo).

4 Progressively slacken the camshaft carrier retaining bolts and, when all tension on the bolts has been relieved, remove them.

5 Raise the camshaft carrier slightly and push

56.26 Removing the cylinder head, complete with manifolds and carburettor

58.1 Remove the camshaft carrier covers

58.3 Withdraw the camshaft locating plate

58.8 Carefully withdraw the camshaft from the carrier

58.9 Lift out the tappet buckets, complete with shims

58.10 Remove the camshaft carrier from the cylinder head

down the tappet buckets until the cam lobes are clear.

6 Move the camshaft towards the rotor arm end until sufficient clearance exists to enable the oil seal at the sprocket end to be removed. Hook the seal out using a screwdriver.

7 Now move the camshaft towards the sprocket end and remove the remaining oil seal in the same way.

8 The camshaft can now be carefully removed from the rotor arm end of the carrier (photo).

9 Lift out each of the tappet buckets in turn and keep them in strict order (photo). Make sure that the small adjustment shim has remained in place inside the bucket.

10 Withdraw the camshaft carrier from the cylinder head (photo) noting the location of the O-ring oil seal.

59 Cylinder head - dismantling

Note: *If the cylinder head was removed with the engine in the car, refer to the relevant Sections and Chapters of this manual and remove the following components:*
(a) *Inlet and exhaust manifolds and carburettor*
(b) *Distributor cap, rotor arm and shield*
(c) *Thermostat housing and water inlet elbow*
(d) *Camshaft and tappets*

1 Using a valve spring compressor, compress each valve spring in turn until the split collets can be removed (photo). Release the compressor and lift off the cap and spring.

2 If, when the valve spring compressor is screwed down, the valve spring cap refuses to free and expose the split collets, gently tap the top of the tool directly over the cap with a light hammer. This will free the cap.

3 Remove the valve through the combustion chamber then prise the valve stem oil seals off the valve guides using a screwdriver (photos).

4 It is essential that the valves are kept in their correct sequence unless they are so badly worn that they are to be renewed. If they are going to be kept and used again, place them in a sheet of card having eight holes numbered 1 to 8 corresponding to the relative fitted positions of the valves. **Note** that No 1 valve is nearest to the crankshaft pulley end of the engine.

60 Sump - removal

Note: *If the engine is still in the car, carry out the following operations:*
(a) *Drain the engine oil*
(b) *Disconnect the breather hose from the oil separator on the front face of the sump*

1 Undo the bolts securing the sump to the gearbox adaptor plate.

2 Progressively slacken the sump retaining bolts and then remove them. Make a note of the locations of the different lengths of bolts and of the ones which also secure cable clips and support brackets.

3 Tap the sump with a soft-faced mallet to free the joint face, then remove the sump from the crankcase. Recover the one-piece rubber gasket.

4 If necessary undo the two bolts and one nut securing the oil pick-up tube to the oil pump housing and main bearing cap and remove the tube. Recover the O-ring oil seal at the base of the pick-up tube.

61 Oil pump and housing - removal

Note: *If the engine is in the car, carry out the following operations with reference to the relevant Sections and Chapters of this manual:*
(a) *Remove the timing belt*
(b) *Remove the sump and oil pick-up tube*
(c) *Disconnect the oil pressure switch wire*

1 Undo the bolt securing the crankshaft pulley to the crankshaft. If the engine is in the car, engage 1st gear (manual transmission) and firmly apply the footbrake to prevent crankshaft rotation as the bolt is undone. On automatic transmission models it is necessary to remove the starter motor (Chapter 10) and prevent the crankshaft from turning by

59.1 Compress the valve springs and lift out the split collets

59.3A Remove the valve . . .

59.3B . . . then prise off the valve stem oil seals

61.1 Using two bolts and a stout bar to lock the crankshaft

62.2 Sump retaining bolt locations (arrowed) in the gearbox adaptor plate

63.1 Identify the connecting rod and cap with centre dots if manufacturer's marks are not apparent

inserting a suitable bar into the driveplate ring gear. If the engine is on the bench, refit two of the clutch pressure plate retaining bolts to the crankshaft and engage a stout bar between them (photo).

2 Withdraw the crankshaft pulley followed by the crankshaft sprocket and guide plate.

3 Undo the pump retaining bolts, noting their lengths and locations, and also the retaining plate fitted under the top centre bolt.

4 Withdraw the oil pump housing and recover the gasket.

62 Gearbox adaptor plate - removal

Note: If the engine is in the car, carry out the following operations with reference to the relevant Sections and Chapters of this manual:
(a) Remove the manual gearbox or automatic transmission
(b) Remove the clutch assembly and flywheel
(c) Remove the sump
(d) Remove the oil filler tube
(e) Remove the crankshaft sensor

1 Undo the bolts securing the adaptor plate to the cylinder block.

2 Tap the adaptor plate using a soft-faced mallet to free it from the locating dowels and remove it from the engine. Remove the two sump retaining bolts and gearbox retaining

bolt from their captive recesses in the adaptor plate (photo).

63 Pistons and connecting rods - removal

Note: If the engine is in the car, carry out the following operations with reference to the relevant Sections and Chapters of this manual:
(a) Remove the cylinder head (this is not necessary if only the big-end bearings are to be removed)
(b) Remove the sump and oil pick-up tube

1 Check the big-end caps for identification marks. If necessary use a centre punch on the caps and rods to identify them; mark them 1 to 4 on the dipstick tube side to ensure correct refitting (photo). Note that No 1 is nearest to the crankshaft pulley end of the engine.

2 Turn the crankshaft so that No 1 crankpin is at its lowest point. Using a suitable socket, undo the two nuts securing the connecting rod cap to the rod.

3 Withdraw the cap, complete with bearing shell.

4 Using the handle of a hammer, carefully push the piston and connecting rod up through the bore and withdraw it from the top of the cylinder block.

5 Loosely refit the cap to the connecting rod.

6 Repeat the procedure given in paragraphs 1 to 5 on No 4 piston and connecting rod, then turn the crankshaft through half a turn and repeat the procedure on No 2 and No 3 piston and connecting rod assemblies.

64 Crankshaft and main bearings - removal

1 With the engine removed from the car and dismantled as described in the previous Sections of this Chapter, the crankshaft and main bearings can now be removed.

2 Check the crankcase and main bearing caps for identification marks (photo) and if no marks are present, use a centre punch to mark them.

3 Undo the bolts securing the main bearing caps and remove the caps, complete with bearing shells.

4 Before removing the crankshaft, check that the endfloat is within the specified limits by inserting feeler blades between No 4 crankshaft web and the thrust washers (photo). If the clearance is not as specified, new thrust washers will be required for reassembly.

5 Lift the crankshaft out of the crankcase (photo) then remove the main bearing shell upper halves and the thrust washers (photo).

64.2 Identification marks on the main bearing cap and crankcase

64.4 Checking crankshaft endfloat

64.5A Lift out the crankshaft . . .

1

64.5B . . . and remove the thrust washers and bearing shells

Keep the main bearing shells in order with their respective caps.

65 Crankcase ventilation system - description

The crankcase ventilation system consists of an oil separator attached to the engine sump, a breather filter located in the oil filler cap and a hose connecting the oil separator and filler cap to the carburettor.

Air is drawn into the crankcase through the filter in the filler cap. Inlet manifold depression draws the crankcase fumes from the oil separator and oil filler tube through the hose into the carburettor airstream where they mix with the incoming fuel/air mixture passing to the cylinders for combustion.

The breather filter should be cleaned at the specified service intervals (see Routine Maintenance) and the hoses periodically checked for condition and security.

66 Examination and renovation - general

With the engine completely dismantled, clean all the components and examine them

Fig. 1.14 Piston ring details (Sec 69)

1 Compression ring upper faces (marked TOP)
2 Compression ring gaps positioned at 90° to each other towards the dipstick tube side of the engine
3 Oil control ring rails and spreader spring

for wear. Each part should be checked and where necessary renewed or renovated, as described in the following Sections. All oil seals, gaskets and O-rings should be renewed as a matter of course and also main and big-end shell bearings unless they have had little wear and are in perfect condition.

67 Cylinder block and crankcase - examination and renovation

Refer to Section 23, paragraphs 1 to 5.

68 Crankshaft and main bearings - examination and renovation

Refer to Section 22.

69 Pistons and connecting rods - examination and renovation

Refer to Section 24, but note that, when arranging the piston rings, the compression ring gaps should be positioned at 90° to each

Fig. 1.15 Oil pump housing and pump components (Sec 71)

1	Oil pressure switch	6	Pressure relief valve spring
2	Outer rotor	7	Pressure relief valve cap
3	Pump backplate	8	Oil pump housing
4	Inner rotor	9	Crankshaft front oil seal
5	Pressure relief valve plunger		

other towards the dipstick tube side of the cylinder block.

70 Gearbox adaptor plate - examination and renovation

Refer to Section 27.

71 Oil pump and housing - examination and renovation

1 Remove the oil filter from the pump housing if not already done.
2 Undo the six screws and lift off the pump backplate (photo).
3 Lift out the two rotors from the pump body (photo).
4 Unscrew the pressure relief valve cap using a wide-bladed tool and remove the spring and plunger (photos).
5 Clean all the parts in paraffin or a suitable

71.2 Undo the screws and remove the oil pump backplate

71.3 Lift out the oil pump rotors

71.4A Unscrew the pressure relief valve cap . . .

71.4B . . . and withdraw the relief valve components

71.6A Checking the oil pump rotor lobe clearance . . .

71.6B . . . outer rotor-to-body clearance . . .

solvent and dry with a lint-free cloth. Examine the components for signs of scoring, wear ridges or other damage and renew the pump as a complete assembly if any of these conditions are apparent.

6 If the pump is satisfactory so far, refit the rotors to the pump body and check the rotor lobe clearance, outer rotor-to-body clearance and the outer rotor endfloat using feeler gauges and a straight-edge (photo). Renew the pump if any of the clearances are outside the figures given in the Specifications.

7 If the pump is serviceable, renew the crankshaft front oil seal in the pump housing. Tap the old seal out from the inside using a punch (photo) and fit a new seal using a tube, block of wood or socket by tapping it squarely into the housing (photo).

8 Lubricate the pressure relief valve plunger with clean engine oil and refit plunger followed by the spring and cap. Tighten the cap securely.

9 Liberally lubricate the two rotors with clean engine oil and place them in position in the pump housing.

10 Refit the pump backplate and secure with the six screws.

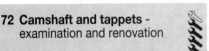

72 Camshaft and tappets - examination and renovation

1 The camshaft itself should show no signs of wear, but if very slight score marks on the

cams are noticed, they can be removed by gently rubbing down with very fine emery cloth or an oilstone. *The greatest care must be taken to keep the cam profiles smooth.*

2 Carefully examine the camshaft bearing surfaces for wear and, if evident, the camshaft must be renewed.

3 Check the fit of the camshaft in the carrier and if excessive bearing journal clearance is apparent a new carrier must be obtained. The camshaft bearings run directly in the machined journals of the carrier: renewable bearings are not used.

4 The faces of the tappet buckets which bear on the camshaft lobes should exhibit no signs of pitting, scoring, cracks or other forms of wear and should be a smooth sliding fit in the carrier. Slight scuffing and blackening of the tappet bucket sides is normal, providing this is not accompanied by scoring or wear ridges.

5 The small shims found inside the tappet bucket should show no signs of indentation from contact with the valve stem. Renew the shim with one of an identical size if wear has taken place. Make sure that each shim is kept with its tappet bucket and not interchanged.

73 Timing belt, sprockets and tensioner - examination and renovation

1 Carefully examine the belt for any sign of cracking, particularly at the root of the teeth, fraying, oil contamination or any other sign of

deterioration. Renew the belt if any of these conditions are found, or as a matter of course if the belt is nearing the end of its recommended service life (see Routine Maintenance).

2 Check the sprockets for signs of cracked or chipped teeth and the tensioner for roughness of its bearings or excessive endfloat. Renew the sprockets or tensioner as necessary. Note that the water pump sprocket is an integral part of the pump and cannot be renewed separately. If this sprocket is damaged or if there is any play in the pump spindle, a complete water pump must be obtained (see Chapter 2).

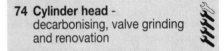

74 Cylinder head - decarbonising, valve grinding and renovation

1 Decarbonising can be carried out with the engine either in or out of the car. With the cylinder head off, carefully remove, with a wire brush and blunt scraper, all traces of carbon deposits from the combustion spaces and the ports. The valve stems and valve guides should also be free from any carbon deposits. Wash the combustion spaces and ports down with paraffin and scrape the cylinder head surface free of any foreign matter with the side of a steel rule or similar article. Take care not to scratch the surfaces.

2 Clean the pistons and top of the cylinder bores. If the pistons are still in the cylinder

71.6C . . . and the outer rotor endfloat

71.7A Remove the crankshaft front oil seal from the pump housing . . .

71.7B . . . and fit a new seal using a block of wood or socket

bores, it is essential that great care is taken to ensure that no carbon gets into the bores as this could scratch the cylinder walls or cause damage to the piston and rings. To ensure that this does not happen, first turn the crankshaft so that two of the pistons are at the top of the bores. Place clean lint-free rags into the two bores, or seal them off with paper and masking tape. The water and oil ways should also be covered with a small piece of masking tape to prevent particles of carbon entering the cooling system and damaging the water pump, or entering the lubrication system and causing damage to a bearing surface.

3 Before starting, press a little grease into the gap between the cylinder walls and the two pistons which are to be worked on. With a blunt scraper carefully scrape away the carbon from the piston crowns, taking care not to scratch the aluminium. Also scrape away the carbon from the surrounding lip of the cylinder wall. When all carbon has been removed, scrape away the grease which will now be contaminated with carbon particles, taking care not to press any into the bore. To assist prevention of carbon build-up, the piston crown can be polished with metal polish. Remove the rags or masking tape from the other two cylinders and turn the crankshaft so that the two pistons which were at the bottom are now at the top. Place rag into the other two bores, or seal them with paper and masking tape. Do not forget the waterways and oilways as well. Proceed as previously described.

4 With the valves removed from the cylinder head, examine the heads for signs of cracking, burning away and pitting of the edges where they seat in the ports. The seats of the valves in the cylinder head should also be examined for the same signs. Usually it is the valve that deteriorates first, but if a bad valve is not rectified the seat will suffer and this is more difficult to repair.

5 Provided there are no obvious signs of serious pitting, the valve should be ground to its seat. This may be done by placing a smear of carborundum paste on the edge of the valve head and using a suction type valve holder, grinding the valve *in situ*. Use a semi-rotary action, rotating the handle of the valve holder between the hands and lifting it occasionally to redistribute the traces of paste. Start with a coarse paste and finish with a fine paste.

6 As soon as a matt grey unbroken line appears on both the valve and seat, the valve is 'ground in'. All traces of carbon should also be cleaned from the head and neck of the valve stem. A wire brush mounted in a power drill is a quick and effective way of doing this.

7 If the valve requires renewal, the new one should be ground into the seat in the same way as the old valve.

8 Another form of valve wear can occur on the stem where it runs in the guide in the cylinder head. This can be detected by trying to rock the valve from side-to-side. If there is any movement at all it is an indication that the valve stem or guide is worn. Check the stem first with a micrometer at points along and around its length, and if they are not within the specified tolerance, new valves will probably solve the problem. If the guides are worn, however, they will need reboring for oversize valves to be fitted. The valve seats will also need recutting to ensure they are concentric with the stems. This work should be given to your local BL garage or engineering works.

9 When the valve seats are badly burnt or pitted, requiring renovation, inserts may be fitted - or renewed if previously fitted - and once again this is a specialist task to be carried out by a suitable engineering firm.

10 When all valve grinding is completed it is essential that every trace of grinding paste is removed from the valves and ports in the cylinder head. This should be done by thorough washing in paraffin and blowing out with a jet of air. If particles of carborundum paste should work their way into the engine, this would cause havoc with bearings or cylinder walls.

75 Engine mountings - removal and refitting

Left-hand mounting

1 Jack up the front of the car and support it on axle stands.
2 Remove the left-hand front roadwheel and the access panel under the wheel arch.
3 Remove the air cleaner cold air intake tube from the front body panel and air cleaner body.
4 Disconnect the two reversing lamp wires from the switch on top of the gearbox casing.
5 Position a jack beneath the gearbox with an interposed block of wood, and just take the weight of the engine and gearbox assembly.
6 Undo the two bolts securing the mounting to the gearbox and the through-bolt securing the mounting to the body bracket.
7 Lower the gearbox slightly and manipulate the mounting out of its location.
8 Refitting is the reverse sequence to removal. Tighten the retaining bolts to the specified torque and centralize the front snubber, as described in paragraph 22.

Right-hand mounting

9 Position a jack beneath the engine sump with an interposed block of wood, and just take the weight of the engine.
10 Lift off the timing belt upper cover then undo the two upper bolts securing the lower cover.
11 Undo the bolts securing the right-hand mounting to the cylinder block and head.
12 Undo the through-bolt securing the mounting to the body bracket.

13 Undo the four bolts securing the support plate to the body and body bracket.
14 Ease the mounting out of the body bracket and manipulate it out of its location.
15 Refitting is the reverse sequence to removal. Tighten the retaining bolts to the specified torque and centralize the front snubber, as described in paragraph 22.

Rear mounting

16 Jack up the front of the car and support it on axle stands.
17 Undo the two bolts securing the rear mounting support bracket to the crossmember. Recover the thread plate from the mounting bracket.
18 Undo the two nuts securing the mounting to the gearbox casing, slide the mounting off the casing studs and remove the assembly from under the car.
19 Refitting is the reverse sequence to removal. Tighten the retaining bolts to the specified torque and centralize the front snubber, as described in paragraph 22.

Front snubber

20 Undo the nuts from the starter motor retaining bolts, remove the crankshaft sensor wiring plug bracket and lift off the front snubber bracket and snubber.
21 Refit the snubber using the reverse of this procedure, tightening the starter motor retaining bolts to the specified torque.
22 Slacken the snubber cup retaining bolts (photo), centralize the snubber cup around the snubber rubber then tighten the bolts. This should be done whenever **any** of the engine mountings are renewed or in any way disturbed.

76 Engine reassembly - general

1 To ensure maximum life with minimum trouble from a rebuilt engine, not only must everything be correctly assembled, but it must also be spotlessly clean. All oilways must be clear, and locking washers and spring washers must be fitted where indicated. Oil all

75.22 Engine front snubber cup retaining bolts (arrowed)

Fig. 1.16 Engine mounting component details (Sec 75)

1 Right-hand mounting support plate
2 Washers
3 Right-hand mounting
4 Through-bolt
5 Right-hand mounting body bracket
6 Right-hand mounting distance spacers
7 Rear mounting thread plate
8 Rear mounting
9 Rear mounting support bracket
10 Left-hand mounting
11 Left-hand mounting body bracket
12 Through-bolt
13 Washers
14 Front snubber bracket
15 Snubber cup retaining bolts
16 Snubber cup
17 Snubber rubber

bearings and other working surfaces thoroughly with engine oil during assembly.

2 Before assembly begins, renew any bolts or studs with damaged threads.

3 Gather together a torque wrench, oil can, clean rags and a set of engine gaskets and oil seals, together with a new oil filter.

4 A tube of Loctite 574 sealant will be required for the camshaft carrier to cylinder head joint face and an RTV silicone sealant for the remainder of the joint faces that do not have gaskets. These compounds, together with conventional gasket jointing compound, are available from BL dealers or motor factors.

77.2 Fit the main bearing shells to the cylinder block

77 Crankshaft and main bearings - refitting

1 Clean the backs of the bearing shells and the bearing recesses in both the cylinder block and main bearing caps.

2 Press the main bearing shells into the cylinder block and caps and oil them liberally (photo).

3 Using a little grease, stick the thrust washers to each side of No 4 main bearing with their oilways facing away from the bearing (photo).

4 Lower the crankshaft into position, then fit the main bearing caps in their previously noted locations (photos).

5 Insert and tighten evenly the main bearing cap bolts to the specified torque. Check that the crankshaft rotates freely, then check that the endfloat is within the specified limits by inserting a feeler blade between the crankshaft web and the thrust washers.

78 Pistons and connecting rods - refitting

1 Clean the backs of the bearing shells and the recesses in the connecting rods and big-end caps.

77.3 Fit the thrust washers with their oilways facing away from the bearing

77.4A Lower the crankshaft into the crankcase . . .

77.4B . . . then fit the main bearing caps

78.3A With the rings compressed, insert the piston and connecting rod into its cylinder . . .

78.3B . . . then tap it down into the bore

78.3C Ensure that the word FRONT is towards the crankshaft pulley end of the engine

2 Fit the big-end bearing shells into their connecting rod and cap locations and oil them liberally.

3 Position a piston ring compressor around No 1 piston then insert the connecting rod and piston into No 1 cylinder. With No 1 crankpin at its lowest point, drive the piston carefully into the cylinder with the wooden handle of a hammer, and at the same time guide the connecting rod onto the crankpin. Make sure that the mark FRONT, A or an arrow on the piston crown is towards the crankshaft pulley end of the engine (photos).

4 Fit the big-end cap in its previously noted position, then screw on the nuts and tighten them to the specified torque (photos).

5 Check that the crankshaft turns freely.

6 Repeat the procedures given in paragraphs 3 to 5 for No 4 piston, then turn the crankshaft through half a turn and repeat the procedure on No 2 and No 3 piston.

7 If the engine is in the car, refit the sump and oil pick-up tube, and the cylinder head with reference to the relevant Sections and Chapters of this manual.

79 Gearbox adaptor plate - refitting

1 Ensure that the mating faces of the cylinder block and adaptor plate are thoroughly clean

then apply a bead of RTV sealant to the adaptor plate face (photo).

2 Make sure that the two sump retaining bolts and the gearbox retaining bolt are fitted in their adaptor plate locations and apply additional sealant to their bolt heads (photo).

3 Liberally lubricate the lips of the crankshaft rear oil seal in the adaptor plate then carefully fit the adaptor plate to the cylinder block (photo).

4 Refit the retaining bolts and tighten them evenly to the specified torque.

5 If the engine is in the car, refer to Section 62 and refit the items listed, in the reverse sequence to removal, with reference to the relevant Sections and Chapters of this manual.

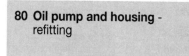

80 Oil pump and housing - refitting

1 Make sure that the mating faces of the pump and cylinder block are clean then place a new gasket in position on the pump housing.

2 Wrap some insulating tape around the end of the crankshaft to protect the oil seal as the pump is fitted.

3 Liberally lubricate the lips of the oil seal and the insulating tape with engine oil.

78.4A Fit the big-end cap . . .

78.4B . . . and tighten the nuts to the specified torque

79.1 Apply RTV sealant to the adaptor plate mating face

79.2 Apply additional sealant to the sump bolt heads and gearbox retaining bolt head (arrowed)

79.3 Fit the adaptor plate to the cylinder block

80.4 Fit the oil pump housing to the cylinder block using tape on the crankshaft to protect the seal

80.5 Refit and tighten the oil! pump housing retaining bolts (arrowed)

81.1A Insert a new O-ring into the oil pick-up tube groove . . .

4 Position the flats of the pump inner rotor to correspond with the flats on the crankshaft and carefully fit the pump to the cylinder block (photo). Remove the tape.

5 Refit the pump retaining bolts (photo) with the exception of the top centre bolt which also secures the water pump. This bolt is fitted later unless the water pump is already in place.

6 Tighten the bolts evenly to the specified torque.

7 If the engine is in the car, refer to Section 61 and refit the items listed, in the reverse sequence to removal, with reference to the relevant Sections and Chapters of this manual.

81 Sump - refitting

1 Insert a new O-ring seal into the groove in the oil pick-up tube then refit the tube to the oil pump housing and main bearing cap (photos). Refit the retaining bolts and nut and tighten them securely.

2 Ensure that all traces of old sealant are removed from the sump and cylinder block mating faces and from around the one-piece rubber gasket if this in intact and to be re-used.

3 Apply a thick bead of RTV sealant to the semi-circular joint faces of the sump, oil pump housing and gearbox adaptor plate. Extend the bead of sealant about 0.5 in (12 mm) beyond the ends of the semi-circular joint faces (photo).

4 Place the rubber gasket on the sump then position the sump on the engine (photo).

5 Refit the sump retaining bolts and nuts with the longer bolts, cable clips and brackets in the positions noted during removal (photo). Progressively tighten the bolts in a diagonal sequence to the specified torque.

6 With a new gasket in place, fit the oil separator and secure with the two nuts (photo).

7 Refit the bolts securing the sump to the gearbox adaptor plate (photo).

8 If the engine is in the car, refer to Section 60

81.1B . . . then secure the tube to the pump housing and bearing cap

81.3 Apply RTV sealant to the semi-circular joint faces

81.4 Position the sump on the engine . . .

81.5. . . and secure with the nuts. Note the cable clip locations (arrowed)

81.6 Refit the oil separator to the sump

81.7 Refit the sump-to-adaptor plate bolts

Fig. 1.17 Valve stem oil seals (Sec 82)

A Standard size stem oil seal with one flange ring
B Oversize stem oil seal with two flange rings

82.1A Place new valve stem oil seals over the valve guides . . .

82.1B . . . and push them fully into place

and refit the items listed, in the reverse sequence to removal. with reference to the relevant Sections and Chapters of this manual.

82 Cylinder head - reassembly

1 Place the new valve stem oil seals in place over the valve guides and push them fully into place using a small tube or socket (photos). Note that, in service, new oil seals are only supplied for the inlet valves and if valves with oversize stems are being fitted, oil seals with two rings on their flange must be used (Fig. 1.17).

2 Oil the valve stems liberally and fit each valve to its original guide, or if new valves have been obtained, to the seat in which they have been ground (photo).

3 Working on one valve at a time, fit the spring and cap then compress the spring with the compressor and insert the split collets (photos). Release the compressor and remove it.

4 Repeat the procedure given in paragraph 3 on the remaining valves. After fitting, tap the end of each valve stem with a mallet to settle the collets.

83 Camshaft and tappets - refitting

1 Smear the tappet shims with petroleum jelly and then locate the shims in the recesses of their respective tappet buckets.

2 Place the camshaft carrier in position on the cylinder head and fit the tappet buckets to their locations in the carrier.

3 Lift the carrier slightly, push the tappet buckets down and carefully insert the camshaft. Fit the camshaft locating plate to the carrier front bearing journal.

4 Fit the camshaft carrier retaining bolts and progressively tighten them to the specified torque.

5 Before proceeding further the tappet clearances should be checked and adjusted using the procedure described in Section 86, paragraphs 2 to 6. For the purposes of tappet clearance checking the camshaft may be turned using an adjustable wrench on the square protrusion between No 6 and 7 camshaft lobe (photo).

6 With the tappet clearance checked and the correct new shims obtained as necessary, remove the camshaft, camshaft carrier and the tappet buckets (if not already done).

7 Locate a new O-ring seal in the carrier recess then fill the carrier groove with Loctite 574 sealant (photos).

B2.2 Fit the valves to their original guides

82.3A Fit the valve spring and cap . . .

82.3B . . . then compress the spring and insert the split collets

83.5 Camshaft square protrusion (arrowed) for spanner engagement

83.7A Locate a new O-ring in the camshaft carrier recess . . .

83.7B . . . then fill the carrier groove with the special sealant

83.8A Place the carrier in position on the cylinder head . . .

83.8B . . . then fit the tappet buckets to their original bores

8 Place the carrier in position on the cylinder head once more and insert the tappet buckets in their respective locations (photos).

9 Lift the carrier slightly, push down the tappet buckets and slide the camshaft into the carrier. Refit the camshaft locating plate.

10 Fit the camshaft carrier retaining bolts and progressively tighten them to the specified torque.

11 Thoroughly lubricate the lips of new camshaft front and rear oil seals and carefully locate them over the camshaft journals and into their positions in the carrier (photos). Tap the seals squarely into the carrier.

12 Place the camshaft sprocket on the camshaft and use the retaining bolt and washer to draw the sprocket fully home

(photo). Tighten the retaining bolt to the specified torque.

13 Locate the one-piece rubber gaskets in the camshaft carrier covers (photo) using new gaskets if necessary.

14 Apply a continuous bead of RTV sealant, 3 mm wide, to the cover mating faces in the camshaft carrier (photo).

15 Fit the two covers, retaining bolts and brackets, where applicable (photo). Tighten the cover bolts progressively to the specified torque.

16 If the engine is in the car refer to Section 58 and refit the items listed, in the reverse sequence to removal, with reference to the relevant Sections and Chapters of this manual.

84 Cylinder head - refitting

1 Ensure that the cylinder block and head mating faces are perfectly clean and free from any traces of oil, grease or water.

2 Place a new head gasket in position over the cylinder block dowels (photo). The gasket is pre-coated and jointing compound should not be used.

3 Lower the cylinder head into position (photo) and, with their threads lightly oiled, refit the retaining bolts.

4 Tighten the cylinder head bolts in the

1

83.11A Fit new camshaft front . . .

83.11B . . . and rear oil seals

83.12 Refit the camshaft sprocket and retaining bolt

83.13 Locate the rubber gaskets in the camshaft carrier covers

83.14 Apply RTV sealant to the camshaft carrier . . .

83.15. . . then fit the covers, noting the cable clip locations under the retaining bolts

84.2 Lay a new cylinder head gasket over the cylinder block dowels . . .

84.3. . . then lower the head onto the gasket

Fig. 1.18 Cylinder head bolt tightening sequence (Sec 84)

sequence shown in Fig. 1.18, to the specified torque.

5 If the engine is in the car reverse the procedure given in Section 56, paragraphs 2 to 23 then refit the timing belt, as described in Section 85.

6 After running the engine, retorque the cylinder head as described in Section 90.

85 Timing belt - refitting and adjustment

1 If the engine is being reassembled after major overhaul, refer to Chapter 2 and refit the water pump.

2 Place the crankshaft sprocket guide plate on the crankshaft followed by the sprocket and crankshaft pulley (photos). Fit the pulley retaining bolt and washer and tighten the pulley to the specified torque (photo).

3 Turn the camshaft as necessary, using a spanner on the sprocket bolt, until the dimple on the rear face of the sprocket is aligned with the notch on the camshaft carrier (photo). Turn the crankshaft until the notch on the pulley is aligned with the timing mark on the oil pump housing .

4 Refit the timing belt tensioner, but do not tighten the two retaining bolts at this stage.

5 Slip the belt over the sprockets and around

the tensioner so that it is taut on the straight (driving) side (photo).

6 To tension the belt, engage a torque wrench of the type having a dial gauge scale or sliding pointer scale and 3/8 in square drive into the hole in the tensioner bracket. Tension the belt to the torque figure given in the Specifications and tighten the two tensioner retaining bolts (photo).

7 Turn the crankshaft clockwise through three quarters of a turn so that the crankshaft pulley notch is at approximately 90° BTDC.

8 Slacken the tensioner retaining bolts again and re-tension the belt, as described in paragraph 6.

9 Turn the crankshaft clockwise through one

85.2A Place the crankshaft sprocket guide plate on the crankshaft . . .

85.2B . . . followed by the sprocket . . .

85.2C . . . and crankshaft pulley

85.2D Secure the pulley with the retaining bolt and washer

85.3 Camshaft timing marks aligned

85.5 Slip the timing belt over the sprockets and tensioner

85.6 Using a torque wrench to adjust the timing belt tension

86.2 Checking tappet clearance with a feeler blade

86.5 Tappet adjusting shim with reference number stamped on its face

and a quarter turns and realign the crankshaft pulley timing notch with the mark on the oil pump housing. Check that the camshaft sprocket and carrier timing marks are aligned. If not, repeat the belt refitting and adjustment procedure, starting at paragraph 3.

10 If the engine is in the car, refit the timing belt upper and lower covers, followed by the alternator drivebelt. Adjust the drivebelt as described in Chapter 2.

11 Refit the access cover and roadwheel, lower the car to the ground and reconnect the battery.

86 Tappet clearances - checking and adjustment

1 To check the tappet clearances, disconnect the battery negative terminal then undo the retaining bolts and lift off the camshaft carrier covers. Note which bolts also secure cable and hose retaining clips.

2 Using a feeler gauge, check the clearance between the cam lobe and the tappet bucket of each valve (photo) in the order given in the following table and record each clearance. The engine may be turned using a spanner or socket on the crankshaft pulley bolt. If necessary remove the access panel from under the right-hand wheel arch to provide greater access to the pulley bolt.

Check No 1 tappet with No 8 valve fully open
Check No 3 tappet with No 6 valve fully open
Check No 5 tappet with No 4 valve fully open
Check No 2 tappet with No 7 valve fully open
Check No 8 tappet with No 1 valve fully open
Check No 6 tappet with No 3 valve fully open
Check No 4 tappet with No 5 valve fully open
Check No 7 tappet with No 2 valve fully open

3 Once the readings have been tabulated for all valves it should be noted that, unless new parts have been fitted or the valve seats reground, adjustment of the valve tappet clearance to the standard setting is only necessary if the clearance of either inlet or exhaust is less than 0.012 in (0.30 mm).

4 If adjustment is necessary, refer to Section 58 and remove the camshaft and tappets.

5 Remove the adjusting shim from each maladjusted tappet bucket in turn and note its thickness. The shim reference number is stamped on the face of the shim (photo) - see Specifications. By using the following calculation, determine the thickness of the new shim required to give the correct tappet clearance:
A = clearance measured in paragraph 2
B = thickness of existing shim
C = correct clearance
New shim thickness required = A + B - C

6 With new shims obtained as necessary, refer to Section 83 paragraphs 7 to 16, and refit the camshaft and tappets.

87 Ancillary components - refitting

Refer to Section 54 and refit the listed components with reference to the Sections and Chapters specified, where applicable.

88 Engine - attachment to manual gearbox or automatic transmission

Refer to Section 52 and attach the gearbox or transmission to the engine using the reverse of the removal procedure. Tighten the retaining bolts to the specified torque.

89 Engine - refitting with manual gearbox or automatic transmission

Refer to Section 50 or 51, as applicable, and refit the engine and manual gearbox or automatic transmission using the reverse of the removal procedure, noting the following additional points:
(a) Do not tighten any of the engine

mountings fully until all have been fitted, then tighten them in this order: right-hand mounting, left-hand mounting, rear mounting, front snubber. Centralize the front snubber cap as described in Section 75, after tightening the other mountings
(b) Align the marks on the driveshaft joints and drive flanges made during removal
(c) On manual gearbox models, refit the clutch cable with reference to Chapter 5
(d) On automatic transmission models, adjust the selector cable and kickdown cable if necessary, as described in Chapter 7
(e) Adjust the accelerator cable to give a small amount of free play in the cable with the throttle closed
(f) Refill the cooling system, as described in Chapter 2
(g) Refill the engine with oil

90 Engine - adjustments after major overhaul

1 With the engine refitted to the car, make a final check to ensure that everything has been reconnected and that no rags or tools have been left in the engine compartment.

2 Make sure that the oil and water levels are topped up and then start the engine: this may take a little longer than usual as the fuel pump and carburettor float chamber may be empty.

3 As soon as the engine starts, watch for the oil pressure light to go out and check for any oil, fuel or water leaks. Don't be alarmed if there are some odd smells and smoke from parts getting hot and burning off oil deposits.

4 Run the engine for at least 15 minutes or drive the car for approximately 5 miles then switch it off and allow it to cool. Working in the sequence shown in Fig. 1.18, slacken each cylinder head bolt one at a time by half a turn and then tighten it to the specified torque.

5 If new pistons, rings or crankshaft bearings have been fitted, the engine must be run-in for the first 500 miles (800 km). Do not exceed 45 mph (72 kph), operate the engine at full throttle or allow it to labour in any gear.

1

Fault finding - all engines

Engine fails to start

- ☐ Discharged battery
- ☐ Loose battery connection
- ☐ Loose or broken ignition leads
- ☐ Moisture on spark plugs, distributor cap, or HT leads
- ☐ Incorrect spark plug gaps
- ☐ Cracked distributor cap or rotor
- ☐ Other ignition system fault
- ☐ Dirt or water in carburettor
- ☐ Empty fuel tank
- ☐ Faulty fuel pump
- ☐ Other fuel system fault
- ☐ Faulty starter motor
- ☐ Low cylinder compressions

Excessive oil consumption

- ☐ Worn pistons, cylinder bores or piston rings
- ☐ Valve guides and valve stem seals worn
- ☐ Major gasket or oil seal leakage

Engine backfires

- ☐ Carburettor adjustment incorrect
- ☐ Ignition timing incorrect (where applicable)
- ☐ Incorrect valve clearances
- ☐ Inlet manifold air leak
- ☐ Sticking valve

Engine misfires

- ☐ Spark plugs worn or incorrectly gapped
- ☐ Dirt or water in carburettor
- ☐ Carburettor adjustment incorrect
- ☐ Burnt out valve
- ☐ Leaking cylinder head gasket
- ☐ Distributor cap cracked
- ☐ Incorrect valve clearances
- ☐ Uneven cylinder compressions
- ☐ Worn carburettor

Engine idles erratically

- ☐ Inlet manifold air leak
- ☐ Leaking cylinder head gasket
- ☐ Worn rocker arms, timing chain, timing belt or gears
- ☐ Worn camshaft lobes
- ☐ Faulty fuel pump
- ☐ Incorrect valve clearances
- ☐ Loose crankcase ventilation hoses
- ☐ Carburettor adjustment incorrect
- ☐ Uneven cylinder compressions

Engine stalls

- ☐ Carburettor adjustment incorrect
- ☐ Inlet manifold air leak
- ☐ Ignition timing incorrect (where applicable)

Chapter 2 Cooling system

For modifications, and information applicable to later models, see Supplement at end of manual

Contents

Degrees of difficulty

Easy, suitable for novice with little experience	Fairly easy, suitable for beginner with some experience	Fairly difficult, suitable for competent DIY mechanic	Difficult, suitable for experienced DIY mechanic	Very difficult, suitable for expert DIY or professional

Specifications

System type .... Pressurized, pump-assisted thermosyphon with front-mounted radiator and electric cooling fan

Expansion tank cap pressure .... 15 lbf/in² (1.0 bar)

Thermostat
Opening temperature .... 168° to 176°F (76° to 80°C)
Fully open .... 190°F (88°C)
Lift height .... 0.32 in (8.1 mm)

Antifreeze type/specification .... Ethylene glycol-based antifreeze with non-phosphate corrosion inhibitors, suitable for mixed-metal engines, containing no methanol and meeting specifications BS6580 and BS5117

Antifreeze properties and quantities
33% antifreeze (by volume):
  Commences freezing .... -2°F (-19°C)
  Frozen solid .... -33°F (-36°C)
  Quantities (system refill):

	Antifreeze	Water
1.3 litre models	3.5 Imp pints (2.0 litres)	7.5 Imp pints (4.3 litres)
1.6 litre models	5.0 Imp pints (2.8 litres)	10.0 Imp pints (5.7 litres)

50% antifreeze (by volume):
  Commences freezing .... -33°F (-36°C)
  Frozen solid .... -53°F (-48°C)
  Quantities (system refill):

	Antifreeze	Water
1.3 litre models	5.75 Imp pints (3.3 litres)	5.75 Imp pints (3.3 litres)
1.6 litre models	7.5 Imp pints (4.25 litres)	7.5 Imp pints (4.25 litres)

Torque wrench settings

	lbf ft	Nm
1.3 litre models		
Coolant temperature thermistor	40	54
Water outlet elbow bolts	16	22
Water pump bolts	16	22
Water pump pulley	8	11
Cylinder block drain plug	27	37
1.6 litre models		
Coolant temperature thermistor	11	15
Thermostat housing bolts	13	18
Water inlet elbow to cylinder head	18	24
Water outlet elbow to thermostat housing	18	24
Water pump to cylinder block	9	12
Timing belt tensioner bolts	18	24

1 General description

The cooling system is of the pressurised, pump-assisted thermosyphon type. The system consists of the radiator, water pump, thermostat, electric cooling fan, expansion tank and associated hoses.

The system functions as follows. Cold coolant in the bottom of the radiator left-hand tank passes through the hose to the water pump on 1.3 litre models, or water inlet elbow on 1.6 litre models, where it is pumped around the cylinder block and head passages. After cooling the cylinder bores, combustion surfaces and valve seats, the coolant reaches the underside of the thermostat, which is initially closed, and is diverted through the heater inlet hose to the heater. After passing through the heater the coolant travels through the water jacket of the inlet manifold before returning to the water pump inlet hose or water outlet elbow. When the engine is cold the thermostat remains closed and the coolant only circulates around the engine, heater and inlet manifold. When the coolant reaches a predetermined temperature the thermostat opens and the coolant passes through the top hose to the radiator right-hand tank. As the coolant circulates around the radiator it is cooled by the inrush of air when the car is in forward motion. Airflow is supplemented by the action of the electric cooling fan when necessary. Upon reaching the left-hand side of the radiator, the coolant is now cooled and the cycle is repeated.

When the engine is at normal operating temperature the coolant expands and some of it is displaced into the expansion tank. This coolant collects in the tank and is returned to the radiator when the system cools.

The electric cooling fan mounted in front of the radiator is controlled by a thermostatic switch located in the radiator side tank. At a predetermined coolant temperature the switch contacts close, thus actuating the fan.

On 1.3 litre models the water pump is driven by the crankshaft pulley in the conventional way via a drivebelt. On 1.6 litre models the pump is driven by the toothed camshaft timing belt.

2 Maintenance and inspection

1 Check the coolant level in the system weekly and, if necessary, top up with a water and antifreeze mixture until the level is up to the indicator in the expansion tank. With a sealed type cooling system, topping-up is required, it is likely there is a leak in the system. Check all hoses and joint faces for any staining, or actual wetness, and rectify if necessary. If no leaks can be found it is advisable to have the system pressure tested,

Fig. 2.1 Layout of the cooling system and components – 1.3 litre models (Sec 1)

1 Expansion tank filler cap
2 Water outlet elbow
3 Thermostat housing
4 Heater hoses
5 Water pump
6 Cooling fan thermostatic switch
7 Radiator
8 Cooling fan assembly
9 Cylinder block drain plug

Fig. 2.2 Layout of the cooling system and components – 1.6 litre models (Sec 1)

1 Expansion tank filler cap
2 Thermostat housing
3 Radiator top hose
4 Heater hoses
5 Water pump
6 Fan thermostatic switch
7 Radiator
8 Cooling fan assembly

as the leak could possibly be internal. It is a good idea to keep a check on the engine oil level as a serious internal leak can often cause the level in the sump to rise, thus confirming suspicions.

2 At the service intervals given in Routine Maintenance at the beginning of this manual carefully inspect all the hoses, hose clips and visible joint gaskets for cracks, corrosion, deterioration or leakage. Renew any hoses and clips that are suspect and also renew any gaskets, if necessary.

3 At the same service interval check the condition of the water pump and alternator drivebelt and renew it if there is any sign of cracking or fraying. Check and adjust the tension of the belt, as described in Section 13.

4 At the less frequent service intervals indicated, drain, flush and refill the cooling system using fresh antifreeze, as described in Sections 3, 4, and 5 respectively.

5 Also, at this service interval, the drivebelt should be renewed, using the procedure described in Section 13.

3 Cooling system - draining

Note: *It is not possible to completely drain the engine on 1.6 litre models due to the absence of a cylinder block drain plug. To drain all coolant from the engine or to bring the coolant* *level to below that of the water inlet elbow, it will be necessary to remove the water pump.*

1 It is preferable to drain the cooling system when the engine is cold. *If the engine is hot the pressure in the cooling system must be released before attempting to drain the system.* Place the cloth over the pressure cap of the expansion tank and turn the cap anti-clockwise until it reaches its stop.

2 Wait until the pressure has escaped, then press the cap downwards and turn it further in an anti-clockwise direction. Release the downward pressure on the cap very slowly and, after making sure that all the pressure in the system has been relieved, remove the cap.

3 Place a suitable container beneath the left-hand side of the radiator. Slacken the hose clip and carefully ease the bottom hose off the radiator outlet. Allow the coolant to drain into the container. Be prepared for some spillage as the chassis member directly below the radiator outlet blocks the directional flow of the coolant as it flows from the outlet.

4 On 1.3 litre models, place a second container beneath the cylinder block drain plug located on the front left-hand side of the engine. Unscrew the plug and drain the remainder of the coolant into the container.

5 If the system is to be flushed after draining, proceed to the next Section, otherwise refit the drain plug and secure the bottom hose to the radiator.

4 Cooling system - flushing

1 With time the cooling system may gradually lose its efficiency as the radiator core becomes choked with rust, scale deposits from the water and other sediment.

2 To flush the system, first drain the coolant, as described in the previous Section.

3 Disconnect the top hose at the outlet elbow and leave the bottom hose disconnected at the radiator outlet.

4 Insert a hose into the top hose and allow water to circulate through the radiator until it runs clear from the outlet.

5 Disconnect the heater inlet hose from the thermostat housing. Insert the hose and allow water to circulate through the heater and out through the bottom hose until clear. If, after a reasonable period the water still does not run clear, the radiator can be flushed with a good proprietary cleaning agent.

6 In severe cases of contamination the system should be reverse flushed. To do this remove the radiator, as described in Section 7, invert it and insert a hose in the bottom outlet. Continue flushing until clean water runs from the top hose outlet.

7 The engine should also be flushed. To do this remove the thermostat, as described in Section 8, and insert the hose into the cylinder head or thermostat housing. Flush the system until clean water runs from the bottom hose.

5 Cooling system - filling

1 If removed, refit the thermostat, hoses, and cylinder block drain plug (where applicable).

2 Fill the system through the expansion tank with the appropriate mixture of water and antifreeze (see Section 6) until the tank is half full. Do not refit the expansion tank cap at this stage.

3 Start the engine and run it at a fast idle for approximately one minute. During this time compress the top hose several times to release any air pockets in the system.

4 Stop the engine, top up the expansion tank to the indicated level then refit the filler cap.

6 Antifreeze mixture

1 The antifreeze should be renewed at regular intervals (see Routine Maintenance). This is necessary not only to maintain the antifreeze properties, but also to prevent corrosion which would otherwise occur as the corrosion inhibitors become progressively less effective.

2 Use an antifreeze, in the specified concentration, which conforms to the standard given in the Specifications at the beginning of this Chapter. Note that Austin Rover recommend the use of Unipart Superplus antifreeze, and state that no other antifreeze should be mixed with this type, such as when topping up is required. If another type of antifreeze is to be used, the system must be drained and flushed prior to its use.

3 Before adding antifreeze the cooling system should be completely drained and flushed, and all hoses checked for condition and security.

4 The quantity of antifreeze and levels of protection are indicated in the Specifications.

5 After filling with antifreeze, a label should be attached to the radiator stating the type and concentration of antifreeze used and the date installed. Any subsequent topping-up should be made with the same type and concentration of antifreeze.

Fig. 2.3 Expansion tank level indicator (Sec 5)

6 Do not use engine antifreeze in the screen washer system, as it will cause damage to the vehicle paintwork. Use a screen wash in the washer system.

7 Radiator - removal, inspection, cleaning and refitting

1 Disconnect the battery negative terminal.

2 Drain the cooling system, as described in Section 3. Leave the bottom radiator hose disconnected.

3 Slacken the retaining clip and detach the radiator top hose.

4 Detach the electrical connectors from the radiator cooling fan thermostatic switch (photo).

5 Release the upper retaining clips, tip the radiator grille forward at the top and lift it to release the lower mounting lugs from their locations.

6 Undo and remove the three bolts each side securing the front body panel in position. Release the air cleaner cold air intake hose from the panel then withdraw the panel and place it to one side, leaving the bonnet release cable still attached (photos).

7 Release the two plastic panel support clips from the left-hand side of the radiator (photo).

8 Disconnect the cooling fan motor wiring multi-plug (photo) and carefully lift out the radiator.

9 Radiator repair is best left to a specialist, but minor leaks may be sealed using a proprietary coolant additive with the radiator

7.4 Disconnect the wiring at the cooling fan thermostatic switch

7.6A Front body panel retaining bolts (arrowed)

2

7.6B Air cleaner cold air intake hose

7.6C Front body panel removal

7.7 Release the two panel support clips

in situ. Clean the radiator matrix of flies and small leaves with a soft brush, or by hosing.

10 Reverse flush the radiator, as described in Section 4. Renew the top and bottom hoses and clips if they are damaged or have deteriorated.

11 Refitting the radiator is the reverse sequence to removal, but ensure that the lower mounting lugs engage in the rubber grommets (photo). Fill the cooling system, as described in Section 5, after fitting.

8 Thermostat - removal, testing and refitting

1 Remove the expansion tank filler cap. *If the engine is hot, place a cloth over the cap and turn it slowly anti-clockwise until the first stop is reached.* Wait until all the pressure has been released and then remove the cap completely.

2 Place a suitable container beneath the radiator bottom hose outlet. Disconnect the bottom hose and drain approximately 4 pints (2.3 litres) of the coolant. Reconnect the bottom hose and tighten the clip.

3 Slacken the clips and detach the radiator top hose, heater hose and expansion tank hose from the water outlet elbow.

4 Undo and remove the bolts securing the water outlet elbow to the cylinder head or thermostat housing (photo), and lift off the elbow. On 1.3 litre models it will be necessary

to remove the upper retaining bolt and lift away the engine mounting support bracket to facilitate removal of the elbow. After removal, recover the gasket.

5 Withdraw the thermostat from its seat in the thermostat housing.

6 To test whether the unit is serviceable, suspend it on a string in a saucepan of cold water together with a thermometer. Heat the water and note the temperature at which the thermostat begins to open. Continue heating the water until the thermostat is fully open and then remove it from the water.

7 The temperature at which the thermostat should start to open is given in the Specifications and the fully open temperature is stamped on the base of the unit. If the thermostat does not start to open or fully open at the specified temperatures, does not attain the specified lift height or does not fully close when cold, then it must be discarded and a new unit fitted. Under no circumstances should the car be used without a thermostat, as uneven cooling of the cylinder walls and head passages will occur, causing distortion and possible seizure of the engine internal components.

8 Refitting the thermostat is the reverse sequence to removal. Ensure that all traces of old gasket are removed from the mating faces of the water outlet elbow and thermostat housing. Use a new gasket lightly smeared with jointing compound and tighten the retaining bolts to the specified torque. On completion top up the cooling system, with reference to Section 5.

9 Water pump (1.3 litre models) - removal and refitting

Note: *Water pump failure is indicated by coolant leaking from the gland at the front of the pump or by rough and noisy operation. This is usually accompanied by excessive play of the pump spindle which can be checked by moving the pulley from side to side. Repair or overhaul of a faulty pump is not possible, as internal parts are not available separately. In the event of failure a replacement pump must be obtained.*

1 Disconnect the battery negative terminal.

2 Refer to Section 3 and drain the cooling system.

3 Slacken the alternator adjusting arm and pivot bolts, move the alternator towards the engine and slip the drivebelt off the three pulleys.

4 Undo and remove the four water pump pulley retaining bolts.

5 Slacken the retaining clip and disconnect the water hose from the pump.

6 Undo and remove the water pump retaining bolts then tap the pump body with a soft-faced mallet to release it from the locating dowels. Manoeuvre the pump and pulley out from between the cylinder block and engine mounting bracket.

7 Refitting is the reverse sequence to removal, bearing in mind the following points:
(a) Remove all traces of old gasket from the

7.8 Cooling fan motor wiring multi-plug

7.11 Ensure proper location of radiator mounting lugs in the rubber grommets

8.4 Water outlet elbow removal (1.6 litre model shown)

Fig. 2.4 Water pump removal – 1.3 litre models (Sec 9)

cylinder block and pump faces, and ensure that both mating surfaces are clean and dry

(b) *Use a new gasket lightly smeared with jointing compound*

(c) *Adjust the drivebelt tension, as described in Section 13, and refill the cooling system, as described in Section 5*

10 Water pump (1.6 litre models) - removal and refitting

1 Refer to the introductory note at the beginning of Section 9 before proceeding.
2 Disconnect the battery negative terminal.
3 Refer to Section 3 and drain the cooling system.
4 Refer to Chapter 1 and remove the timing belt.
5 Undo the two bolts and lift off the timing belt tensioner (photo).
6 Place a suitable container beneath the water pump to collect the coolant remaining in the cylinder block.
7 Using an Allen key, undo the water pump upper retaining bolt then undo the remaining three bolts using a spanner or socket (photo). Recover the clamp plate on the lower bolt.
8 Ease the water pump off the engine using a screwdriver to lever between the block and

Fig. 2.5 Water pump removal – 1.6 litre models (Sec 10)

1 Water pump
2 Timing belt tensioner retaining bolts
3 Water pump retaining bolts
4 Clamp plate

pump side flanges if necessary.
9 Refitting the pump is the reverse sequence to removal, bearing in mind the following points:
(a) *Remove all traces of old sealant from the cylinder block and pump faces, and ensure that both mating surfaces are clean and dry*
(b) *Apply a bead of RTV sealant around the pump mating face (photo) and, with the pump in position, tighten the retaining bolts to the specified torque.*
(c) *Refit and adjust the timing belt, as described in Chapter 1*
(d) *Refill the cooling system, as described in Section 5.*

11 Cooling fan assembly - removal and refitting

1 Disconnect the battery negative terminal.
2 Release the upper retaining clips, tip the radiator grille forward at the top and lift it to release the lower mounting lugs from their locations.

10.5 Timing belt tensioner retaining bolts (arrowed)

3 Undo and remove the three bolts each side securing the front body panel in position. Release the air cleaner cold air intake hose from the panel then lift the panel upwards and place it to one side, leaving the bonnet release cable still attached (photos 7.6a, 7.6b and 7.6c).
4 Disconnect the fan motor wiring multi-plug.
5 Undo the three nuts securing the fan cowl to the radiator and withdraw the assembly from its location (photo).
6 If required the fan may be removed by pulling it off the motor shaft. Mark the outer face to ensure correct refitment. To remove the fan motor, drill off the rivet heads, tap out the rivets securing the motor to the cowl and lift away the motor.
7 Refitting is the reverse sequence to removal.

12 Cooling fan thermostatic switch - testing, removal and refitting

1 The radiator cooling fan is operated by a thermostatic switch located on the right-hand side of the radiator. When the coolant exceeds a predetermined temperature the switch contacts close and the fan is activated.
2 If the operation of the fan or switch is suspect, run the engine until normal operating temperature is reached and then allow it to idle. If the fan does not cut in within a few minutes, switch off the engine and disconnect the wiring

10.7 Water pump retaining bolts (arrowed)

10.9 Apply RTV sealant to the pump mating face before fitting

11.5 Fan cowl-to-radiator lower retaining nuts (arrowed)

2

12.4 Cooling fan thermostatic switch removal

14.3 Coolant temperature thermistor location (1.6 litre model shown)

Fig. 2.6 Drivebelt adjustment points – 1.3 litre models (Sec 13)

Arrow indicates tension checking point
1 Alternator pivot
2 Adjusting arm bolts mounting bolt

Fig. 2.7 Drivebelt adjustment points – 1.6 litre models (Sec 13)

Arrow indicates tension checking point
1 Alternator pivot mounting bolt
2 Adjusting arm bolts

plug from the thermostic switch. Bridge the two terminals in the wiring plug with a length of wire and switch on the ignition. If the fan now operates, the thermostatic switch is faulty and must be renewed. If the fan still fails to operate check that battery voltage is present at the plug terminals. If not, check for a blown fuse or wiring fault. If voltage is present the fan motor is faulty.

3 To remove the switch, disconnect the battery negative terminal then drain the cooling system, as described in Section 3.

4 Disconnect the wiring plug, release the retaining plate and withdraw the switch and seal from the radiator (photo).

5 Refitting is the reverse sequence to removal, but use a new seal on the switch and refill the cooling system, as described in Section 5.

13 Drivebelt - renewal and adjustment

Note: *On 1.3 litre models the drivebelt runs in the crankshaft, water pump and alternator pulleys. On 1.6 litre models the belt only runs in the crankshaft and alternator pulleys as the water pump is driven by the toothed timing*

belt. However, the renewal and adjustment procedures on all models are similar.

1 To remove the drivebelt, slacken the alternator pivot mounting bolt and the adjusting arm bolts then move the alternator towards the engine. Slip the drivebelt off the pulleys and remove it from the engine.

2 Fit the new drivebelt over the pulleys then lever the alternator away from the engine until moderate tension is obtained. The alternator must only be levered at the drive end bracket.

3 Hold the alternator in this position and tighten the adjusting arm bolts followed by the pivot mounting bolt.

4 Start the engine and run it for five minutes at a fast idle.

5 Switch off the engine and readjust the drivebelt tension so that the belt deflects by 0.25 to 0.50 in (6.0 to 12.0 mm) at the point shown in Fig. 2.6 or 2.7 under moderate finger pressure.

14 Coolant temperature thermistor - removal and refitting

1 The coolant temperature thermistor incorporates a temperature sensitive element, the resistance of which alters according to coolant temperature. The unit controls the operation of the temperature gauge and also influences the settings of the fuel and ignition system electronic control units.

2 Place a suitable container beneath the radiator bottom hose outlet. Slacken the retaining clip, disconnect the bottom hose and drain approximately 4 pints (2.3 litres) of coolant. Refit the hose and tighten the clip.

3 Disconnect the wiring plug from the thermistor which is located at the rear right-hand side of the cylinder head on 1.3 litre models and in the thermostat housing on 1.6 litre models (photo).

4 Unscrew the thermistor and remove it from the engine.

5 Refitting is the reverse sequence to removal, but top up the cooling system with reference to Section 5.

Fault finding - cooling system

Overheating
- [ ] Low coolant level (this may be overheating for other reasons)
- [ ] Drivebelt slipping or broken (1.3 litre models only)
- [ ] Radiator blockage (internal or external), or grille restricted
- [ ] Thermostat defective
- [ ] Ignition timing incorrect or distributor defective (1.3 litre models only)
- [ ] Carburettor maladjustment
- [ ] Faulty cooling fan thermostatic switch
- [ ] Blown cylinder head gasket (combustion gases in coolant)

- [ ] Water pump defective
- [ ] Expansion tank pressure cap faulty
- [ ] Brakes binding

Overcooling
- [ ] Thermostat missing, defective or wrong heat range

Water loss - external
- [ ] Loose hose clips
- [ ] Perished or cracked hoses
- [ ] Radiator core leaking
- [ ] Heater matrix leaking
- [ ] Expansion tank pressure cap leaking

- [ ] Boiling due to overheating
- [ ] Water pump or thermostat housing leaking
- [ ] Core plug leaking

Water loss - internal
- [ ] Cylinder head gasket blown
- [ ] Cylinder head cracked or warped
- [ ] Cylinder block cracked

Corrosion
- [ ] Infrequent draining and flushing
- [ ] Incorrect antifreeze mixture or inappropriate type
- [ ] Combustion gases contaminating coolant

Chapter 3 Fuel and exhaust systems

For modifications, and information applicable to later models, see Supplement at end of manual

Contents

Degrees of difficulty

Easy, suitable for novice with little experience	**Fairly easy,** suitable for beginner with some experience	**Fairly difficult,** suitable for competent DIY mechanic	**Difficult,** suitable for experienced DIY mechanic	**Very difficult,** suitable for expert DIY or professional

Specifications

Air cleaner

Type .... Automatic air temperature control type, with renewable paper element
Application:
   1.3 litre engine .... Champion W135
   1.6 litre engine .... Champion W114

Fuel pump

Type .... Mechanical, operated by eccentric on camshaft
Make .... SU AUF 800
Delivery pressure .... 4.0 lbf/in^2 (0.3 bar)

Fuel tank capacity .... 11.25 Imp gals (51 litres)

Fuel octane rating .... see Supplement

Carburettor (general)

Type .... SU HIF 44 variable choke with electronic mixture control
Identification:
   1.3 litre models .... FZX 1422 or 1468
   1.6 litre models:
      Manual gearbox .... FZX 1424, 1463 or 1476
      Automatic transmission .... FZX 1425
Piston damper .... LZX 1511
Piston spring colour .... Red
Jet size .... 0.100 in (2.54 mm)
Needle identification:
   1.3 litre models .... BCZ
   1.6 litre models .... BFM
Piston damper oil type/specification .... Multigrade engine oil, viscosity SAE 10W/40

Adjustment data

Fast idle rod minimum clearance . . . .   0.005 in (0.13 mm)
Throttle lever lost motion gap . . . .   0.060 to 0.080 in (1.5 to 2.0 mm)
Float height (see text) . . . .   0.040 to 0.060 in (1.0 to 1.5 mm)
Idling speed:
    1.3 litre models . . . .   700 to 800 rpm
    1.6 litre models:
       Manual gearbox . . . .   700 to 800 rpm
       Automatic transmission . . . .   775 to 925 rpm
Fast idle speed:
    1.3 litre models . . . .   1150 to 1225 rpm
    1.6 litre models:
       Manual gearbox . . . .   1150 to 1250 rpm
       Automatic transmission . . . .   1300 to 1400 rpm
Exhaust gas CO content:
    1.3 litre models . . . .   1.5 to 3.5%
    1.6 litre models . . . .   2.0 to 3.5%

Torque wrench settings

	lbf ft	Nm
Carburettor retaining nuts	16	22
Fuel pump retaining nuts or bolts:		
1.3 litre models	16	22
1.6 litre models	11	15
Manifold retaining nuts and bolts	21	28

1 General description

The fuel system consists of a centrally-mounted fuel tank, camshaft-operated mechanical fuel pump and an SU variable choke carburettor with electronic mixture control system.

The air cleaner contains a disposable paper filter element and incorporates an automatic air temperature control system. The system is controlled by a flap valve located at the junction of the air cleaner hot and cold air intakes. The flap is operated by inlet manifold vacuum acting on a thermac unit in conjunction with a temperature-sensitive thermac switch. The system allows hot or cold air to be delivered to the carburettor, depending on the position of the flap valve which varies according to engine temperature and load.

The SU variable choke carburettor incorporates a computer-operated electronic mixture control system working in conjunction with the electronic ignition system to provide a sophisticated engine management package. Further details of this system will be found in Section 11.

The exhaust system is in three sections; the front section incorporates the twin downpipes and is fitted with ball and socket type flexible joints, the intermediate section incorporates the single or twin front silencers and the rear section incorporates the rear silencer and tailpipe. The system is supported on rubber mountings at the centre and rear and is bolted to the exhaust manifold at the front.

The inlet and exhaust manifolds are of cast aluminium and cast iron construction respectively. The inlet manifold is heated by engine coolant to improve fuel vaporisation and additionally, on 1.6 litre models, an electrically-operated manifold heater is used. This unit warms the manifold during initial start-up conditions to improve cold start driveability. The unit is switched off by a thermostatic switch when a predetermined temperature is reached.

Warning: Many of the procedures in this Chapter entail the removal of fuel pipes and connections which may result in some fuel spillage. Before carrying out any operation on the fuel system, refer to the precautions given in Safety First! at the beginning of this manual and follow them implicitly. Petrol is a highly dangerous and volatile liquid and the precautions necessary when handling it cannot be overstressed.

2 Maintenance and inspection

1 At the service intervals given in Routine Maintenance at the beginning of this manual the following checks and adjustments should be carried out on the fuel and exhaust system components.

2 With the car over a pit, raised on a vehicle lift or securely supported on axle stands, carefully inspect the fuel pipes, hoses and unions for chafing, leaks and corrosion. Renew any pipes that are severely pitted with corrosion or in any way damaged. Renew any hoses that show signs of cracking or other deterioration.

3 Examine the fuel tank for leaks, particularly around the fuel gauge sender unit, and for signs of corrosion or damage.

4 Check the condition of the exhaust system, described in Section 17.

5 From within the engine compartment, check the security of all fuel hose attachments and inspect the fuel hoses and vacuum hoses for kinks, chafing or deterioration.

6 Renew the air cleaner element and check the operation of the air cleaner automatic temperature control, described in Sections 3 and 4.

7 Check the operation of the accelerator linkage and lubricate the linkage, cable and pedal pivot with a few drops of engine oil.

8 Top up the carburettor piston damper to the top of the hollow piston rod with engine oil. Note that although this operation is only considered necessary by the manufacturers at the annual major service interval, practical experience has shown that the damper oil may require topping-up more frequently.

9 Check and, if necessary, adjust the carburettor idle, fast idle and mixture settings, as described in Section 12.

3 Air cleaner and element (1.3 litre models) - removal and refitting

1 To remove the air cleaner element unscrew the three large screws and one small screw securing the air cleaner top cover and body. Withdraw the screws, release the cover from the locating tags and withdraw it from the air cleaner body.

2 The paper element can now be removed.

3 If the air cleaner body is to be removed, detach the cold air intake hose from its location in the front body panel.

4 Lift up the air cleaner and detach the vacuum hose from the connector in the main vacuum line adjacent to the carburettor.

Fig. 3.1 Air cleaner assembly and related components – 1.3 litre models (Sec 3)

1 Retaining screw
2 Washer
3 Top cover
4 Paper element
5 Air cleaner body
6 Sealing washer
7 Thermac unit
8 Retaining clip
9 Intake elbow
10 Hot air hose
11 Hot air box
12 Washer
13 Bolt
14 Cold air intake hose adaptor
15 Cold air intake hose

Detach the air cleaner hose from the hot air box on the exhaust manifold and remove the air cleaner from the engine.

5 Thoroughly clean the inside of the air cleaner and check the vacuum pipes and thermac switch for condition and security.

6 To test the operation of the air temperature control system, first slacken the retaining clip and remove the cold air intake hose at the elbow.

7 Observe the position of the air temperature control flap which should be set to receive air from the cold air intake. Apply suction to the air cleaner vacuum pipe that was previously disconnected, and ensure that the flap moves to the hot air delivery position. The flap should move to the cold air delivery position when the ambient temperature reaches 85°F (30°C). This can be tested by heating the thermac

4.1 Air cleaner element renewal

switch in the air cleaner body with a hair dryer while applying suction to the hose. If the operation of the unit is in doubt it should be renewed.

8 Refitting the air cleaner body and element is the reverse sequence to removal. Ensure that the rubber sealing washer is in position around the lip of the carburettor intake flange on the air cleaner body. Also make sure that the element seats correctly in the body before fitting the cover.

4 Air cleaner and element (1.6 litre models) - removal and refitting

1 To remove the air cleaner element, spring back the retaining clips, lift off the top cover and withdraw the element (photo).

2 If the air cleaner body is to be removed, release the cold air intake hose from its attachments on the front body panel and thermac unit then remove the hose (photo).

3 Undo the three bolts securing the air cleaner mounting bracket to the engine.

4 Detach the air cleaner body from the plenum chamber and hot air ducts, disconnect the vacuum hose from the thermac unit (photo) and remove the air cleaner assembly from the engine.

5 To remove the plenum chamber, disconnect the vacuum hose from the thermac switch at the T-piece (photo).

4.2 Cold air intake hose front body panel attachment

4.4 Vacuum hose attachment at air cleaner thermac unit

3

6 Undo the two screws and one nut securing the plenum chamber and support bracket (photo). Withdraw the bracket then remove the plenum chamber from the carburettor (photo).

7 Thoroughly clean the inside of the air cleaner body and check the vacuum pipes and thermac unit for condition and security.

8 To test the operation of the air temperature control system, reconnect the vacuum hose from thermac unit to thermac switch, but leave the other vacuum hose from the thermac switch to the T-piece disconnected.

9 Observe the position of the air temperature control flap in the thermac unit at the base of the air cleaner body. The flap should be set to receive air from the cold air intake. Apply suction to the disconnected vacuum hose and

4.5 Vacuum hose attachment at vacuum line T-piece

4.6A Plenum chamber retaining screws (A) and nut (B)

4.6B Removing the plenum chamber

check that the flap moves to the hot air delivery position. The flap should return to the cold air delivery position when the ambient temperature reaches 85°F (30°C). This can be tested by heating the thermac switch in the plenum chamber with a hair dryer while applying suction to the hose. If the operation of the unit is in doubt, the thermac switch should be renewed.

10 Refitting the plenum chamber and air cleaner is the reverse sequence to removal. Renew the gasket between the plenum chamber and carburettor if the old one shows any sign of deterioration.

5 Fuel pump - removal, testing and refitting

Note: *Refer to the warning note in Section 1 before proceeding.*

1 The mechanical fuel pump is located in the front lower right-hand side of the cylinder block on 1.3 litre engines, and at the rear of the camshaft cover on 1.6 litre units. The pump is of sealed construction and in the event of faulty operation must be renewed as a complete unit.

2 To remove the pump, first disconnect the battery negative terminal.

3 Note the location of the fuel inlet pipe and fuel outlet pipe and then remove the pipes from the pump (photo). Plug the pipe ends with a metal rod or old bolt after removal.

4 Undo and remove the two bolts and washers and withdraw the pump and insulating block from the engine.

5 To test the pump operation, refit the fuel inlet pipe to the pump inlet and hold a wad of rag near the outlet. Operate the pump lever by hand and if the pump is in a satisfactory condition, a strong jet of fuel should be ejected from the pump outlet as the lever is released. If this is not the case, check that fuel will flow from the inlet pipe when it is held below the tank level, if so the pump is faulty.

6 Before refitting the pump, clean all traces of old gasket from the pump flange, insulating block and engine face. Use a new gasket on each side of the insulator block and refit the

Fig. 3.2 Air cleaner assembly and related components – 1.6 litre models (Sec 4)

1 Top cover	6 Adaptor sleeve	12 Hot air duct
2 Paper element	7 Cold air intake hose	13 Hot air box
3 Air cleaner body	8 Plenum chamber	14 Cold air intake hose
4 Air cleaner mounting bracket	9 Support bracket	adaptor
5 Thermac unit	10 Gasket	15 Gasket
	11 Connecting tube	

pump, using the reverse sequence to removal. Ensure that the pump lever locates over the top of the camshaft eccentric as the pump is installed. If this proves difficult, turn the engine over until the large offset of the eccentric is facing downward.

6 Fuel tank - removal, servicing and refitting

Note: *Refer to the warning note in Section 1 before proceeding.*

1 Disconnect the battery negative terminal. Remove the fuel tank filler cap.

2 A drain plug is not provided and it will therefore be necessary to syphon, or hand pump, all the fuel from the tank before removal.

3 Having emptied the tank, jack up the rear of the car and support it securely on axle stands.

4 Disconnect the electrical leads from the fuel gauge sender unit and release the clips securing the leads to the tank (photo).

5 Using pliers, release the fuel feed hose retaining clip and disconnect the hose from the outlet on the sender unit.

6 Unscrew the retaining clip securing the fuel filler hose to the tank and disconnect the hose.

7 Support the tank on blocks, or with a jack, and undo the two rear and two front retaining bolts and stiffener plates (photo).

5.3 Removing the fuel inlet pipe from the pump nozzle

6.4 Electrical leads (A) and fuel feed hose (B) at the fuel gauge sender unit

6.7 Fuel tank front retaining bolts and stiffener plates (arrowed)

8.2 Accelerator inner cable linkage connector (A) and support bracket fitting (B) – 1.3 litre models

9.1 Carburettor linkage lever slot (A) and cable locknuts (B) – 1.6 litre models

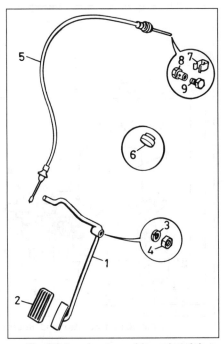

Fig. 3.3 Accelerator cable and pedal components (Secs 8, 9 and 10)

1 Accelerator pedal	6 Pedal stop
2 Pedal pad	7 Cable retaining
3 Washer	clip
4 Retaining nut	8 Cable connector
5 Accelerator cable	9 Connector screw

3

8 Move the tank to the left to clear the brake pipe and lower it sufficiently to allow the breather hose to be detached. Now lower the tank to the ground and withdraw it from under the car.

9 If the tank is contaminated with sediment or water, remove the sender unit, as described in Section 7, and swill the tank out with clean fuel. If the tank is damaged, or leaks, it should be repaired by a specialist or, alternatively, renewed. **Do not** under any circumstances solder or weld the tank.

10 Refitting the tank is the reverse sequence to removal.

7 Fuel gauge sender unit - removal and refitting

Note: Refer to the warning note in Section 1 before proceeding.

1 Follow the procedure given in Section 6, paragraphs 1 to 5 inclusive.

2 Engage a screwdriver, flat bar or other suitable tool with the lugs of the locking ring, and turn the ring anti-clockwise to release it.

3 Withdraw the locking ring, seal and sender unit.

4 Refitting is the reverse sequence to removal, but always use a new seal.

8 Accelerator cable (1.3 litre models) - removal and refitting

1 Disconnect the battery negative terminal then remove the air cleaner assembly, as described in Section 3.

2 Slacken the screw to release the inner cable from the connector on the throttle linkage (photo).

3 Release the outer cable from the support bracket and withdraw the inner cable from the connector.

4 Working inside the car, prise the retaining clip from the top of the accelerator pedal and disconnect the inner cable.

5 Release the cable from the engine compartment bulkhead and remove the cable from the car.

6 Refitting is the reverse sequence to removal but, before tightening the throttle linkage connector, adjust the position of the inner cable to provide a small amount of free play. Check that, with the accelerator pedal fully depressed, the throttle linkage is fully open and, with the pedal released, the linkage is in the closed position.

9 Accelerator cable (1.6 litre models) - removal and refitting

1 Open the throttle linkage on the carburettor fully and slip the inner cable end out of the slot on the linkage lever (photo).

2 Slacken the two locknuts securing the cable to the support bracket on the side of the carburettor. Unscrew the nut nearest the end of the cable fully, then slip the cable out of the slot on the bracket.

3 Working inside the car, prise the retaining clip from the top of the accelerator pedal and disconnect the inner cable.

4 Release the accelerator cable from the engine compartment bulkhead and withdraw the complete cable from the car.

5 Refitting is the reverse sequence to removal, but adjust the outer cable lock nuts to provide a small amount of free play of the cable. Check that, with the accelerator pedal fully depressed, the throttle linkage is fully open and, with the pedal released, the linkage is in the closed position.

6 On models equipped with automatic transmission, check the kickdown cable adjustment, as described in Chapter 7.

10 Accelerator pedal - removal and refitting

1 Disconnect the battery negative terminal.

2 Prise the retaining clip from the top of the accelerator pedal and disconnect the accelerator cable from the pedal arm.

3 Unhook the pedal return spring, undo the retaining nut and washer and slide the pedal off the shaft.

4 Refitting is the reverse sequence to removal. After fitting, check the accelerator cable adjustment, as described in Section 8 or 9, as applicable.

11 SU carburettor - description and operation

The SU HIF (Horizontal Integral Float chamber) carburettor is of the variable choke, constant depression type incorporating a sliding piston which automatically controls the mixture of air and fuel supplied to the engine with respect to the throttle valve position and engine speed. In addition the carburettor is equipped with an electronically operated mixture control device. This alters the mixture strength and engine speed when starting and during slow running, and also controls the operation of a fuel shut-off valve when decelerating or descending a hill.

The carburettor functions as follows. When the engine is started and is allowed to idle, the throttle valve passes a small amount of air. Because the piston is in a low position it offers a larger restriction and the resultant pressure reduction draws fuel from the jet, and atomisation occurs to provide a combustible

Fig. 3.4 Carburettor and electronic mixture control layout (Sec 11)

1 Carburettor
2 Fuel shut-off valve
3 Mixture control stepping motor
4 Vacuum switch
5 Electronic control unit – ECU
6 Ignition coil
7 Ambient air temperature sensor
8 High engine temperature warning lamp
9 Engine temperature gauge
10 Accelerator pedal switch
11 Coolant temperature thermistor
12 Fuse C5
A From ignition switch
B To ignition ECU (1.6 litre models only)
For colour code details refer to the wiring
diagrams at the end of this manual

mixture. Since the inside section of the tapered needle is across the mouth of the jet, a relatively small amount of fuel is passed.

When the throttle valve is opened, the amount of air passing through the carburettor is increased, which causes a greater depression beneath the sliding piston. An internal passageway connects this depression with the suction chamber above the piston, which now rises. The piston offers less of a restriction where the forces of depression, gravity, and spring tension balance out. The tapered needle has now been raised, and more fuel passes from the jet.

Incorporated in the jet adjusting (mixture) screw mechanism is a bi-metal strip which alters the position of the jet to compensate for varying fuel densities resulting from varying fuel temperatures.

Fuel enrichment for cold starting is by an internal valve which admits more fuel into the airstream passing through the carburettor. This valve is operated by a stepping motor which also controls the engine idling speed. An electronic control unit (ECU) which is a small microprocessor, receives inputs from the coolant temperature sensor, ambient air temperature sensor, accelerator pedal switch and ignition coil and adjusts the engine idle speed and mixture accordingly. The ECU also controls the operation of a fuel shut-off valve which comes into operation when decelerating or descending a hill. If, during

these conditions, the engine speed is in excess of 1300 rpm, the ambient air temperature and engine temperature are above a predetermined value, and the accelerator pedal switch is closed (pedal released) the valve will be opened and closed at half second intervals. This introduces a partial vacuum to the top of the float chamber thus weakening the mixture. The fuel shut-off circuit is deactivated if the engine speed suddenly drops, ie when declutching. When accelerating, a vacuum operated switch acts upon the mixture control, allowing more fuel to be drawn through, resulting in the necessary richer mixture.

The overall effect of this type of carburettor is that it will remain in tune during the lengthy service intervals and also under varying operating conditions and temperature changes. The design of the unit and its related systems ensures a fine degree of mixture control over the complete throttle range, coupled with enhanced engine fuel economy.

12 SU carburettor - adjustments

Note: Before carrying out any carburettor adjustment, ensure that the spark plug gaps, valve clearances and, on 1.3 litre models, the

ignition timing, are all correctly set. To carry out the following adjustments an accurate tachometer will be required. The use of an exhaust gas analyser (CO meter) is also preferable, although not essential.

1 Begin by removing the air cleaner on 1.3 litre models, as described in Section 3, or the plenum chamber on 1.6 litre models, as described in Section 4.

2 Unscrew and remove the piston damper from the suction chamber.

3 Undo and remove the three securing screws and lift off the suction chamber, complete with piston and piston spring. After removal avoid rotating the piston in the suction chamber.

4 Invert the suction chamber assembly and drain the oil from the hollow piston rod. Check that the needle guide is flush with the piston face and is secure. Do not be concerned that the needle appears loose in the guide, this is perfectly normal.

5 Observe the position of the jet in relation to the jet guide located in the centre of the carburettor venturi. The jet will probably be slightly below the top face of the jet guide. Turn the mixture adjusting screw until the top of the jet is flush with the top of the jet guide. Now turn the adjusting screw two complete turns clockwise. If the mixture adjusting screw is covered by a small blue or red tamperproof plug, hook this out with a small screwdriver and discard it.

6 Refit the piston and suction chamber assembly, taking care not to turn the piston in the suction chamber any more than is necessary to align the piston groove with its guide. If the piston is turned excessively the spring will be wound up and the assembly will have to be dismantled, as described in Section 14.

7 Check that the piston is free to move in the suction chamber by lifting it and allowing it to drop under its own weight. A definite metallic click should be heard as the piston falls and contacts the bridge in the carburettor body. If this is not the case, dismantle and clean the suction chamber, as described in Section 14. If satisfactory, top up the damper oil with engine oil to the top of the hollow piston rod and refit the damper.

8 Check that the throttle linkage operates smoothly and that there is a small amount of free play in the accelerator cable.

9 Connect a tachometer to the engine in accordance with the manufacturer's instructions, and also a CO meter if this is to be used.

10 Reconnect the vacuum hoses to the air cleaner or plenum chamber and lay the unit alongside the carburettor.

11 Start the engine and run it at a fast idle speed until it reaches its normal operating temperature. Continue to run the engine for a further five minutes before commencing adjustment.

12 Increase the engine speed to 2500 rpm for 30 seconds and repeat this at three minute

Fig. 3.5 Carburettor adjustment points (Sec 12)

1 Piston damper oil level
2 Idle speed adjustment
   screw
3 Accelerator cable
4 Throttle lever adjustment
   screw
5 Fast idle adjustment
   screw
6 Fast idle pushrod
7 Mixture adjustment screw
A = Lost motion gap
B = Fast idle clearance

intervals during the adjustment procedure. This will ensure that any excess fuel is cleared from the inlet manifold.

13 Disconnect the coolant thermistor wiring plug (see Chapter 2 if necessary) and join the two plug terminals together using a suitable length of wire. This will ensure that the mixture control stepping motor is not actuated during adjustment.

14 If the cooling fan is running, wait until it stops then turn the idle speed adjustment screw as necessary until the engine is idling at the specified speed.

15 Switch off the engine.

16 Check the clearance between the fast idle pushrod and fast idle adjustment screw using feeler gauges (position B in Fig. 3.5). Turn the fast idle adjustment screw as necessary to obtain the specified clearance.

17 Check the throttle lever lost motion gap using feeler gauges (position A in Fig. 3.5) and, if necessary, turn the throttle lever adjustment screw to obtain the specified clearance.

18 Start the engine and slowly turn the mixture adjustment screw clockwise (to enrich) or anti-clockwise (to weaken) until the fastest idling speed which is consistent with smooth even running is obtained. If a CO meter is being used, adjust the mixture screw to obtain the specified idling exhaust gas CO content.

19 Reset the idling speed, if necessary, using the idle speed adjustment screw then switch off the engine once more.

20 To adjust the fast idle speed, disconnect the two wires at the ambient air temperature sensor located in the engine compartment behind the left-hand headlamp (photo). Remove the sensor and join the two wires

together using a male-to-male connector or suitable length of wire.

21 Remove the wire connecting the coolant thermistor wiring plug terminals together, but leave the plug disconnected.

22 Start the engine again. The mixture control stepping motor should move the fast idle pushrod to the fast idle position. Compare the engine fast idle speed with the specified setting and if necessary adjust by turning the fast idle adjustment screw as required.

23 Switch off the engine, reconnect the ambient air temperature sensor and coolant thermistor wiring plug. **Note:** *after carrying out this adjustment, ensure that the specified minimum clearance still exists between pushrod and screw, as described in paragraph 16. Adjust the screw if the clearance is less than specified.*

24 Make a final check that the idling speed and mixture are correct after refitting the air cleaner or plenum chamber then switch off the engine and disconnect the instruments.

13 SU carburettor - removal and refining

1 Disconnect the battery negative terminal.
2 On 1.3 litre models remove the air cleaner assembly, as described in Section 3. On 1.6 litre models remove the plenum chamber, as described in Section 4.
3 On 1.3 litre models slacken the retaining screw and release the accelerator inner cable from the throttle lever connector. Release the outer cable from the support bracket and place the cable to one side. On 1.6 litre models open the throttle by hand and slip the cable end out of the slot on the throttle lever. Slacken the outer cable locknuts, unscrew the inner locknut and release the cable from the support bracket. Place the cable to one side.
4 If automatic transmission is fitted, disconnect the kickdown cable from the throttle lever, slip the cable out of the support bracket and place it to one side.
5 Disconnect the wiring connectors at the fuel shut-off valve solenoid and stepping motor (photos).

3

12.20 Ambient air temperature sensor location (arrowed) behind left-hand headlamp

13.5A Detach the fuel shut-off valve wiring connector . . .

13.5B . . . and the stepping motor wiring connector

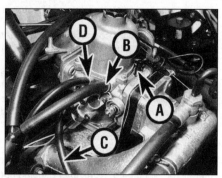

13.6 Ignition vacuum advance hose (A), crankcase breather hose (B), fuel inlet hose (C), and float chamber vent hose (D)

13.7 Removing the carburettor from the manifold – 1.6 litre model

6 Detach the ignition vacuum advance hose, crankcase breather hose, fuel inlet hose and float chamber vent hose (photo). Plug the fuel hose after removal.

7 Undo the two nuts, remove the washers and withdraw the carburettors from the manifold studs (photo). Recover the insulating block and gaskets. On 1.3 litre models remove the air cleaner mounting bracket, gaskets and insulating block as required, noting the arrangement of gaskets.

8 Refitting is the reverse sequence to removal. Ensure that all mating faces are perfectly clean and always use new gaskets. After refitting, connect the accelerator cable referring to Section 8 or 9 and, if necessary, adjust the carburettor as described in Section 12.

14 SU carburettor - dismantling, overhaul and reassembly

1 Remove the carburettor, as described in the previous Section.
2 Clean off the exterior of the carburettor using paraffin, or a suitable solvent and wipe dry.
3 Unscrew the three retaining screws and lift off the suction chamber and piston assembly (photo).
4 Unscrew the damper from the suction chamber (photo), and drain the oil from the piston rod.

Fig. 3.6 Exploded view of the carburettor (Sec 14)

14.3 Removing the carburettor suction chamber and piston assembly

14.4 Unscrew the damper and drain the oil

1 Piston damper
2 Retaining circlip
3 Suction chamber
4 Piston
5 Piston spring
6 Needle guide locking screw
7 Needle bias spring
8 Jet needle
9 Needle guide
10 Idle speed screw
11 Idle screw seal
12 Mixture adjustment screw
13 Fuel shut-off valve and housing

14 Fuel shut-off valve solenoid
15 Throttle return spring
16 Throttle spindle seal
17 Throttle plate
18 Throttle spindle
19 Carburettor body
20 Vacuum switch
21 Mixture control stepping motor
22 Fast idle pushrod
23 Jet bearing
24 Jet bearing nut
25 Jet assembly

26 Float needle seat
27 Float needle
28 Bi-metal jet lever
29 Float
30 Jet lever retaining screw
31 Float chamber cover seal
32 Float chamber cover
33 Throttle lever and return spring
34 Fast idle adjustment screw
35 Lost motion link and return spring
36 Throttle lever adjustment screw

5 Push the piston up to expose the retaining circlip (photo). Extract the circlip and withdraw the piston and spring assembly (photo).

6 Unscrew the needle guide locking screw and withdraw the needle guide and spring (photo).

7 Mark the relationship of the float chamber cover to the carburettor body. Unscrew the four retaining screws and lift off the cover and O-ring seal (photo).

8 Unscrew the jet adjusting lever retaining screw and withdraw the jet and adjusting lever assembly (photo). Disengage the jet from the lever.

9 Unscrew the float pivot screw (photo) and lift out the float and fuel needle valve (photo). Unscrew the needle valve seat from the base of the float chamber (photo).

10 Unscrew the jet bearing locking nut (photo) and remove the jet bearing (photo).

11 Undo the three retaining screws and remove the fuel shut-off valve and solenoid assembly (photo). Recover the gasket.

12 Dismantling the remaining components is not recommended, as these parts are not available separately. If the throttle levers, linkage or spindle appear worn, or in any way damaged, it will be necessary to renew the complete carburettor. **Do not** remove the mixture control stepping motor or vacuum switch. These components are set to each individual carburettor during manufacture and may not operate correctly if disturbed.

14.5A Extract the retaining circlip . . .

14.5B . . . to allow removal of the piston and spring

14.6 Slacken the needle guide locking screw and withdraw the needle, guide and spring

14.7 Lift off the float chamber cover after removing the four screws

3

14.8 Removing the jet and adjusting lever assembly

14.9A Unscrew the float pivot screw and remove the float . . .

14.9B . . . followed by the fuel needle valve . . .

14.9C . . . then unscrew the needle valve seat

14.10A Unscrew the jet bearing locknut . . .

14.10B . . . and lift out the jet bearing

14.11 Remove the fuel shut-off valve and solenoid

14.13 Ensure that the filter in the fuel needle valve seat is clean

Fig. 3.7 Carburettor float height adjustment (Sec 14)

A = specified float level height
Arrows indicate checking and adjustment points

13 Check the condition of the float needle valve and seat and renew these components if there is any sign of pitting or wear ridges, particularly on the needle. Ensure that the filter in the seat assembly is clean (photo).

14 Examine the carburettor body for cracks and damage, and ensure that the brass fittings and piston guide are secure.

15 Clean the inside of the suction chamber and the outer circumference of the piston with a petrol-moistened rag and allow to air dry. Insert the piston into the suction chamber without the spring. Hold the assembly in a horizontal position and spin the piston. If there is any tendency for the piston to bind, renew the piston and dashpot assembly.

16 Connect a 12 volt supply to the terminals of the fuel shut-off valve solenoid and ensure that the valve closes. If not, renew the solenoid.

17 Check the piston needle and jet bearing for any signs of ovality, or wear ridges.

18 Shake the float and listen for any trapped fuel which may have entered through a tiny crack or fracture.

19 Check the condition of all gaskets, seals and connecting hoses and renew any that show signs of deterioration.

20 Begin reassembly by refitting the jet bearing and retaining nut to the carburettor body.

21 Refit the fuel needle valve and seat, followed by the float and float pivot screw.

22 Allow the float to close the needle valve

under its own weight and measure the distance from the centre of the float to the face of the carburettor body, as shown in Fig. 3.7. If the measured dimension is outside the float level height setting given in the Specifications, carefully bend the brass contact pad on the float to achieve the required setting.

23 Engage the jet with the cut-out in the adjusting lever, ensuring that the jet head moves freely. Position the jet in the jet bearing and, at the same time, engage the slot in the adjusting lever with the protruding tip of the mixture adjustment screw. Secure the assembly with the retaining screw.

24 Turn the mixture adjustment screw as necessary to bring the top of the jet flush with the jet bearing upper face when viewed from above. Now turn the adjustment screw two complete turns clockwise to obtain an initial mixture setting.

25 Fit a new O-ring seal to the float chamber cover. Fit the cover with the previously made marks aligned and secure with the four retaining screws.

26 Refit the piston needle, spring and needle guide to the piston (photo), ensuring that the needle guide is flush with the underside of the piston and the triangular etch mark on the guide is between the two transfer holes in the piston (photo). Refit and tighten the locking screw.

27 Temporarily refit the piston and dashpot to the carburettor body without the spring. Engage the piston in its guide and, with the suction chamber in its correct position relative

to the retaining screws, mark the piston-to-suction chamber relationship. Remove the suction chamber and piston.

28 Fit the spring to the piston, align the previously made marks and slide the suction chamber over the piston and spring. Avoid turning the piston in the suction chamber, otherwise the spring will be wound up.

29 Push the piston rod up and refit the circlip to the piston rod.

30 Refit the piston and suction chamber, and secure with the three retaining screws tightened evenly. Fill the piston damper with engine oil up to the top of the piston and refit the damper.

31 Refit the fuel shut-off valve using a new gasket, if necessary, and secure the unit with the three screws.

15 Inlet and exhaust manifolds (1.3 litre models) - removal and refitting

1 Disconnect the battery negative terminal, and then remove the carburettor, as described in Section 13.

2 Pull the vacuum hose off the banjo union connector in the centre of the inlet manifold (photo). Undo and remove the banjo union

15.2 Banjo union components

A Vacuum hose   D Banjo union
B Union nut   E Sealing washer
C Sealing washer

14.26A Refit the needle, spring and guide to the piston . . .

14.26B . . . with the guide flush with the piston base and the etch mark (arrowed) positioned as shown

Fig. 3.8 Inlet and exhaust manifold assemblies – 1.3 litre models (Sec 15)

1 Manifold gasket
2 Inlet manifold
   locating ring
3 Inlet manifold
4 Support bracket
5 Steady bracket
6 Hot air box
7 Exhaust manifold

bolt and recover the two washers. Place the servo vacuum hose to one side.

3 Remove the cooling system filler cap from the expansion tank. *If the engine is hot, unscrew the cap slowly to release the pressure and use a rag as protection against scalding.*

4 Place a suitable receptacle beneath the inlet manifold and slacken the two clips

16.3 Manifold induction heater wiring connector

securing the water hoses to the manifold. Ease off the hoses and allow the water to drain into the receptacle.

5 Undo and remove the bolt securing the steady bracket to the exhaust manifold and the nuts and large washers securing the inlet manifold to the cylinder head. Withdraw the inlet manifold from the cylinder head and recover the vent hose.

6 To remove the exhaust manifold, remove the front portion of the hot air box to provide access to the exhaust downpipe.

7 Undo and remove the nuts securing the downpipe to the manifold, and the remaining nuts and washers securing the manifold to the cylinder head. Withdraw the exhaust manifold from the cylinder head.

8 With the manifolds removed, recover the gaskets from the cylinder head and exhaust downpipe flange, and remove the inlet manifold locating rings.

9 Refitting the manifolds is the reverse sequence to removal. Use new gaskets and make sure all mating faces are clean. Tighten the manifold-to-cylinder head nuts evenly to the specified torque before fully tightening the downpipe and steady bracket nuts and bolts. Refit the carburettor as described in Section 13, and top up the cooling system, as described in Chapter 2.

16 Inlet and exhaust manifolds (1.6 litre models) - removal and refitting

1 Disconnect the battery negative terminal then remove the air cleaner and plenum chamber, as described in Section 4, and the carburettor, as described in Section 14.

2 Pull the vacuum hose off the banjo union connector in the centre of the inlet manifold (photo 15.2). Undo and remove the banjo union bolt and recover the two washers. Place the servo vacuum hose to one side.

3 Disconnect the induction heater lead at the wiring connector (photo).

4 Disconnect the two wires at the induction temperature sensor (photo).

5 Remove the cooling system filler cap from the expansion tank. **Note:** *If the engine is hot, unscrew the cap slowly to release the*

Fig. 3.9 Inlet and exhaust manifold assemblies – 1.6 litre models (Sec 16)

1 Manifold gasket
2 Heat shield
3 Inlet manifold
4 Induction
   temperature
   sensor
5 Induction heater
6 Exhaust manifold
7 Hot air box
8 Support strut
9 Support strut

pressure and use a rag as protection against scalding.

6 Place a suitable container beneath the inlet manifold and slacken the clips securing the three hoses to the manifold outlets. Ease off the hoses and allow the coolant to drain into the receptacle.

7 Undo the bolts securing the left-hand and right-hand support struts to the manifold (photos).

8 Jack up the front of the car and securely support it on axle stands.

9 Undo the nuts securing the exhaust downpipes to the manifold and ease the flange off the manifold studs.

10 Undo the bolts securing the right-hand engine mounting to the cylinder head. Ease the engine away from the mounting sufficiently to allow removal of the manifold. Wedge the engine in this position.

16.4 Wiring connectors at the induction temperature sensor

16.7A Inlet manifold left-hand . . .

16.7B . . . and right-hand support strut attachments (arrowed)

3

16.11 Heat shield retaining screws (arrowed)

16.12 Removing the inlet manifold . . .

16.13. . . followed by the exhaust manifold

11 Undo the two screws and remove the heat shield from the inlet manifold (photo).
12 Undo all the bolts, clamp plates and nuts securing the inlet manifold to the cylinder head and remove the manifold

Fig. 3.10 Exhaust system components (Sec 17)

(photo). Recover the carburettor vent hose.
13 Undo the remaining nuts and bolts and remove the exhaust manifold (photo).
14 Refitting the manifolds is the reverse sequence to removal. Use new gaskets and make sure all mating faces are clean. Tighten the manifold-to-cylinder head nuts and bolts evenly and to the specified torque before fully tightening the downpipe and steady bracket nuts and bolts. Refit the carburettor, as described in Section 13, the air cleaner and plenum chamber, as described in Section 4, then top up the cooling system, as described in Chapter 2.

17 Exhaust system - checking, removal and refitting

1 The exhaust system should be examined for leaks, damage and security at regular intervals (see Routine Maintenance). To do this, apply the handbrake and allow the engine to idle. Lie down on each side of the car in turn and check the full length of the exhaust system for leaks while an assistant temporarily places a wad of cloth over the end of the tailpipe. If a leak is evident stop the engine and use a proprietary repair kit to seal it. If a leak is excessive or damage is evident, renew the section. Check the rubber mountings for deterioration and renew them if necessary.
2 To remove the exhaust system, jack up the

front and/or rear of the car and support it securely on axle stands. Alternatively drive the front or rear wheels up on ramps.
3 The system consists of three sections which can be individually removed. If the intermediate section is to be removed it will, however, be necessary to remove the front or rear section first. To remove the rear section of the system, unscrew the retaining nuts and remove the U-shaped retaining clamp. Release the mounting bracket from the rubber mounting block (photo) and twist the section free. If the joint is stubborn, liberally apply penetrating oil and leave it to soak. Tap the joint with a hammer and it should now be possible to twist it free. If necessary, carefully heat the joint with a blowlamp to assist removal, *but shield the fuel tank, fuel lines and underbody adequately from heat.*
4 To remove the front section, first remove the anti-roll bar if working on a 1.6 litre model, as described in Chapter 11. Undo and remove the nuts securing the downpipes to the exhaust manifold (photo) and, where fitted, remove any additional support brackets. Unhook the compression spring from the flexible joint, remove the U-shaped clamp (photo) and release the section.
5 Refitting is the reverse sequence to removal. Position the joints so that there is adequate clearance between all parts of the system and the underbody, and ensure that there is equal load on all mounting blocks. Always use a new gasket on the downpipe-to-manifold joint face.

17.3 Exhaust rear section rubber mounting block

17.4A Exhaust downpipe flexible joint – 1.6 litre model

17.4B Front-to-intermediate exhaust section retaining clamp

Fault finding - fuel and exhaust systems

Unsatisfactory engine performance, bad starting and excessive fuel consumption are not necessarily the fault of the fuel system or carburettor. In fact they more commonly occur as a result of ignition and timing faults. Before acting on the following, it is necessary to check the ignition system first Even though a fault may lie in the fuel system, it will be difficult to trace unless the ignition system is correct. The faults below, therefore, assume that where applicable, this has been attended to first. If during the fault diagnosis procedure it is suspected that the carburettor electronic mixture control or any of its related systems may be at fault, it is recommended that the help of a reputable BL dealer is sought. Accurate testing of the system and its components entails the use of a systematic checking procedure using specialist equipment and this is considered beyond the scope of the average home mechanic.

Difficult starting when cold

- [ ] Faulty electronic mixture control system or related component
- [ ] Carburettor piston sticking
- [ ] Fuel tank empty or pump defective
- [ ] Incorrect float chamber fuel level

Difficult starting when hot

- [ ] Faulty electronic mixture control system or related component
- [ ] Air cleaner choked
- [ ] Carburettor piston sticking
- [ ] Float chamber flooding or incorrect fuel level
- [ ] Fuel tank empty or pump defective
- [ ] Carburettor idle mixture adjustment incorrect

Excessive fuel consumption

- [ ] Leakage from tank, pipes, pump or carburettor
- [ ] Air cleaner choked
- [ ] Carburettor idle mixture adjustment incorrect
- [ ] Carburettor float chamber flooding
- [ ] Faulty fuel shut-off solenoid or control system
- [ ] Carburettor worn
- [ ] Excessive engine wear or other internal fault
- [ ] Tyres underinflated
- [ ] Brakes binding

Fuel starvation

- [ ] Fuel level flow
- [ ] Leak on suction side of pump
- [ ] Fuel pump faulty
- [ ] Float chamber fuel level incorrect
- [ ] Fuel tank breather restricted
- [ ] Fuel tank inlet or carburettor inlet filter blocked

Poor performance, hesitation or erratic running

- [ ] Carburettor idle mixture adjustment incorrect
- [ ] Faulty carburettor vacuum switch
- [ ] Carburettor piston damper oil level low
- [ ] Leaking manifold gasket
- [ ] Fuel starvation
- [ ] Carburettor worn
- [ ] Excessive engine wear or other internal fault

3

Notes

Chapter 4 Ignition system

For modifications, and information applicable to later models, see Supplement at end of manual

Contents

Degrees of difficulty

Easy, suitable for novice with little experience	Fairly easy, suitable for beginner with some experience	Fairly difficult, suitable for competent DIY mechanic	Difficult, suitable for experienced DIY mechanic	Very difficult, suitable for expert DIY or professional

Specifications

Part A: 1.3 litre models

System type . . . . Electronic breakerless, inductive type

Ignition coil
Type . . . . Ducellier 520029A
Current consumption - engine idling . . . . 2.3 to 2.7 amps
Primary resistance at 20°C (68°F) . . . . 0.82 ohms ± 5%

Distributor
Type . . . . Lucas 59 DM4
Direction of rotation . . . . Anti-clockwise
Reluctor air gap . . . . 0.008 to 0.014 in (0.20 to 0.35 mm)
Ignition amplifier . . . . Lucas AB14 or Ducellier 54403505
Firing order 1-3-4-2
Location of No 1 cylinder . . . . Crankshaft pulley end
Lubricant type/specification . . . . Multigrade engine oil, viscosity SAE 10W/40

Spark plugs
Type . . . . Champion RN9YCC or RN9YC
Electrode gap* . . . . 0.032 in (0.8 mm)
The gap quoted is that recommended by Champion for the plug specified. The gap for other makes of spark plug may vary, and reference should be made to their manufacturers' recommendations

HT leads . . . . Champion LS-02 boxed set

Ignition timing
Stroboscopic at 1500 rpm with vacuum pipe disconnected . . . . 12° BTDC
Timing marks . . . . Crankshaft pulley groove and 4° pointers on timing cover scale

Torque wrench settings	lbf ft	Nm
Spark plugs	18	24
Distributor clamp bolt	16	22

Part B: 1.6 litre models

System type . . . . Microprocessor-controlled programmed electronic ignition

Ignition coil
Type . . . . Lucas 45328
Current consumption - engine idling . . . . 2.3 to 2.7 amps
Primary resistance at 20°C (68°F) . . . . 0.82 ohms ± 5%

Programmed ignition system
Electronic control unit type . . . . Lucas AB17-84185
Distributor cap type . . . . Lucas 544-03944
Rotor arm type . . . . Lucas 544-04286
Rotor arm rotation . . . . Anti-clockwise
Knock sensor type . . . . Lucas or Lamerholm VP50/1-M 12
Crankshaft sensor type . . . . Lucas 547-42886
Firing order 1-3-4-2
Location of No 1 cylinder . . . . Crankshaft pulley end

Spark plugs
Type . . . . Champion RC9YCC or RC9YC
Electrode gap* . . . . 0.032 in (0.8. mm)
*The gap quoted is that recommended by Champion for the plug specified. The gap for other makes of spark plug may vary, and reference should be made to their manufacturers' recommendations

HT leads . . . . Champion LS-04 boxed set

Ignition timing*
With vacuum pipe disconnected . . . . 10° to 16° BTDC @ 1000 rpm
With vacuum pipe connected . . . . 23° to 27° BTDC @ 1000 rpm
* Non-adjustable; for reference purposes only - see text

Torque wrench settings

	lbf ft	Nm
Spark plugs	13	18
Knock sensor	9	12

Part A: 1.3 litre models

1 General description

A breakerless inductive type electronic ignition system is used; consisting of the battery, coil, distributor, ignition amplifier, spark plugs and HT leads. The distributor is located on the rear facing side of the engine and is driven by a driveshaft in mesh with the camshaft.

In order that the engine can run correctly, it is necessary for an electrical spark to ignite the fuel/air mixture in the combustion chamber at exactly the right moment in relation to engine speed and load. The ignition system is based on feeding low tension voltage from the battery to the coil, where it is converted to high tension voltage. The high tension voltage is powerful enough to jump the spark plug gap in the cylinders many times a second under high compression, providing that the system is in good condition and that all adjustments are correct.

The ignition system is divided into two circuits, the low tension circuit and the high tension circuit. The low tension circuit consists of the battery, lead to the ignition

switch, lead from the ignition switch to the low tension coil windings, leads from the coil windings to the ignition amplifier and leads from the ignition amplifier to the pick-up coil assembly in the distributor. The high tension circuit consists of the high tension coil windings, the heavy lead from the coil to the distributor cap, the rotor arm, spark plug leads and spark plugs.

The system functions in the following manner. Low tension voltage is changed in the coil into high tension voltage by the action of the ignition amplifier in conjunction with the pick-up coil assembly. As each of the reluctor teeth passes through the magnetic field of the pick-up coil in the distributor an electrical signal is sent to the ignition amplifier which triggers the coil in the same way as the opening of the contact breaker points in a conventional system. High tension voltage is then fed via the carbon brush in the centre of the distributor cap to the distributor rotor arm. The voltage passes across to the appropriate metal segment in the cap and via the spark plug lead to the spark plug where it finally jumps the spark plug gap to earth. The ignition is advanced and retarded automatically, to ensure that the spark occurs at just the right instant for the particular load

at the prevailing engine speed. The ignition advance is controlled both mechanically and by a vacuum-operated system. The mechanical governor mechanism consists of two weights, which move out from the distributor shaft as the engine speed rises due to centrifugal force. As they move outwards they rotate the cam relative to the distributor shaft, and so advance the spark. The weights are held in position by two light springs and it is the tension of the springs which is largely responsible for correct spark advancement.

The vacuum control consists of a diaphragm, one side of which is connected via a small bore tube to the carburettor, and the other side to the distributor baseplate. Depression in the inlet manifold and carburettor, which varies with engine speed and throttle opening, causes the diaphragm to move, so moving the baseplate, and advancing or retarding the spark. A fine degree of control is achieved by a spring in the vacuum assembly.

Due to the nature of the electronic ignition system, no current is consumed by the ignition coil with the ignition switched on and the engine stationary. A ballast resistor is not required in the starting circuit.

Warning: *The voltages produced by the electronic ignition system are considerably higher than those produced by conventional systems. Extreme care must be used when working on the system with the ignition switched on. Persons with surgically-implanted cardiac pacemaker devices should keep well clear of the ignition circuits, components and test equipment.*

2 Maintenance and inspection

1 At the intervals specified in Routine Maintenance at the beginning of this manual remove the distributor cap and thoroughly clean it inside and out with a dry lint-free rag. Examine the four HT lead segments inside the cap. If the segments appear badly burnt or pitted, renew the cap. Make sure that the carbon brush in the centre of the cap is free to move and that it protrudes by approximately 0.1 in (3 mm) from its holder.

2 With the distributor cap removed, lift off the rotor arm and the plastic anti-flash shield. Carefully apply two drops of engine oil to the felt pad in the centre of the cam spindle. Also lubricate the centrifugal advance mechanism by applying two drops of oil through the square hole in the baseplate. Wipe away any excess oil and refit the antiflash shield, rotor arm and distributor cap.

3 Renew the spark plugs at the specified interval. Using a stroboscopic timing light check and, if necessary, reset the ignition timing, as described in Section 5.

3 Distributor –
removal and refitting

1 Disconnect the battery negative terminal.
2 Pull off the HT lead and remove No 1 spark plug (nearest the crankshaft pulley).
3 Place a finger over the plug hole and turn the engine in the normal direction of rotation (clockwise from the crankshaft pulley end) until pressure is felt in No 1 cylinder. This indicates that the piston is commencing its compression stroke. The engine can be turned with a socket and bar on the crankshaft pulley bolt after removing the access cover from the inner wheel arch.
4 Continue turning the engine until the notch in the crankshaft pulley is aligned with the TDC pointer on the timing scale. This is the last pointer on the scale, nearest the front of the car.
5 Make a reference mark on the side of the distributor body adjacent to the No 1 cylinder spark plug lead position in the cap. Spring back the clips, or remove the two screws, and lift off the cap. Check that the rotor arm is pointing toward the reference mark.

Fig. 4.1 Distributor lubrication points (Sec 2)

6 Make a further mark on the cylinder block in line with the mark on the distributor body.
7 Detach the vacuum advance and disconnect the ignition amplifier wiring harness at the connector.
8 Unscrew the distributor clamp retaining bolt, lift away the clamp and withdraw the distributor from the engine.
9 To refit the distributor, first check that the engine is still at the TDC position with No 1 cylinder on compression. If the engine has been turned while the distributor was removed, return it to the correct position, as previously described.
10 With the vacuum unit pointing toward No 1 spark plug, slide the distributor into the cylinder block and turn the rotor arm slightly until the offset slot on the distributor drive dog positively engages with the driveshaft.
11 Turn the distributor body until the rotor arm is pointing toward the No 1 spark plug lead segment in the distributor cap, or if the original distributor is being refitted, align the previously made reference marks. Hold the distributor in this position and refit the clamp and retaining bolt.
12 Reconnect the vacuum advance pipe and the wiring harness connector. Refit the distributor cap, No 1 spark plug and the HT lead.
13 Reconnect the battery and, if removed, refit the access panel to the inner wheel arch.
14 The ignition timing should now be adjusted, as described in Section 5.

4 Distributor –
dismantling and reassembly

1 Remove the distributor, as described in the previous Section.
2 Lift off the rotor arm, followed by the anti-flash shield (photo).
3 Using circlip pliers, extract the retaining circlip (photo) and lift off the washer and O-ring (photo).
4 Withdraw the reluctor and coupling ring (photos) using a screwdriver very carefully to ease them off the shaft if they are initially tight.
5 Undo and remove the screws securing the vacuum unit to the distributor body.

Fig. 4.2 Exploded view of the distributor (Sec 4)

1 *Distributor cap*	6A *Pick-up limb*
2 *Rotor arm*	7 *Wiring guide*
3 *Anti-flash shield*	8 *Felt pad*
4 *O-ring, washer*	9 *Distributor shaft*
and circlip	10 *Distributor body*
5 *Reluctor and*	11 *O-ring*
coupling ring	12 *Vacuum unit*
6 *Pick-up coil and*	
baseplate assembly	

4.2 Lift off the rotor arm and anti-flash shield

4

4.3A Extract the circlip . . .

4.3B . . . and lift off the washer and O-ring

4.4A Withdraw the reluctor . . .

Disengage the vacuum unit operating link from the peg on the underside of the baseplate using a twisting movement and withdraw the unit (photo).

6 Release the wiring harness rubber grommet and remove the two baseplate securing screws. Lift the baseplate out of its location in the distributor body (photo).

7 This is the limit of dismantling, as the parts located below the baseplate, the distributor shaft and distributor body can only be renewed as an assembly.

8 With the distributor dismantled, renew any parts that show signs of wear, or damage, and any that are known to be faulty. Pay close attention to the centrifugal advance mechanism (photo), checking for loose or broken springs, wear in the bob weight

pivots and play in the distributor shaft.
9 Begin reassembly by lubricating the distributor shaft, bob weight pivots, vacuum link and baseplate sliding surfaces with engine oil.
10 Place the baseplate assembly in position, with the peg on the underside adjacent to the vacuum unit aperture. Refit and tighten the two securing screws.
11 Refit the coupling ring to the underside of the reluctor and slide this assembly over the distributor shaft. Align the broad lug of the coupling ring with the broad slot in the shaft and push the ring and reluctor fully into place.
12 Position the O-ring and washer over the shaft and secure them with the circlip.
13 Insert the vacuum unit operating link into its aperture and manipulate the unit and

baseplate until the link can be engaged with the peg. Refit and tighten the retaining screws.
14 Refit the harness leads and grommet to the slot in the distributor body .
15 Position the reluctor so that one of the teeth is adjacent to the limb on the pick-up assembly. Using feeler gauges, preferably of plastic or brass, measure the air gap between the reluctor tooth and pick-up assembly (photo). If the measured dimension is outside the tolerance given in the Specifications, slacken the adjusting nuts on the pick-up assembly and reposition the unit as necessary.
16 Refit the anti-flash shield and rotor arm, then refit the distributor, as described in Section 3.

4.4B . . . followed by the coupling ring

4.5 Disengage the vacuum unit operating link from the baseplate peg and withdraw the unit

4.6 Remove the screws and lift out the baseplate

4.8 Check the components below the baseplate for wear

4.15 Using feeler gauges to measure the reluctor air gap

Fig. 4.3 Reluctor air gap adjustment (Sec 4)

Dimension A = specified air gap
1 Adjusting nuts   3 Pick-up limb
2 Pick-up coil assembly   4 Reluctor tooth

5 Ignition timing - adjustment

Note: *With electronic ignition systems the only suitable method which may be used to accurately time the ignition is with a stroboscopic timing light. However, for initial setting up purposes (ie after major overhaul, or if the timing has been otherwise completely lost) a basic initial static setting may be used to get the engine started. Once the engine is running, the timing should be accurately set using the timing light. A further method, employing the light emitting diode (LED) sensor bracket, and timing disc on the crankshaft pulley may be used, but the equipment for use with this system is not normally available to the home mechanic.*

1 In order that the engine can run efficiently, it is necessary for a spark to occur at the spark plug and ignite the fuel/air mixture at the instant just before the piston on the compression stroke reaches the top of its travel. The precise instant at which the spark occurs is determined by the ignition timing. and this is quoted in degrees before top-dead-centre (BTDC).

2 If the timing is being checked as a maintenance or servicing procedure, refer to paragraph 11. If the distributor has been dismantled or renewed, or if its position on the engine has been altered, obtain an initial static setting as follows.

Static setting

3 Pull off the HT lead and remove No 1 spark plug (nearest the crankshaft pulley).

4 Place a finger over the plug hole and turn the engine in the normal direction of rotation (clockwise from the crankshaft pulley end) until pressure is felt in No 1 cylinder. This indicates that the piston is commencing its compression stroke. The engine can be turned with a socket and bar on the crankshaft pulley bolt after removing the access cover from the inner wheel arch.

5 Continue turning the engine until the notch in the crankshaft pulley is aligned with the TDC pointer on the timing scale (photo 5.12). This is the last pointer on the scale, nearest the front of the car.

6 Remove the distributor cap and check that the rotor arm is pointing toward the No 1 spark plug HT lead segment in the cap.

7 Lift off the rotor arm and anti-flash shield and observe the position of the reluctor in relation to the pick-up coil. One of the teeth on the reluctor should be aligned with, or very near to, the small pip, or limb, of the pick-up coil.

8 Slacken the distributor clamp retaining bolt and turn the distributor body until the reluctor tooth and pick-up limb are directly in line (photo).

9 Tighten the distributor clamp, or pinch-bolt,

5.8 Reluctor tooth (A) aligned with pick-up limb (B)

refit the anti-flash shield, rotor arm and distributor cap. Refit No 1 spark plug and HT lead.

10 It should now be possible to start and run the engine enabling the timing to be accurately checked with a timing light as follows.

Stroboscopic setting

11 Disconnect the vacuum advance pipe at the distributor and plug its end.

12 The timing marks are located on a scale just above the crankshaft pulley, with a corresponding V-notch in the rim of the pulley (photo). The pointer peak at the far right of the scale (ie nearest the front of the car) is the TDC position and is marked with a 'O'. The pointer peaks to the left of the TDC are in increments of 4° BTDC. If a timing light with a strong light source is being used the marks will be clearly visible from above, however, for greater clarity, the access panel under the inner wheel arch may be removed - enabling the timing light to be held very close to the marks.

13 Refer to the Specifications for the timing setting applicable to the engine being worked on, and then highlight the appropriate mark and pulley V-notch with white chalk or paint.

14 Connect a timing light to the engine in accordance with the manufacturer's instructions (usually between No 1 spark and its HT lead). If the car is not equipped with a tachometer, connect a suitable unit to the engine in accordance with the manufacturer's instruction.

15 Start the engine and run it at the speed specified for ignition timing.

16 Point the timing light at the timing marks and they should appear to be stationary with the crank pulley notch in alignment with the appropriate pointer.

17 If adjustment is necessary (ie the pulley notch does not line up with the appropriate point), loosen the distributor clamp retaining bolt, or pinch-bolt, and turn the distributor body clockwise to advance the timing and anti-clockwise to retard it. Tighten the securing bolt when the setting is correct.

18 Gradually increase the engine speed while still pointing the timing light at the marks. The pulley notch should appear to advance

5.12 Crankshaft pulley timing notch and timing scale

Pulley notch shown positioned at TDC

further, indicating that the centrifugal advance mechanism is operating correctly. If the timing marks remain stationary when the engine speed is increased, or if the movement is erratic or jerky, then the distributor should be dismantled for inspection, as described in Section 4.

19 Reconnect the vacuum pipe to the distributor and check that the advance alters when the pipe is connected. If not, the vacuum unit on the distributor may be faulty.

20 Switch off the engine and disconnect the timing light and tachometer. Where applicable, refit the access panel to the inner wheel arch.

6 Ignition coil - description and testing

4

1 The coil is bolted to the centre of the engine compartment bulkhead and it should be periodically wiped over to prevent high tension (HT) voltage loss through arcing.

2 To ensure correct HT polarity at the spark plugs, the LT coil leads must always be connected correctly. The LT leads from the ignition amplifier should be connected as follows. White/black leads to the coil **negative** terminal. White leads to the coil **positive** terminal. Incorrect connections can cause bad starting, misfiring and short spark plug life.

3 Apart from the tests of the low tension circuit contained in the ignition system test procedure (Section 9), accurate checking of the coil output requires special equipment and for the home mechanic the easiest test is by substitution of a new unit.

4 If a new coil is to be fitted, ensure that it is of the correct type and suitable for use on electronic ignition systems. Failure to do so could cause irreparable damage to the ignition amplifier or distributor pick-up assembly.

5 To remove the coil, disconnect the HT and LT wires from the terminals. Undo and remove the two retaining bolts and lift away the coil complete with bracket. Refitting is the reverse sequence to removal.

7 Ignition amplifier - general

1 The ignition amplifier is mounted on the engine compartment bulkhead, just below the coil. The amplifier controls the function of the ignition coil in response to signals received from the pick-up coil in the distributor.

2 The unit may be tested using the procedure described in Section 9. If the amplifier is found to be faulty it must be renewed as a complete unit, repairs to the components or circuitry are not possible due to its sealed construction.

3 To remove the unit, disconnect the battery negative terminal and then disconnect the wiring plug from the end of the amplifier. Remove the two small retaining screws and withdraw the unit from the car. Refitting is the reverse sequence to removal.

8 Spark plugs and HT leads - general

1 The correct functioning of the spark plugs is vital for the correct running and efficiency of the engine. It is essential that the plugs fitted are appropriate for the engine, and the suitable type is specified at the beginning of this chapter. If this type is used and the engine is in good condition, the spark plugs should not need attention between scheduled replacement intervals. Spark plug cleaning is rarely necessary and should not be attempted unless specialised equipment is available as damage can easily be caused to the firing ends.

2 To remove the plugs, first mark the HT leads to ensure correct refitment, and then pull them off the plugs. Using a spark plug spanner, or suitable deep socket and extension bar, unscrew the plugs and remove them from the engine.

3 The condition of the spark plugs will also tell much about the overall condition of the engine.

4 If the insulator nose of the spark plug is clean and white, with no deposits, this is indicative of a weak mixture, or too hot a plug. (A hot plug transfers heat away from the electrode slowly - a cold plug transfers it away quickly.)

5 If the tip and insulator nose are covered with hard black-looking deposits, then this is indicative that the mixture is too rich. Should the plug be black and oily, then it is likely that the engine is fairly worn, as well as the mixture being too rich.

6 If the insulator nose is covered with light tan to greyish brown deposits, then the mixture is correct and it is likely that the engine is in good condition.

7 The spark plug gap is of considerable importance, as, if it is too large or too small, the size of the spark and its efficiency will be seriously impaired. The spark plug gap should be set to the figure given in the Specifications at the beginning of this Chapter.

8 To set it, measure the gap with a feeler gauge, and then bend open, or close, the outer plug electrode until the correct gap is achieved. The centre electrode should never be bent as this may crack the insulation and cause plug failure, if nothing worse.

9 When fitting new plugs screw them in by hand initially and then fully tighten to the specified torque. If a torque wrench is not available, tighten the plugs until initial resistance is felt as the sealing washer contacts its seat and then tighten by a further eighth of a turn. Refit the HT leads in the correct order, ensuring that they are a tight fit over the plug ends. Periodically wipe the leads clean to reduce the risk of HT leakage by arcing.

HAYNES HiNT

It's often difficult to insert spark plugs into their holes without cross-threading them. To avoid this possibility, fit a short piece of rubber hose over the end of the spark plug. The flexible hose acts as a universal joint, to help align the plug with the plug hole. Should the plug begin to cross-thread, the hose will slip on the spark plug, preventing thread damage.

9 Fault finding - electronic ignition system

There are two main symptoms indicating ignition faults. Either the engine will not start or fire, or the engine is difficult to start and misfires. If it is a regular misfire, ie the engine is only running on two or three cylinders, the fault is almost sure to be in the high tension circuit. If the misfiring is intermittent, the fault could be in either the high or low tension circuits. If the car stops suddenly, or will not start at all, it is likely that the fault is in the low tension circuit. Loss of power and overheating, apart from faulty carburation settings, are normally due to faults in the distributor or incorrect ignition timing.

The first part of this Section deals with the diagnosis of faults in the high tension circuit. If these tests prove negative or indicate a possible fault in the electronic ignition or low tension circuit, a separate test procedure should be followed. This is contained in the latter part of this Section and entails the use of a 0 to 12 volt voltmeter and an ohmmeter.

Engine fails to start

1 If the engine fails to start and the car was running normally when it was last used, first check there is fuel in the petrol tank. If the engine turns over normally on the starter motor and the battery is evidently well charged, then the fault may be either in the high or low tension circuits. First check the HT circuit. If the battery is known to be fully charged, the ignition light comes on and the starter motor fails to turn the engine, check the tightness of the leads on the battery terminals and the security of the earth lead to its connection to the body. It is quite common for the leads to have worked loose, even if they look and feel secure. If one of the battery terminal posts gets very hot when trying to work the starter motor, this is a sure indication of a faulty connection to that terminal.

2 One of the most common reasons for bad starting is wet or damp spark plug leads and distributor. Remove the distributor cap. If condensation is visible internally a moisture dispersant can be very effective. Refit the cap.

3 If the engine still fails to start, check that current is reaching the plugs, by disconnecting each plug lead in turn at the spark plug end, and holding the end of the cable about 0.2 in (5 mm) away from the cylinder block. Spin the engine on the starter motor.

4 Sparking between the end of the cable and the block should be fairly strong with a regular blue spark. (Hold the lead with rubber to avoid electric shocks). If current is reaching the plugs, then remove and regap them. The engine should now start.

5 If there is no spark at the plug leads, take off the HT lead from the centre of the distributor cap and hold it to the block as before. Spin the engine on the starter once more. A rapid succession of blue sparks between the end of the lead and the block indicates that the coil is in order and that the distributor cap is cracked, the rotor arm faulty or the carbon brush in the top of the distributor cap is not making good contact with the rocker arm.

6 If there are no sparks from the end of the lead from the coil, check the connection at the coil end of the lead. If it is in order carry out the checks contained in the electronic ignition test procedure.

Engine misfires

7 If the engine misfires regularly, run it at a fast idling speed. Pull off each of the plug caps in turn and listen to the note of the engine. Hold the plug cap in a dry cloth or with a rubber glove as additional protection against a shock from the HT supply.

8 No difference in engine running will be

noticed when the lead from the defective circuit is removed. Removing the lead from one of the good cylinders will accentuate the misfire.

9 Remove the plug lead from the end of the defective plug and hold it about 0.2 in (5 mm) away from the block. Restart the engine. If the sparking is fairly strong and regular, the fault must lie in the spark plug.

10 The plug may be loose, the insulation may be cracked, or the points may have burnt away giving too wide a gap for the spark to jump. Worse still, one of the points may have broken off. Either renew the plug, or reset the gap, and then test it.

11 If there is no spark at the end of the plug lead, or if it is weak and intermittent, check

the ignition lead from the distributor to the plug. If the insulation is cracked or perished, renew the lead. Check the connections at the distributor cap.

12 If there is still no spark, examine the distributor cap carefully for tracking. This can be recognised by a very thin black line running between two or more electrodes, or between an electrode and some other part of the distributor. These lines are paths which now conduct electricity across the cap, thus letting it run to earth. The only answer in this case is a new distributor cap.

13 Apart from the ignition timing being incorrect, other causes of misfiring have already been dealt with under the section dealing with the failure of the engine to start.

To recap, these are that:
(a) The coil may be faulty giving an intermittent misfire
(b) There may be a damaged wire or loose connection in the low tension circuit
(c) There may be a fault in the electronic ignition system
(d) There may be a mechanical fault in the distributor

14 If the ignition timing is too far retarded it should be noted that the engine will tend to overheat, and there will be a quite noticeable drop in power. If the engine is overheating and the power is down, and the ignition timing is correct, then the carburettor should be checked, as it is likely that this is where the fault lies.

Electronic ignition system test procedure

Test	Remedy
1 Is the reluctor air gap set to the specified dimension?	Yes: Proceed to Test 2 No: Adjust the gap, as described in Section 4
2 Is the battery voltage greater than 11.5 volts?	Yes: Proceed to Test 3 No: Recharge the battery
3 Is the voltage at the coil '+' terminal more than 1 volt below battery voltage?	Yes: Faulty wiring or connector between ignition switch and coil. Faulty ignition switch No: Proceed to Test 4
4 Is the voltage at the coil - terminal more than 1 volt	Yes: Disconnect the wiring connector between distributor and ignition amplifier and proceed to Test 7 No: Disconnect the ignition amplifier lead at the coil - terminal and proceed to Test 5
5 Is the voltage at the coil - terminal now more than 1 volt below battery voltage?	Yes: Proceed to Test 6 No: Renew the ignition coil
6 Is the voltage at the ignition amplifier earth more than 0.1 volts?	Yes: Clean and/or repair the earth connection No: Renew the ignition amplifier
7 Is the pick-up coil resistance measured at the wiring connector terminals between 2.2 k ohms and 4.8 k ohms?	Yes: Reconnect the wiring connector between distributor and ignition amplifier and proceed to Test 8 No: Renew the pick-up coil assembly in the distributor
8 Does the voltage at the coil - terminal drop when the starter motor is operated?	Yes: Check and adjust the ignition timing. If the fault still exists the problem may lie with the engine internal components No: Renew the ignition amplifier

4

Part B: 1.6 litre models

10 General description

The programmed electronic ignition system operates on an advanced principle whereby the main functions of the distributor are replaced by an electronic control unit (ECU).

The mechanical operation of the contact breaker points in a conventional distributor is

simulated electronically by the reluctor disc on the periphery of the clutch pressure plate and by the crankshaft sensor whose inductive head runs between the reluctor disc teeth. 34 teeth are used on the reluctor disc, spaced at 10° intervals with two spaces 180° apart which correspond to TDC for Nos 1 and 4 pistons and Nos 2 and 3 pistons respectively. As the crankshaft rotates, the reluctor disc teeth pass over the crankshaft sensor which transmits a pulse to the ECU every time a tooth passes over it. The ECU recognises the

absence of a pulse every 180° and consequently establishes the TDC position. Each subsequent pulse then represents 10° of crankshaft rotation. This, and the time interval between pulses, allows the ECU to accurately determine engine position and speed.

A small bore pipe connecting the inlet manifold to a pressure transducer within the ECU, supplies the unit with information on engine load. From this constantly changing data the ECU selects a particular advance setting from a range of ignition characteristics

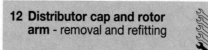

16.2 Electronic control unit wiring multi-plug (A) and vacuum connection (B)

Fig. 4.4 Programmed electronic ignition system component layout (Sec 10)

1 Ignition coil	4 Electronic control unit	6 Crankshaft sensor
2 Coolant thermistor	(ECU)	7 Knock sensor
3 Distributor cap	5 Reluctor disc	

stored in its memory. This basic setting can be further advanced or retarded according to information sent to the ECU from the coolant temperature thermistor and knock sensor.

With the firing point established, the ECU triggers the ignition coil which delivers HT voltage to the spark plugs in the conventional manner. The cycle is then repeated, many times a second for each cylinder in turn.

11 Maintenance and inspection

1 The only components of the system which require periodic maintenance are the distributor cap, HT leads and spark plugs. The spark plugs and HT leads should be treated in the same way as for 1.3 litre models, as described in Section 8. Attend to the distributor cap and rotor arm as described in Section 12.
2 On this system, dwell angle and ignition timing are a function of the electronic control unit and there is no provision for adjustment. It is possible to check the ignition advance using a stroboscopic timing light, but this

should only be necessary as part of a fault finding procedure. Further details will be found in Section 19.

12 Distributor cap and rotor arm - removal and refitting

1 Undo the two screws and lift the cap off the camshaft carriers. Thoroughly clean the cap inside and out with a dry lint-free rag. Examine the four HT lead segments inside the cap. If the segments appear badly burned or pitted, renew the cap. Make sure that the carbon brush in the centre of the cap is free to move and stands proud of its holders. If renewal of the cap is necessary, mark the position of the HT leads then pull them off. Transfer the leads to a new cap, fitting them in the same position.
2 To remove the rotor arm, undo the retaining screw using a suitable Allen key and withdraw the rotor arm from the end of the camshaft. If necessary remove the rotor arm shield.
3 Refitting the shield, rotor arm and distributor cap is the reverse sequence to removal.

13 Crankshaft sensor - removal and refitting

1 Disconnect the battery negative terminal.
2 Disconnect the wiring multi-plug and undo the wiring plug screw. Undo the two bolts and withdraw the unit from the gearbox or automatic transmission adaptor plate.
3 To refit the sensor, ensure that the correct spacer is fitted to the sensor then position the unit on the adaptor plate and secure with the two retaining bolts and one screw.
4 Reconnect the wiring multi-plug and the battery negative terminal.

14 Knock sensor - removal and refitting

1 The knock sensor is located on the front facing side of the cylinder block in the centre. To remove the unit, disconnect the battery negative terminal and the wiring multi-plug then unscrew the sensor from its location.
2 Refitting is the reverse sequence to removal, but ensure that the sensor and cylinder block mating faces are clean.

15 Coolant thermistor - removal and refitting

1 Removal and refitting procedures for this component are contained in Chapter 2.

16 Electronic control unit - removal and refitting

1 Disconnect the battery negative terminal.
2 Release the catch and disconnect the wiring multi-plug from the front of the unit (photo).

3 Disconnect the ignition vacuum supply hose.

4 Undo the retaining screw, slip the unit out of the retaining tags and remove it from the engine compartment.

5 Refitting is the reverse sequence to removal.

17 Ignition coil - description and testing

1 The coil is bolted to the centre of the engine compartment bulkhead (photo) and it should be periodically wiped over to prevent high tension (HT) voltage loss through arcing.

2 To ensure correct HT polarity at the spark plugs, the LT coil leads must always be connected correctly, ie white lead to the coil **positive** terminal and white/black lead to the coil **negative** terminal. Incorrect connections can cause bad starting, misfiring and short spark plug life.

3 Apart from the tests of the low tension circuit contained in the fault diagnosis test procedure (Section 19), accurate checking of the coil output requires special equipment

17.1 Ignition coil location on bulkhead

and for the home mechanic the easiest test is by substitution of a new unit.

4 If a new coil is to be fitted, ensure that it is of the correct type, specifically for use on the programmed electronic ignition system. Failure to do so could cause irreparable damage to the electronic control unit.

5 To remove the coil, disconnect the HT and LT wiring, undo the two retaining bolts and lift away the coil. Refitting is the reverse sequence to removal.

18 Spark plugs and HT leads - general

Refer to Section 8.

19 Fault finding - programmed electronic ignition system

Problems associated with the programmed electronic ignition system can usually be grouped into one of two areas, those caused by the more conventional HT side of the system such as spark plugs, HT leads, rotor arm and distributor cap, and those caused by the LT circuitry including the electronic control unit and its related components. It is recommended that the checks described in Section 9 under the headings 'Engine fails to start' or 'Engine misfires' should be carried out first, according to the symptoms. If the fault still exists the following step-by-step test procedure should be used. For these tests a good quality 0 to 12 volt voltmeter and an ohmmeter will be required.

4

Engine fails to start

Test	Remedy
1 Connect a voltmeter across pins 9 (+) and 12 - of the electronic control unit (ECU) wiring connector. Does the voltmeter indicate battery voltage 10 seconds after switching on the ignition?	Yes: Proceed to Test 2 No: Check the wiring between the ignition switch and pin 9, and between pin 12 and earth. Rectify as required
2 Connect a voltmeter across pins 10 (+) and 12 - of the ECU wiring connector. Does the voltmeter indicate battery voltage 10 seconds after switching on the ignition?	Yes: Proceed to test 3 No: Check the wiring between the ignition switch and coil (+) terminal and between pin 10 and the coil - terminal. Rectify as required
3 Connect an ohmmeter across the coil terminals. Is the coil primary winding resistance between 0.73 and 0.83 ohms?	Yes: Proceed to test 4 No: Renew the coil
4 Connect a voltmeter between the battery (+) terminal and the coil - terminal. Does the reading on the voltmeter increase when the engine is cranking?	Yes: Engine should start. If not check ignition HT components, fuel system and engine internal components No: Proceed to test 5
5 Switch ignition off and connect an ohmmeter across terminals 4 and 6 of the ECU. Does the ohmmeter register 1.5 k ohms approximately?	Yes: Probable ECU fault No: Check crankshaft sensor wiring and connections. If satisfactory, sensor is suspect

Engine misfires and performance is unsatisfactory

Test	Remedy
1 Set engine at TDC with No 1 cylinder on compression. Highlight mark on crankshaft pulley with white chalk. Make a corresponding mark on timing belt cover. Connect a stroboscopic timing light, disconnect vacuum pipe at manifold and start engine. Does the pulley mark advance as engine speed is increased?	Yes: Proceed to test 2 No: Probable ECU fault
2 With the engine operating as in test 1, apply suction to the end of the vacuum pipe. Does the pulley mark advance as vacuum is increased?	Yes: Ignition system is satisfactory, fault lies elsewhere No: Check for leaks in vacuum pipe and connections. If satisfactory, ECU is faulty

Notes

Chapter 5 Clutch

For modifications, and information applicable to later models, see Supplement at end of manual

Contents

Degrees of difficulty

Easy, suitable for novice with little experience	**Fairly easy,** suitable for beginner with some experience	**Fairly difficult,** suitable for competent DIY mechanic	**Difficult,** suitable for experienced DIY mechanic	**Very difficult,** suitable for expert DIY or professional

Specifications

Type . . . . Cable-operated single dry plate, with diaphragm spring

Clutch disc diameter
1.3 litre models . . . . 7.48 in (190.0 mm)
1.6 litre models . . . . 7.87 in (200.0 mm)

Clutch pedal free travel (all models) . . . . 0.47 to 1.10 in (12.0 to 28.0 mm)

Torque wrench settings	lbf ft	Nm
Pressure plate to crankshaft	55	75
Flywheel to pressure plate:		
1.3 litre models	15	20
1.6 litre models	11	15
Gearbox end cover (four-speed gearbox)	11	15

5

1 General description

Unlike the clutch on most engines, the clutch pressure plate is bolted to the crankshaft flange. The flywheel, which is dish shaped, is bolted to the pressure plate with the friction disc being held between them. This is, in effect, the reverse of the more conventional arrangement where the flywheel is bolted to the crankshaft flange and the clutch pressure plate bolted to the flywheel.

The release mechanism consists of a metal disc, or release plate, which is clamped in the centre of the pressure plate by a retaining ring. In the centre of the release plate is a boss into which the clutch pushrod is fitted. The pushrod passes through the centre of the gearbox input shaft and is actuated by a release bearing located in the gearbox end housing. A single finger lever presses on this bearing when the shaft to which it is splined is turned by operation of the cable from the clutch pedal. In effect the clutch lever pushes

Fig. 5.1 Exploded view of the clutch assembly (Sec 1)

1	Pressure plate (1.3 models)	4	Release plate	7	Flywheel
2	Locking plate	5	Retaining ring	8	Flywheel retaining bolt
3	Pressure plate retaining bolts	6	Friction disc	9	Pressure plate (1.6 models)

Fig. 5.2 Clutch cable and self-adjusting mechanism (Sec 2)

1 Clutch operating lever
2 Cable retaining clip
3 Cable seating plate
4 Rubber pad
5 Outer cable – gearbox end
6 Spring retaining clip
7 Self-adjusting spring
8 Outer cable – bulkhead end
9 Clutch pedal

the clutch pushrod, which in turn pushes the centre of the release plate inwards towards the crankshaft. The outer edge of the release plate presses on the pressure plate fingers forcing them back towards the engine and removing the pressure plate friction face from the friction disc, thus disconnecting the drive. When the clutch pedal is released, the pressure plate reasserts itself, clamping the friction disc firmly against the flywheel and restoring the drive.

Clutch adjustment is carried out automatically by a ratchet and spring type self-adjusting mechanism incorporated in the clutch cable.

2 Clutch cable - removal and refitting

1 Working in the engine compartment, release the clutch cable from its retaining clips and cable ties.

2 Using pliers, withdraw the retaining clip from the cable at the end of the self-adjusting spring (photo).
3 Release the inner cable from the clutch operating lever by sliding out the retaining clip and cable seating plate located on the underside of the lever (photos).
4 Withdraw the inner cable end from the operating lever rubber pad, release the rubber retainer and withdraw the cable assembly from the gearbox bracket (photos).
5 From inside the car, unhook the cable end from the clutch pedal and withdraw the cable into the engine compartment. Remove the cable assembly from the car.
6 To refit the cable, feed the hooked end through the engine compartment bulkhead and connect it to the pedal. Ensure that the outer cable is located correctly in the bulkhead tube.
7 Route the cable through the engine compartment, locating it in its retaining clips and cable ties.
8 Feed the cable through the transmission bracket until the guide sleeve is seated squarely in the bracket.
9 Feed the inner cable through the rubber pad of the operating lever and slide on the cable seating plate and retaining clip.
10 Refit the retaining clip to the cable at the end of the self-adjusting spring. Press down on the clutch operating lever and at the same time pull up on the cable to operate the self-adjusting mechanism.

3 Clutch pedal - removal and refitting

The clutch pedal and brake pedal are hinged on a common pivot and reference should be made to Chapter 9, Section 21 for the removal and refitting procedures.

4 Clutch assembly - removal and refitting

1 Refer to Chapter 6 and remove the gearbox.
2 In a diagonal sequence, half a turn at a

2.2 Remove the cable self-adjusting spring retaining clip

2.3A Slide out the cable retaining clip . . .

2.3B . . . and seating plate

2.4A Withdraw the inner cable from the operating lever rubber pad . . .

2.4B . . . release the rubber retainer and remove the cable from the gearbox

4.2A Undo the flywheel-to-pressure plate retaining bolts (arrowed) . . .

4.2B . . . while locking the ring gear to prevent rotation

4.5 Lock the pressure plate using a screwdriver or flat bar engaged with the U-shaped cut-out while undoing the bolts

time, slacken the six bolts securing the flywheel to the pressure plate. Use a screwdriver or stout bar engaged with the ring gear teeth and a suitable bolt to prevent the crankshaft turning (photos).

3 When all the bolts are slack, take them out and lift off the flywheel and the clutch friction disc. It may be necessary to carefully ease the flywheel off using a screwdriver, due to the tight fit of the locating dowels.

4 Note the fitted position of the clutch release plate retaining ring as a guide to reassembly, and then prise the ring out using a screwdriver. Lift off the release plate.

5 It is not necessary to remove the pressure plate unless it is visibly worn or is to be renewed for other reasons. If the plate is to

be removed, undo the retaining bolts in a diagonal sequence, lift off the locking plate and withdraw the pressure plate. To prevent the crankshaft turning as the bolts are undone, lock it using a spanner or socket on the pulley bolt if a 1.3 litre model is being worked on. On 1.6 litre models use a screwdriver or stout bar located in one of the U-shaped cut-outs in the pressure plate and in contact with a bolt engaged in the starter top mounting bolt hole (photo). **Do not**, under any circumstances, lock the crankshaft using the reluctor ring teeth on the pressure plate periphery. Note that after removal of the pressure plate retaining bolts, new bolts must be obtained before reassembly. The bolts are of the

encapsulated type containing a thread locking and sealing compound the properties of which are impaired after removal.

6 With the clutch assembly removed from the engine, refer to Section 5 and carry out a careful inspection of the components.

7 To refit the clutch, place the pressure plate and locking plate in position on the end of the crankshaft and secure with new encapsulated bolts, tightened to the specified torque (photos).

8 Position the release plate over the pressure plate diaphragm fingers (photo) and refit the retaining ring. Ensure that the retaining ring is correctly located, as noted during removal, and as shown in the accompanying illustrations.

5

4.7A Fit the pressure plate . . .

4.7B . . . and locking plate . . .

4.7C . . . followed by new encapsulated bolts . . .

4.7D . . . tightened to the specified torque

Fig. 5.3 Fitted position of release plate retaining ring (Sec 4)

Fig. 5.4 Fitted position of alternative type release plate retaining ring (Sec 4)

4.8 Fit the release plate . . .

4.9 . . . and then the friction disc and flywheel

4.10 Using vernier calipers to check the clutch friction disc centralisation

9 Hold the clutch friction disc against the flywheel (photo), with the greater projecting boss incorporating the torsion springs facing away from the engine. Refit the flywheel and the six retaining bolts. Tighten the bolts finger tight so that the friction disc is gripped, but can still be moved.

10 The clutch friction disc must now be centralised to allow the gearbox input shaft to pass through the friction disc hub splines. This can be done by obtaining the manufacturer's special service tool, or by centralising the disc using vernier calipers or a pair of dividers (photo). Once the clutch disc is centred correctly, tighten the retaining bolts in a diagonal sequence to the specified torque and recheck the centralisation.

5 Clutch assembly - inspection

1 With the clutch assembly removed, clean off all traces of asbestos dust using a dry cloth. This is best done outside or in a well ventilated area; *asbestos dust is harmful, and must not be inhaled*.

2 Examine the linings of the friction disc for wear and loose rivets, and the disc for rim distortion, cracks, broken torsion springs and worn splines. The surface of the friction linings may be highly glazed, but, as long as the friction material pattern can be clearly seen, this is satisfactory. If there is any sign of oil contamination, indicated by a continuous, or patchy, shiny black discoloration, the disc must be renewed and the source of the contamination traced and rectified. This will be either a leaking crankshaft oil seal or gearbox input shaft oil seal - or both. Renewal procedures are given in Chapter 1 and Chapter 6 respectively. The disc must also be renewed if the lining thickness has worn down to, or just above, the level of the rivet heads.

3 Check the machined faces of the flywheel and pressure plate. If either is grooved, or heavily scored, renewal is necessary. The pressure plate must also be renewed if any cracks are apparent, or if the diaphragm spring is damaged or its pressure suspect.

4 With the gearbox removed it is advisable to check the condition of the release bearing, as described in the following Sections.

6 Clutch release bearing (four-speed gearbox) - removal, inspection and refitting

1 If the gearbox has not been removed, apply the handbrake, prise off the wheel trim and slacken the left-hand front roadwheel nuts. Jack up the front left-hand side of the car and support it securely on axle stands. Remove the roadwheel.

2 From under the wheel arch, undo and remove the retaining screws and lift away the access panel from the inner wing.

3 Refer to Section 2 and disconnect the clutch cable from the gearbox operating lever and bracket.

4 Place a suitable receptacle beneath the gearbox end cover as there is likely to be some oil spillage when the cover is removed.

5 Undo and remove the four retaining bolts and lift off the end cover. Recover the gasket.

Fig. 5.5 Release bearing components – four-speed gearbox (Sec 6)

1 Gearbox	5 Gasket
2 Release hearing	6 End Cover
3 Sleeve	7 End cover bolt
4 Operating lever	

6 Move the operating lever sufficiently to allow the release bearing and sleeve to be withdrawn, and then remove the bearing from the sleeve.

7 Check the release bearing for smoothness of operation and renew it if there is any roughness or harshness as the bearing is spun.

8 Refitting is the reverse sequence to removal, bearing in mind the following points.

(a) Use a new end cover gasket, lightly smeared with jointing compound

(b) Tighten the end cover retaining bolts to the specified torque in a progressive diagonal sequence

(c) Reconnect the clutch cable, as described in Section 2

(d) Check the gearbox oil level and top up if necessary

7 Clutch release bearing (five-speed gearbox) - removal, inspection and refitting

1 If the gearbox has not been removed, apply the handbrake, prise off the wheel trim and

Fig. 5.6 Release bearing components – five-speed gearbox (Sec 6)

1 Gearbox	3 Release bearing
2 Operating lever	4 End cap

slacken the left-hand front roadwheel nuts. Jack up the front left-hand side of the car and support it securely on axle stands. Remove the roadwheel.

2 From under the wheel arch, undo and remove the retaining screws and lift away the access panel from the inner wing.

3 Refer to Section 2 and disconnect the clutch cable from the gearbox operating lever and bracket.

4 Place a suitable receptacle beneath the gearbox end cap as there is likely to be some oil spillage when the cover is removed.

5 Using a suitable sharp instrument, pierce the end cap and lever it out of its location in the gearbox housing. Discard the end cap, as a new one will be needed when refitting.

6 Remove the operating lever stop clip and then move the lever sufficiently to allow the release bearing to be withdrawn.

7 Check the release bearing for smoothness of operation and renew it if there is any roughness or harshness as the bearing is spun.

8 Refitting is the reverse sequence to removal, bearing in mind the following points.

(a) *Use a block of wood or suitable drift to drive in a new end cap and ensure that the cap is kept square as it is fitted*

(b) *Reconnect the clutch cable, as described in Section 2*

(c) *Check the gearbox oil level and top up if necessary*

Fault finding - clutch

Judder when taking up drive

☐ Loose or worn engine/gearbox mountings
☐ Friction disc linings contaminated with oil, or worn clutch cable
☐ sticking or defective
☐ Friction disc hub sticking on input shaft splines

Clutch fails to disengage (clutch spin)*

☐ Clutch cable sticking or defective
☐ Excessive free play in the cable or release mechanism
☐ Friction disc linings contaminated with oil
☐ Friction disc hub sticking on input shaft splines

Noise when depressing clutch pedal

☐ Worn release bearing
☐ Defective release mechanism
☐ Faulty pressure plate or diaphragm assembly

Noise when releasing clutch pedal

☐ Faulty pressure plate assembly
☐ Broken friction disc torsion springs
☐ Gearbox internal wear

Clutch slips

☐ Clutch cable sticking or defective
☐ Clutch release mechanism sticking or partially seized
☐ Faulty pressure plate or diaphragm assembly
☐ Friction disc linings worn or contaminated with oil

Self-adjusting mechanism not working

☐ Adjuster body not fully home in bulkhead
☐ Incorrect free play in clutch pedal
☐ Cable end fitting at pedal not in contact with trigger tube of adjusting
☐ mechanism when clutch engaged

This condition may also be due to the friction disc being rusted to the flywheel or pressure plate. It is possible to free it by applying the handbrake, engaging top gear, depressing the clutch and operating the starter motor. If really badly corroded. then the engine will not turn over, but in the majority of cases the friction disc will free. Once the engine starts, rev it up and slip the clutch several times to clear the rust deposits.

5

Notes

Chapter 6 Manual gearbox

For modifications, and information applicable to later models, see Supplement at end of manual

Contents

Degrees of difficulty

Easy, suitable for novice with little experience	**Fairly easy,** suitable for beginner with some experience	**Fairly difficult,** suitable for competent DIY mechanic	**Difficult,** suitable for experienced DIY mechanic	**Very difficult,** suitable for expert DIY or professional

Specifications

Type . . . . Four or five forward speeds (all synchromesh) and reverse. Final drive integral with main gearbox

Gearbox ratios
1.3 litre models:
  1st . . . . 3.45 : 1
  2nd . . . . 1.94 : 1
  3rd . . . . 1.29 : 1
  4th . . . . 0.91 : 1
  Reverse . . . . 3.17 : 1
1.6 litre models:
  1st . . . . 3.45 : 1
  2nd . . . . 1.94 : 1
  3rd . . . . 1.29 : 1
  4th . . . . 0.91 : 1
  5th . . . . 0.71 : 1
  Reverse . . . . 3.17 : 1

6

Final drive ratios
1.3 litre models . . . . 4.25 : 1
1.6 litre models . . . . 3.94 : 1

Gearbox overhaul data
3rd gear axial movement . . . . 0 to 0.008 in (0 to 0.20 mm)
Axial movement adjustment . . . . Selective circlips
Minimum baulk ring-to-gear clearance:
  1st and 2nd gear:
    New ring . . . . 0.043 to 0.067 in (1.1 to 1.7 mm)
    Wear limit . . . . 0.020 in (0.5 mm)
  3rd gear:
    New ring . . . . 0.045 to 0.069 in (1.15 to 1.75 mm)
    Wear limit . . . . 0.020 in (0.5 mm)
  4th and 5th gear:
    New ring . . . . 0.051 to 0.075 in (1.3 to 1.9 mm)
    Wear limit . . . . 0.020 in (0.5 mm)

Lubricant
Type/specification . . . . Hypoid gear oil, viscosity SAE 80EP
Capacity:
  Four-speed gearbox . . . . 2.75 pints (1.6 litres)
  Five-speed gearbox . . . . 3.5 pints (2.0 litres)

Torque wrench settings

	lbf ft	Nm
Gearbox to adaptor plate:		
M7 bolts	4	5
M10 bolts	38	52
M12 bolts	67	91
Main casing to gear carrier housing	18	24
End cover bolts:		
Four-speed gearbox	11	15
Five-speed gearbox	18	24
Selector shaft locking screw	15	20
Engine mounting bracket to end cover or casing	30	41
Mainshaft bearing retaining nuts or screws	11	15
Pinion shaft bearing retaining plate bolts	30	41
Shift fork set retaining bolts	18	24
Reverse idler shaft retaining bolt:		
Four-speed gearbox	15	20
Five-speed gearbox	22	30
5th gear synchro-hub retaining screw	110	149
Oil filler/level plug and drain plug	18	24
Reverse lamp switch	22	30

1 General description

The gearbox is of Volkswagen manufacture and is equipped with either four forward and one reverse gear or five forward and one reverse gear, according to model. Synchromesh gear engagement is used on all forward gears.

The final drive (differential) unit is integral with the main gearbox and is located between the main casing and the bearing housing. The gearbox and differential both share the same lubricating oil.

Gearshift is by means of a floor-mounted lever connected by a remote control housing and shift rod to the gearbox selector shaft and relay lever.

If gearbox overhaul is necessary, due consideration should be given to the costs involved since it is often more economical to obtain a service exchange or good second-hand gearbox rather than fit new parts to the existing unit.

2 Maintenance and inspection

1 At the intervals specified in Routine Maintenance at the beginning of this manual, inspect the gearbox joint faces and oil seals for any sign of damage, deterioration or oil leakage.
2 At the same service interval check and, if necessary, top up the gearbox oil. The filler plug is located on the end of the gearbox casing and the oil level should be maintained up to the level of the filler plug orifice.
3 Although not considered necessary by the

HAYNES HiNT *Removal of the filler plug entails the use of a large Allen key. A suitable alternative, however, is to lock two nuts together on the thread of a suitable bolt, insert the hexagonal head of the bolt into the filler plug and then unscrew the plug using a spanner on the innermost nut.*

manufacturers, the diligent home mechanic may wish to renew the gearbox oil, in the interests of extended gearbox life, every 24 000 miles (40 000 km) or two years.
4 It is also advisable to check for excess free play or wear in the gear linkage joints and levers, and check the gear lever adjustment, as described in Section 5. If any repair or adjustment work is to be carried out on the gear linkage, lubricate all sliding joints and contact surfaces (with the exception of the nylon balljoints) using Unipart Solid Lubricating Paste.

3 Gearbox - removal and refitting

1 Disconnect the battery negative terminal.
2 Slide back the rubber cap and disconnect the two reversing lamp switch wires from the switch terminals.
3 Release the clutch cable adjustment by removing the retaining clip at the end of the cable self-adjusting spring (photo).
4 Slide out the clip securing the clutch cable to the gearbox operating lever then withdraw the seating plate. Disengage the rubber retainer from the guide sleeve and pull the cable and guide sleeve out of the operating lever and gearbox bracket (photo).
5 Undo and remove the bolt securing the speedometer cable to the gearbox casing. Carefully withdraw the cable and pinion assembly and place them aside (photo).

3.3 Remove the cable self-adjusting spring retaining clip

3.4 Remove the cable and guide sleeve from the gearbox bracket

3.5 Withdraw the speedometer cable and pinion assembly

Fig. 6.1 Exploded view of the four-speed gearbox (Sec 1)

1 Plastic cap
2 Circlip
3 Spring washer
4 Drive coupling
5 Spring
6 Spring collar
7 Konusring
8 Differential oil seal
9 Blanking plug
10 Gear carrier housing
11 Sleeve
12 Shim
13 Bearing outer race
14 Pinion shaft bearing
15 Pinion shaft
16 Pinion shaft bearing
17 Bearing outer race and
   retaining plate assembly
18 Retaining plate bolt
19 Thrust washer
20 Needle roller bearing
21 1st gear
22 1st gear baulk ring
23 Synchro key

24 Spring
25 1st/2nd gear
   synchroniser hub
26 1st/2nd gear
   synchroniser sleeve and
   reverse gear
27 Baulk ring
28 Needle roller bearing
   inner race
29 Needle roller bearing
30 2nd gear
31 3rd gear
32 Selective circlip
33 4th gear
34 Circlip
35 Bearing retaining screw
36 Needle roller bearing
37 Shim
38 Bearing outer race
39 Taper roller bearing
40 Thrust washer
41 Differential shaft
42 Circlip
43 Final drivegear

44 Bolt, lockplate and nut
45 Differential cage
46 Reverse lamp switch
   and washer
47 Selector shaft peg bolt
   and washer
48 Selector shaft oil seal
49 Selector shaft boot
50 Main casing
51 Casing retaining bolt
52 Clutch pushrod
53 Release bearing
54 Release bearing sleeve
55 Dowel
56 Magnet
57 Drain plug
58 Differential gear
59 Pinion pin
60 Circlip
61 Differential pinion
62 Mainshaft bearing
   retaining clamps
63 Clutch release shaft
64 Release shaft oil seal

65 Filler/level plug
66 Clutch return spring
67 Circlip
68 Clutch lever
69 Main casing end cover
70 End cover bolt
71 Reverse idler gear
72 Bush
73 Reverse idler shaft
74 Selector shaft
75 Yoke
76 Circlip
77 Detent plate
78 Spring
79 Roll pin
80 Selector finger
81 Spring
82 Oil deflector
83 End cover
84 Selector rod
85 Spring
86 Relay lever pillar
87 Pillar retaining bolt
88 Reverse gear relay lever

89 1st/2nd selector fork
90 Reverse selector fork
91 3rd/4th selector fork
92 Reverse idler shaft bolt
93 Needle roller bearing
94 Clutch pushrod oil seal
95 Clutch pushrod bush
96 Mainshaft
97 Needle roller bearing
98 3rd gear
99 Baulk ring
100 Synchro key
101 Spring
102 3rd/4th synchroniser
    hub
103 3rd/4th synchroniser
    sleeve
104 Circlip
105 Baulk ring
106 Needle roller bearing
107 4th gear
108 Mainshaft bearing
109 Circlip
110 Shim (if fitted)

6

Fig. 6.2 Exploded view of the five-speed gearbox (Sec 1)

1 Plastic cap	27 Baulk ring	53 Thrust washer	80 Clutch release shaft	108 Selector rod
2 Circlip	28 Needle roller bearing	54 Circlip	81 Clutch pushrod	109 Reverse idler shaft bolt
3 Spring washer	inner race	55 5th gear selector fork	82 Dowel	110 Relay lever pillar
4 Drive coupling	29 Needle roller bearing	56 Lock plate	83 Magnet	111 Pillar bolt
5 Spring	30 2nd gear	57 Bearing retainer screw	84 Drain plug	112 Reverse gear relay
6 Spring collar	31 3rd gear	58 Needle roller bearing	85 Differential gear	lever
7 Konusring	32 Selective circlip	59 Clutch return spring	86 Pinion pin	113 1st/2nd selector fork
8 Differential oil seal	33 4th gear	60 Circlip	87 Circlip	114 Reverse selector fork
9 Blanking plug	34 Circlip	61 Clutch lever	88 Differential pinion	115 3rd/4th selector fork
10 Gear carrier housing	35 Needle roller bearing	62 Thrust washer	89 Mainshaft bearing	116 5th gear selector link
11 Sleeve	36 Shim	63 Bearing retaining plate	retaining plate	and tube
12 Shim	37 Bearing outer race	screw	90 Mainshaft bearing	117 Needle roller bearing
13 Bearing outer race	38 Taper roller bearing	64 Needle roller bearing	91 Reverse idler gear	118 Clutch pushrod oil seal
14 Pinion shaft bearing	39 Thrust washer	65 5th gear	92 Bush	119 Clutch pushrod bush
15 Pinion shaft	40 Differential shaft	66 Baulk ring	93 Reverse idler shaft	120 Mainshaft
16 Pinion shaft bearing	41 Circlip	67 Spring	94 Selector shaft	121 Needle roller bearing
17 Bearing outer race and	42 Final drivegear	68 Synchro key	95 Yoke	122 3rd gear
retaining plate assembly	43 Bolt, lockplate and nut	69 5th gear synchroniser	96 Circlip	123 Baulk ring
18 Retaining plate bolt	44 Differential cage	hub	97 Detent plate	124 Synchro key
19 Thrust washer	45 Selector shaft peg bolt	70 Washer	98 Spring	125 Spring
20 Needle roller bearing	and washer	71 Synchroniser hub screw	99 Roll pin	126 3rd/4th synchroniser
21 1st gear	46 5th gear detent plunger	72 5th gear synchroniser	100 Selector finger	hub
22 1st gear baulk ring	and washer	sleeve	101 Sleeve	127 3rd/4th synchroniser
23 Synchro key	47 Main casing	73 Stop plate	102 Spring	sleeve
24 Spring	48 Selector shaft oil seal	74 End cover	103 Spring plate	128 Circlip
25 1st/2nd gear	49 Selector shaft boot	75 End cover bolt	104 Circlip	129 Baulk ring
synchroniser hub	50 Casing retaining bolt	76 Filler/level plug	105 Spring	130 Needle roller bearing
26 1st/2nd gear	51 Reverse lamp switch	77 Clutch release bearing	106 End cover	131 4th gear
synchroniser sleeve	and washer	78 End cap	107 Spring	132 Shim (if fitted)
and reverse gear	52 5th gear	79 Release shaft oil seal		

3.6 Undo the bolt and release the cable harness clip

3.7 Remove the gearchange rod clip (A) and the selector rod balljoint (B) – shown removed – to allow removal of the linkage

3.15 Remove the left-hand engine mounting through-bolt and flat washers (1.3 litre model shown)

6 Disconnect the battery earth cable and cable harness retaining clip from the top of the gearbox (photo).

7 Extract the clip securing the gearchange rod to the selector shaft lever and slide the rod out of the lever bush (photo). Prise off the rear selector rod nylon balljoint from the relay lever using a screwdriver and move the rod to one side.

8 Make a note of the wiring harness connections at the starter motor solenoid and disconnect them.

9 Undo the starter motor retaining bolts, withdraw the starter and, where fitted, the front snubber and its bracket.

10 Prise off the left-hand front wheel trim and slacken the wheel nuts. Jack up the car, support it securely on axle stands and remove the roadwheel.

11 Undo and remove the retaining screws and lift off the access panel from under the wheel arch.

12 From underneath the front of the car, mark the drive flange to inner constant velocity joint flange relationship using paint or a file.

13 Lift off the protective covers and then undo and remove the bolts securing the constant velocity joints to the drive flanges, using an Allen key. Tie the driveshafts out of the way using string or wire.

14 Using a suitable jack and interposed block of wood, support the engine and gearbox assembly under the engine sump.

15 Undo and remove the left-hand engine mounting through-bolt (photo). On 1.6 litre models undo the bolts securing the left-hand mounting to the gearbox and remove the mounting. Undo the nuts and bolts securing the rear engine mounting to the crossmember and gearbox and remove the mounting.

16 Position a second jack beneath the gearbox and remove all the bolts securing the gearbox to the engine adaptor plate. Make a note of the different lengths of bolts and their locations and also, on 1.6 litre models, the arrangement of nuts and washers at the inlet manifold support strut.

17 With all the bolts removed, make a final check that everything attached to the gearbox has been disconnected.

18 With the help of an assistant, lower the jacks until sufficient clearance exists to enable the gearbox to be drawn off the side of the engine. Keep the gearbox supported on the jack, as it is quite heavy, and, after releasing the gearbox from the adaptor plate dowels, lower the unit slowly and carefully to the ground.

19 Refitting the gearbox is the reverse sequence to removal, bearing in mind the following points.

(a) Tighten all retaining and mounting bolts to the specified torque

(b) Refill the gearbox with the specified lubricant to the level of the filler plug orifice

(c) Align the marks on the drive flanges and inner constant velocity joints before refitting the retaining bolts

(d) Lubricate the selector linkage rod and gearchange rod with a lithium-based grease before refitting

(e) On models equipped with a front snubber, slacken the snubber cup retaining bolts, position the cup centrally around the snubber then tighten the bolts

(f) With the clutch cable connected, refit the spring retaining clip then press down on the operating lever and pull up on the outer cable to operate the self-adjusting mechanism

4 Gearbox overhaul - general

The overhaul of the gearbox requires the use of a number of special tools, and also certain critical adjustments, if the job is to be done successfully. For this reason it is not recommended that a complete overhaul be attempted by the home mechanic unless he has access to the tools required and feels reasonably confident.

Repair or overhaul of the differential unit is not considered to be within the scope of the home mechanic, since special jigs and fixtures are required for this work.

Before starting any repair work on the gearbox, drain the oil and thoroughly clean the exterior of the casings, using paraffin or a suitable solvent. Dry the unit with a lint-free rag. Make sure that an uncluttered working area is available with some small containers and trays handy to store the various parts. Label everything as it is removed.

Before starting reassembly all the components must be spotlessly clean and should be lubricated with the recommended grade of gear oil during assembly.

5 Gear lever - adjustment

Note: *It will be necessary to obtain BL service tool 18G 1455 to enable the following adjustment to be carried out.*

1 Jack up the front of the car and support it securely on axle stands.

2 From under the car remove the plastic cap from the gear lever rubber boot. Ensure that the gearbox is in neutral.

3 Slacken the clamp bolt (arrowed in Fig. 6.4) which secures the selector rod to the linkage lever, and make sure that the linkage slides freely on the rod. The angular setting of the linkage cannot be altered, as the splines on the selector rod will have cut unique grooves in the bore of the lever. A new lever is the only solution.

4 Refer to Fig. 6.5 and fit tool 18G 1455 over the lip of the stop plate and with the gear linkage reverse stop engaged with the cutaway portion of the tool.

5 Pull the tool rearward so that the lug on the tool leading edge is in firm contact with the edge of the stop plate.

6 Insert an 0.080 in (2.0 mm) thick feeler gauge between the end of the reverse stop and the tool cutaway. Move the reverse stop until the feeler gauge is a tight sliding fit.

7 Have an assistant hold the selector shaft lever in the vertical position and tighten the selector rod clamp bolt.

8 Remove the feeler gauge and tool, refit the plastic cap to the rubber boot and lower the car to the ground.

6

Fig. 6.3 Selector rod to linkage clamp bolt location – four and five-speed gearboxes (Sec 6)

Fig. 6.4 Gear lever adjustment – four- and five-speed gearboxes (Sec 6)

1 Stop plate   3 Reverse stop
2 Service tool 18G 1455   4 Feeler gauges

9.6 Gearshift linkage clamp bolt (A), selector rod support bracket retaining bolts (B) and (C)

6 Gear lever and linkage - removal and refitting

1 Jack up the front of the car and support it securely on stands.
2 From under the car, remove the plastic cap from the gear linkage rubber boot. Undo and remove the nut, washer and through-bolt securing the gear lever to the selector rod.

3 From inside the car, remove the centre console, as described in Chapter 12, undo and remove the two nuts and washers securing the gear lever to the floor and lift out the lever assembly.
4 To remove the selector rod and remote control linkage, extract the retaining clip and slide the gearchange rod out of the bush on the gearbox selector lever.
5 Disconnect the rear selector rod from the relay lever on the gearbox housing by prising off the balljoint using a screwdriver.

6 Undo and remove the two bolts securing the selector rod support bracket to the vehicle floor, and the nuts and bolts securing the linkage support bracket to the steering gear (photo).
7 Withdraw the linkage from under the car.
8 Refitting is the reverse sequence to removal, but adjust the gear lever, as described in the previous Section. Lubricate all sliding joints and contact surfaces (with the exception of the nylon balljoints) using Unipart Solid Lubricating Paste.

Fault finding - manual gearbox

Gearbox noisy in neutral
☐ Mainshaft (input shaft) bearings worn

Gearbox noisy only when moving (in all gears)
☐ Pinion shaft (output shaft) bearings worn
☐ Differential bearings worn
☐ Countershaft bearings worn

Gearbox noisy in only one gear
☐ Worn, damaged or chipped gear teeth
☐ Worn bearings

Jumps out of gear
☐ Worn synchro-hub or baulk rings
☐ Gearshift mechanism out of adjustment
☐ Worn selector forks
☐ Worn detent mechanisms

Ineffective synchromesh
☐ Worn baulk rings or synchro-hubs

Difficulty in engaging gears
☐ Clutch fault
☐ Gearshift mechanism out of adjustment or broken
☐ Worn synchromesh

Chapter 7 Automatic transmission

Contents

Degrees of difficulty

Easy, suitable for novice with little experience ⚒	Fairly easy, suitable for beginner with some experience ⚒	Fairly difficult, suitable for competent DIY mechanic ⚒	Difficult, suitable for experienced DIY mechanic ⚒	Very difficult, suitable for expert DIY or professional ⚒

Specifications

Type . . . . Hydraulically-controlled epicyclic geartrain with three element torque converter

Gear ratios

1st	2.71:1
2nd	1.50:1
3rd	1.00:1
Reverse	2.43:1
Final drive ratio	3.409:1

Lubricant

Type/specification:	
Automatic transmission	Dexron IID type ATF
Final drive	Hypoid gear oil, viscosity SAE 90EP
Capacity:	
Automatic transmission:	
Drain and refill	5.25 pints (3.0 litres)
Total (dry unit including torque converter)	10.5 pints (6.0 litres)
Final drive	1.25 pints (0.71 litre)

Torque wrench settings

	lbf ft	Nm
Torque converter to driveplate	22	30
Oil strainer to valve block	2	3
Oil pan to transmission	15	20
Transmission to engine and adaptor plate:		
M10 bolts	33	45
M12 bolts	66	89
Dipstick tube lower mounting bolt	7	9
Dipstick tube upper mounting bolt	18	24

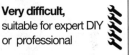

1 General description

A three-speed automatic transmission is available as an option on Montego 1.6 HL models. The transmission consists of a torque converter, an epicyclic geartrain and hydraulically-operated clutches and brakes.

The torque converter provides a fluid coupling between engine and transmission which acts as an automatic clutch and also provides a degree of torque multiplication when accelerating.

The epicyclic geartrain provides either of the three forward or one reverse gear ratios according to which of its component parts are held stationary or allowed to turn. The components of the geartrain are held or released by brakes and clutches which are activated by hydraulic valves. An oil pump within the transmission provides the necessary hydraulic pressure to operate the brakes and clutches.

Driver control of the transmission is by a six position selector lever which allows fully automatic operation with a hold facility on the first and second gear ratios.

Due to the complexity of the automatic

1 Transmission casing
2 Oil pan seal
3 Oil pan
4 Dipstick
5 Dipstick/filler tube
6 Final drive housing
7 Valve block
8 Gasket
9 Oil strainer
10 Strainer cover
11 Torque converter
12 Driveplate

Fig. 7.1 Exploded view of the transmission casings and components (Secs 1, 5 and 6)

Fig. 7.2 Transmission fluid dipstick/filler tube details (Sec 3)

transmission, any repair or overhaul work must be left to a BL dealer or automatic transmission specialist with necessary equipment for fault diagnosis and repair. The contents of the following Sections are therefore confined to supplying general information and any service information and instructions that can be used by the owner.

2 Maintenance and inspection

1 At the intervals specified in Routine Maintenance, carefully inspect the transmission joint faces and oil seals for any signs of damage, deterioration or oil leakage.
2 At the same service intervals check the transmission fluid level and the final drivegear oil level, as described in Sections 3 and 4.

Fig. 7.3 Final drivegear oil level/filler plug location (Sec 4)

3 At less frequent intervals (see Routine Maintenance) drain the transmission fluid, clean the oil strainer then refill with fresh fluid, using the procedure described in Section 5.
4 Carry out a thorough road test ensuring that all gear changes occur smoothly and, when under kickdown acceleration, at the speeds given in Section 7. With the vehicle at rest, check the operation of the parking pawl when P is selected.

3 Automatic transmission fluid level checking

1 The automatic transmission fluid level should be checked when the engine is at normal operating temperature, preferably after a short journey.
2 With the car standing on level ground and with the engine running, apply the handbrake and slowly move the selector lever through all gear positions.
3 Return the selector lever to N and with the engine still idling, withdraw the dipstick from the filler tube and wipe it on paper or a non-fluffy cloth.
4 Reinsert the dipstick, withdraw it immediately and observe the fluid level. This should be between the upper and lower 'O' marks on the dipstick.
5 If topping-up is necessary, switch off the engine and add the required quantity of the specified fluid through the dipstick tube. Use a funnel with a fine mesh screen to avoid spillage and to ensure that any foreign matter

is trapped. Take care not to overfill the transmission; noting that the difference between the upper and lower 'O' marks on the dipstick is 0.75 pint (0.4 litre).
6 After topping-up, re-check the level again, as described above, refit the dipstick and switch off the engine.

4 Final drive gear oil level checking

1 With the car raised to provide working clearance, but in a level position, wipe clean the area around the filler/level plug then unscrew the plug.
2 Allow any oil lodged behind the plug to trickle out and then check the level which should be up to the filler plug orifice. If topping-up is necessary, inject the correct grade of oil until it just runs out of the orifice then refit the plug. Note that gear oil is used for lubrication of the final drivegears - not automatic transmission fluid.
3 After checking the level and topping-up as required, lower the car to the ground.
4 Draining and refilling of the final drive oil is not a service requirement and no provision is made for this purpose.

5 Automatic transmission fluid - draining and refilling

Note: *To avoid the risk of scalding, only drain the fluid when cold or after the vehicle has been standing for some time.*
1 Jack up the front of the car and support it on stands.
2 Wipe around the oil pan-to-transmission case joint to avoid the risk of dirt or grit entry.
3 Place a suitable container beneath the transmission oil pan and slacken the oil pan retaining bolts. Carefully separate the oil pan-to-transmission joint if it is stuck, and allow the fluid to drain.
4 When most of the fluid has drained, remove the bolts and lift off the oil pan. Recover the seal.

5 Undo the bolts securing the oil strainer to the valve block and withdraw the strainer, strainer cover and gasket.

6 Thoroughly clean the strainer in paraffin, or a suitable solvent, and dry with compressed air.

7 Using a new gasket if necessary, refit the strainer assembly and secure with the retaining bolts tightened to the specified torque.

8 Ensure that the mating faces of the oil pan and transmission casing are clean and refit the pan, using a new seal if necessary. Tighten the retaining bolts to the specified torque.

9 Lower the car to the ground and fill the transmission with the specified type and quantity of transmission fluid, through the dipstick filler tube.

10 With the car standing on level ground, apply the handbrake, select P and start the engine.

> **HAYNES HiNT** *Use a funnel with a fine mesh screen to avoid spillage and to ensure that any foreign matter is trapped.*

11 Move the selector lever through all gear positions, pausing at each position.

12 With the engine idling, select N, withdraw the dipstick and wipe it on paper or a lint-free cloth.

13 Reinsert the dipstick fully then withdraw it again and observe the fluid level. Top up if necessary until the level reaches the lower 'O' mark on the dipstick.

14 Run the engine until normal operating temperature is reached or, preferably, drive the car for a short journey. Carry out a final level check and top up, as described in Section 3.

6 Automatic transmission - removal and refitting

1 Disconnect the battery negative terminal.

2 Remove the air cleaner assembly, as described in Chapter 3.

3 Disconnect the speedometer cable from its transmission attachment.

4 Undo the bolts securing the dipstick/filler tube to the transmission and remove the dipstick and tube. Note the O-ring at the base of the tube and also the cable clip on the upper retaining bolt.

5 Refer to Chapter 10 and remove the starter motor.

6 Prise off the left-hand front wheel trim and slacken the wheel nuts. Jack up the front of the car, support it on axle stands and remove the roadwheel.

7 Undo and remove the retaining screws and lift off the access panel from under the wheel arch.

8 From underneath the front of the car, mark the drive flange to inner constant velocity joint flange relationship using paint or a file.

9 Lift off the protective covers and then undo and remove the bolts securing the constant velocity joints to the drive flanges, using an Allen key. Tie the driveshafts out of the way using string or wire.

10 Undo the nut securing the selector cable trunnion to the selector lever. Slip the trunnion out of the lever.

11 Release the kickdown cable end from the transmission lever, undo the cable support bracket retaining bolts and place the cables and bracket to one side.

12 Turn the crankshaft as necessary using a socket or spanner on the pulley bolt until one of the torque converter retaining bolts becomes accessible through the starter motor aperture. Undo the bolt then turn the crankshaft and remove the remaining two bolts in the same way.

13 Place a jack beneath the engine sump with a block of wood between the jack head and sump.

14 Slacken, but do not remove, the upper front transmission-to-engine retaining bolt then remove all the other remaining bolts securing the transmission to the engine and adaptor plate.

15 Undo the bolts securing the left-hand mounting bracket to the body. Lower the engine slightly, undo the mounting-to-transmission bolts, remove the earth cable and the mounting assembly.

16 Remove the engine front snubber bracket and the rear mounting-to-crossmember assembly.

17 Place a second jack beneath the transmission with interposed block of wood and just take the weight of the unit.

18 Remove the remaining transmission-to-engine bolt then lower both jacks until the transmission is clear of the body side-member.

19 Withdraw the transmission and torque

Fig. 7.4 Kickdown cable and selector cable adjustment points (Secs 7 and 8)

1 Kickdown cable adjuster and locknut
2 Selector cable trunnion
3 Move selector lever towards left-hand roadwheel to adjust

converter from the engine and remove the assembly from under the car.

20 Refitting the transmission is the reverse sequence to removal, bearing in mind the following points:

(a) Tighten all retaining and mounting bolts to the specified torque where applicable

(b) Top up or refill the transmission and final drive with the specified lubricants as described earlier in this Chapter

(a) Align the marks on the drive flanges and inner constant velocity joints before refitting the retaining bolts

(d) Adjust the front snubber cup position so that it is central around the snubber rubber

(e) Check and, if necessary, adjust the kickdown cable and selector cable, as described in Sections 7 and 8

7 Kickdown cable - adjustment

1 Fully depress the accelerator pedal and check that there is full movement at the carburettor linkage. If the kickdown cable is preventing full movement, slacken the locknut and back off the cable adjuster slightly (Fig. 7.4).

2 Drive the car until normal operating temperature is reached and then find a quiet, straight stretch of road.

3 Accelerate the car from rest with the selector lever in D and the accelerator pedal fully depressed in the kickdown position. Note the road speeds at which the 1st/2nd and 2nd/3rd gear changes occur, these should be:

1st to 2nd   38 to 41 mph (61 to 66 km/h)
2nd to 3rd   67 to 69 mph (108 to 112 km/h)

If the gearchange speeds are too low, decrease the cable tension. If the gearchange speeds are too high, increase the cable tension.

4 To adjust the cable tension, switch off the engine and slacken the kickdown cable locknut. Turn the cable adjuster to increase or decrease the cable tension as required then screw the locknut back up to the bracket. Hold the locknut and tighten the adjuster by hand. Do not hold the adjuster and tighten the locknut.

5 Repeat the procedure described in paragraphs 3 and 4, making small adjustments each time until the gear changes occur at the specified speeds.

8 Selector cable - adjustment

1 Move the selector lever to the P position.

2 Slacken the selector cable trunnion at the transmission selector lever then move the lever towards the left-hand roadwheel as far as it will go (Fig. 7.4).

7

3 Hold the lever in this position and tighten the trunnion.

4 Check that the trunnion pivots are without any free play, that the selector lever moves through all gear positions and that the starter only operates with the lever in the P or N positions.

9 Selector cable - removal and refitting

1 Refer to Chapter 12 and remove the centre console.

2 Move the selector lever to the P position.

3 Extract the retaining spring clip and disconnect the cable end from the selector lever. Undo the outer cable locknut and release the cable from the selector lever housing.

4 Attach a drawstring to the disconnected cable end.

5 Working in the engine compartment, slacken the cable-to-transmission selector lever trunnion and the locknut securing the cable to the support bracket. Remove the cable from the trunnion and bracket.

6 Release the grommet from the engine compartment bulkhead, pull the cable through and into the engine compartment then untie the drawstring. Remove the cable from the car.

7 Attach the drawstring to the new cable and insert the cable into the bulkhead as far as possible.

8 Pull the carpet up from behind the left-hand side of the heater ducts. Pull the drawstring and guide the cable below the heater ducts and through the selector lever housing. Remove the drawstring.

9 Lubricate both ends of the inner cable with multi-purpose grease and connect the cable using the reverse of the removal sequence.

10 Refit the centre console then adjust the cable, as described in Section 8.

10 Starter inhibitor/reversing lamp switch - removal and refitting

1 Refer to Chapter 12 and remove the centre console.

2 Place the selector lever in N then undo the retaining Allen screw and remove the selector lever handle.

3 Remove the selector panel and light screen. Withdraw the bulb holders and remove the guide plate.

Fig. 7.5 Exploded view of the selector lever assembly (Sec 11)

4 Disconnect the switch wiring connectors, undo the two screws and lift out the switch.

5 Before refitting the switch, check the condition and operation of the switch contact on the selector lever and renew the contact if worn. Also check that the selector cable trunnion on the transmission selector lever pivots freely but without free play. Free play in the trunnion or selector cable will affect the operation of the starter inhibitor/reversing lamp switch. If free play is evident, renew the nylon bush in the selector lever trunnion.

6 Fit the switch and secure with the two screws, finger tight only at this stage.

7 With the selector lever at N align the mark on the upper face of the switch with the mark on the contact bracket, then tighten the retaining screws.

8 Connect the wiring, refit the selector handle and check that the starter only operates in P or N and the reversing lamps operate in R. Realign the switch if necessary.

9 Remove the selector handle, refit the guide plate, bulb holders, light screen and selector panel.

10 Refit the selector handle, followed by the centre console.

11 Selector lever assembly - removal and refitting

1 Refer to Chapter 12 and remove the centre console.

2 Place the selector lever in the P position.

3 Extract the spring clip securing the selector cable to the lever and disconnect the cable end. Undo the outer cable retaining locknut and withdraw the selector cable from the selector lever assembly.

4 Disconnect the electrical wiring at the starter inhibitor/reversing lamp switch.

5 Undo the retaining bolts and remove the selector lever assembly from the car.

6 Refitting is the reverse sequence to removal. Check the selector cable adjustment, as described in Section 8 after refitting.

Fault finding - automatic transmission

In the event of a fault occurring on the transmission, it is first necessary to determine whether it is of a mechanical or hydraulic nature and to do this the transmission must be in the car. Special test equipment is necessary for this purpose, together with a systematic test procedure, and the work should be entrusted to a suitably equipped BL dealer or automatic transmission specialist.

Do not remove the transmission from the car for repair or overhaul until professional fault diagnosis has been carried out.

Chapter 8 Driveshafts

For modifications, and information applicable to later models, see Supplement at end of manual

Contents

Degrees of difficulty

Easy, suitable for novice with little experience	**Fairly easy,** suitable for beginner with some experience	**Fairly difficult,** suitable for competent DIY mechanic	**Difficult,** suitable for experienced DIY mechanic	**Very difficult,** suitable for expert DIY or professional

Specifications

Type .... Unequal length, solid (left-hand), tubular (right-hand), splined to inner and outer constant velocity joints

Lubrication
Assembly only - see text
Type:
Outer constant velocity joint	Molycote grease VN2461/C, or equivalent
Inner constant velocity joint	Mobil 525 grease, or equivalent
Hub bearing water shield	Duckhams LBM 10, or equivalent

Quantity:
Outer constant velocity joint:
1.3 litre models	78 cc
1.6 litre models	90 cc

Inner constant velocity joint:
All models	180 cc

Torque wrench settings

	lbf ft	Nm
Driveshaft nut*	150	203
Inner joint to drive flange	33	45
Suspension strut to swivel hub nuts	66	89
Roadwheel nuts	53	72

*Refer to Chapter 13, Section 10

1 General description

Drive is transmitted from the differential to the front wheels by means of two unequal length driveshafts. The right-hand driveshaft is a hollow construction and is of a larger diameter than the solid left-hand shaft. This is necessary to balance the torsional stiffness of both driveshafts so that an equal torque is applied to the front wheels under acceleration.

Both driveshafts are fitted with constant velocity joints at each end. The outer joints are of the Rzeppa ball and cage type and are splined to accept the driveshaft and wheel hub drive flange. The inner joints are of the sliding tripod type allowing lateral movement of the driveshaft during suspension travel. The inner joints are splined to the driveshafts and bolted to the differential drive flanges.

2 Maintenance and inspection

1 At regular intervals (see Routine Maintenance) carry out a thorough inspection of the driveshafts and joints as follows.
2 Jack up the front of the car and support it securely on axle stands.
3 Slowly rotate the roadwheel and inspect the condition of the outer joint rubber boots. Check for signs of cracking, splits or deterioration of the rubber which may allow the grease to escape and lead to water and grit entry into the joint. Also check the security and condition of the retaining clips. Repeat these checks on the inner constant velocity joints. If any damage or deterioration is found, the joints should be attended to, as described in Sections 4 or 5.
4 Continue rotating the roadwheel and check for any distortion or damage to the driveshafts. Check for any free play in the joints by holding the driveshaft firmly and attempting to rotate the wheel. Repeat this check whilst holding the differential drive flange. Any noticeable movement indicates wear in the joints, wear in the driveshaft splines or loose joint retaining bolts or hub nut.
5 Check the tightness of the inner joint retaining bolts using an Allen key, after removing the protective caps.
6 Lower the car to the ground, prise off the wheel trim, extract the split pin and check the tightness of the hub retaining nut. Fit a new split pin after aligning the holes and slots in the joint and hub nut. Refit the wheel trim.
7 Road test the car and listen for a metallic clicking from the front, as the car is driven slowly in a circle on full lock. If a clicking noise is heard, this indicates wear in the outer constant velocity joint caused by excessive clearance between the balls in the joint and the

3.5A Remove the protective caps . . .

3.5B . . . to expose the inner constant velocity joint retaining bolts (arrowed)

3.10 Undo the screws and lift off the access panel

recesses in which they operate. Remove and inspect the joint, as described in Section 5.

8 If vibration, consistent with road speed, is felt through the car when accelerating, there is a possibility of wear in the inner constant velocity joint. Remove and inspect the joint, as described in Section 4.

3 Driveshaft - removal and refitting

Note: First refer to Chapter 13, Section 10 for details of modification

1 While the vehicle Is standing on its wheels, firmly engage the handbrake and put the transmission in gear or in the P position if automatic transmission is fitted.

2 Prise off the wheel trim and extract the driveshaft nut retaining split pin. Using a suitable socket and bar, slacken the nut, but do not remove it at this stage.

3 Slacken the wheel nuts, jack up the front of the car and support it on axle stands. Remove the roadwheel and return the transmission to neutral. Remove the driveshaft nut and washer.

4 From underneath the car, make an alignment mark between the inner constant velocity joint flange and the differential drive flange, as an aid to reassembly.

5 Remove the protective caps over the inner joint retaining bolts and using an Allen key of the appropriate size, unscrew and remove the bolts (photos).

6 The procedure now varies slightly depending on whether the left-hand or right-hand driveshaft is being removed.

Left-hand driveshaft

7 On vehicles with manual transmission ease the inner constant velocity joint away from the differential drive flange and lower the inner end of the shaft. Withdraw the outer constant velocity joint from the wheel hub, lower the driveshaft to the ground and remove it from

under the car. Withdraw the bearing water shield from the outer joint.

8 On vehicles with automatic transmission, undo and remove the nuts and washers, then withdraw the two bolts securing the suspension strut to the upper part of the swivel hub. Separate the swivel hub from the strut, ease the inner constant velocity joint away from the differential drive flange and withdraw the outer constant velocity joint from the wheel hub. Remove the driveshaft from under the car and slide the bearing water shield off the outer joint.

Right-hand driveshaft

9 On vehicles with manual transmission, select reverse gear. Check that the linkage has moved sufficiently to allow clearance for the inner joint to be raised and the outer CV joint withdrawn from the wheel hub. If the clearance is insufficient, extract the retaining clip and flat washer from the gearchange linkage pivot point directly above the inner constant velocity joint, then release the linkage from the pivot location and place it to one side.

10 On all vehicles undo and remove the retaining screws and lift off the access cover from the inner wheel arch (photo).

11 Ease the inner constant velocity joint away from the differential drive flange, raise

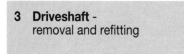

Fig. 8.1 Left-hand driveshaft and related components (Sec 3)

1 Inner constant velocity joint
2 Rubber boot
3 Retaining bolt
4 Protective caps
5 Driveshaft
6 Lower suspension arm
7 Brake caliper
8 Suspension strut
9 Disc shield
10 Disc
11 Wheel stud
12 Flat washer
13 Driveshaft nut
14 Split pin

Fig. 8.2 Gearchange linkage disconnection point (Sec 3)

1 Retaining clip
2 Linkage arm
3 Pivot
4 Inner constant velocity joint

3.12 Withdraw the outer constant velocity joint from the wheel hub

3.13 Position the bearing water shield on the outer joint flange before refitting

Fig. 8.3 Exploded view of the constant velocity joints (Secs 4 and 5)

1	Grease retaining plate	6	Rubber boot
2	Circlip	7	Retaining ring
3	Inner joint inner member	8	Driveshaft
		9	Circlip
4	Inner joint outer member	10	Retaining clip
		11	Rubber boot
5	Retaining clip	12	Retaining clip
		13	Outer joint

the inner end of the shaft and allow the joint to rest on the flange.

12 Withdraw the outer constant velocity joint from the wheel hub (photo) and remove the driveshaft from under the wheel arch. Withdraw the bearing water shield from the outer joint.

Refitting

13 Refitting both driveshafts is the reverse sequence to removal, bearing in mind the following points:

(a) *Fill the bearing water shield with the specified grease and position the shield on the outer joint flange before fitting the joint to the hub (photo)*

(b) *If the original inner constant velocity joint is being refitted, ensure that the marks on the joint and differential drive flange made during removal are aligned*

(c) *Apply a thread-locking compound to the*

4.9 Slide the rubber boot inner retaining ring onto the driveshaft up to the shoulder

threads of the inner joint retaining bolts prior to refitting

(d) *Tighten the inner joint retaining bolts, swivel hub retaining nuts (where fitted) and driveshaft nut to the specified torque and use a new split pin to secure the driveshaft nut* **Do not attempt to fully tighten the driveshaft nut until the weight of the car is on its wheels**

4 Inner constant velocity joint - removal, inspection and refitting

1 Remove the driveshaft from the car, as described in Section 3.

2 With the driveshaft on the bench, carefully prise up the tags securing the grease retaining plate to the joint outer member. Lift off the plate.

3 Cut off the outer metal retaining clip and inner rubber ring securing the rubber boot to the driveshaft and joint outer member.

4 Using circlip pliers, extract the circlip securing the joint inner member to the driveshaft.

5 Make an alignment mark between the end of the driveshaft and joint inner member to ensure correct reassembly. Withdraw the inner member, outer member, and the rubber boot.

6 Thoroughly clean the constant velocity joint inner and outer members using paraffin, or a suitable solvent. Dry with a lint-free rag, or compressed air, and then inspect the joint as follows.

7 Examine the bearing tracks in the outer member for signs of scoring, wear ridges or

evidence of lack of lubrication. Similarly examine the three bearing caps on the inner member. Check that each bearing cap turns evenly and smoothly on its roller bearings with no trace of tight spots. Insert the inner member into the outer member and check for excessive side movement of the bearing caps in their tracks, and of the inner member in the bearing caps.

8 If any of the above checks indicate wear in the joint, it will be necessary to renew the driveshaft and inner joint as an assembly. they are not available separately. If the joint is in satisfactory condition, obtain a repair kit consisting of a new rubber boot, retaining clips, and the correct quantity of grease.

9 Apply a little rubber grease to the boot inner rubber retaining ring and slide it onto the shaft up to the shoulder (photo).

10 Slide on the new rubber boot (photo) and ease the retaining ring over its end to secure it in position.

11 Place the joint outer member in position and carefully ease the rubber boot over its inner end using a screwdriver, or other suitable flat tool (photo).

8

4.10 Fit the rubber boot and secure the inner end of the boot with the retaining ring

4.11 Ease the other end of the boot over the joint outer member

4.12 Hook the retaining clip slot over the clip tag, making sure it is tight

4.13 Tighten the clip fully by squeezing the raised portion

4.14A Pack the outer member with the special grease . . .

4.14B . . . and then slide on the inner member

4.15 Secure the inner member with the retaining circlip

4.16 Secure the grease retaining plate in position by bending over the tags

12 Position the metal retaining ring over the rubber boot and engage one of the slots in the clip end over the small tag. Make sure the clip is as tight as possible and, if necessary, use a screwdriver to ease the slot over the tag (photo).
13 Fully tighten the clip by squeezing the raised portion with pliers (photo).
14 Pack the joint inner and outer members with the specified quantity of the grease supplied in the kit (photo) and then slide the inner member onto the shaft (photo). Ensure that the reference marks made during removal are aligned.
15 Secure the joint inner member with the retaining circlip (photo).
16 Place the grease retaining plate over the end of the outer member, and bend over the tags to secure it in place (photo).
17 The driveshaft can now be refitted to the car, as described in Section 3.

5 Outer constant velocity joint - removal, inspection and refitting

1 Remove the driveshaft, as described in Section 3.

2 With the driveshaft on the bench, cut off the two rubber boot retaining clips and fold back the boot to expose the outer joint.
3 Firmly grasp the driveshaft, or support it in a vice. Using a hide, or plastic mallet, sharply strike the outer edge of the joint and drive it off the shaft. The outer joint is retained on the driveshaft by an internal circular section circlip and striking the joint in the manner described forces the circlip to contract into a groove, so allowing the joint to slide off.
4 With the constant velocity joint removed from the driveshaft, thoroughly clean the joint using paraffin, or a suitable solvent, and dry it, preferably using compressed air. Carry out a careful visual inspection of the joint, paying particular attention to the following areas.
5 Move the inner splined driving member from side to side to expose each ball in turn at the top of its track. Examine the balls for cracks, flat spots or signs of surface pitting.
6 Inspect the ball tracks on the inner and outer members. If the tracks have widened, the balls will no longer be a tight fit. At the same time check the ball cage windows for wear or for cracking between the balls. Wear in the balls, ball tracks and ball cage windows will lead to the characteristic clicking noise on full lock described previously.

7 If any of the above checks indicate wear in the joint it will be necessary to renew it complete, as the internal parts are not available separately. If the joint is in a satisfactory condition, obtain a repair kit consisting of a new rubber boot, retaining clips and the correct quantity of grease.
8 The help of an assistant will be necessary whilst refitting the joint to the driveshaft. Ensure that the circlip is undamaged and correctly located in its groove in the driveshaft. Position the new rubber boot over the shaft and locate its end in the shaft groove.
9 Place the retaining clip over the rubber boot and wrap it round until the slot in the clip end can be engaged with the tag. Make sure the clip is as tight as possible using pliers, or a screwdriver, if necessary. Fully tighten the clip by squeezing the raised portion with pliers.
10 Fold back the rubber boot and position the constant velocity joint over the splines on the driveshaft until it abuts the circlip.
11 Using two small screwdrivers placed either side of the circlip, compress the clip and at the same time have your assistant firmly strike the end of the joint with a hide, or plastic, mallet.
12 The joint should slide over the compressed circlip and into position on the shaft. It will probably take several attempts until you achieve success. If the joint does not spring into place the moment it is struck, remove it, reposition the circlip and try again. Do not force the joint, otherwise the circlip will be damaged.
13 With the joint in position against the retaining collar, pack it thoroughly with the specified quantity of the grease supplied in the repair kit. Work the grease well into the ball tracks while twisting the joint, and fill the rubber boot with any excess.
14 Ease the rubber boot over the joint and secure it with the retaining clip, as described in paragraph 9.
15 The driveshaft can now be refitted to the car, as described in Section 3.

Fault finding - driveshafts

Vibration and/or noise on turns
☐ Worn constant velocity outer joint(s)

Vibration when accelerating
☐ Worn constant velocity inner joint(s)
☐ Bent or distorted driveshaft

Noise on taking up drive
☐ Worn driveshaft or constant velocity joint splines
☐ Loose driveshaft nut
☐ Worn constant velocity joints

See also Fault finding - suspension and steering

Chapter 9 Braking system

For modifications, and information applicable to later models, see Supplement at end of manual

Contents

Degrees of difficulty

Easy, suitable for novice with little experience	**Fairly easy,** suitable for beginner with some experience	**Fairly difficult,** suitable for competent DIY mechanic	**Difficult,** suitable for experienced DIY mechanic	**Very difficult,** suitable for expert DIY or professional

Specifications

System type	Diagonally split dual circuit hydraulic with pressure regulating valve in rear hydraulic circuit. Cable-operated handbrake on rear wheels. Servo assistance on all models

Front brakes

Type	Disc with single piston sliding calipers
Disc diameter	9.5 in (241.3 mm)
Disc thickness	0.497 to 0.507 in (12.623 to 12.878 mm)
Maximum disc run-out	0.006 in (0.15 mm)
Minimum pad thickness	0.125 in (3.2 mm)

Rear brakes

Type	Single leading shoe drum, self-adjusting
Drum diameter	8.0 in (203.0 mm)
Lining width	1.5 in (38.1 mm)
Minimum lining thickness	0.0625 in (1.6 mm)
Wheel cylinder diameter:	
Saloon	0.687 in (17.45 mm)
Estate	0.750 in (19.05 mm)
Handbrake lever stop endfloat	0 to 0.080 in (0 to 2.03 mm)

General

Master cylinder bore diameter	0.81 in (20.57 mm)
Servo unit boost ratio	3:1
Brake fluid type/specification	Hydraulic fluid to FMVSS 116 DOT 4 or SAE J1703C

Torque wrench settings	lbf ft	Nm
Bleed screws	7	9
Brake caliper anchor bracket-to-swivel hub bolts	53	72
Twin GP valve mounting bolts	9	12
Guide pin bolts	24	33
Master cylinder mounting nuts	9	12
Servo unit mounting nuts	9	12
Wheel cylinder-to-backplate bolts	5	7
Rear hub retaining nut *(tighten to torque then align next split pin hole)* .	50	68
Wheel nuts	53	72
Brake disc to drive flange	8	11

9

1 General description

The braking system is of the servo-assisted, dual circuit hydraulic type with disc brakes at the front and drum brakes at the rear. A diagonally split dual circuit hydraulic system is employed in which each circuit operates one front and one diagonally opposite rear brake from a tandem master cylinder. Under normal conditions both circuits operate in unison; however, in the event of hydraulic failure in one circuit, full braking force will still be available at two wheels. A pressure regulating device or 'twin GP' (Gravity Pressure) valve is incorporated in the rear brake hydraulic circuit. This valve regulates the pressure applied to each rear brake and reduces the possibility of the rear wheels locking under heavy braking.

The front disc brakes are operated by single piston sliding type calipers. At the rear, leading and trailing brake shoes are operated by twin piston wheel cylinders and are self-adjusting by footbrake application.

Driver warning lights are provided for brake pad wear, low brake hydraulic fluid level and handbrake applied.

2 Maintenance and inspection

1 At the intervals given in Routine Maintenance at the beginning of this manual the following service operations should be carried out on the braking system components.

2 Check the brake hydraulic fluid level and if necessary top up with the specified fluid to the MAX mark on the reservoir. Any need for frequent topping-up indicates a fluid leak somewhere in the system which must be investigated and rectified immediately.

3 Check the front disc pads and the rear brake shoe linings for wear and inspect the condition of the discs and drums. Details will be found in Sections 3 and 6 respectively.

4 Check the condition of the hydraulic pipes and hoses as described in Section 14. At the same time check the condition of the handbrake cables, lubricate the exposed cables and linkages and, if necessary, adjust the handbrake, as described in Section 16.

5 The three braking system warning lights should be tested as follows. Check the operation of the handbrake warning light by applying the handbrake with the ignition switched on. The light should illuminate when the handbrake is applied. To test the low brake hydraulic fluid level warning light, place the car in gear (or P if automatic transmission is fitted), release the handbrake and switch on the ignition. The light should illuminate when the flexible contact cover in the centre of the brake fluid reservoir filler cap is depressed. To check the disc pad wear warning indicator, locate the twin terminal black plastic socket which is in the wiring harness adjacent to the right-hand brake caliper. Switch on the ignition and connect a bridging wire between the terminals of one socket; the pad wear warning light should be illuminated on the instrument panel when the bridging wire is earthed. If any of the lights fail to illuminate in the test condition, then either the bulb is blown, a fuse is at fault or there is a fault in the circuit.

6 Renew the brake hydraulic fluid at the specified intervals by draining the system and refilling with fresh fluid, as described in Section 15.

7 The flexible brake hoses and rubber seals in the brake calipers, wheel cylinders and master cylinder should also be renewed at the less frequent intervals given, as should the air filter in the vacuum servo unit. Details of these operations will be found in the relevant Sections of this Chapter.

3 Front disc pads - inspection and renewal

1 Apply the handbrake, prise off the front wheel trim and slacken the wheel nuts. Jack up the front of the car and support it securely on axle stands. Remove the roadwheels.

2 The thickness of the disc pads can now be checked by viewing through the slot in the front of the caliper body. If the lining on any of the pads is at, or below, the minimum specified thickness, all four pads must be renewed as a complete set.

3 To renew the pads, first remove the protective cap over the caliper bleed screw (photo). Obtain a plastic or rubber tube of suitable diameter to fit snugly over the bleed screw and submerge the free end in a jar containing a small quantity of brake fluid.

4 Open the bleed screw half a turn and pull the caliper body toward you. This will push the piston back into its bore to facilitate removal and refitting of the pads. When the piston has moved in as far as it will go, close the bleed screw, remove the tube and refit the protective cap.

5 Disconnect the pad wear indicator wiring connector (right-hand caliper only) and, using a suitable spanner, unscrew the lower guide pin bolt while holding the guide pin with a second spanner (photo).

6 Pivot the caliper body upwards (photo), withdraw the two disc pads and, where fitted, the anti-squeal shim(s).

1	Guide pin bolt	5	Anchor bracket
2	Caliper body	6	Disc pads
3	Guide pin	7	Bleed screw
4	Dust cover	8	Friction material

Fig. 9.1 Front disc pad renewal (Sec 3)

3.3 Front caliper bleed screw (A) and pad wear indicator wiring connector (B)

7 Brush the dust and dirt from the caliper, piston, disc and pads, but **do not inhale,** as it is injurious to health.

8 Rotate the brake disc by hand and scrape away any rust and scale. Carefully inspect the entire surface of the disc and if there are any signs of cracks, deep scoring or severe abrasions, the disc must be renewed. Also inspect the caliper for signs of fluid leaks around the piston, corrosion, or other damage. Renew the piston seals or the caliper body as necessary.

9 To refit the pads, first attach any anti-squeal shim(s) to them. If a single shim is fitted, it must be fitted to the outer pad. Later models are fitted with an anti-squeal shim behind both pads; in this instance the inner pad's shim can be identified by the cut-out section to facilitate the location of the pad wear warning leads. Very lightly smear the pad and caliper contact areas with a silicone grease, ensuring that no grease is allowed to come into contact with the friction material.

10 Place the pads in position against the disc, noting that the pad with the wear indicator lead is fitted to the inner position on the right-hand caliper.

11 Place the caliper body over the pads and refit the guide pin bolt. Tighten the bolt to the specified torque.

12 Reconnect the wear indicator wiring connector (where applicable), and refit the roadwheels - do not tighten the wheel nuts fully until the weight of the car is on the wheels.

13 Depress the brake pedal several times to bring the piston into contact with the pads and then lower the car to the ground. Check and, if necessary, top up the fluid in the master cylinder reservoir.

4 Front brake caliper - removal, overhaul and refitting

1 Apply the handbrake, prise off the front wheel trim and slacken the wheel nuts. Jack up the front of the car and support it securely on axle stands. Remove the roadwheel.

2 Using a suitable spanner, unscrew the guide pin bolts while holding the guide pins with a second spanner.

3 Disconnect the pad wear indicator wiring connector (right-hand side caliper only) and lift away the disc pads and anchor bracket still in position. It is not necessary to remove the anchor bracket unless it requires renewal because of accident damage or severe corrosion.

4 With the flexible brake hose still attached to the caliper body, very slowly depress the brake pedal until the piston has been ejected just over halfway out of its bore.

5 Using a brake hose clamp, or self-locking wrench with protected jaws, clamp the flexible brake hose. This will minimise brake fluid loss during subsequent operations.

6 Slacken the brake hose-to-caliper body

3.5 Unscrew the lower caliper guide pin bolt

union, and then, while holding the hose, rotate the caliper to unscrew it from the hose. Lift away the caliper and plug or tape over the end of the hose to prevent dirt entry.

7 With the caliper on the bench wipe away all traces of dust and dirt, but *avoid inhaling the dust as it is injurious to health.*

8 Withdraw the partially ejected piston from the caliper body and remove the dust cover.

9 Using a suitable blunt instrument, such as a knitting needle, carefully extract the piston seal from the caliper bore.

10 Clean all the parts in methylated spirit, or clean brake fluid, and wipe dry using a lint free cloth. Inspect the piston and caliper bore for signs of damage, scuffing or corrosion and if these conditions are evident renew the caliper body assembly. Also renew the guide pins if bent or damaged.

11 If the components are in a satisfactory condition, a repair kit consisting of new seals and dust cover should be obtained.

12 Thoroughly lubricate the components and new seals with clean brake fluid and carefully fit the seal to the caliper bore.

13 Position the dust cover over the innermost end of the piston so that the caliper bore sealing lip protrudes beyond the base of the piston. Using a blunt instrument, if necessary, engage the sealing lip of the dust cover with the groove in the caliper. Now push the piston into the bore until the other sealing lip of the dust cover can be engaged with the groove in the piston. Having done this, push the piston fully into its bore. Ease the piston out again slightly, and make sure that the cover lip is correctly seating in the piston groove.

14 Remove the guide pins from the anchor bracket and smear them with a high melting-point brake grease. Fit new dust covers to the guide pins and refit them to the anchor bracket.

15 Hold the flexible brake hose and screw the caliper body back onto the hose.

16 With the piston pushed fully into its bore, refit the caliper and secure it with the guide pin bolts. Tighten the bolts to the specified torque.

17 Fully tighten the brake hose union and remove the clamp. If working on the right-hand caliper, reconnect the pad warning light wiring connector.

3.6 Pivot the caliper body upwards and withdraw the disc pads

18 Refer to Section 15 and bleed the brake hydraulic system; noting that, if precautions were taken to minimise fluid loss, it should only be necessary to bleed the relevant front wheel.

19 Refit the roadwheel and lower the car to the ground before fully tightening the wheel nuts and refitting the wheel trim.

5 Front brake disc - removal and refitting

1 Apply the handbrake, remove the front wheel trim and slacken the wheel nuts. Jack the front of the car up and support it securely on axle stands. Remove the roadwheel.

2 Rotate the disc by hand and examine it for deep scoring, grooving or cracks. Light scoring is normal, but if excessive the disc must be renewed. Any loose rust and scale around the outer edge of the disc can be removed by lightly tapping it with a small hammer while rotating the disc.

Fig. 9.2 Front brake caliper components (Sec 4)

1 Piston   2 Piston seal   3 Dust cover

6.3 Rear hub retaining nut and flat washer

6.4 Remove the hub and brake drum assembly from the stub axle

6.8 Layout and position of the rear brake components

3 To remove the disc undo and remove the two bolts securing the brake anchor bracket to the swivel hub. Withdraw the caliper assembly complete with pads, off the disc and support it to one side. Avoid straining the flexible brake hose.

4 Undo and remove the two screws securing the disc to the drive flange and withdraw the disc.

5 Refitting is the reverse sequence to removal. Ensure that the mating face of the disc and drive flange are thoroughly clean and tighten all retaining bolts to the specified torque. Prior to refitting the caliper unit, check that the run-out of the brake disc is within the specified limits. If not, the disc is warped and must be renewed.

Fig. 9.3 Rear brake assembly – left-hand side (Sec 6)

1 Wheel cylinder
2 Brake shoes
3 Hold-down springs
4 Lower return spring
5 Upper return springs
6 Self-adjust quadrant pivot pin
7 Hollow pin
8 Quadrant
9 Ratchet wheel
10 Operating spring

6 Rear brake shoes - inspection and renewal

1 Chock the front wheels, remove the rear wheel trim and slacken the rear wheel nuts. Jack up the rear of the car and support it securely on axle stands. Remove the roadwheel and release the handbrake.

2 By judicious tapping and levering remove the hub cap and extract the split pin from the hub retaining nut.

3 Using a large socket and bar, undo and remove the hub retaining nut and flat washer (photo). *Note that the left-hand nut has a left-hand thread and the right-hand nut has a conventional right-hand thread.* **Take care not to tip the car from the axle stands.** If the hub nuts are particularly tight, temporarily refit the roadwheel and lower the car to the ground. Slacken the nut in this more stable position and then raise and support the car before removing the nut.

4 Withdraw the hub and brake drum assembly from the stub axle (photo). If it is not possible to withdraw the hub due to the brake drum binding on the brake shoes, the following procedure should be adopted. Refer to Section 16, if necessary, and slacken off the handbrake cable at the adjuster. From the rear of the brake backplate, prise out the handbrake lever stop, which will allow the brake shoes to retract sufficiently from the

hub assembly to be removed. It will, however, be necessary to remove the brake shoes and fit a new handbrake lever stop to the backplate.

5 With the brake drum assembly removed, brush or wipe the dust from the brake drum, brake shoes and backplate. *Take great care not to inhale the dust, as it is injurious to health.*

6 Measure the brake shoe lining thickness. If it is worn down to the specified minimum amount, or if it is nearly worn down to the rivets, renew all four rear brake shoes. The shoes must also be renewed if any are contaminated with brake fluid or grease, or show signs of cracking or glazing. If contamination is evident, the cause must be traced and cured before fitting new brake shoes.

7 If the brake shoes are in a satisfactory condition proceed to paragraph 19; if removal is necessary, proceed as follows.

8 First make a careful note of the location and position of the various springs and linkages as an aid to refitting (photo).

9 Depress the brake shoe hold-down springs (photo) while supporting the hold-down pin from the rear of the backplate with your finger. Turn the springs through 90° and lift off. Withdraw the hold-down pins.

10 Using a screwdriver, if necessary, release the shoes from their lower pivots and disengage the lower return spring (photo).

11 Using long-nosed pliers, release the

6.9 Brake shoe hold-down spring and pin

6.10 Brake shoe lower return spring

6.11 Brake shoe upper return spring removal

6.12 Detach the handbrake cable from the trailing shoe operating lever

6.13A Apply a trace of silicone grease to the brake shoe contact areas (arrowed)

upper return spring from the leading shoe and the arm of the self-adjust mechanism (photo). Detach the leading shoe from the wheel cylinder and self-adjust mechanism, and remove it from the backplate.

12 Withdraw the trailing shoe from the backplate, move the handbrake operating lever away from the shoe and unhook the handbrake cable (photo). Release the upper return spring and detach the self-adjust mechanism from the trailing brake shoe.

13 Before fitting the new brake shoes, clean off the brake backplate with a rag and apply a trace of silicone grease to the brake shoe contact areas (photo). Clean the self-adjust mechanism and make sure that it is free to move in its elongated slot (photo).

14 Refit the self-adjust mechanism to the trailing brake shoe and secure with the return spring.

15 Position the self-adjust mechanism in the fully retracted position by moving the quadrant away from the ratchet wheel and turning it until the hollow pin locates the inner cutaway (photo).

16 Connect the handbrake cable to the operating lever and position the trailing shoe on the backplate.

17 Refit the leading shoe to the backplate, ensuring that the shoe is properly located around the pin on the self-adjust mechanism (photo).

18 Refit the upper and lower return springs and the hold-down springs and pins.

19 Refit the brake drum and hub assembly, flat washer and hub retaining nut. Tighten the hub retaining nut to the specified torque and then tighten further until a split pin hole is aligned. Fit a new split pin and tap on the hub cap.

20 Refit the roadwheel, but do not fully tighten the wheel nuts.

21 If it was necessary to slacken the handbrake cable to enable the brake drum to be removed, adjust the cable as described in Section 16.

22 Lower the car to the ground, tighten the wheel nuts to the specified torque and refit the wheel trim. Depress the footbrake two or three times to operate the brake adjusters.

7 Rear wheel cylinder - removal and refitting

1 Begin by removing the rear hub and brake drum assembly, as described in Section 6, paragraphs 1 to 5 inclusive.

2 Using a screwdriver, or other suitable tool, carefully ease the upper end of the leading brake shoe (the one nearest the front of the car) away from the wheel cylinder piston. Take care not to damage the wheel cylinder rubber boot as you do this. As the leading shoe is moved away from the wheel cylinder, the self-adjust mechanism will expand and hold both brake shoes in the expanded position. This

will provide sufficient clearance to allow removal of the wheel cylinder.

3 Using a brake hose clamp, or self-locking wrench with protected jaws, clamp the flexible brake hose just in front of the rear axle pivot mounting. This will minimise brake fluid loss during subsequent operations.

4 At the rear of the brake backplate, unscrew the union nut securing the brake pipe to the wheel cylinder. Carefully ease the pipe out of the cylinder and plug or tape over its end to prevent dirt entry.

5 Undo and remove the two bolts securing the wheel cylinder to the backplate and withdraw the cylinder from between the brake shoes.

6 To refit the wheel cylinder, place it in position on the backplate and engage the brake pipe and union. Screw in the union nut two or three turns to ensure the thread has started.

7 Refit the wheel cylinder retaining bolts and tighten them to the specified torque. Now fully tighten the brake pipe union nut.

8 Using a screwdriver or other suitable tool, as before, ease the leading brake shoe away from the wheel cylinder and retract the self-adjust mechanism. To do this move the quadrant, in its elongated slot, away from the ratchet wheel and turn it until the hollow pin contacts the cutaway in the operating lever. As you do this, ease the brake shoes back into their upper locations in the wheel cylinder pistons.

6.13B Brake shoe self-adjust mechanism

6.15 Self-adjust mechanism pin (arrowed) in fully retracted position

6.17 Brake shoe correctly located around self-adjust mechanism hollow pin (arrowed)

9

Fig. 9.4 Exploded view of the right-hand rear wheel cylinder (Sec 8)

1 *Dust cover retainers (where fitted)*
2 *Dust cover*
3 *Trailing shoe piston*
4 *Piston seal*
5 *Bleed screw and dust cap*
6 *Wheel cylinder body*
7 *Piston spring*
8 *Leading shoe piston*
9 *Leading shoe tappet*

9 Refit the brake drum and hub assembly, flat washer and hub retaining nut. Tighten the hub retaining nut to the specified torque and then tighten further until a split pin hole is aligned. Fit a new split pin and tap on the hub cap.
10 Remove the clamp from the brake hose and bleed the brake hydraulic system, as described in Section 15. Providing suitable precautions were taken to minimise loss of fluid, it should only be necessary to bleed the relevant rear brake.
11 If it was necessary to slacken the handbrake cable to remove the brake drum, adjust the cable, as described in Section 16.
12 Refit the roadwheel, but do not tighten the wheel nuts fully.
13 Lower the car to the ground and tighten the wheel nuts. Depress the footbrake two or three times to operate the brake adjusters.

8 Rear wheel cylinder - overhaul

1 Remove the wheel cylinder from the car, as described in the previous Section.
2 With the wheel cylinder on the bench, remove the dust cover retainers, where fitted, and withdraw the dust covers from the ends of the piston and cylinder body.
3 Withdraw the pistons and piston spring. Remove the seals from the pistons and unscrew the bleed screw from the cylinder body.
4 Thoroughly clean all the components in methylated spirits or clean brake fluid and dry with a lint-free rag.
5 Carefully examine the surfaces of the pistons and cylinder bore for wear, score marks or corrosion and, if evident, renew the complete wheel cylinder. If the components are in a satisfactory condition, obtain a repair

10.4 Brake pipe union nuts (A) and master cylinder retaining nuts (B)

kit consisting of new seals and dust covers.
6 Dip the new seals and pistons in clean brake fluid and assemble the components wet, as follows.
7 Using your fingers, fit the new seals to the pistons with their sealing lips facing inwards.
8 Lubricate the cylinder bore with clean brake fluid and insert the spring, followed by the two pistons. Note that the piston with the slot in its end must face toward the front of the car when fitted.
9 Place the dust covers over the pistons and cylinder and, where applicable, refit the dust cover retainers.
10 Screw the bleed screw into the cylinder body and then refit the wheel cylinder to the car, as described in the previous Section.

9 Rear brake backplate - removal and refitting

The rear brake backplate is removed in conjunction with the stub axle and details of this procedure will be found in Chapter 11, Section 12.

10 Master cylinder - removal and refitting

1 Working under the front of the car, remove the dust cover from the bleed screw on each front brake caliper. Obtain two plastic or rubber tubes of suitable diameter to fit snugly over the bleed screws, and place the other ends in a suitable receptacle.
2 Open the bleed screws half a turn and operate the brake pedal until the master cylinder reservoir is empty. Tighten the bleed screws and remove the tubes. Discard the expelled brake fluid.
3 Disconnect the wiring connectors from the reservoir filler cap terminals.
4 Unscrew the two brake pipe union nuts and carefully withdraw the pipes from the master cylinder. Plug or tape over the ends of the pipes to prevent dirt entry, and place rags beneath the master cylinder to protect the surrounding paintwork (photo).
5 Undo and remove the two retaining nuts and washers and withdraw the master cylinder from the servo unit.
6 Refitting the master cylinder is the reverse sequence to removal.
Tighten the retaining nuts to the specified torque and, on completion, bleed the brake hydraulic system, as described in Section 15.

11 Master cylinder - overhaul

1 Remove the master cylinder from the car, as described in the previous Section. Drain any fluid remaining in the reservoir and prepare a clean uncluttered working surface, ready for dismantling.

1 *Reservoir*
2 *Cylinder body*
3 *Reservoir sealing washers*
4 *Secondary piston stop pin*
5 *Roll pin*
6 *Primary piston assembly*
7 *Secondary piston spring*
8 *Seal retainer*
9 *Secondary piston seal and washer*
10 *Secondary piston*
11 *Secondary piston seal*

Fig. 9.5 Master cylinder components and assembly details (Sec 11)

2 Remove the primary piston assembly and then mount the cylinder horizontally in a soft-jawed vice. Using a parallel pin punch, drive out the two roll pins securing the reservoir to the cylinder body.

3 Lift off the reservoir and withdraw the two reservoir sealing washers from the master cylinder inlet ports.

4 Using a blunt instrument, push the secondary piston in as far as it will go and withdraw the secondary piston stop pin from its location in the secondary inlet port.

5 Slowly release the secondary piston, remove the cylinder from the vice and tap it on a block of wood to release the secondary piston from the cylinder bore.

6 Note the location and position of the components on the secondary piston and then remove the piston spring. Withdraw the seal retainer, followed by the seal and washer. Now remove the remaining seal from the other end of the secondary piston.

7 The primary piston should not be dismantled, as parts are not available separately. If the master cylinder is in a serviceable condition, and is to be re-used, a complete new primary piston assembly is included in the repair kit.

8 With the master cylinder completely dismantled, clean all the components in methylated spirits, or clean brake fluid, and dry with a lint-free rag.

9 Carefully examine the cylinder bore and secondary piston for signs of wear, scoring or corrosion, and if evident renew the complete cylinder assembly.

10 If the components are in a satisfactory condition, obtain a repair kit consisting of new seals, springs and primary piston assembly.

11 Lubricate the master cylinder bore, pistons and seals thoroughly in clean brake fluid, and assemble them wet.

Fig. 9.6 Hydraulic pipe arrangement at twin GP valve (Sec 13)

Primary circuit hydraulic pipes (11 mm unions)
1A From master cylinder
1B To right-hand front brake
1C To left-hand rear brake
Secondary circuit hydraulic pipes (13 mm unions)
2A From master cylinder
2B To left-hand front brake
2C To right-hand rear brake

12 Fit the washer and seal onto the inner end of the secondary piston using your fingers only. Use the notes made during dismantling and the accompanying illustrations as a guide to the direction of fitment of the seal. Place the seal retainer over the seal and refit the spring. Fit the remaining seal to the other end of the secondary piston.

13 Insert the secondary piston into the cylinder bore, taking care not to turn over the lips of the seals as the piston is inserted.

14 Push the secondary piston down the cylinder bore as far as it will go and refit the stop pin into its hole in the inlet port.

15 Insert the new primary piston assembly into the cylinder bore, again taking care not to turn over the seal lips as they enter the bore.

16 Place the two reservoir seals into the inlet ports and refit the reservoir. Secure the reservoir with the two roll pins.

17 The master cylinder can now be refitted to the car, as described in the previous Section.

12 Twin GP valve - description and testing

1 The twin GP valve is mounted in the engine compartment and contains two gravity/pressure valves, one for each hydraulic circuit.

2 The purpose of the valve is to distribute brake fluid to the front and rear brakes, and to limit the fluid pressure supplied to the rear brakes under heavy braking.

3 The operation of the valve may be suspect if one or both rear wheels continually lock during normal braking. It is essential, however, before condemning the valve to ensure the fault does not lie with the brake shoe assemblies or wheel cylinders, and that adverse road conditions are also not responsible.

4 In the event of failure of the valve it must be renewed as an assembly, as parts are not available separately.

13 Twin GP valve - removal and refitting

1 Remove the master cylinder reservoir filler cap and place a piece of polythene over the filler neck. Secure the polythene in place with an elastic band ensuring that an airtight seal is obtained. This will minimise brake fluid loss during subsequent operations.

2 Place some rags around the valve to protect the paintwork from brake fluid spillage.

HAYNES HiNT *Wash off any brake fluid that comes into contact with the body immediately using copious amounts of cold water. Brake fluid is a very effective paint stripper.*

3 Clean the area around the brake pipe unions thoroughly and unscrew the union nuts. Note that the nuts securing the primary brake pipes are of a smaller diameter than the secondary nuts. Very carefully withdraw the brake pipes from the valve.

4 Undo and remove the two bolts securing the valve to the inner member and withdraw the unit from the engine compartment.

5 Refitting is the reverse sequence to removal. Refer to Fig. 9.6 if in any doubt about the pipe locations, and bleed the brake hydraulic system, as described in Section 15, after refitting.

14 Hydraulic pipes and hoses - inspection, removal and refitting

1 At intervals given in Routine Maintenance carefully examine all brake pipes, hoses, hose connections and pipe unions.

2 First check for signs of leakage at the pipe unions. Then examine the flexible hoses for signs of cracking, chafing and fraying.

3 The brake pipes must be examined

Fig. 9.7 Layout of brake hydraulic pipes and hoses (Sec 14)

Secondary circuit
1 Master cylinder to GP valve
2 GP valve to left-hand front hose
3 GP valve to right-hand rear hose
Primary circuit
4 Master cylinder to GP valve
5 GP valve to right-hand front hose
6 GP valve to left-hand rear hose

9

14.7 Front brake hose and retaining nut (arrowed)

15.10 Front brake caliper bleed screw (arrowed)

15.14 Bleed tube attached to front caliper bleed screw

carefully and methodically. They must be cleaned off and checked for signs of dents, corrosion or other damage. Corrosion should be scraped off and, if the depth of pitting is significant, the pipes renewed. This is particularly likely in those areas underneath the vehicle body where the pipes are exposed and unprotected.

4 If any section of pipe or hose is to be removed, first unscrew the master cylinder reservoir filler cap and place a piece of polythene over the filler neck. Secure the polythene with an elastic band ensuring that an airtight seal is obtained. This will minimise brake fluid loss when the pipe or hose is removed.

5 Brake pipe removal is usually quite straight-forward. The union nuts at each end are undone, the pipe and union pulled out and the centre section of the pipe removed from the body clips. Where the unions nuts are exposed to the full force of the weather they can sometimes be quite tight. As only an open ended spanner can be used, burring of the flats on the nuts is not uncommon when attempting to undo them. For this reason a self-locking wrench, or special brake union spanner, is often the only way to separate a stubborn union.

6 To remove a flexible hose, wipe the unions and brackets free of dirt and undo the union nut from the brake pipe end(s).

7 Next extract the hose retaining clip, or unscrew the nut, and lift the end of the hose out of its bracket (photo). If a front hose is being removed, it can now be unscrewed from the brake caliper.

8 Brake pipes can be obtained individually, or in sets, from most accessory shops or garages with the end flares and union nuts in place. The pipe is then bent to shape, using the old pipe as a guide, and is ready for fitting to the car.

9 Refitting the pipes and hoses is a reverse of the removal procedure. Make sure that the hoses are not kinked when in position and also make sure that the brake pipes are securely supported in their clips. After refitting, remove the polythene from the reservoir and bleed the brake hydraulic system, as described in Section 15.

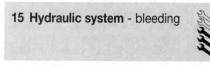

15 Hydraulic system - bleeding

1 The correct functioning of the brake hydraulic system is only possible after removal of all air from the components and circuit; this is achieved by bleeding the system. Note that only clean unused brake fluid, which has remained unshaken for at least 24 hours, must be used.

2 If there is any possibility of incorrect fluid being used in the system, the brake lines and components must be completely flushed with uncontaminated fluid and new seals fitted to the components.

3 *Never re-use* brake fluid which has been bled from the system.

4 During the procedure, do not allow the level of brake fluid to drop more than halfway down the reservoir.

5 Before starting work, check that all pipes and hoses are secure, unions tight and bleed screws closed. Take great care not to allow brake fluid to come into contact with the car paintwork, otherwise the finish will be seriously damaged. Wash off any spilled fluid immediately with cold water.

6 There is a number of one-man, do-it-yourself, brake bleeding kits currently available from motor accessory shops. If one of these kits is not available, it will be necessary to gather together a clean jar and a suitable length of clear plastic tubing which is a tight fit over the bleed screw, and also to engage the help of an assistant.

7 If brake fluid has been lost from the master cylinder due to a leak in the system, ensure that the cause is traced and rectified before proceeding further.

8 If the hydraulic system has only been partially disconnected and suitable precautions were taken to prevent further loss of fluid, it should only be necessary to bleed that part of the system (ie primary or secondary circuit).

9 If the complete system is to be bled then it should be done in the following sequence.

Secondary circuit: Left-hand front then right-hand rear

Primary circuit: Right-hand front then left-hand rear

10 To bleed the system, first clean the area around the bleed screw (photo) and fit the bleed tube. If necessary, top up the master cylinder reservoir with brake fluid.

11 If the system incorporates a vacuum servo, destroy the vacuum by giving several applications of the brake pedal in quick succession.

Bleeding - two-man method

12 Gather together a clean jar and a length of rubber or plastic tubing which will be a tight fit on the brake bleed screws.

13 Engage the help of an assistant.

14 Push one end of the bleed tube onto the first bleed screw and immerse the other end in the jar which should contain enough hydraulic fluid to cover the end of the tube (photo).

15 Open the bleed screw one half turn and have your assistant depress the brake pedal fully then slowly release it. Tighten the bleed screw at the end of each pedal downstroke to obviate any chance of air or fluid being drawn back into the system.

16 Repeat this operation until clean hydraulic fluid, free from air bubbles, can be seen coming through into the jar.

17 Tighten the bleed screw at the end of a pedal downstroke and remove the bleed tube. Bleed the remaining screws in a similar way.

Bleeding - using one-way valve kit

18 There is a number of one-man, one-way brake bleeding kits available from motor accessory shops. It is recommended that one of these kits is used wherever possible as it will greatly simplify the bleeding operation and also reduce the risk of air or fluid being drawn back into the system, quite apart from being able to do the work without the help of an assistant.

19 To use the kit, connect the tube to the bleed screw and open the screw one half turn.

20 Depress the brake pedal fully and slowly release it. The one-way valve in the kit will prevent expelled air from returning at the end of each pedal downstroke. Repeat this operation several times to be sure of ejecting

all air from the system. Some kits include a translucent container which can be positioned so that the air bubbles can be seen being ejected from the system.

21 Tighten the bleed screw, remove the tube and repeat the operations on the remaining brakes.

22 On completion, depress the brake pedal. If it still feels spongy repeat the bleeding operations, as air must still be trapped in the system.

Bleeding - using a pressure bleed kit

23 These kits are also available from motor accessory shops and are usually operated by air pressure from the spare tyre.

24 By connecting a pressurised container to the master cylinder fluid reservoir, bleeding is then carried out by simply opening each bleed screw in turn and allowing the fluid to run out, rather like turning on a tap, until no air is visible in the expelled fluid.

25 By using this method, the large reserve of hydraulic fluid provides a safeguard against air being drawn into the master cylinder during bleeding which often occurs if the fluid level in the reservoir is not maintained.

26 Pressure bleeding is particularly effective when bleeding 'difficult' systems or when bleeding the complete system at the time of routine fluid renewal.

All methods

27 When bleeding is completed, check and top up the fluid level in the master cylinder reservoir.

28 Check the feel of the brake pedal. If it feels at all spongy, air must still be present in the system and further bleeding is indicated. Failure to bleed satisfactorily after a reasonable repetition of the bleeding operations may be due to worn master cylinder seals.

29 Discard brake fluid which has been expelled. It is almost certain to be contaminated with moisture, air and dirt making it unsuitable for further use. Clean fluid should always be stored in an airtight container as it is hygroscopic (absorbs moisture readily) which lowers its boiling point and could affect braking performance under severe conditions.

16.5 Location of the handbrake cable adjuster (arrowed) in front of the rear axle

16 Handbrake cable - adjustment

1 Chock the front wheels, jack up the rear of the car and support it securely on axle stands. Release the handbrake.

2 Apply the footbrake firmly two or three times to ensure full movement of the self-adjust mechanism on the rear brake shoes. This is particularly important if the brake drums have recently been removed.

3 Apply the handbrake sharply and then release it to equalise the cable loads.

4 From under the rear of the car, measure the endfloat of the handbrake lever stops located on the rear of each brake backplate. If the movement of the stops is not as given in the Specifications, adjustment is necessary and is carried out as follows.

5 Turn the cable adjuster, located just in front of the rear axle (photo), clockwise to increase

the cable tension and anti-clockwise to decrease it. The direction of rotation assumes the adjuster is being viewed from the rear of the car, ie facing forwards.

6 Turn the cable adjuster until the endfloat of the handbrake lever stops is as specified and the travel of the handbrake lever necessary to lock the wheels is between 5 and 8 clicks of the ratchet. Do not overtighten the cable.

7 After adjustment, ensure that the wheels are free to turn, without binding when the handbrake is released, and then lower the car to the ground.

17 Handbrake cable (front) - removal and refitting

1 Chock the front wheels, jack up the rear of the car and support it securely on axle stands.

2 From under the rear of the car slacken the handbrake cable adjuster to remove all

Fig. 9.8 Layout of the handbrake mechanism (Secs 16 to 20)

1 Brake shoe inspection aperture	4 Compensator assembly	8 Handbrake lever
2 Handbrake cable adjuster	5 Handbrake cable – rear	9 Handbrake cable – intermediate
3 Cable connector	6 Handbrake lever stop	
	7 Handbrake cable – front	

9

tension from the cable. Refer to Section 16, if necessary.

3 From inside the car remove the centre console, as described in Chapter 12.

4 Slide both the front seats fully forward then undo and remove the rear bolts securing the inner seat rails to the floor. Now remove the centre console rear mounting bracket.

5 Undo and remove the seat belt centre stalk mounting bolts and remove the two stalks.

6 Undo and remove the bolt securing the left-hand seat belt to the inner sill. Remove the carpet retaining screws and lift up the rear carpet sufficiently to gain access to the handbrake cable cover plate. Remove the cover plate and seal.

7 Extract the split pin and withdraw the clevis pin securing the handbrake cable to the handbrake lever. Remove the cable from the lever and feed it through the cover plate aperture.

8 Disconnect the front cable from the intermediate cable at the connector and withdraw it from under the car.

9 Refitting the cable is the reverse sequence to removal. Ensure that the seat belt mounting bolts are tightened to the specified torque (Chapter 12) and adjust the cable, as described in Section 16, after refitting.

18 Handbrake cable (intermediate) - removal and refitting

1 Chock the front wheels, jack up the rear of the car and support it securely on axle stands.

2 From under the rear of the car, slacken the handbrake cable adjuster to remove all tension from the cable. Refer to Section 16 if necessary.

3 Disconnect the intermediate cable from the front cable at the connector (photo), release the cable adjuster from its bracket and pull the cable through the bracket.

4 Disconnect both rear cables from the connectors located to the rear of the rear axle transverse member. Release the intermediate cable from its mounting bushes and withdraw it from under the car.

18.3 Handbrake intermediate cable-to-front cable connector located just forward of the fuel tank

5 Refitting is the reverse sequence to removal but adjust the cable, as described in Section 16, after fitting.

19 Handbrake cable (rear) - removal and refitting

1 Chock the front wheels, prise off the rear wheel trim and slacken the wheel nuts. Jack the car up and support it securely on axle stands. Remove the roadwheel.

2 Disconnect the rear cable at the connector just behind the rear axle transverse member.

3 Using circlip pliers, extract the retaining circlip and withdraw the rear cable from its mounting bracket on the rear cable.

4 Refer to Section 6, paragraphs 2 to 4 inclusive, and remove the rear hub and brake drum assembly.

5 With the drum removed, ease the handbrake operating lever on the trailing brake shoe forward and disengage the inner cable nipple from the elongated slot on the lever.

6 Withdraw the cable from the brake backplate and remove the spring collar and felt seal.

7 Refitting is the reverse sequence to removal. Adjust the cable, as described in Section 16, after refitting.

20 Handbrake lever and switch - removal and refitting

1 Refer to Chapter 12, and remove the centre console.

2 If only the warning light switch is to be removed, disconnect the wires from the switch terminals, remove the securing screws and withdraw the switch.

3 To remove the lever assembly, extract the split pin, withdraw the clevis pin and detach the handbrake cable from the lever.

4 Undo and remove the two mounting bolts and lift away the handbrake lever assembly.

5 Refitting is a straightforward reversal of the removal sequence.

21 Footbrake pedal - removal and refitting

1 From inside the car extract the split pin and withdraw the clevis pin and washer securing the servo unit pushrod to the brake pedal.

2 Undo and remove the nut and washer at the clutch pedal end of the pedal pivot bolt.

3 Draw the pivot bolt toward the side of the car to release the clutch pedal. Recover the washer from the pivot shaft (where fitted), unhook the top of the clutch pedal from the cable and withdraw the pedal.

4 Fully remove the pivot bolt and withdraw the brake pedal after detaching the return spring. Where fitted, recover the pivot bolt washers.

5 With the pedal removed, examine the pivot bushes and, if worn, renew them.

6 Refitting the pedals is the reverse sequence to removal. Smear the pivot bolt and bushes with a little lithium-based grease prior to fitting.

22 Stop-light switch - removal. refitting and adjustment

1 To remove the switch, first disconnect the battery negative terminal.

2 Undo and remove the bolts on the right-hand side of the pedal securing the switch bracket in position.

3 Disconnect the wiring connector and remove the switch. Unscrew the switch from the plastic insert.

4 To refit the switch, screw it fully into the plastic insert and position the switch with the terminal in the vertical position.

5 Refit the wiring connector and secure the switch bracket to the pedal bracket with the bolts, finger tight only at this stage.

6 To adjust the switch, reconnect the battery negative terminal and switch on the ignition.

7 Depress the brake pedal by 0.25 in (6 mm) and adjust the switch position so that the stop-lights just come on.

8 Tighten the switch bracket retaining bolts and recheck the stoplight operation.

23 Vacuum servo unit - description

A vacuum servo unit is fitted into the brake hydraulic circuit in series with the master cylinder, to provide assistance to the driver when the brake pedal is depressed. This reduces the effort required by the driver to operate the brakes under all braking conditions.

The unit operates by vacuum obtained from the inlet manifold and comprises basically a booster diaphragm, control valve, and a non-return valve.

The servo unit and hydraulic master cylinder are connected together so that the servo unit piston rod acts as the master cylinder pushrod. The driver's braking effort is transmitted through another pushrod to the servo unit piston and its built-in control system. The servo unit piston does not fit tightly into the cylinder, but has a strong diaphragm to keep its edges in constant contact with the cylinder wall, so ensuring an airtight seal between the two parts. The forward chamber is held under vacuum conditions created in the inlet manifold of the engine and, during periods when the brake pedal is not in use, the controls open a passage to the rear chamber so placing it under vacuum conditions as well. When the brake pedal is depressed, the vacuum passage to the rear chamber is cut off and the chamber opened to atmospheric pressure. The consequent rush of air pushes the servo piston forward in the vacuum chamber and operates the main pushrod to the master cylinder.

24 Vacuum servo unit - removal and refitting

1 Undo and remove the two nuts and washers securing the brake master cylinder to the servo unit. Carefully withdraw the master cylinder, taking great care not to strain the brake pipes, and tie it to one side, just clear of the servo.

2 Using a wide-bladed screwdriver, carefully prise the vacuum hose elbow out of the grommet on the front face of the servo.

3 From inside the car, extract the split pin and withdraw the clevis pin securing the servo pushrod to the brake pedal.

4 Undo and remove the two nuts and washers securing the servo to the bulkhead and withdraw the unit from the engine compartment.

5 Refitting the servo unit is the reverse sequence to removal. Tighten the servo and master cylinder retaining nuts to the specified torque and use a new split pin in the servo pushrod clevis pin.

Fig. 9.9 Vacuum servo unit attachments (Sec 24)

1 Servo unit retaining nuts
2 Clevis pin
3 Split pin
4 Servo pushrod
5 Brake pedal

25 Vacuum servo unit - servicing

1 At the intervals given in Routine Maintenance the servo unit air filter should be renewed as follows. Note that this is the only work that can be carried out on the servo and no attempt should be made to dismantle the unit or alter the setting of the domed nut in the output rod (where fitted).

2 From inside the car, extract the split pin and

Fig. 9.10 Servo unit air filter renewal (Sec 25)

1 Dust cover
2 End cap
3 Filter
4 Position of cut in filter

withdraw the clevis pin securing the servo pushrod to the brake pedal.

3 Pull back the rubber dust cover, release the end cap and extract the old filter. Cut the new filter, as shown in Fig. 9.10, place it over the pushrod and push the filter into the neck of the servo. Refit the end cap and dust cover.

4 To test the operation of the servo, depress the footbrake and then start the engine. As the engine starts there should be a noticeable 'give' in the brake pedal. Allow the engine to run for at least two minutes and then switch it off. If the brake pedal is now depressed again, it should be possible to detect a hiss from the servo when the pedal is depressed. After about four or five applications no further hissing will be heard and the pedal will feel considerably firmer.

Fault finding - braking system

Excessive pedal travel
- [ ] Rear brake self-adjust mechanism inoperative
- [ ] Air in hydraulic system
- [ ] Faulty master cylinder

Brake pedal feels spongy
- [ ] Air in hydraulic system
- [ ] Faulty master cylinder

Judder felt through brake pedal or steering wheel when braking
- [ ] Excessive run-out or distortion of front discs or rear drums
- [ ] Brake pedals or linings worn
- [ ] Brake backplate or disc caliper loose
- [ ] Wear in suspension or steering components or mountings - see Chapter 11

Brakes binding
- [ ] Wheel cylinder or caliper piston seized
- [ ] Handbrake incorrectly adjusted
- [ ] Faulty master cylinder

Excessive pedal pressure required to stop car
- [ ] Faulty servo unit, disconnected, damaged or insecure vacuum hose
- [ ] Wheel cylinder(s) or caliper piston seized
- [ ] Brake pads or brake shoe linings worn or contaminated
- [ ] Brakes shoes incorrectly fitted
- [ ] Incorrect grade of pads or linings fitted
- [ ] Primary or secondary hydraulic circuit failure

Brakes pull to one side
- [ ] Brake pads or linings worn or contaminated
- [ ] Wheel cylinder or caliper piston seized
- [ ] Seized rear brake self-adjust mechanism
- [ ] Brake pads or linings renewed on one side only
- [ ] Faulty twin GP valve
- [ ] Tyre, steering or suspension defect - see Chapter 11

Rear wheels locking under normal braking
- [ ] Rear brake shoe linings contaminated
- [ ] Faulty twin GP valve

9

Notes

Chapter 10 Electrical system

For modifications, and information applicable to later models, see Supplement at end of manual

Contents

Degrees of difficulty

Easy, suitable for novice with little experience	**Fairly easy,** suitable for beginner with some experience	**Fairly difficult,** suitable for competent DIY mechanic	**Difficult,** suitable for experienced DIY mechanic	**Very difficult,** suitable for expert DIY or professional

Specifications

System type . . . . 12 volt, negative earth

Battery

Type . . . . Unipart - 'Sealed for life'
Performance - cold start current (amps)/reserve capacity (minutes)
    1.3 litre models 280/50
    1.6 litre models 360/70

Starter motor

Type:
    1.3 litre models . . . . Lucas 8M90 pre-engaged
    1.6 litre models . . . . Lucas 9M90 pre-engaged
Minimum brush length . . . . 0.4 in (10.0 mm)
Brush spring tension . . . . 32 to 36 ozf (9 to 10 N)
Commutator minimum skimmed thickness . . . . 0.08 in (2.0 mm)
Wiper blades . . . . Champion X-5103 (front) and X-3603 (rear)
Wiper arms . . . . Champion CCA6

10

Alternator

Type	Lucas 127/55
Maximum output	55 amps
Brush length:	
New	0.8 in (20.0 mm)
Minimum	0.4 in (10.0 mm)
Brush spring tension (brush face flush with brushbox)	4.7 to 9.8 ozf (1.3 to 2.7 N)

Relays and control units

Component:	Location
Direction indicator/hazard warning flasher unit	In fusebox on right-hand side of facia
Starter solenoid relay	In fusebox on right-hand side of facia
Ignition auxiliary relay	In fusebox on right-hand side of facia
Heated rear screen relay	In fusebox on right-hand side of facia
Headlamp relay	In fusebox on right-hand side of facia
Inlet manifold heater (if fitted)	In fusebox on right-hand side of facia
Fuel system electronic mixture control unit - ECU	Attached to panel on glovebox roof
Wipe/wash programme control unit	Attached to panel on glovebox roof
Programmed ignition system control unit (if fitted)	Attached to engine compartment left-hand valance
Electric window lift relay and control unit (if fitted)	Behind the driver's door inner trim panel
Central locking control unit (if fitted)	Behind the driver's door inner trim panel

Fuses

Fuse colour coding:	Current rating
Violet	3 amp
Tan	5 amp
Red	10 amp
Blue	15 amp
Natural	25 amp
Green	30 amp
Fusible links:	
Link A	150 mm long, 28/0.3 wire
Link B	200 mm long, 28/0.3 wire
Link C	450 mm long, 14/0.3 wire

Bulbs

	Wattage
Headlamps	60/55
Sidelamps	4
Direction indicators	21
Reverse lamps	21
Stop/tail lamps	21/5
Tail lamps	5
Rear foglamps	21
Number plate lamp	5
Interior and luggage compartment lamps	10
Glovebox lamp	5
Switch illumination	0.36
Selector illumination lamp (automatic transmission models)	3
Instrument panel illumination and warning lamps	1.2
Ignition warning lamp	2
Heater control illumination	0.36 and 1.2

Torque wrench settings

	lbf ft	Nm
Alternator adjustment arm to alternator	18	24
Alternator adjustment arm to engine:		
1.3 litre models	28	38
1.6 litre models	67	91
Alternator pivot mounting bolt:		
1.3 litre models	16	22
1.6 litre models	13	18
Alternator pulley nut	28	38
Battery tray to body	18	24
Starter motor retaining bolts:		
Manual gearbox models	38	52
Automatic transmission models	18	24
Wiper arm retaining nuts	7	9
Wiper motor spindle nuts:		
M18	3	4
Plastic nut	2	3

1   General description

The electrical system is of the 12 volt negative earth type, and consists of a 12 volt battery, alternator, starter motor and related electrical accessories, components and wiring. The battery is of the maintenance free, 'sealed for life' type and is charged by an alternator which is belt-driven from the crankshaft pulley. The starter motor is of the pre-engaged type incorporating an integral solenoid. On starting, the solenoid moves the drive pinion into engagement with the flywheel ring gear before the starter motor is energised. Once the engine has started, a one-way clutch prevents the motor armature being driven by the engine until the pinion disengages from the flywheel.

Further details of the major electrical systems are given in the relevant Sections of this Chapter.

Caution: Before carrying out any work on the vehicle electrical system, read through the precautions given in Safety First! at the beginning of this manual and in Section 2 of this Chapter.

2   Electrical system - precautions

It is necessary to take extra care when working on the electrical system to avoid damage to semi-conductor devices (diodes and transistors), and to avoid the risk of personal injury. In addition to the precautions given in Safety First! at the beginning of this manual, observe the following items when working on the system.

1 *Always remove rings, watches, etc., before working on the electrical system.* Even with the battery disconnected, capacitive discharge could occur if a component live terminal is earthed through a metal object. This could cause a shock or nasty burn.

2 *Do not reverse the battery connections.* Components such as the alternator or any other having semi-conductor circuitry could be irreparably damaged.

3 If the engine is being started using jump leads and a slave battery, connect the batteries *positive to positive and negative to negative.* This also applies when connecting a battery charger.

4 Never disconnect the battery terminals, or alternator multi-plug connector, when the engine is running.

5 The battery leads and alternator multi-plug must be disconnected before carrying out any electric welding on the car.

6 Never use an ohmmeter of the type incorporating a hand-cranked generator for circuit or continuity testing.

7 1.6 litre models are equipped with an inlet manifold heater which will operate whenever the ignition is switched on and the coolant temperature is below 90°F (32°C). Due to the high current consumption of this unit, always disconnect the wiring connector if the ignition is to be left on for any length of time with the engine stopped. Further details will be found in Chapter 3.

3   Maintenance and inspection

1 At regular intervals (see Routine Maintenance) carry out the following maintenance and inspection operations on the electrical system components.

2 Check the operation of all the electrical equipment, ie wipers, washers, lights, direction indicators, horn, etc. Refer to the appropriate Sections of this Chapter if any components are found to be inoperative.

3 Visually check all accessible wiring connectors, harnesses and retaining clips for security, or any signs of chafing or damage. Rectify any problems encountered.

4 Check the alternator drivebelt for cracks, fraying or damage. Renew the belt if worn or, if satisfactory, check and adjust the belt tension. These procedures are covered in Chapter 2.

5 Check the condition of the wiper blades and if they are cracked or show signs of deterioration, renew them, as described in Section 33. Check the operation of the windscreen and headlamp washers (if fitted). Adjust the nozzles using a pin, if necessary.

6 Check the battery terminals and, if there is any sign of corrosion, disconnect and clean them thoroughly. Smear the terminals and battery posts with petroleum jelly before refitting the plastic covers. If there is any corrosion on the battery tray, remove the battery, clean the deposits away and treat the affected metal with an anti-rust preparation. Repaint the tray in the original colour after treatment.

7 Top up the windscreen washer reservoir and check the security of the pump wires and water pipes.

8 It is advisable to have the headlight aim adjusted using optical beam setting equipment.

9 While carrying out a road test check the operation of all the instruments and warning lights, and the operation of the direction indicator self-cancelling mechanism.

10 At less frequent intervals (see Routine Maintenance) renew the alternator drivebelt, as described in Chapter 2.

4   Battery - removal and refitting

1 The sealed for life battery is located on the left-hand side of the engine compartment.

2 To remove the battery, slacken the negative (-) terminal clamp bolt and lift the terminal off the battery post (photo).

3 Lift the plastic cover from the positive (+) terminal, loosen the clamp bolt and lift the terminal off the battery post.

4 Undo and remove the retaining bolt and lift off the battery clamp plate (photo).

5 Withdraw the battery from the carrier tray.

6 Refitting is the reverse sequence to removal, but make sure that the polarity is correct before connecting the leads, and do not overtighten the clamp bolts.

5   Battery - charging

1 In winter when a heavy demand is placed on the battery, such as when starting from cold and using more electrical equipment, it may be necessary to have the battery fully charged from an external source.

2 Charging is best done overnight at a 'trickle' rate of 1 to 1.5 amps. Due to the design of certain maintenance-free batteries, rapid or boost charging is not recommended. If in any doubt about the suitability of certain types of charging equipment for use with maintenance-free batteries, consult a BL dealer or automotive electrical specialist.

3 Battery charging must be carried out with the battery removed from the vehicle and in a well-ventilated area.

4 The terminals of the battery and the leads of the charger must be connected positive to positive and negative to negative.

4.2 Battery terminal identification

4.4 Battery clamp retaining bolt

10

6.2 Alternator wiring multi-plug

Fig. 10.1 Alternator mounting details (Sec 6)

*A 1.3 litre models B 1.6 litre models 1 Pivot mounting bolt 2 Adjustment arm nuts and bolts
Arrows indicate belt tension checking point*

6 Alternator - removal and refitting

1 Disconnect the battery negative terminal.
2 Release the retaining clip and remove the multi-plug from the rear of the alternator (photo).
3 Slacken the adjustment arm bolt and the pivot mounting bolt and move the unit in towards the engine. Slip the drivebelt off the pulleys.
4 Remove the adjustment arm bolt and washers. Remove the pivot bolt, nuts and washers, taking note of the position of any additional spacers. Withdraw the alternator from the engine.

5 Refitting is a reverse of the removal procedure, but before tightening the mounting bolts and the adjustment arm bolt tension the drivebelt, as described in Chapter 2.

7 Alternator - fault tracing and rectification

Due to the specialist knowledge and equipment required to test or repair an alternator, it is recommended that, if the performance is suspect, the car be taken to an automobile electrician who will have the facilities for such work. Because of this recommendation, information is limited to the inspection and renewal of the brushes. Should the alternator not charge, or the system be suspect, the following points should be checked before seeking further assistance:
(a) Check the drivebelt condition and tension
(b) Ensure that the battery is fully charged
(c) Check the ignition warning light bulb, and renew it if blown

8 Alternator brushes - removal, inspection and refitting

1 Remove the alternator, as described in Section 6.
2 Disconnect the electrical lead and remove the suppression capacitor from the rear of the alternator.
3 Undo the retaining screws, lift off the regulator and brushbox assembly and disconnect the electrical lead.
4 Check the brush length and the brush spring tension against the figures given in the Specifications. New brushes are supplied as an assembly complete with brushbox and regulator.
5 Refitting is the reverse sequence to removal.

9 Starter motor - testing in the car

1 If the starter motor fails to operate, first check the condition of the battery by switching on the headlamps. If they glow brightly then gradually dim after a few seconds, the battery is in an uncharged condition.
2 If the battery is satisfactory, check the starter motor main terminal and the engine earth cable for security. Check the terminal connections on the starter solenoid located on top of the starter motor.
3 If the starter still fails to turn, use a voltmeter, or 12 volt test lamp and leads, to ensure that there is battery voltage at the

Fig 10.2 Exploded view of the alternator (Sec 8)

1 Suppression capacitor
2 Regulator and brushbox assembly
3 Slip ring end bracket
4 Bearing
5 Rectifier
6 Phase terminal and washer assembly
7 Main terminal and washer assembly
8 Slip rings
9 Rotor assembly
10 Stator
11 Through-bolts
12 Drive end bracket
13 Spacers
14 Bearing
15 Pulley retaining nut and washer

10.2 Wiring connections at the starter motor solenoid

10.3 Removing the front snubber bracket

11 Starter motor - overhaul

1 Remove the starter motor from the car, as described in the previous Section.
2 At the rear of the solenoid, unscrew the nut and lift away the lead from the solenoid STA terminal.
3 Undo and remove the two screws securing the solenoid to the drive end housing. Disengage the solenoid plunger from the engaging lever and withdraw the solenoid.
4 Withdraw the end cap from the commutator

solenoid main terminal (containing the cable from the battery positive terminal).
4 With the ignition switched on and the ignition key in position III, check that voltage is reaching the solenoid terminal with the Lucar connector, and also the starter main terminal.
5 If there is no voltage reaching the Lucar connector there is a wiring or ignition switch fault. If voltage is available, but the starter does not operate, then the starter or solenoid is likely to be at fault.

10 Starter motor - removal and refitting

1 Disconnect the battery negative terminal.
2 Disconnect the electrical leads at the solenoid terminals noting their respective locations (photo). **Note:** *Take care when disconnecting the leads from the Lucar type terminal connections as they are easily broken. Pull back the cover along the lead to expose the connector, then using a small screwdriver, depress the lock tag in the centre of the connector to release it.*

Manual gearbox models

3 Using a suitable Allen key, undo and remove the two bolts, nuts and washers securing the starter to the gearbox flange and lift the unit off. Note that on 1.6 litre models the starter motor bolts also retain the engine front snubber bracket (photo) and ignition system crankshaft sensor bracket.
4 Refitting the starter motor is the reverse sequence to removal, but tighten the retaining bolts to the specified torque.

Automatic transmission models

5 Jack up the front of the car and securely support it on axle stands.
6 From under the car undo and remove the three bolts securing the starter motor to the transmission and manipulate the motor out from under the car.
7 Refitting is the reverse sequence to removal, but tighten the retaining bolts to the specified torque.

Fig 10.3 Exploded view of the starter motor (Sec 11)

1 Housing retaining screws
2 Drive end housing
5 End cover
6 Solenoid
7 Jump ring
8 Thrust collar
9 Drive assembly
10 Engaging lever and bush
11 Armature
12 Thrust washer
13 Field coil assembly
14 Field brush
15 Commutator end housing
16 Through-bolt
17 Bush
18 'Spire' washer
19 End cap
20 Drive end housing
21 Solenoid
22 Drive and engaging lever assembly
23 Eccentric pivot pin
A Alternative components fitted to automatic transmission models
B Eccentric pivot pin mark and housing arrow alignment

10

end housing and then prise off the spire-retaining washer from the armature shaft.

5 Undo and remove the two through-bolts and withdraw the end housing sufficiently to gain access to the brushes.

6 Release the field brushes from their brushbox locations and then remove the end housing.

7 On models fitted with automatic transmission, slacken the locknut and unscrew the eccentric pivot pin from the drive end housing.

8 Mark the relationship of the field coil assembly to the drive end housing, unscrew the two housing retaining screws and withdraw the drive end housing.

9 Slide the armature and drive assembly out of the field coil assembly.

10 Mount the armature in a vice and, using a suitable tubular drift, tap the thrust collar on the end of the shaft toward the pinion to expose the jump ring. Prise the jump ring out of its groove and slide it off the shaft. Withdraw the thrust collar and the drive assembly.

11 With the starter motor now completely dismantled, clean all the components in paraffin or a suitable solvent and wipe dry.

12 Check the length of the brushes and the tension of the brush springs. If the length and tension are not as given in the Specifications renew the brushes and springs. Note that the field brushes must be soldered in place.

13 Check that the brushes move freely in their holders, and clean the holders and brushes with a petrol-moistened rag if they show any tendency to stick.

> **HAYNES HINT** *Use a fine file on the brushes if they still stick after cleaning.*

14 Check the armature shaft for distortion, and examine the commutator for excessive scoring, wear or burns. If necessary, the commutator may be skimmed in a lathe and then polished with fine glass paper. Make sure that it is not reduced below the specified minimum thickness and do not undercut the mica insulation.

15 Check the taping of the field coils, check all joints for security and check the coils and commutator for signs of burning.

16 Check the drive pinion assembly, drive end housing, engaging lever and solenoid for wear or damage. Make sure that the drive pinion one-way clutch permits movement of the pinion in one direction only and renew the complete assembly, if necessary.

17 Check the condition of the bush in the commutator end housing and, if necessary, renew it. Note that on manual gearbox models the armature is supported at the drive end by a bush in the gearbox housing, and that access to this bush entails removal of the gearbox from the car unless the BL special removing tool can be obtained. Soak the new bushes in engine oil for 24 hours before fitting.

18 Accurate checking of the armature, commutator and field coil windings and insulation requires the use of special test equipment. If the starter motor was inoperative when removed from the car and the previous checks have not highlighted the problem, then it can be assumed that there is a continuity or insulation fault and the unit should be renewed.

19 If the starter is in a satisfactory condition, or if a fault has been traced and rectified, the unit can be reassembled using the reverse of the dismantling procedure. When refitting the eccentric pivot pin (automatic transmission models) screw the pin fully into the housing, unscrew it one full turn then align the mark with the arrow on the housing. Hold the pin in this position and tighten the locknut.

12 Fuses, relays and control units - general

Fuses

1 The fusebox is situated below the facia on the right-hand side, adjacent to the steering column. To gain access to the fusebox, release the two turnbuckles using a coin and lift off the fusebox cover (photo). The fuse locations, current rating and circuits protected are shown on the fusebox cover (photo). Each fuse is colour-coded and has its rating stamped on it.

2 To remove a fuse from its location, hook it out using the small plastic removal tool provided. This is located, together with the spare fuses, in a holder on the left-hand side of the fusebox. Hook the tool over the fuse and pull up to remove. Refit the fuse by pressing it firmly into its location.

3 Always renew a fuse with one of an identical rating. Never renew a fuse more than once without finding the source of the trouble.

4 Circuits protected by fuses C1, C2 and C3 operate when the ignition switch is at positions I or II. Circuits A1, A2, C5 and C6 only operate when the ignition switch is at position II. All other circuits operate irrespective of ignition switch position.

Relays and control units

5 The relays are located in the fusebox under the right-hand side of the facia.

6 The relays can be removed by simply pulling them from their respective locations. If a system controlled by a relay becomes inoperative, and the relay is suspect, operate the system and if the relay is functioning it should be possible to hear it click as it is energized. If the relay is not being energized then the relay is not receiving a main supply voltage, a switching voltage, or the relay itself is faulty.

7 Control units for the wiper delay and fuel system electronic mixture control are located on a panel attached to the roof of the glovebox. Release the two turnbuckles using a coin and lower the panel to gain access (photo).

8 Where applicable, the programmed ignition system control unit will be found on the left-hand valance in the engine compartment. The electric window lift relay and control unit together with the central locking control unit are located inside the driver's door behind the trim panel.

12.1A Fuse and relay locations in the fusebox . . .

12.1B . . . and circuit details on the fusebox cover

12.7 Control unit locations on glovebox roof panel

16.4 Removing the fibre optic guide from the steering column switch bulb housing

16.5 Depress the retainers to release the switch. . .

16.6. . . then disconnect the wiring multi-plugs

13 Fusible link - general

1 Certain electrical circuits on Montego models are protected by fusible links which form the first part of the battery positive (+) cable. The links consist of fusible cable of different thicknesses and lengths according to the circuits they protect. The wire size and fusible link lengths are given in the Specifications.
2 If power to a number of related electrical circuits is lost, the relevant fusible link may be suspect. The circuits protected by the fusible links are as follows.
Link A Ignition circuit
Link B Window lift circuit
Link C Interior lights, lighter, clock circuit
3 To renew a fusible link, disconnect the battery leads then remove the leads from the battery positive (+) terminal.
4 Carefully cut back the binding and pull the sleeve from the cables. Identify the link to be renewed by referring to the Specifications.
5 Remove the joint cover and unsolder the fusible link at both ends.
6 Solder a new fusible link into place and seal the joints with insulating tape. Retape the sleeve to the cables and reconnect the battery terminals.

14 Direction indicator and hazard flasher system - general

1 The flasher unit is located in the fusebox situated under the right-hand side of the facia.
2 Should the flashers become faulty in operation, check the bulbs for security and make sure that the contact surfaces are not corroded. If one bulb blows or is making a poor connection due to corrosion, the system will not flash on that side of the car.
3 If the flasher unit operates in one direction and not the other, the fault is likely to be in the bulbs, or wiring to the bulbs. If the system will not flash in either direction, operate the

hazard flashers. If these function, check for a blown fuse in position C6. If the fuse is satisfactory renew the flasher unit.

15 Ignition switch/steering column lock - removal and refitting

The ignition switch can be separated from the steering column lock (see Chapter 11, Section 19), after extracting the grub screw.

16 Steering column switches - removal and refitting

1 Disconnect the battery negative terminal.
2 Remove the steering wheel, as described in Chapter 11.
3 Undo the retaining screws and lift off the left- and right-hand steering column cowls.
4 Carefully lift up the retaining clip and slip the fibre optic guide out of the bulb housing (photo).
5 Depress the retainers at the top and bottom of the switch then pull the switch out of the steering column boss (photo).
6 Disconnect the wiring multi-plug(s) as applicable and remove the switch (photo).
7 Refitting is the reverse sequence to removal. Position the switch striker bush with the arrow pointing towards the direction indicator switch before refitting the steering wheel.

17.3A . . . undo the two screws (arrowed) . . .

17 Facia switches - removal and refitting

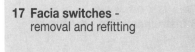

1 Disconnect the battery negative terminal.
2 Undo the retaining screws and withdraw the right-hand steering column cowl from the column (photo). Position the steering wheel so that the spokes are facing away from the cowl to provide sufficient clearance for removal.
3 Undo the two retaining screws and withdraw the switch panel from the facia (photos).
4 Disconnect the wiring multi-plug and push the switch out of the panel.
5 Refitting is the reverse sequence to removal.

17.2 Remove the steering column cowl . . .

10

17.3B . . . then withdraw the switch panel

19.2A Undo the retaining screws . . .

19.2B . . . then withdraw the instrument panel surround and disconnect the clock wiring

19.4 Disconnect the instrument panel wiring multi-plugs

18 Instrumentation - description

Electro-mechanical instrumentation is used on Montego models covered by this manual. On all versions the instrumentation consists of a speedometer, fuel gauge, temperature gauge and driver warning lights. Additionally, according to model, a tachometer, digital clock and additional warning lights for low fuel and high engine temperature may be fitted. A multi-function unit attached to the rear of the instrument panel provides a stabilized 10 volt supply for the instruments and warning lights and controls the tachometer operation, where applicable.

19 Instrument panel and instruments - removal and refitting

1 Disconnect the battery negative terminal.
2 Undo the two retaining screws and ease the instrument panel surround from its location (photo). Disconnect the clock wiring harness plug and remove the surround (photo).
3 Undo the five screws securing the instrument panel mounting brackets to the facia. Ease the panel down slightly and tip it towards the steering wheel at the top.
4 Disconnect the wiring harness multi-plugs

(photo) then reach round behind the panel and disconnect the speedometer cable by pulling the retainer straight from the speedometer head. It may be necessary to push the cable through the bulkhead grommet from the engine compartment side to facilitate removal.
5 Withdraw the instrument panel from the facia.
6 Refitting is the reverse sequence to removal.

20 Instrument panel and instruments - dismantling and reassembly

1 Remove the instrument panel from the car, as described in the previous Section.

Panel illumination and warning lamp bulbs

2 The bulb holders are secured to the rear of the instrument panel by a bayonet fitting and are removed by turning the holders anti-clockwise (photo). Note that only the no-charge warning lamp bulb can be separated from its bulb holder (coloured red). All the other illumination and warning lamp bulbs are renewed complete with their bulb holders.
3 To gain access to the panel front illumination lamp bulb, remove the upper instrument panel mounting bracket (photo).
4 Refit the bulb holders by turning clockwise to lock.

Multi-function unit

5 Undo the three nuts and lift off the multi-function unit cover (photo).
6 Undo the four nuts securing the fuel and temperature gauges and, where fitted, the three nuts securing the tachometer.
7 Undo the multi-function unit retaining screws and withdraw the unit from the instrument panel.
8 Refit the multi-function unit using the reverse sequence to removal.

Printed circuit

9 Remove all the instrument panel warning and illumination bulb holders as previously described.
10 Undo the three nuts and remove the multi-function unit cover.
11 Carefully extract the pegs securing the printed circuit to the instrument panel. Remove the tape, ease the printed circuit off the pegs and studs and lift off.
12 Refitting the printed circuit is the reverse sequence to removal.

Speedometer

13 Release the retaining wires and lift off the instrument panel shroud and window assembly on the front illuminated panel. Note that the two parts will be connected by the printed circuit.
14 Ease the face plate from the case noting that it is secured between the fuel and temperature gauges with double-sided tape.

20.2 Remove the instrument panel bulb holders by turning them anti-clockwise

20.3 Panel mounting bracket retaining nuts (arrowed)

20.5 Multi-function unit cover retaining nuts (arrowed)

20.15 Speedometer retaining screws (arrowed)

Fig. 10.4 Instrument panel connections and component locations (Sec 20)

1 Printed circuit
2 Printed circuit retaining pegs
3 Panel illumination bulbs
4 Speedometer retaining screws
5 Wiring multi-plug connections
6 Warning lamp bulb holders

6A Ignition no-charge warning lamp bulb holder
7 Fuel and temperature gauge retaining nuts
8 Tachometer retaining nuts (where fitted)
9 Multi-function unit

15 Undo the retaining screws and withdraw the speedometer from the instrument panel (photo).
16 Refitting is the reverse sequence to removal, but use new double-sided tape to secure the face plate.

Fuel gauge, temperature gauge and tachometer

17 Carry out the operations described in paragraphs 13 and 14.
18 Undo the retaining nuts and remove the cover from the multifunction unit.
19 Undo the nuts securing the fuel and temperature gauges and, where fitted, the tachometer to the printed circuit and instrument panel .
20 With the panel held face down, carefully remove the instruments. Recover the wavy washers from the gauge studs.

21 Refitting is the reverse sequence to removal bearing in mind the following points:
(a) Ensure that an equal number of wavy washers are positioned on each of the fuel and temperature gauge studs.
(b) Position all the instruments in the panel before tightening the retaining nuts; where fitted, tighten the tachometer retaining nuts first.

21 Clock - removal and refitting

1 Disconnect the battery negative terminal.
2 Undo the two retaining screws and ease the instrument panel surround from its location.
3 Disconnect the clock wiring harness plug and remove the surround.

4 Undo the two screws securing the clock to the surround and carefully lift the clock from its location (photo).
5 The clock time set push rods should not be disturbed. If they become dislodged, the longest legs must be positioned horizontally.
6 Refitting the clock is the reverse sequence to removal. Reset the hour and minute display by depressing first the hour then the minute control buttons using a pencil or ballpoint pen. To zero the display depress both control buttons simultaneously.

22 Headlamp and sidelamp bulbs - renewal

1 From within the engine compartment pull off the wiring connector at the rear of the headlamp bulb (photo).
2 Slip off the rubber cover to gain access to the bulbs (photo).

Headlamp bulb

3 Release the bulb retaining clip and withdraw the bulb from its location in the headlamp (photos). Take care not to touch the bulb glass with your fingers; if touched, clean the bulb with methylated spirits.
4 Fit the bulb ensuring that the lugs on the bulb engage with the slots in the headlamp.

10

21.4 Clock retaining screws (arrowed)

22.1 Disconnect the headlamp bulb wiring connector . . .

22.2. . . then slip off the rubber cover

22.3A Release the headlamp bulb retaining clip

22.3B . . . and withdraw the bulb

22.6 The sidelamp bulb holder is a push fit in the lens assembly

5 Refit the retaining clip, rubber cover and wiring connector.

Sidelamp bulb

6 Withdraw the bulb holder from the headlamp and remove the bulb from the holder by turning anti-clockwise (photo).
7 Fit the new bulb to the holder, push the holder into the headlamp and refit the rubber cover.

23 Headlamp lens assembly - removal and refitting

1 From within the engine compartment, pull off the wiring connector at the rear of the headlamp bulb.

24.1A Release the direction indicator lamp body spring retainer . . .

2 Slip off the rubber cover then withdraw the sidelamp bulb holder.
3 Undo the two nuts securing the top of the lens unit to the body, release the two lower plastic ball pegs from their sockets and remove the assembly from the car.
4 Remove the headlamp bulb from the lens assembly if required, as described in the previous Section.
5 Refitting is the reverse sequence to removal, but have the headlamp aim adjusted using optical beam setting equipment (see Section 32).

24 Front direction indicator bulb - renewal

1 Working in the engine compartment, release the spring retainer (photo) and ease the lamp body and seal from the body panel (photo). Release the bulb holder by turning anti-clockwise.
2 Remove the bulb from the holder by turning anti-clockwise.
3 Fit the bulb and holder to the lamp body, locate the lamp flange behind the panel and push the unit into position. Make sure the seal seats correctly.
4 Secure the lamp body with the spring retainer.

25 Rear lamp cluster bulbs - renewal

1 Working in the luggage compartment, press and disengage the retainers then withdraw the bulb panel from the lens unit (photos).
2 The bulb can now be removed from the panel as required. All the bulbs except the tail lamp bulb are removed by turning them anti-clockwise. The tail lamp bulb is a push fit.
3 Fit the bulbs and bulb panel using the reverse sequence to removal.

26 Number plate lamp bulb - renewal

1 Push the lens housing forward and lift up to release it from the bumper (photo).
2 Turn the bulb holder anti-clockwise and withdraw it from the lens housing. The bulb is a push fit in the holder.
3 Refit using the reverse sequence to removal.

27 Interior courtesy lamp bulbs - renewal

1 Carefully ease the lamp lens from its location and then withdraw the bulb by turning anti-clockwise.
2 Fit the bulb and push the unit into place.

24.1B . . . to gain access to the bulb holder and bulb

25.1A Depress the plastic retainers . . .

25.1B . . . then withdraw the rear lamp cluster bulb panel

26.1 Push the lens housing forward and lift to release from bumper

Fig. 10.5 Interior courtesy lamp bulb and holder arrangement (Sec 27)

29.2 Switch panel bulbs located in wiring multi-plug

28 Instrument panel illumination and warning lamp bulbs - renewal

Refer to Section 20.

29 Switch illumination bulbs - renewal

1 Remove the facia switch panel, as described in Section 17, to gain access to the illumination bulbs.
2 With the wiring multi-plug disconnected, remove the relevant bulb which is a push fit in the holder (photo).
3 To renew the hazard warning switch bulb, lift off the switch lens and remove the push-fit bulb (photo).
4 Refitting is the reverse sequence to removal.

30 Heater control illumination bulbs - removal

1 Carefully prise off the switch blanking plate on the right-hand side of the heater control knobs.
2 Undo the retaining screw located behind the switch blanking plate (photo).
3 Centralize the heater control knobs and

ease the control panel, complete with knobs, off the facia.
4 Disconnect the switch multi-plug to gain access to the push-fit bulbs.
5 The panel illumination bulb holder and bulb are removed by turning anti-clockwise (photo).
6 Refitting is the reverse sequence to removal.

31 Selector lever illumination bulbs (automatic transmission models) - renewal

1 Remove the centre console sufficiently to gain access to the bulbs, using the procedure given in Chapter 12.
2 Pull the relevant bulb holder from the side of the selector housing and remove the push-fit bulb.
3 Refitting is the reverse sequence to removal.

32 Headlamp aim - adjustment

1 At regular intervals (see Routine Maintenance) headlamp aim should be checked and, if necessary, adjusted.

Fig. 10.6 Selector lever illumination bulb location (Sec 31)

1 Console retaining screws
2 Centre console
3 Illumination bulb holder

2 Due to the light pattern of the homofocal headlamp lenses fitted to Montego models, optical beam setting equipment must be used to achieve satisfactory aim of the headlamps. It is recommended therefore that this work be entrusted to a BL dealer.

33 Wiper blades and arms - removal and refitting

Wiper blades

1 The wiper blades should be renewed when they no longer clean the windscreen effectively.
2 Lift the wiper arm away from the window.

29.3 Lift off the switch lens to renew the hazard warning switch bulb

10

30.5 Heater panel illumination bulbs located in wiring multi-plug (A) and at rear of panel (B)

30.2 Undo the heater control panel retaining screw (arrowed)

33.3 Release the catch and separate the wiper blade from the arm

33.5 Lift the hinged cover to gain access to the wiper arm retaining nut

35 Windscreen wiper linkage - removal and refitting

3 Release the spring retaining catch and separate the blade from the wiper arm (photo).
4 Insert the new blade into the arm, making sure that the spring retainer catch is engaged correctly.

Wiper arms

5 To remove a wiper arm, open the bonnet, lift the hinged cover and unscrew the retaining nut (photo).
6 Carefully prise the arm off the spindle.
7 Before refitting the arm switch the wipers on and off, allowing the mechanism to return to the park position.
8 Noting that the longer arm is fitted to the driver's side, refit the arm to the spindle with the blade positioned on the finisher at the bottom edge of the windscreen.
9 Refit and tighten the retaining nut then close the hinged cover.

34 Windscreen wiper motor - removal and refitting

1 Disconnect the battery negative terminal.
2 Undo the screws securing the washer reservoir in place and move the reservoir to one side.
3 Pull the rubber edge seal off the top of the closure panel, undo the retaining screws and lift away the panel (photo).

4 Remove the wiper arms, as described in Section 33.
5 Undo the retaining nut and remove the wiper linkage rotary link from the motor spindle (photo).
6 Undo the three bolts securing the wiper motor mounting bracket to the bulkhead.
7 Ease the motor assembly out of its fitted position and prise the wiring harness grommet out of the bulkhead.
8 From inside the car, open the glovebox lid and lower the relay panel from the roof of the glovebox.
9 Identify the wiper motor wiring harness (coloured grey) and disconnect the multi-plugs.
10 Pull the wiring harness through the bulkhead and remove the wiper motor assembly from its location.
11 Refitting is the reverse sequence to removal, bearing in mind the following points:
(a) *Before reconnecting the linkage to the motor spindle, switch the wipers on and then off again to set the motor in the 'park' position. Apply silicone grease to the rotary link and gimbal, hold the primary link and turn the rotary link anti-clockwise to set the cam in its extended position. Hold the primary link and rotary link in a straight line, as shown in Fig. 10.7, and refit the link to the wiper motor spindle*
(b) *Switch the wipers on and off once more so that the linkage is in the 'park' position then refit the wiper arms, as described in Section 33*

1 Disconnect the battery negative terminal.
2 Undo the screws securing the washer reservoir in place and move the reservoir to one side.
3 Pull the rubber edge seal off the top of the closure panel, undo the retaining screws and lift away the panel.
4 Remove the wiper arms, as described in Section 33.
5 Carefully prise the primary link arm socket off the rotary link assembly.
6 Remove the wiper spindle sealing covers followed by the retaining nuts, washers and upper spacers.
7 Push the wiper spindles through the body then withdraw the linkage assembly and central water shield from the engine compartment.
8 Remove the central water shield and lower spindle spacers.
9 Refitting is the reverse sequence to removal, bearing in mind the following points:
(a) *Apply silicone grease to the primary link ball and socket then press the two parts together, using a lightly adjusted self-locking wrench*
(b) *Switch the wipers on and off to set the linkage in the 'park' position then refit the wiper arms as described in Section 33*

36 Windscreen wiper primary link - removal and refitting

1 Disconnect the battery negative terminal.
2 Undo the screws securing the washer reservoir in place and move the reservoir to one side.
3 Pull the rubber edge seal off the top of the closure panel, undo the retaining screws and lift away the panel.
4 Carefully prise the primary link arm socket off the rotary link assembly.
5 Undo the retaining nut and remove the rotary link from the wiper motor spindle.

34.3A Undo the retaining screws . . .

34.3B . . . and lift out the closure panel

34.5 Wiper linkage rotary link retaining nut (A) and motor bracket retaining bolts (B)

37.2 Windscreen washer reservoir and pump locations

Fig. 10.7 Windscreen wiper motor and linkage layout (Secs 34, 35 and 36)

1 Wiper blade and arm
2 Wiper arm retaining nut
3 Wiper arm
4 Sealing cover
5 Spindle retaining nut and washer
6 Upper spacer
7 Lower spacer
8 Wiper spindle
9 Wiper arm stop
10 Drive link assembly
11 Primary link arm
12 Rotary link assembly
13 Rotary link retaining nut
14 Wiper motor mounting bracket
15 Mounting bracket retaining bolt and washers
16 Wiper motor

6 To refit the primary link, reconnect the battery then switch the wipers on and off again to set the motor in the 'park' position.
7 Hold the primary link and turn the rotary link anti-clockwise to position the cam in the fully extended position.
8 Hold the primary and rotary link together in a straight line, as shown in Fig. 10.7, then refit the rotary link to the wiper motor spindle. Refit and tighten the retaining nut.
9 Apply silicone grease to the primary link ball and socket then press the two parts together, using a lightly adjusted self-locking wrench.
10 With the windscreen wet, check the operation of the wipers; ensuring that they 'park' on the finisher at the bottom edge of the

windscreen. If necessary adjust the wiper arm position, as described in Section 33.
11 Refit the closure panel, edge seal and washer reservoir.

37 Windscreen washer reservoir and pump - removal and refitting

1 Undo the retaining screws and withdraw the reservoir from its location.
2 Disconnect the washer pump wiring connectors and water hoses then remove the reservoir from the car (photo).

3 To remove the pump(s) from the reservoir, lift the pump and pull the inlet nozzle from the seal. Withdraw the pump from the reservoir.
4 Refitting is the reverse sequence to removal.

38 Headlamp washer jet - removal and refitting

1 From within the front bumper panel disconnect the hose from the washer extension tube.
2 Undo the retaining nut, remove the seating collar and withdraw the washer jet assembly.
3 Refitting is the reverse sequence to removal.

39 Horn - removal and refitting

1 Disconnect the battery negative terminal.
2 Working under the left-hand front wing, disconnect the electrical leads, undo the retaining nut and remove the horn from its bracket.
3 The horn is a sealed unit which cannot be dismantled or adjusted. In the event of horn failure, renewal will be necessary.

40 Speedometer cable - removal and refitting

10

1 Refer to Section 19, paragraphs 1 to 4 inclusive and detach the speedometer cable from the instrument panel.
2 Release the grommet from the bulkhead and pull the cable through into the engine compartment.
3 Undo the bolt securing the cable retaining plate to the transmission and withdraw the cable and pinion.
4 Release the cable clips and remove the cable from the car.
5 Refitting the cable is the reverse sequence to removal.

41 Radio, radio/cassette player - removal and refitting

1 Disconnect the battery negative terminal.
2 Pull off the knobs and bezels from the radio or radio/cassette player controls, unscrew the retaining nuts and lift off the finisher and masking plate.
3 Push the unit back into its aperture and remove the mounting plate from inside the panel.
4 Withdraw the unit, disconnect the wiring, speaker and aerial leads then remove it from the car.
5 Refitting is the reverse sequence to removal.

42 Electrically-operated windows - description

Certain Montego models covered by this manual are available with electrically-operated front windows as optional equipment. The system enables both front windows to be raised or lowered independently by two switches on the driver's door armrest. A single switch on the passenger's door armrest allows independent operation of the passenger's window. A 'one-touch' facility incorporated in the driver's door switch circuitry allows the driver's window to be raised or lowered fully when the switch is pressed fully then released.

Each window is operated by an electric motor acting on the window regulator. A relay mounted within the driver's door controls the electrical supply to the circuit and a thermal cut-out in each motor isolates the circuit should any object jam the window during operation.

43 Window lift motor - removal and refitting

1 Remove the front door inner trim panel, as described in Chapter 12.
2 If the door window is not closed, temporarily reconnect the switch multi-plugs and the battery and close the window.
3 Undo the retaining screws and remove the inner trim panel mounting bracket.
4 Carefully remove the polythene condensation barrier from the door.
5 Support the window in the raised position using wooden wedges then undo the three nuts securing the motor unit to the door.
6 Release the three nylon wheels of the lift arms from the lifting channel and auxiliary channel.
7 Operate the motor so that the lift arms are

set in the fully lowered position. Disconnect the switch wiring multi-plug and manoeuvre the motor unit out of the door aperture.
8 Refitting is the reverse sequence to removal, bearing in mind the following points.
(a) Lubricate the lifting and auxiliary channels with graphite grease
(b) Install the motor unit with the lifting arms in the lowered position then engage the nylon wheels of the arms into the channels with the arms in the raised position
(c) With the motor unit installed, check the operation of the window and adjust the lower ends of the window channels if necessary
(d) Ensure that all wiring is neatly secured in its clips

44 Window lift 'one-touch' control unit - removal and refitting

1 Remove the front door inner trim panel, described in Chapter 12. Carefully peel back the polythene condensation barrier as necessary, starting at the lower front corner of the door.
2 Disconnect the wiring multi-plug, undo the retaining screws and withdraw the control unit from inside the door.
3 Refitting is the reverse sequence to removal.

45 Central door locking - description

A central door locking system is available as an option on certain Montego models covered by this manual. The system enables the passenger's front door lock, both rear door locks and the boot lid lock to be operated simultaneously by the action of the driver's door interior lock button or exterior private lock.

The passenger's door, both rear doors and the boot lid each incorporate a solenoid which is connected to the lock mechanism.

The driver's door is equipped with the normal private lock and interior lock button arrangement and is also fitted with a control unit. Operation of the driver's door lock causes the control unit to supply an electric current to each of the door lock solenoids, thus locking or unlocking the doors in unison with the driver's door.

46 Central locking solenoid - removal and refitting

1 To remove a passenger door solenoid or driver's door control unit, first remove the inner trim panel from the relevant door, as described in Chapter 12.

Fig. 10.8 Electric window and central locking door compartment locations (Secs 43 to 46)

1 Window auxiliary channel retaining screws	4 Inner trim panel retainers	8 Inner trim panel mounting bracket
2 Speaker wiring connector	5 Window lift relay	9 Window lift motor
3 Window lift 'one-touch' control unit	6 Window lift multi-plugs	10 Central locking switch unit
	7 Inner trim panel retaining studs	11 Interior light door switch

2 If the door window is not closed, temporarily reconnect the switch multi-plugs and battery if electrically-operated windows are fitted, and close the window.

3 Undo the retaining screws and remove the inner trim panel mounting bracket.

4 Carefully remove the polythene condensation barrier from the door.

5 Undo the retaining screws, disconnect the wiring multi-plug and cable clips then lift the solenoid or control unit off the door panel. Detach the lock lever link and remove the unit.

6 Refitting is the reverse sequence to removal.

47 Boot lock solenoid - removal and refitting

1 Disconnect the battery negative terminal.

2 Open the boot lid and undo the nut securing the solenoid mounting plate to the lock barrel. Remove the lock barrel.

3 Disconnect the wiring multi-plug then position the solenoid mounting plate in the left-hand boot lid aperture.

4 Undo the retaining screws and withdraw the solenoid from behind the mounting plate.

5 Refitting is the reverse sequence to removal.

48 Accessory wiring - general

1 If an electrical accessory is to be fitted, electrical connections should be made at the

Fig. 10.9 Wiring harness connections for towing bracket installation (Sec 48)

1 Left-hand tail lamps	5 Earth point	9 Interior lamp (live feed)
2 Left-hand indicator	6 Right-hand tail lamps	10 Flasher unit relay
3 Stop lamps	7 Right-hand rear foglamp	connector
4 Left-hand rear foglamp	8 Right-hand indicator	

Cable colour code

B Black	N Brown	P Purple	U Blue	Y Yellow
G Green	O Orange	R Red	W White	

The second code letter indicates the tracer colour

fusebox, on the feed side of the following fuses.

(a) If the accessory is to operate through the ignition switch, connect to fuse C1, C2 or C3 (light green/white wire)

(b) If the accessory is to operate independently of the ignition switch, connect to fuse A6 (brown wire)

2 Always use a separate line fuse of the appropriate rating to protect the accessory being fitted.

3 To avoid the risk of damage resulting from overloading the vehicle electrical circuits, **do** **not** plug any accessory into the cigarette lighter socket unless it is approved by BL for such fitment.

4 For towing bracket installations, connection for the towing socket can be made at the wiring harness behind the rear light clusters. To gain access, fold back the floor covering and release the rear of the side panel covers. The cable colours, locations and their respective circuits are shown in Fig. 10.9. Note: a special plug-in type relay is also required. Always disconnect the battery negative terminal before making any wiring conections.

Fault Finding commences overleaf

10

Fault finding - electrical system

Starter fails to turn engine

- [ ] Battery discharged or defective
- [ ] Battery terminal and/or earth leads loose
- [ ] Starter motor connections loose
- [ ] Starter solenoid faulty
- [ ] Starter brushes worn or sticking
- [ ] Starter commutator dirty or worn
- [ ] Starter field coils earthed
- [ ] Starter inhibitor switch faulty (automatic transmission only)

Starter turns engine very slowly

- [ ] Battery discharged
- [ ] Starter motor connections loose
- [ ] Starter brushes worn or sticking

Starter spins but does not turn engine

- [ ] Pinion or flywheel ring gear teeth broken or badly worn
- [ ] Starter pinion sticking

Starter noisy

- [ ] Pinion or flywheel ring gear teeth badly worn
- [ ] Mounting bolts loose

Battery will not hold charge for more than a few days

- [ ] Battery defective internally
- [ ] Battery terminals loose
- [ ] Alternator drivebelt slipping
- [ ] Alternator or regulator faulty
- [ ] Short circuit

Ignition light stays on

- [ ] Alternator faulty
- [ ] Alternator drivebelt broken

Ignition light fails to come on

- [ ] Warning bulb blown
- [ ] Indicator light open circuit
- [ ] Alternator faulty

Instrument readings increase with engine speed

- [ ] Faulty instrument multi-function unit

Fuel or temperature gauge gives no reading

- [ ] Wiring open circuit
- [ ] Sender or thermistor faulty
- [ ] Faulty instrument multi-function unit

Fuel or temperature gauge gives continuous maximum reading

- [ ] Wiring short circuit
- [ ] Sender or thermistor faulty
- [ ] Faulty instrument multi-function unit
- [ ] Faulty gauge

Lights inoperative

- [ ] Bulb blown
- [ ] Fuse blown
- [ ] Fusible link blown
- [ ] Battery discharged
- [ ] Switch faulty
- [ ] Relay faulty
- [ ] Wiring open circuit
- [ ] Bad connection due to corrosion

Failure of component motor

- [ ] Commutator dirty or burnt
- [ ] Armature faulty
- [ ] Brushes sticking or worn
- [ ] Armature bearings dry or misaligned
- [ ] Field coils faulty
- [ ] Fuse blown
- [ ] Relay faulty
- [ ] Fusible link blown
- [ ] Poor or broken wiring connections

Failure of an individual component

- [ ] Fuse blown
- [ ] Relay faulty
- [ ] Fusible link blown
- [ ] Poor or broken wiring connections
- [ ] Switch faulty
- [ ] Component faulty

Chapter 11 Suspension and steering

For modifications, and information applicable to later models, see Supplement at end of manual

Contents

Degrees of difficulty

Easy, suitable for novice with little experience	Fairly easy, suitable for beginner with some experience	Fairly difficult, suitable for competent DIY mechanic	Difficult, suitable for experienced DIY mechanic	Very difficult, suitable for expert DIY or professional

Specifications

Front suspension

Type .... Independent by MacPherson struts with coil springs and integral telescopic shock absorbers. Anti-roll bar on 1.6 litre models only

Coil spring free length:
    1.3 litre models (white spring) .... 14.48 in (368.0 mm)
    1.6 litre models:
        Manual gearbox (purple spring) .... 14.72 in (373.9 mm)
        Automatic transmission (yellow spring) .... 15.16 in (385.1 mm)
Trim height (measured from the centre of the front hub
to the edge of the wheel arch) .... 14.7 to 16.0 in (375.0 to 405.0 mm)
Trim height permissible side difference .... 1.02 in (26.0 mm)

Rear suspension

Type .... Trailing twist axle with coil springs and telescopic shock absorbers
Coil spring free length .... 13.5 in (343.0 mm)
Trim height (measured from the centre of the rear hub to the edge
of the wheel arch):
    Up to VIN 131623 .... 13.9 to 15.1 in (352.0 to 382.0 mm)
    From VIN 131624 .... 14.5 to 15.7 in (368.0 to 398.0 mm)
Trim height permissible side difference .... 1.02 in (26.0 mm)
Rear wheel toe setting .... 0°20' to 0°40' toe-in
Rear wheel camber angle .... 0° to 1° negative

Steering

Type .... Rack and pinion
Turns lock to lock 4.3
Steering wheel diameter .... 15 in (381.0 mm)
Camber angle .... 0°05' negative to 0°26' negative
Castor angle .... 0°30' positive to 1°30' positive
Steering axis inclination .... 12°0' to 13°0'
Toe setting .... Parallel ± 0°8'
Steering gear lubricant .... Semi-fluid grease (Duckhams Adgear 00)

Roadwheels

Wheel size:
1.3 litre models	5.00J x 13
1.6 litre models	120 x 365 mm 'TD' type

Tyres

Tyre size:
1.3 litre models	165 SR 13 steel braced radial ply
1.6 litre models	180/65 R365 'TD' type steel braced radial ply

Tyre pressures (cold):	**Front**	**Rear**
Saloon	26 lbf/in^2 (1.8 bar)	28 lbf/in^2 (1.9 bar)
Estate	28 lbf/in^2 (1.9 bar)	31 lbf/in^2 (2.1 bar)

When fully loaded, or for high speed use, increase the front pressure by 3.0 lbf/in^2 (0.2 bar) and the rear pressure by 2.0lbf/in^2 (0.1 bar) for Saloons or 7.0 lbf/in^2 (0.5 bar) for Estates

Torque wrench settings

	lbf ft	Nm
Front suspension		
Anti-roll bar bush to lower arm:		
10 mm nut	13	18
12 mm nut	30	41
Anti-roll bar clamp bolts	33	45
Balljoint-to-lower arm (service replacement bolts)	22	30
Balljoint-to-swivel hub clamp nut	33	45
Driveshaft nut*	150	203
Suspension strut-to-swivel hub nuts	66	90
Suspension strut upper retaining nut	41	56
Suspension strut bearing retaining nut	33	45
Lower arm rear mounting bolts	30	41
Lower arm front mounting bolt	53	72
Subframe to body	67	91
Subframe supports to body	55	75
Subframe supports to subframe	67	91
Refer to Chapter 13, Section 10		
Rear suspension		
Rear axle pivot bolts (marked '8.8')	41	56
Rear axle pivot bolts (marked '10.9')	63	85
Rear hub retaining nut	50	68
Stub axle-to-trailing arm nuts	39	53
Suspension strut lower mounting	55	75
Suspension strut upper mounting nut	33	45
Suspension strut spring retainer nut	18	24
Steering		
Steering column mounting bolts	18	24
Intermediate shaft clamp nuts	18	24
Rack and pinion assembly mounting bolts	33	45
Steering wheel nut	35	47
Steering wheel bolt	24	33
Tie-rod inner balljoint to rack	60	81
Tie-rod outer balljoint to steering arm	22	30
Roadwheels		
Wheel nuts (all models)	53	72

1 General description

The independent front suspension is of the MacPherson strut type, incorporating coil springs and integral telescopic shock absorbers. Lateral and longitudinal location of each strut assembly is by pressed steel lower suspension arms utilizing rubber inner mounting bushes and incorporating a balljoint at their outer ends. On 1.6 litre models both lower suspension arms are interconnected by an anti-roll bar. The front swivel hubs, which carry the wheel bearings, brake calipers and the hub/disc assemblies, are bolted to the MacPherson struts and connected to the lower arms via the balljoints.

The rear suspension is of the trailing twist axle type, whereby the two trailing arms are welded to an 'L' section transverse member. This arrangement allows considerable independent up-and-down movement of each trailing arm whilst providing lateral rigidity and anti-roll capability in a structure of minimum unsprung weight. Suspension and damping is by strut assemblies containing coil springs and integral telescopic shock absorbers.

The steering gear is of the conventional rack and pinion type, located behind the front wheels. Movement of the steering wheel is transmitted to the steering gear by an intermediate shaft containing two universal joints. The front wheels are connected to the steering gear by tie-rods, each having an inner and outer balljoint.

23 Upper bearing
24 Spring seat
25 Spring aid
26 Upper insulator ring
27 Rubber boot
28 Strut-to-swivel hub retaining
   bolt
29 Bearing water shield
30 Inner oil seal
31 Oil seal spacer
32 Hub inner bearing
33 Brake caliper mounting bolt
34 Disc shield retaining screw
   and clip
35 Lower balljoint clamp bolt
36 Swivel hub
37 Hub outer bearing
38 Outer oil seal
39 Disc shield halves
40 Disc shield retaining bolt
41 Wheel stud
42 Drive flange
43 Brake disc
44 Disc retaining screw
45 Flat washer
46 Driveshaft nut
47 Split pin
48 Wheel nut
49 Bleed screw
50 Caliper retaining (guide pin)
   bolt
51 Caliper body
52 Inner brake pad
53 Outer brake pad
54 Piston
55 Guide pin
56 Dust cover
57 Piston dust cover
58 Anchor bracket

1 Anti-roll bar
2 Mounting block
3 Clamp
4 Clamp retaining bolts
5 Lower arm front mounting bolt
6 Rubber bush
7 Lower suspension arm
8 Anti-roll bar mounting bush
9 Lower suspension arm
   balljoint
10 Rivet (replaced by nut and
   bolt after balljoint renewal)
11 Front suspension strut
12 Lower insulator ring
13 Rubber bush
14 Rear mounting bracket
15 Mounting bolt
16 Coil spring
17 Upper mounting nut
18 Washer
19 Cup and washer assembly
20 Upper mounting rubber
21 Bearing retainer nut
22 Bearing housing

Fig. 11.1 Exploded view of the front suspension (Sec 1)

1 Pivot bolt
2 Pivot bush
3 Rear axle
4 Suspension strut
   lower mounting
   bolt
5 Rear suspension
   strut spindle
6 Rubber boot
7 Spring aid
8 Circlip
9 Spring aid
   retaining collar
10 Coil spring
11 Insulator ring
12 Spring seat
13 Large mounting
   rubber
14 Spacer
15 Spring retainer nut
16 Small mounting
   rubber

17 Flat washer
18 Upper mounting
   nut
19 Stub axle retaining
   nut
20 Stub axle
21 Wheel cylinder
   retaining bolt
22 Brake shoe hold-
   down pin
23 Inspection plug
24 Brake backplate
25 Wheel cylinder
   mounting seal
26 Bleed screw
27 Wheel cylinder
28 Brake self-adjust
   mechanism
29 Trailing brake
   shoe
30 Leading brake
   shoe

31 Brake shoe hold-
   down spring
32 Brake shoe return
   spring
33 Handbrake lever
34 Brake shoe return
   spring
35 Backplate retaining
   stud
36 Brake shoe return
   spring
37 Hub oil seal

38 Hub inner
   bearing
39 Spacer
40 Wheel stud
41 Brake drum
42 Hub outer
   bearing
43 Flat washer
44 Hub retaining
   nut
45 Split pin
46 Hub cap
47 Wheel nut

Fig. 11.2 Exploded view of the rear suspension (Sec 1)

11

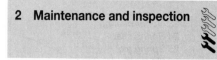

2 Maintenance and inspection

1 At the intervals given in Routine Maintenance at the beginning of this manual a thorough inspection of all suspension and steering components should be carried out using the following procedure as a guide.

Front suspension and steering

2 Apply the handbrake, jack up the front of the car and support it securely on axle stands.
3 Visually inspect the lower balljoint dust covers and the steering rack and pinion gaiters for splits, chafing, or deterioration. Renew the rubber gaiters or the balljoint assembly, as described in Sections 21 and 8 respectively, if any damage is apparent.
4 Grasp the roadwheel at the 12 o'clock and 6 o'clock positions and try to rock it. Very slight free play may be felt, but if the movement is appreciable further investigation is necessary to determine the source. Continue rocking the wheel while an assistant depresses the footbrake. If the movement is now eliminated or significantly reduced, it is likely that the hub bearings are at fault. If the free play is still evident with the footbrake depressed, then there is wear in the suspension joints or mountings. Pay close attention to the lower balljoint and lower arm mounting bushes. Renew any worn components, as described in the appropriate Sections of this Chapter.
5 Now grasp the wheel at the 9 o'clock and

3.3 Remove the driveshaft nut and washer

3 o'clock positions and try to rock it as before. Any movement felt now may again be caused by wear in the hub bearings or the steering tie-rod inner or outer balljoints. If the outer balljoint is worn the visual movement will be obvious. If the inner joint is suspect, it can be felt by placing a hand over the rack and pinion rubber gaiter and gripping the tie-rod. If the wheel is now rocked, movement will be felt at the inner joint if wear has taken place. Repair procedures are described in Sections 20 and 23.
6 Using a large screwdriver or flat bar check for wear in the anti-roll bar mountings (where fitted) and lower arm mountings by carefully levering against these components. Some movement is to be expected, as the mountings are made of rubber, but excessive wear should be obvious. Renew any bushes that are worn.
7 With the car standing on its wheels, have an assistant turn the steering wheel back and forth about one eighth of a turn each way. There should be no lost movement whatever between the steering wheel and roadwheels. If this is not the case, closely observe the joints and mountings previously described, but in addition check the intermediate shaft universal joints for wear and also the rack and pinion steering gear itself. Any wear should be visually apparent and must be rectified, as described in the appropriate Sections of this Chapter.

Rear suspension

8 Chock the front wheels, jack up the rear of the car and support it securely on axle stands.
9 Visually inspect the rear suspension components, attachments and linkages for any visible signs of wear or damage.
10 Grasp the roadwheel at the 12 o'clock and 6 o'clock positions and try to rock it. Any excess movement here indicates wear in the hub bearings which may also be accompanied by a rumbling sound when the wheel is spun. Repair procedures are described in Section 11.

Wheels and tyres

11 Carefully inspect each tyre, including the spare, for signs of uneven wear, lumps, bulges or damage to the sidewalls or tread face. Refer to Section 25 for further details.
12 Check the condition of the wheel rims for distortion, damage and excessive run-out.

Also make sure that the balance weights are secure with no obvious signs that any are missing. Check the torque of the wheel nuts and check the tyre pressures.

Shock absorbers

13 Check for any signs of fluid leakage around the shock absorber body or from the rubber boot around the piston rod. Should any fluid be noticed the shock absorber is defective internally and renewal is necessary.
14 The efficiency of the shock absorber may be checked by bouncing the car at each corner. Generally speaking the body will return to its normal position and stop after being depressed. If it rises and returns on a rebound, the shock absorber is probably suspect. Examine also the shock absorber upper and lower mountings for any sign of wear. Renewal procedures are contained in Sections 6 and 14.

3 Front swivel hub assembly - removal and refitting

1 Securely apply the handbrake, chock the rear wheels and remove the wheel trim from the front roadwheel.
2 Extract the split pin, then, using a socket and long bar, slacken, but do not remove, the driveshaft nut.
3 Slacken the roadwheel retaining nuts then jack up the front of the car and support it securely on axle stands. Remove the roadwheel. Remove the driveshaft retaining nut and washer (photo).
4 Undo and remove the two bolts securing the disc brake caliper to the anchor bracket (photo). Slide the caliper, complete with brake pads, off the anchor bracket (photo), and suspend it from a convenient place under the wheel arch using string or wire. Take care not to strain the flexible hydraulic hose.
5 Undo and remove the nut securing the tie-rod balljoint to the steering arm on the swivel hub. Release the balljoint from the steering arm using a suitable extractor (see Section 20).
6 At the base of the swivel hub unscrew and remove the nut and washer, withdraw the lower balljoint clamp bolt (photo).

3.4A Brake caliper-to-anchor bracket upper retaining bolt (arrowed)

3.4B Remove the caliper and brake pads from the anchor bracket

3.6 Undo the nut and withdraw the lower balljoint clamp bolt (arrowed)

3.7 Remove the two nuts and bolts (arrowed) securing the swivel hub to the suspension strut

3.8 Withdraw the hub assembly from the driveshaft

3.9A Remove the brake caliper anchor bracket

7 Undo and remove the nuts and washers, then withdraw the two bolts securing the suspension strut to the upper part of the swivel hub (photo) .

8 Release the swivel hub from the strut and then lift the hub, while pushing down on the suspension arm, to disengage the lower balljoint. Withdraw the swivel hub assembly from the driveshaft and remove it from the car (photo).

Fig. 11.3 Cross-sectional view of the front hub (Sec 4)

1 Split pin	8 Outer bearing
2 Driveshaft nut	9 Inner bearing
3 Flat washer	10 Spacer
4 Brake disc	11 Inner oil seal
5 Drive flange	12 Bearing
6 Hub	watershield
7 Outer oil seal	13 Driveshaft

9 Secure the swivel hub in a vice, undo the two bolts and remove the brake caliper anchor bracket. Separate the drive flange and disc from the hub using a hammer and suitable tube or socket, if necessary (photos).
10 If required, the two halves of the disc shield can now be removed after unscrewing the retaining bolt and screw.
11 Refitting the swivel hub is the reverse of the removal sequence, bearing in mind the following points:
(a) Ensure that the bearing water shield is in position on the driveshaft before fitting the swivel hub. Fill the groove in the water shield with a general purpose grease
(b) Where applicable tighten all retaining nuts and bolts to the specified torque. **Do not attempt to fully tighten the driveshaft nut until the weight of the car is on the roadwheels**
(c) Tighten the driveshaft retaining nut to the specified torque, with reference to Chapter 13 Section 10

4 Front hub bearings - removal and refitting

1 Remove the swivel hub assembly from the car, as described in the previous Section.
2 With the hub assembly on the bench, prise out the inner and outer oil seals using a screwdriver or suitable flat bar. Note that

there is a spacer fitted between the inner oil seal and the bearing.
3 With the hub supported on blocks use a hammer and drift to drive out one of the bearing inner races from the centre of the hub. Take care not to lose the balls which will be dislodged as the inner race is released. Turn the hub over and repeat the procedure for the other inner race. The outer races can now be driven out in the same way.
4 Wipe away any surplus grease from the bearings and swivel hub and then clean these components thoroughly using paraffin, or a suitable solvent. Dry with a lint-free rag. Remove any burrs or score marks from the hub bore with a fine file or scraper.
5 Carefully examine the bearing inner and outer races, the balls and ball cage for pitting, scoring or cracks, and if at all suspect renew the bearings as a pair. It will also be necessary to renew the oil seals as they will have been damaged during removal.
6 If the old bearings are in satisfactory condition and are to be re-used, reassemble the ball cage, holding the balls in position with grease, and then place this assembly in the outer race. Lay the inner race over the balls and push it firmly into place.
7 Before refitting the bearings to the hub, pack them thoroughly with a high melting-point grease.
8 Place one of the bearings in position on the hub with the word THRUST, or the markings stamped on the edge of the inner race, facing away from the centre of the hub (photo).

11

3.9B Use a hammer and tube to drift out the drive flange if tight . . .

3.9C . . . then withdraw the drive flange and disc assembly from the hub

4.8 Bearing fitted with THRUST marking (arrowed) facing away from the hub centre

4.11A Fit the outer oil seal with its sealing lip facing inwards

4.11B Place the spacer in position over the bearing . . .

4.11C . . . then fit the inner oil seal, with its sealing lip facing inwards

9 Using a tube of suitable diameter, a large socket or a soft metal drift, drive the bearing into the hub bore until it contacts the shoulder in the centre of the hub. Ensure that the bearing does not tip slightly and bind as it is being fitted. *If this happens the outer race may crack, so take great care to keep it square.*

10 Turn the hub over and repeat this procedure for the other bearing.

11 Dip the new oil seals in oil and carefully fit them to the hub using a tube of suitable diameter or one of the old seals to drive them in. Note that both oil seals are fitted with their sealing lips inward (photo) and that the inner seal has a second lip on its outer face. Don't forget to fit the spacer between the bearing and inner oil seal (photos).

12 The swivel hub can now be refitted to the car, as described in the previous Section.

5 Front suspension strut - removal and refitting

1 Securely apply the handbrake, chock the rear wheels and remove the trim from the front roadwheel.

2 Slacken the roadwheel retaining nuts, then jack up the front of the car and support it securely on axle stands. Remove the roadwheel.

3 From within the engine compartment prise off the small plastic cap in the centre of the strut upper mounting (photo), and remove the upper mounting cover.

4 Insert an Allen key of the appropriate size into the centre of the strut spindle and, while

holding the key to prevent the spindle turning, unscrew the mounting nut (photo). Lift off the spring washer and the cup and washer assembly.

5 Undo and remove the two nuts, bolts and spring washers securing the suspension strut to the swivel hub (photo). Release the strut from the hub and withdraw it from under the wheel arch (photo).

6 Refitting is the reverse sequence to removal. Ensure that all retaining nuts and bolts are tightened to the specified torque, where applicable.

6 Front suspension strut - dismantling and reassembly

Note: *Before attempting to dismantle the front suspension strut a suitable tool to hold the coil spring in compression must be obtained. Adjustable coil spring compressors are readily available and are recommended for this operation. Any attempt to dismantle the strut without such a tool is likely to result in damage or personal injury.*

1 Proceed by removing the front suspension strut, as described in the previous Section.

2 Position the spring compressors on either side of the spring (photo) and compress the spring evenly until there is no tension on the upper spring seat or upper mounting.

5.3 Prise off the plastic cap and remove the front strut upper mounting cover

5.4 Undo the strut upper mounting nut whilst holding the spindle

5.5A Undo the strut-to-swivel hub retaining nuts and bolts (arrowed). . .

5.5B . . . then remove the strut assembly from under the wheel arch

6.2 Compressors in position on the front coil spring

6.3A Lift off the upper mounting rubber . . .

6.3B . . . and bearing housing (arrowed)

Fig. 11.4 Suspension strut bearing retainer nut removal tool (Sec 6)

3 Lift off the upper mounting rubber (photo) and bearing housing (photo).
4 To remove the bearing retainer nut it will be necessary to make up a suitable tool which will engage in the slots of the nut enabling it to be unscrewed. A tool can be made out of a large nut with one end suitably shaped by cutting or filing so that two projections are left which will engage with the slots in the retainer nut (Fig. 11.4).
5 While holding the strut spindle with an Allen key, unscrew the bearing retainer nut. Lift off the upper bearing, spring seat and insulator ring.
6 The coil spring can now be removed, with compressors still in position if desired, followed by the spring aid, rubber boot and lower insulator ring.
7 With the strut completely dismantled, the components can be examined as follows.
8 Examine the strut for signs of fluid leakage. Check the strut spindle for signs of wear or pitting along its entire length and check the strut body for signs of damage or elongation of the mounting bolt holes. Test the operation of the strut, while holding it in an upright position, by moving the spindle through a full stroke and then through short strokes of 2 to 4 in (50 to 100 mm). In both cases the resistance felt should be smooth and continuous. If the resistance is jerky or uneven, or if there is any visible sign of wear or damage to the strut, renewal is necessary.
9 If any doubt exists about the condition of the coil spring, remove the spring compressors and check the spring for distortion. Also measure the free length of the spring and compare the measurement with the figure given in the Specifications. Renew the spring if it is distorted or outside the specified length.
10 Begin assembly by fitting the rubber boot and spring aid to the strut.
11 Place the lower insulator ring in position, followed by the spring, ensuring that the end of the bottom coil locates in the step of the spring seat.
12 With the spring suitably compressed, withdraw the strut spindle as far as it will go and refit the upper insulator ring and spring seat. Make sure that the end of the spring

upper coil locates in the step of the spring seat.
13 Place the bearing, with the small internal diameter downwards, over the spindle and refit the bearing retainer nut. Tighten the nut to the specified torque and remove the spring compressors.
14 Finally refit the bearing housing and the upper mounting rubber, large opening uppermost.
15 The strut can now be refitted to the car, as described in the previous Section.

7 Front lower suspension arm - removal and refitting

1 Apply the handbrake, chock the rear wheels and remove the front wheel trim. Slacken the wheel nuts. Jack up the front of the car, support it securely on axle stands and remove the roadwheel.
2 Undo and remove the nut and washer and then withdraw the clamp bolt securing the lower balljoint to the swivel hub.
3 Lever the lower suspension arm downwards to release the balljoint from the hub.
4 Undo and remove the three bolts securing the suspension arm rear mounting to the underbody (photo).
5 Undo and remove the nut and bolt securing the front mounting to the crossmember (photo).

Fig. 11.5 Front suspension strut upper mounting details (Sec 6)

1 Mounting nut	5 Bearing housing
2 Cup and washer assembly	6 Bearing retainer nut
3 Inner front wing valance	7 Upper bearing
4 Upper mounting rubber	8 Spring seat

6 On models equipped with an anti-roll bar, undo and remove the nut and washer securing the anti-roll bar mounting bush to the suspension arm.
7 Ease the front mounting out of the subframe, lift the suspension arm to disengage the anti-roll bar (where fitted) and manoeuvre the arm out from beneath the vehicle.
8 With the arm removed from the car,

7.4 Front suspension arm rear mounting bolts (arrowed)

7.5 Front suspension arm front mounting retaining bolt (arrowed)

11

carefully examine the rubber mounting bushes for swelling or deterioration, the balljoint for slackness, and check for damage to the rubber boot. Renewal of the balljoint is described in Section 8. Renewal of the suspension arm mounting bushes may be carried out as follows.

9 Using a two-legged puller, or similar tool, draw the rear bush assembly off its spigot. The rear bush can be removed from its mounting bracket by pressing it out in a vice with the aid of tubes of suitable length and diameter. Removal of the front bush in the arm follows the same procedure.

10 To refit the new bushes first lubricate them with rubber grease and then press them fully into place using a vice. Slide the rear bush assembly onto its spigot on the suspension arm. Note that the rear bush housings are handed and must now be interchanged from side to side. When fitted the small hole in the bush housing must be toward the centre of the car.

11 Refitting the lower suspension arm is the reverse sequence to removal. Ensure that all retaining nuts and bolts are tightened to the specified torque.

8 Front lower suspension arm balljoint - removal and refitting

1 Remove the lower suspension arm, as described in the previous Section.

2 Drill out the heads of the three rivets securing the balljoint to the arm and drive out the rivets with a punch.

3 Withdraw the balljoint from the suspension arm.

4 Replacement balljoint kits are supplied with nuts and bolts to secure the joint in place of the factory fitted rivets. Slide the new balljoint into position and fit the bolts so that the bolt heads are located above the arm. Screw on the nuts and tighten them to the specified torque.

5 The lower suspension arm can now be fitted to the arm as described in the previous Section.

9 Anti-roll bar - removal and refitting

Note: *For this operation the front suspension must be kept in a laden condition. If a vehicle lift or inspection pit are not available it will be necessary to drive the front of the car up on ramps.*

1 Undo and remove the nuts and washers securing the anti-roll bar mounting bush, one each side, to the lower suspension arms.

2 Undo and remove the four bolts securing the anti-roll clamps to the subframe. Lift away the clamps, disengage the mounting bushes from the lower suspension arms and lower the anti-roll bar to the ground.

3 If the mounting blocks require renewal, slip them off the bar and place new blocks in position after lubricating liberally with rubber grease.

4 To renew the mounting bushes first measure and record the distance from the outer face of the bush to the end of the anti-roll bar. Now draw off the bushes using a two-legged puller.

5 Lubricate the new bushes with rubber grease and drive them onto the anti-roll bar using a hammer and tube of suitable diameter. Use the measurement recorded during removal as a setting dimension.

6 To refit the anti-roll bar to the car, first locate the bush assemblies in the lower suspension arms and fit the washers and retaining nuts finger tight.

7 Place the clamps over the mounting blocks and refit the retaining bolts, noting that the long bolts locate in the rear holes.

8 First tighten the clamp bolts to the specified torque, followed by the bush retaining nuts.

9 Lower the car to the ground (if applicable).

10 Rear hub assembly - removal and refitting

1 Chock the front wheels, remove the rear wheel trim and slacken the wheel nuts. Jack up the rear of the car and support it securely on axle stands. Remove the roadwheel and release the handbrake.

2 By judicious tapping and levering, extract the hub cap and withdraw the retaining split pin from the hub retaining nut.

3 Using a large socket and bar, undo and remove the hub retaining nut and flat washer. *Note that the left-hand nut has a left-hand thread and the right-hand nut has a conventional right-hand thread.* **Take care not to tip the car from the axle stands**. If the hub nuts are particularly tight, temporarily refit the roadwheel and lower the car to the ground. Slacken the nut in this more stable position and then raise and support the car before removing the nut.

4 Withdraw the hub and brake drum assembly from the stub axle (photo). If it is not possible to withdraw the hub due to the brake

drum binding on the brake shoes, the following procedure should be adopted. Refer to Chapter 9, if necessary, and slacken off the handbrake cable at the cable adjuster. From the rear of the brake backplate, prise out the handbrake lever stop, which will allow the brake shoes to retract sufficiently for the hub assembly to be removed. It will, however, be necessary to remove the brake shoes and fit a new handbrake lever stop to the backplate.

5 Refitting the hub assembly is the reverse sequence to removal. Tighten the hub retaining nut to the specified torque and then align the next split pin hole. Always use a new split pin.

11 Rear hub bearings - removal and refitting

1 Remove the rear hub assembly from the car, as described in the previous Section.

2 With the hub on the bench, prise out the rear oil seal using a stout screwdriver or suitable flat bar.

3 Support the hub on blocks and, using a soft metal drift, tap out the two bearing inner races. Take care not to lose any of the balls which will be released from the ball cage as the inner races are removed.

4 Withdraw the spacer located between the two bearings and then drive the two outer races from the centre of the hub.

5 Wipe away any surplus grease and then thoroughly clean all the parts in paraffin or a suitable solvent. Dry with a lint-free rag.

6 Carefully examine the bearing inner and outer races, the ball cage and the balls for scoring, pitting or wear ridges. Renew both bearings as a set if any of these conditions are apparent. The hub oil seal must be renewed as it will have been damaged during removal. If the bearings are in a satisfactory condition, reassemble the balls and ball cage on the outer race, holding them in place with grease, and then press the inner race back into position (photo).

7 Before refitting the bearings, remove any burrs that may be present in the bore of the hub using a fine file or scraper.

8 Pack the bearings with a high melting-point

10.4 Withdraw the hub and brake drum from the stub axle

11.6 Reassemble the balls in the hub bearing cage then press the inner race into position

11.10 Fit the spacer between the bearings, smaller diameter outward

11.11A Fit the bearings with the word THRUST or the markings facing away from the hub centre

11.11B Fit the inner bearing to the hub . . .

grease and place the outer bearing in position with the word THRUST, or the markings stamped on the edge of the inner race, facing outwards. Drive the bearing into position using a tube of suitable diameter, or a drift, in contact with the bearing outer race. Take great care to keep the bearing square as it is installed, otherwise it will jam in the hub bore which could crack the outer race.

9 Dip a new oil seal in clean engine oil and position it over the outer bearing with its sealing lip facing inwards. Using a hammer and block of wood, tap the seal into the hub until it is flush with the end face of the hub.

10 Turn the hub over and lay the spacer over the installed outer bearing, with the smaller diameter of the spacer facing outwards (photo).

11 Fit the inner bearing and oil seal to the hub, using the same procedure as for the outer bearing, with the word THRUST, or the bearing markings, also facing out from the hub centre (photos).

12 The rear hub assembly can now be refitted to the car, as described in the previous Section.

12 Rear stub axle - removed and refitting

1 Remove the rear hub assembly, as described in Section 10.

11.11C . . . followed by the oil seal

2 Working under the car, disconnect the handbrake inner cable at the cable connector located beneath the rear axle transverse member.

3 Using circlip pliers, extract the circlip securing the handbrake outer cable to the bracket on the rear axle.

4 Using a brake hose clamp, or self-locking wrench with protected jaws, clamp the flexible brake hose located just in front of the rear axle. This will minimise brake fluid loss during subsequent operations.

5 Unscrew the brake pipe union nut at the rear of the wheel cylinder and carefully ease the pipe out of the cylinder. Plug the end of the pipe to prevent dirt entry.

6 Undo and remove the four nuts and spring washers securing the stub axle to the trailing arm and lift away the stub axle and brake backplate as an assembly.

7 Support the stub axle in a vice and drive out the four mounting studs using a soft metal drift. Take care not to damage the ends of the threads during this operation.

8 With the studs removed, separate the backplate from the stub axle.

Fig. 11.6 Cross-sectional view of the rear hub (Sec 11)

1 Hub cap	5 Hub and brake
2 Split pin	drum assembly
3 Hub retaining	6 Outer bearing
nut	7 Spacer
4 Flat washer	8 Inner bearing
	9 Oil seal

9 Refitting the stub axle is the reverse sequence to removal. Tighten all retaining nuts and bolts to the specified torque and, on completion, bleed the brake hydraulic system, as described in Chapter 9; if suitable precautions were taken to minimise fluid loss, as described, it should only be necessary to bleed the relevant wheel and not the entire system.

13 Rear suspension strut - removal and refitting

1 Chock the wheels, prise off the rear wheel trim and slacken the wheel nuts. Jack up the rear of the car and support it securely on axle stands. Remove the roadwheel.

2 As a safety precaution place a jack on suitable blocks beneath, and in contact with, the suspension trailing arm.

3 From inside the luggage compartment release the plastic cap from the strut upper mounting by rotating it whilst at the same time lifting upwards.

4 Engage a suitable small spanner on the flats of the strut spindle to prevent it turning and unscrew the upper mounting nut (photo). Lift off the flat washer and small mounting rubber.

5 From underneath the car, undo and remove the bolt securing the strut lower mounting to

13.4 Rear suspension upper mounting, accessible from inside the luggage compartment

11

13.5 Rear suspension lower mounting bolt
(arrowed)

Fig. 11.7 Rear suspension strut upper
mounting details (Sec 13)

1 Upper mounting nut	5 Large mounting rubber
2 Flat washer	6 Spring retainer nut
3 Small mounting rubber	7 Spacer
4 Rear wheel arch	8 Spring seat

15.8 Rear axle pivot bolt retaining nut
(arrowed)

the rear suspension trailing arm (photo). Withdraw the strut from under the wheel arch and remove the large mounting rubber.

6 Refitting the suspension strut is the reverse sequence to removal. Ensure that the upper and lower mountings are tightened to the specified torque.

14 Rear suspension strut - dismantling and reassembly

Note: *Before attempting to dismantle the rear suspension strut a suitable tool to hold the coil spring in compression must be obtained. Adjustable coil spring compressors are readily available and are recommended for this operation. Any attempt to dismantle the strut without such a tool is likely to result in damage or personal injury.*

1 Proceed by removing the rear suspension strut, as described in the previous Section.

2 Position the spring compressors on either side of the spring and compress the spring evenly until all the tension on the spring retainer nut is released.

3 With a spanner engaged with the flats of the strut spindle to stop it turning, unscrew the spring retainer nut. Lift off the spacer, spring seat and insulator ring.

4 The coil spring can now be removed. with the compressors still in position, if desired.

5 Carefully tap the spring aid retaining collar off the strut spindle then lift off the spring aid and the protective rubber boot.

6 With the strut completely dismantled, the components can be examined as follows.

7 Examine the strut body for signs of damage or corrosion, and for any trace of fluid leakage. Check the strut spindle for distortion, wear, pitting, or corrosion along its entire length. Test the operation of the strut, while holding it in an upright position, by moving the spindle through a full stroke and then through short strokes of 2 to 4 in (50 to 100 mm). In both cases the resistance felt should be smooth and continuous. If the resistance is jerky or uneven, or if there is any sign of wear

or damage to the strut, renewal is necessary.

8 If the strut is in a satisfactory condition check the condition of the circlip on the strut spindle and, if it is in any way damaged or distorted, fit a new circlip.

9 If any doubt exists about the condition of the coil spring, remove the spring compressors and check the spring for distortion. Also measure the free length of the spring and compare the measurement with the figure given in the Specifications. Renew the spring if it is distorted or not of the specified length.

10 Begin reassembly by fitting the rubber boot to the strut, followed by the spring aid and retaining collar.

11 Place the spring in position, ensuring that the end of the bottom coil locates in the step of the retainer.

12 With the spring suitably compressed, withdraw the strut spindle as far as it will go and refit the insulator ring and spring seat, ensuring that the end of the coil locates in the step of the spring seat.

13 Refit the spacer, followed by the spring retainer nut. Tighten the nut to the specified torque.

14 The spring compressors can now be removed and the strut assembly refitted to the car, as described in the previous Section.

15 Rear axle - removal and refitting

1 Chock the wheels, prise off the rear wheel trim and slacken the wheel nuts. Jack up the

rear of the car and support it securely on axle stands. Remove the roadwheel and release the handbrake.

2 Disconnect the two rear handbrake inner cables at the connectors located behind the rear axle transverse member.

3 Using two brake hose clamps, or self-locking wrenches with protected jaws, clamp the brake hydraulic flexible hoses, one located on each side of the car, adjacent to the rear axle front pivot bolts. This will minimise brake fluid loss during subsequent operations.

4 Undo and remove the two rear brake pipes unions at their connections with the flexible hoses. Plug or tape over the pipe and hose ends after disconnection to prevent dirt entry.

5 Using pliers extract the retaining clips and release the flexible hoses from the brackets on the rear axle.

6 Place a jack beneath one of the rear axle trailing arms and just take the weight of the axle.

7 Undo and remove the single bolt each side securing the rear suspension strut lower mountings to the rear axle trailing arms.

8 Undo and remove the nuts from the rear axle pivot bolts (one each side) (photo). Suitably support the axle beneath the transverse member and drift the pivot bolts from their locations.

9 Lever the axle out of its pivot mountings, lower it to the ground and withdraw it from under the car.

10 If necessary the axle can be completely dismantled by removing the rear hub assemblies and stub axles, as described in Sections 10 and 12 respectively.

11 If the axle pivot bushes require renewal, the old ones may be prised out and new ones inserted after lubricating them thoroughly with rubber grease.

12 Refitting the axle to the car is a straightforward reversal of the removal sequence. Ensure that all nuts and bolts are tightened to the specified torque and, on completion, bleed the brake hydraulic system, as described in Chapter 9.

16.2 Ease off the steering wheel pad . . .

16.3. . . undo the nut . . .

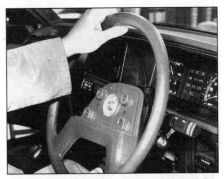

16.4. . . then pull the steering wheel off the inner column

16 Steering wheel - removal and refitting

1 Set the front wheels in the straight-ahead position.
2 Ease off the steering wheel pad to provide access to the retaining nut (photo).
3 Using a socket and bar, undo and remove the retaining nut and lockwasher (photo).
4 Mark the steering wheel and inner column in relation to each other and withdraw the wheel from the inner column splines (photo). If it is tight, tap it upwards near the centre, using the palm of your hand. *Refit the steering wheel retaining nut two turns before doing this for obvious reasons.*
5 Refitting is the reverse of removal, but align the previously made marks and tighten the retaining nut to the specified torque. Note that there is a small arrow stamped on the striker bush of the multifunction switch and this must point towards the direction indicator switch when fitting the steering wheel.

17 Steering column assembly - removal, overhaul and refitting

1 Disconnect the battery negative terminal.
2 Remove the steering wheel, as described in the previous Section.
3 Undo and remove the screws securing the two steering column cowl halves to the column and lift off both cowls.
4 Disconnect the wiring multi-plugs from the steering column multi-function switches and from the ignition switch. Release any cable ties securing the wiring harness to the column.
5 From under the facia, remove the steering column cover and seal and then, to assist refitting, mark the inner column in relation to the intermediate shaft.
6 Undo and remove the intermediate shaft clamp bolt and nut securing the intermediate shaft to the inner column.
7 Undo and remove the upper and lower steering column mounting bolts, lift the

column off the intermediate shaft and remove the assembly from the car.
8 Slacken the clamp screw and lift the multifunction switch off the steering column. Release the wiring from the clip.
9 Carefully support the outer column in a vice and withdraw the inner column from the top of the outer column.
10 Lift out the top bush, bend back the retaining tag and extract the bottom bush.

11 Clean the parts in paraffin, or a suitable solvent, and wipe dry. Examine the bushes for wear and renew, if necessary.
12 Reassembly and refitting is a reverse of removal and dismantling, bearing in mind the following points:
(a) *Smear the outer surfaces and inner grooves of the bushes with graphite grease before fitting*
(b) *Ensure that the marks made on the inner*

Fig. 11.8 Exploded view of the steering column assembly (Sec 17)

1 Steering column cowl	5 Lockwasher	9 Ignition switch
2 Steering wheel	6 Shear bolt	10 Inner column
3 Steering wheel pad	7 Steering lock/ignition	11 Outer column
4 Steering wheel retaining	switch	12 Bottom bush
nut	8 Top bush	

11

column and intermediate shaft are aligned when fitting the column
(c) Adjust the position of the outer column so that it is 3.25 in (82.6 mm) below the top of the inner column before tightening the retaining bolts
(d) Position the arrow on the striker bush of the multi-function switch so that it points towards the direction indicator switch before fitting the steering wheel
(e) Tighten all retaining nuts and bolts to the specified torque

18 Steering column intermediate shaft - removal and refitting

1 Disconnect the battery negative terminal.
2 Apply the handbrake, chock the rear wheels, jack up the front of the car and support it securely on axle stands.
3 From inside the car, pull back the carpet and unscrew the nut and bolt securing the intermediate shaft lower universal joint to the pinion shaft.
4 From under the facia remove the steering column cover and seal.
5 Unscrew the nut and bolt securing the intermediate shaft upper universal joint to the inner column.
6 Release the intermediate shaft from the pinion and inner column, and withdraw it from the car.
7 Before refitting it is first necessary to centralize the steering gear. To do this move the rubber band on the rack housing to one side to expose the centralizing hole. Turn the pinion shaft or move the roadwheels until a corresponding hole in the rack is in alignment. Insert a 6 mm bolt or drill into the hole to hold the steering gear in the central position.
8 From inside the car, engage the intermediate shaft upper universal joint with the inner column. Refit the clamp bolt and nut and tighten to the specified torque.
9 Position the steering wheel in the straight-ahead position and engage the intermediate shaft lower universal joint with the pinion shaft. Refit and tighten the clamp nut and bolt.
10 Refit the steering column cover and seal and place the carpet in position.

11 Remove the centralizing bolt or drill from the rack housing, refit the rubber band over the hole and lower the car to the ground. Reconnect the battery.

19 Steering column lock/ignition switch - removal and refitting
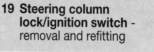

1 Remove the steering column, as described in Section 17.
2 With the column assembly on the bench, drill out the shear bolt heads and remove the clamp plate and lock/ignition switch from the outer column. The ignition switch can be removed from the lock after extracting the small grub screw.
3 Refit the ignition switch and secure it with the grub screw. Locate the new lock body centrally over the slot in the outer column. Lightly bolt the clamp plate into position, but take care not to shear the bolt heads.
4 Refit the steering column, as described in Section 17, but before fitting the cowls check that the lock and ignition switch operate correctly.
5 Tighten the shear bolts until the heads break off, and then refit the cowls.

20 Tie-rod outer balljoint - removal and refitting

1 Apply the handbrake, chock the rear wheels, prise off the front wheel trim and slacken the wheel nuts. Jack up the front of the car and support it securely on axle stands. Remove the roadwheel.
2 Using a suitable spanner, slacken the balljoint locknut on the tie-rod by a quarter of a turn.
3 Undo and remove the locknut securing the balljoint to the steering arm and then release the tapered ball-pin using a balljoint separator tool (photos).
4 Unscrew the balljoint from the tie-rod.
5 Refitting is the reverse sequence to removal. Tighten the nuts to the specified torque and check the front wheel alignment, as described in Section 24.

21 Steering rack rubber gaiter - removal and refitting

1 Remove the tie-rod outer balljoint, as described in the previous Section.
2 Release the retaining wire or unscrew the securing clip screws and slide the gaiter off the rack and pinion housing and tie-rod.
3 Slide on a new gaiter and position it over the housing and tie-rod.
4 Using new clips, or two or three turns of soft iron wire, secure the gaiter in position.
5 Refit the outer balljoint, as described in the previous Section.

22 Rack and pinion steering gear - removal and refitting

1 Disconnect the battery negative terminal.
2 Apply the handbrake, chock the rear wheels and remove the trim from both front roadwheels. Slacken the wheel nuts before jacking up the front of the car and then support it securely on axle stands. Remove the roadwheels.
3 Unscrew the nuts securing the tie-rod outer balljoints to the steering arms and release the tapered ballpins using a balljoint separator tool.
4 From inside the car pull back the carpet and unscrew the nut and bolt securing the intermediate shaft lower universal joint to the pinion shaft.
5 Using a sharp knife make diagonal cuts in the sound-deadening material around the pinion shaft to provide access to the pinion cover plate. The pinion cover plate can now be removed.
6 Undo and remove the two nuts and washers securing the gearchange linkage relay lever bracket to the rack housing. Move the linkage clear of the steering gear.
7 Undo and remove the two bolts and washers securing the pinion end of the steering gear to the bulkhead. Now remove the two bolts and washers, clamp plate and plastic seating securing the other end of the rack housing to the bulkhead.
8 Slacken the front crossmember support strut bolts on the driver's side. Remove the two short bolts, but leave the long bolt in position. Pivot the support strut outward at the top.
9 Ease the pinion shaft out of the intermediate shaft splines, manoeuvre the steering gear as necessary and withdraw the assembly out through the driver's side wheel arch.
10 To refit the steering gear, manoeuvre it into position through the wheel arch and locate the pinion in the bulkhead aperture.
11 Fit the retaining bolts, finger tight, to the pinion end of the steering gear. At the other

20.3A Using a separator tool to release the tie-rod outer balljoint

20.3B Withdraw the balljoint from the steering arm after releasing the taper

1 Intermediate shaft
2 Pinion cover seal
3 Rubber gaiter inner clip
4 Rubber gaiter
5 Rubber gaiter outer clip
6 Tie-rod and inner balljoint assembly
7 Centralizing hole rubber band
8 Gearchange linkage relay lever bracket
9 Plastic seating
10 Clamp plate
11 Rack housing
12 Tie-rod outer balljoint

Fig. 11.9 Exploded view of the rack and pinion steering gear (Sec 22)

end place the plastic seating and clamp in position, refit the retaining bolts and tighten them to the specified torque. Now tighten the pinion end retaining bolts to the specified torque.

12 Refit the gearchange linkage relay lever bracket and the two crossmember support strut bolts. Do not tighten the support strut bolts until the weight of the car is on its wheels.

13 Move the rubber band on the rack housing to one side to expose the centralizing hole. Move the rack as necessary, by turning the pinion, until a 6 mm drill or bolt can be inserted through the hole in the housing and into the corresponding hole in the rack.

14 From inside the car, refit the pinion cover plate, position the steering wheel in the straight-ahead position and refit the intermediate shaft universal joint to the pinion shaft. Refit and tighten the clamp bolt and nut.

15 Reposition the sound-deadening material around the pinion shaft and tape over the diagonal cuts. Refit the carpets.

16 Remove the centralizing bolt or drill and cover the hole with the rubber band.

17 Refit the two nuts and washers securing the gearchange linkage bracket to the rack housing.

18 Refit the tie-rod outer balljoints to the steering arms and secure with the retaining nuts tightened to the specified torque.

19 Refit the roadwheels and wheel nuts, lower the car to the ground and fully tighten the wheel nuts. Tighten the crossmember support strut bolts and refit the wheel trim.

23 Rack and pinion steering gear - dismantling and reassembly

Note: *The rack and pinion steering gear fitted to Montego models cannot be fully dismantled for repair or overhaul and, with one exception individual parts are not available separately. Should repair of the steering gear be necessary due to wear or damage a complete assembly must be obtained. It is however possible to renew the tie-rods individually and this Section describes the procedure.*

1 Begin by removing the steering gear from the car, as described in the previous Section.

2 Measure the distance between the ball-pin centres of the two outer balljoints and record this figure as an aid to reassembly.

3 Slacken the tie-rod outer balljoint locknut and unscrew the balljoint, followed by the locknut.

4 Remove the wire or retaining clips securing the rubber gaiter to the rack housing. Slide the gaiter off the rack housing and tie-rod.

5 Turn the pinion to extend the rack fully and support the exposed portion of rack between protected vice jaws.

6 Unscrew the ballhousing and withdraw the tie-rod and ballhousing from the rack.

7 Repeat paragraphs 3 to 6 inclusive for the other tie-rod, if required.

8 Liberally lubricate the tie-rod and ballhousing, using the specified lubricant.

9 Refit the ballhousing and tie-rod to the rack and tighten the housing fully. Secure the

ballhousing by staking its edge into the groove in the rack.

10 Liberally lubricate the rack teeth with the specified lubricant and refit the rubber gaiter. Secure the gaiter with the retaining clips or two to three turns of soft iron wire.

11 Refit the outer balljoint locknut and balljoint to the tie-rod, but do not tighten the locknut at this stage.

12 Repeat paragraphs 8 to 11 inclusive for the other tie-rod, if this was also removed.

13 Position the two balljoints so that the dimension between the ballpin centres is as recorded during dismantling with an equal number of exposed threads visible on each tie-rod. Now secure the balljoints with the locknuts.

14 The steering gear can now be refitted to the car, as described in the previous Section. It will, however, be necessary to adjust the toe setting after refitting, as described in Section 24.

24 Front wheel alignment and steering angles

1 Accurate front wheel alignment is essential to provide positive steering and prevent excessive tyre wear. Before considering the steering/suspension geometry, check that the tyres are correctly inflated, the front wheels are not buckled and the steering linkage and suspension joints are in good order, without slackness or wear.

2 Wheel alignment consists of four factors:

Camber is the angle at which the front wheels are set from the vertical when viewed from the front of the car. 'Positive camber' is the amount (in degrees) that the wheels are tilted outward at the top from the vertical.

Castor is the angle between the steering axis and a vertical line when viewed from each side of the car. 'Positive castor' is when the steering axis is inclined rearward.

Steering axis inclination is the angle (when viewed from the front of the car) between the vertical and an imaginary line drawn between the suspension strut upper mounting and the lower suspension arm balljoint.

Toe setting is the amount by which the distance between the front inside edges of the roadwheels (measured at hub height) differs from the diametrically opposite distance measured between the rear inside edges of the front roadwheels.

3 With the exception of the toe setting, all other steering angles on Montego models are set during manufacture and no adjustment is possible. It can be assumed, therefore, that unless the car has suffered accident damage all the preset steering angles will be correct. Should there be some doubt about their accuracy it will be necessary to seek the help of a BL dealer, as special gauges are needed to check the steering angles.

11

Fig. 11.10 Toe setting adjustment (Sec 24)

1 Rubber gaiter clip
2 Tie-rod
3 Outer balljoint locknut

A Standard wheel
B TD wheel

Arrows indicate tyre bead retaining grooves

Fig. 11.11 Roadwheel identification (Sec 25)

4 Two methods are available to the home mechanic for checking the toe setting. One method is to use a gauge to measure the distance between the front and rear inside edges of the roadwheels. The other method is to use a scuff plate in which each front wheel is rolled across a movable plate which records any deviation, or scuff, of the tyre from the straight-ahead position as it moves across the plate. Relatively inexpensive equipment of both types is available from accessory outlets to enable these checks, and subsequent adjustments, to be carried out at home.

5 If, after checking the toe setting using whichever method is preferable, it is found that adjustment is necessary, proceed as follows.

6 Turn the steering wheel onto full left lock and record the number of exposed threads on the right-hand steering tie-rod. Now turn the steering onto full right lock and record the number of threads on the left-hand tie-rod. If there are the same number of threads visible on both tie-rods then subsequent adjustments can be made equally on both sides. If there are more threads visible on one side than the other it will be necessary to compensate for this during adjustment. *After adjustment there must be the same number of threads visible on each tie-rod. This is most important.*

7 To alter the toe setting slacken the locknut on the tie-rod and turn the rod using a self-grip wrench to achieve the desired setting.

When viewed from the side of the car, turning the tie-rod clockwise will increase the toe-in, turning it anti-clockwise will increase the toe-out. Only turn the tie-rods by a quarter of a turn each time and then recheck the setting using the gauges, or scuff plate.

8 After adjustment tighten the locknuts and reposition the steering gear rubber gaiters, if necessary, to remove any twist caused by turning the tie-rods.

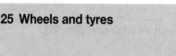

25 Wheels and tyres

1 Check the tyre pressures regularly (see Routine Maintenance) when the tyres are cold, and periodically check the tread depth using a depth gauge.

2 Frequently inspect the tyre walls and treads for damage and pick out any stones which have become trapped in the tread pattern.

3 In the interests of extending tread life, the wheels and tyres can be moved between front and rear on the same side of the car and the spare incorporated in the rotational pattern. If the wheels have previously been balanced on the car it will be necessary to have them rebalanced after rotation.

4 Never mix tyres of different construction, or very dissimilar tread patterns. This is particularly important on models equipped with TD (Total Deflation) wheels and tyres on which two grooves running around the wheel retain the tyre in place in the event of a

puncture. TD tyres and wheels are not interchangeable with wheels and tyres of different design and construction, and replacement must be of identical specification to those originally fitted to the car.

5 Always keep the roadwheel nuts tightened to the specified torque and if the wheel stud holes become elongated or flattened, renew the wheel.

6 Occasionally clean the inner faces of the roadwheels and, if there is any sign of rust or corrosion, paint them with metal preservative paint.

7 Before removing a roadwheel which has been balanced on the car, always mark one wheel stud hole and the wheel, so that the roadwheel may be refitted in the same position, to maintain the balance.

8 Should unexpected excessive wear be noticed on any of the tyres, its cause must be identified and rectified immediately. Generally speaking the wear pattern can be used as a guide to the cause. If a tyre is worn excessively in the centre of the tread face, but not on the edges, over inflation is indicated. Similarly if the edges are worn, but not the centre, this may be due to under inflation. If both the front or rear tyres are wearing on their inside or outside edges, this is likely to be due to incorrect toe setting. If only one tyre is exhibiting this tendency then there may be a problem with the steering geometry, a worn steering or suspension component, or a faulty tyre. Wheel and tyre imbalance is indicated by irregular and uneven wear patches appearing periodically around the tread face.

Fault finding - suspension and steering

Note: *Before diagnosing steering or suspension faults, be sure that the trouble is not due to incorrect tyre pressures mixture of tyre types or binding brakes*

Vehicle pulls to one side

☐ Incorrect wheel alignment
☐ Wear in front suspension or steering components
☐ Accident damage to steering or suspension components

Steering stiff or heavy

☐ Lack of steering gear lubricant
☐ Seized balljoint
☐ Wheel alignment incorrect
☐ Steering rack or column bent or damaged

Tyre wear uneven

☐ Wheel alignment incorrect
☐ Worn steering or suspension components
☐ Wheels out of balance
☐ Accident damage

Excessive play in steering

☐ Worn steering or suspension joints
☐ Wear in intermediate shaft universal joints
☐ Worn rack and pinion assembly

Wheel wobble and vibration

☐ Roadwheels out of balance
☐ Roadwheels buckled or distorted
☐ Faulty or damaged tyre
☐ Worn steering or suspension joints
☐ Wheel nuts loose
☐ Worn rack and pinion assembly

Chapter 12 Bodywork

For modifications, and information applicable to later models, see Supplement at end of manual

Contents

Degrees of difficulty

Easy, suitable for novice with little experience | **Fairly easy,** suitable for beginner with some experience | **Fairly difficult,** suitable for competent DIY mechanic | **Difficult,** suitable for experienced DIY mechanic | **Very difficult,** suitable for expert DIY or professional

Specifications

Torque wrench settings	lbf ft	Nm
Seat belt mountings	24	32
Bumper bracket retaining bolts	18	24
Front body panel retaining bolts	6	8
Door lock retaining bolts	6	8
Door striker pins	33	45
Bonnet lock retaining bolts	6	8
Boot lock retaining bolts	6	8
Boot lock striker retaining bolts	18	24

1 General description

The bodyshell and underframe is of all-steel welded construction and is of computer-based design. The assembly and welding of the main body unit is completed entirely by computer-controlled robots, and the finished unit is checked for dimensional accuracy using modern computer and laser technology.

The front wings are bolted in position and are detachable should renewal be necessary after a front end collision.

2 Maintenance - bodywork and underframe

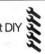

The general condition of a vehicle's bodywork is the one thing that significantly affects its value. Maintenance is easy, but needs to be regular. Neglect, particularly after minor damage, can lead quickly to further deterioration and costly repair bills. It is important also to keep watch on those parts of the vehicle not immediately visible, for instance the underside, inside all the wheel arches, and the lower part of the engine compartment.

The basic maintenance routine for the bodywork is washing - preferably with a lot of water, from a hose. This will remove all the loose solids which may have stuck to the vehicle. It is important to flush these off in such a way as to prevent grit from scratching the finish. The wheel arches and underframe need washing in the same way, to remove any accumulated mud, which will retain moisture and tend to encourage rust. Paradoxically enough, the best time to clean the underframe and wheel arches is in wet weather, when the mud is thoroughly wet and soft. In very wet weather, the underframe is usually cleaned of large accumulations

12

automatically, and this is a good time for inspection.

Periodically, except on vehicles with a wax-based underbody protective coating, it is a good idea to have the whole of the underframe of the vehicle steam-cleaned, engine compartment included, so that a thorough inspection can be carried out to see what minor repairs and renovations are necessary. Steam-cleaning is available at many garages, and is necessary for the removal of the accumulation of oily grime, which sometimes is allowed to become thick in certain areas. If steam-cleaning facilities are not available, there are some excellent grease solvents available which can be brush-applied; the dirt can then be simply hosed off. Note that these methods should not be used on vehicles with wax-based underbody protective coating, or the coating will be removed. Such vehicles should be inspected annually, preferably just prior to Winter, when the underbody should be washed down, and any damage to the wax coating repaired. Ideally, a completely fresh coat should be applied. It would also be worth considering the use of such wax-based protection for injection into door panels, sills, box sections, etc, as an additional safeguard against rust damage, where such protection is not provided by the vehicle manufacturer.

After washing paintwork, wipe off with a chamois leather to give an unspotted clear finish. A coat of clear protective wax polish will give added protection against chemical pollutants in the air. If the paintwork sheen has dulled or oxidised, use a cleaner/polisher combination to restore the brilliance of the shine. This requires a little effort, but such dulling is usually caused because regular washing has been neglected. Care needs to be taken with metallic paintwork, as special non-abrasive cleaner/polisher is required to avoid damage to the finish. Always check that the door and ventilator opening drain holes and pipes are completely clear, so that water can be drained out. Brightwork should be treated in the same way as paintwork. Windscreens and windows can be kept clear of the smeary film which often appears, by the use of proprietary glass cleaner. Never use any form of wax or other body or chromium polish on glass.

3 Maintenance - upholstery and carpets

Mats and carpets should be brushed or vacuum-cleaned regularly, to keep them free of grit. If they are badly stained, remove them from the vehicle for scrubbing or sponging, and make quite sure they are dry before refitting. Seats and interior trim panels can be kept clean by wiping with a damp cloth. If they do become stained (which can be more apparent on light-coloured upholstery), use a little liquid detergent and a soft nail brush to scour the grime out of the grain of the material. Do not forget to keep the headlining clean in the same way as the upholstery. When using liquid cleaners inside the vehicle, do not over-wet the surfaces being cleaned. Excessive damp could get into the seams and padded interior, causing stains, offensive odours or even rot.

> **HAYNES HINT** *If the inside of the vehicle gets wet accidentally, it is worthwhile taking some trouble to dry it out properly, particularly where carpets are involved.* Do not leave oil or electric heaters inside the vehicle for this purpose.

4 Minor body damage - repair

Note: *For more detailed information about bodywork repair, Haynes Publishing produce a book by Lindsay Porter called "The Car Bodywork Repair Manual". This incorporates information on such aspects as rust treatment, painting and glass-fibre repairs, as well as details on more ambitious repairs involving welding and panel beating.*

Repairs of minor scratches in bodywork

If the scratch is very superficial, and does not penetrate to the metal of the bodywork, repair is very simple. Lightly rub the area of the scratch with a paintwork renovator, or a very fine cutting paste, to remove loose paint from the scratch, and to clear the surrounding bodywork of wax polish. Rinse the area with clean water.

Apply touch-up paint to the scratch using a fine paint brush; continue to apply fine layers of paint until the surface of the paint in the scratch is level with the surrounding paintwork. Allow the new paint at least two weeks to harden, then blend it into the surrounding paintwork by rubbing the scratch area with a paintwork renovator or a very fine cutting paste. Finally, apply wax polish.

Where the scratch has penetrated right through to the metal of the bodywork, causing the metal to rust, a different repair technique is required. Remove any loose rust from the bottom of the scratch with a penknife, then apply rust-inhibiting paint to prevent the formation of rust in the future. Using a rubber or nylon applicator, fill the scratch with bodystopper paste. If required, this paste can be mixed with cellulose thinners to provide a very thin paste which is ideal for filling narrow scratches. Before the stopper-paste in the scratch hardens, wrap a piece of smooth cotton rag around the top of a finger. Dip the finger in cellulose thinners, and quickly sweep it across the surface of the stopper-paste in the scratch; this will ensure that the surface of the stopper-paste is slightly hollowed. The scratch can now be painted over as described earlier in this Section.

Repairs of dents in bodywork

When deep denting of the vehicle's bodywork has taken place, the first task is to pull the dent out, until the affected bodywork almost attains its original shape. There is little point in trying to restore the original shape completely, as the metal in the damaged area will have stretched on impact, and cannot be reshaped fully to its original contour. It is better to bring the level of the dent up to a point which is about 3 mm below the level of the surrounding bodywork. In cases where the dent is very shallow anyway, it is not worth trying to pull it out at all. If the underside of the dent is accessible, it can be hammered out gently from behind, using a mallet with a wooden or plastic head. Whilst doing this, hold a suitable block of wood firmly against the outside of the panel, to absorb the impact from the hammer blows and thus prevent a large area of the bodywork from being "belled-out".

Should the dent be in a section of the bodywork which has a double skin, or some other factor making it inaccessible from behind, a different technique is called for. Drill several small holes through the metal inside the area - particularly in the deeper section. Then screw long self-tapping screws into the holes, just sufficiently for them to gain a good purchase in the metal. Now the dent can be pulled out by pulling on the protruding heads of the screws with a pair of pliers.

The next stage of the repair is the removal of the paint from the damaged area, and from an inch or so of the surrounding "sound" bodywork. This is accomplished most easily by using a wire brush or abrasive pad on a power drill, although it can be done just as effectively by hand, using sheets of abrasive paper. To complete the preparation for filling, score the surface of the bare metal with a screwdriver or the tang of a file, or alternatively, drill small holes in the affected area. This will provide a really good "key" for the filler paste.

To complete the repair, see the Section on filling and respraying.

Repairs of rust holes or gashes in bodywork

Remove all paint from the affected area, and from an inch or so of the surrounding "sound" bodywork, using an abrasive pad or a wire brush on a power drill. If these are not available, a few sheets of abrasive paper will do the job most effectively. With the paint removed, you will be able to judge the severity of the corrosion, and therefore decide whether to renew the whole panel (if this is possible) or to repair the affected area. New body panels are not as expensive as most people think, and it is often quicker and more satisfactory to fit a new panel than to attempt to repair large areas of corrosion.

Remove all fittings from the affected area, except those which will act as a guide to the original shape of the damaged bodywork (eg headlight shells etc). Then, using tin snips or a hacksaw blade, remove all loose metal and any other metal badly affected by corrosion. Hammer the edges of the hole inwards, in order to create a slight depression for the filler paste.

Wire-brush the affected area to remove the powdery rust from the surface of the remaining metal. Paint the affected area with rust-inhibiting paint, if the back of the rusted area is accessible, treat this also.

Before filling can take place, it will be necessary to block the hole in some way. This can be achieved by the use of aluminium or plastic mesh, or aluminium tape.

Aluminium or plastic mesh, or glass-fibre matting, is probably the best material to use for a large hole. Cut a piece to the approximate size and shape of the hole to be filled, then position it in the hole so that its edges are below the level of the surrounding bodywork. It can be retained in position by several blobs of filler paste around its periphery.

Aluminium tape should be used for small or very narrow holes. Pull a piece off the roll, trim it to the approximate size and shape required, then pull off the backing paper (if used) and stick the tape over the hole; it can be overlapped if the thickness of one piece is insufficient. Burnish down the edges of the tape with the handle of a screwdriver or similar, to ensure that the tape is securely attached to the metal underneath.

Bodywork repairs - filling and respraying

Before using this Section, see the Sections on dent, deep scratch, rust holes and gash repairs.

Many types of bodyfiller are available, but generally speaking, those proprietary kits which contain a tin of filler paste and a tube of resin hardener are best for this type of repair. A wide, flexible plastic or nylon applicator will be found invaluable for imparting a smooth and well-contoured finish to the surface of the filler.

Mix up a little filler on a clean piece of card or board - measure the hardener carefully (follow the maker's instructions on the pack), otherwise the filler will set too rapidly or too slowly. Using the applicator, apply the filler paste to the prepared area; draw the applicator across the surface of the filler to achieve the correct contour and to level the surface. As soon as a contour that approximates to the correct one is achieved, stop working the paste - if you carry on too long, the paste will become sticky and begin to "pick-up" on the applicator. Continue to add thin layers of filler paste at 20-minute intervals, until the level of the filler is just proud of the surrounding bodywork.

Once the filler has hardened, the excess can be removed using a metal plane or file. From then on, progressively-finer grades of abrasive paper should be used, starting with a 40-grade production paper, and finishing with a 400-grade wet-and-dry paper. Always wrap the abrasive paper around a flat rubber, cork, or wooden block - otherwise the surface of the filler will not be completely flat. During the smoothing of the filler surface, the wet-and-dry paper should be periodically rinsed in water. This will ensure that a very smooth finish is imparted to the filler at the final stage.

At this stage, the "dent" should be surrounded by a ring of bare metal, which in turn should be encircled by the finely "feathered" edge of the good paintwork. Rinse the repair area with clean water, until all of the dust produced by the rubbing-down operation has gone.

Spray the whole area with a light coat of primer - this will show up any imperfections in the surface of the filler. Repair these imperfections with fresh filler paste or bodystopper, and once more smooth the surface with abrasive paper. Repeat this spray-and-repair procedure until you are satisfied that the surface of the filler, and the feathered edge of the paintwork, are perfect. Clean the repair area with clean water, and allow to dry fully.

HAYNES HiNT *If bodystopper is used, it can be mixed with cellulose thinners to form a really thin paste which is ideal for filling small holes.*

The repair area is now ready for final spraying. Paint spraying must be carried out in a warm, dry, windless and dust-free atmosphere. This condition can be created artificially if you have access to a large indoor working area, but if you are forced to work in the open, you will have to pick your day very carefully. If you are working indoors, dousing the floor in the work area with water will help to settle the dust which would otherwise be in the atmosphere. If the repair area is confined to one body panel, mask off the surrounding panels; this will help to minimise the effects of a slight mis-match in paint colours. Bodywork fittings (eg chrome strips, door handles etc) will also need to be masked off. Use genuine masking tape, and several thicknesses of newspaper, for the masking operations.

Before commencing to spray, agitate the aerosol can thoroughly, then spray a test area (an old tin, or similar) until the technique is mastered. Cover the repair area with a thick coat of primer; the thickness should be built up using several thin layers of paint, rather than one thick one. Using 400-grade wet-and-dry paper, rub down the surface of the primer until it is really smooth. While doing this, the work area should be thoroughly doused with water, and the wet-and-dry paper periodically rinsed in water. Allow to dry before spraying on more paint.

Spray on the top coat, again building up the thickness by using several thin layers of paint. Start spraying at one edge of the repair area, and then, using a side-to-side motion, work until the whole repair area and about 2 inches of the surrounding original paintwork is covered. Remove all masking material 10 to 15 minutes after spraying on the final coat of paint.

Allow the new paint at least two weeks to harden, then, using a paintwork renovator, or a very fine cutting paste, blend the edges of the paint into the existing paintwork. Finally, apply wax polish.

5 Major body damage - repair

Where serious damage has occurred or large areas need renewal due to neglect, it means that completely new sections or panels will need welding in, and this is best left to professionals. If the damage is due to impact, it will also be necessary to completely check the alignment of the bodyshell structure. Due to the principle of construction, the strength and shape of the whole car can be affected by damage to one part. In such instances the services of a BL agent with specialist checking jigs are essential. If a body is left misaligned, it is first of all dangerous, as the car will not handle properly, and secondly uneven stresses will be imposed on the steering, engine and transmission, causing abnormal wear or complete failure. Tyre wear may also be excessive.

6 Maintenance - hinges and locks
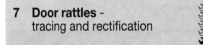

1 Oil the hinges of the bonnet, boot lid and doors with a drop or two of light oil at regular intervals (see Routine Maintenance).
2 At the same time, lightly oil the bonnet release mechanism and all door locks.
3 Do not attempt to lubricate the steering lock.

7 Door rattles - tracing and rectification

1 Check first that the door is not loose at the hinges, and that the latch is holding the door firmly in position. Check also that the door lines up with the aperture in the body. If the door is out of alignment, adjust it, as described in Sections 22 and 28.
2 If the latch is holding the door in the correct position, but the latch still rattles, the lock mechanism is worn and should be renewed.
3 Other rattles from the door could be caused by wear in the window operating mechanism, interior lock mechanism, or loose glass channels.

12

8.2 Slacken the bonnet hinge retaining bolts

9.1 Bonnet lock adjustment points – locknut (A) and lockpin (B)

8 Bonnet - removal, refitting and adjustment

1 Support the bonnet in its open position and place some cardboard, or rags, beneath the corners by the hinges.
2 Mark the location of the hinges with a soft pencil, then loosen the four retaining nuts and bolts (photo).
3 With the help of an assistant, release the stay, unscrew and remove the retaining bolts and withdraw the bonnet from the car.
4 Refitting is a reversal of removal, but adjust the hinges to their original positions. The bonnet rear edge should be flush with the scuttle, and the gaps at either side equal.

9 Bonnet lock - adjustment

1 Adjustment is possible by screwing the rubber buffers at each end of the front top rail in or out, or by repositioning the lockpin mounted on the bonnet (photo).
2 Slacken the locknut and use a screwdriver to adjust the length of the lockpin so that the bonnet closes easily and is held firmly in place.
3 Tighten the locknut.

11.3 Lift the grille up to release the lower edge

10 Bonnet lock and release cable - removal and refitting

1 Working inside the car, remove the bonnet release lever and disconnect the cable.
2 Working in the engine compartment, release the outer cable from the support bracket on the lock, and detach the inner cable from the lock lever.
3 Release the cable from its retaining clips, pull the cable through the bulkhead grommet and remove it from the car.
4 To remove the lock, undo and remove the retaining bolts and remove the lock assembly through the aperture in the front body panel.
5 Refitting is the reverse sequence to removal. Adjust the bonnet lock as described in the previous Section, if necessary.

11 Radiator grille - removal and refitting

1 Open the bonnet and support it in the raised position.
2 Very carefully lift the three plastic retaining tags, one at a time, and tip the grille outward at the top.
3 Lift the grille up to release the lower legs (photo) and remove the grille from the car.
4 Refitting is the reverse sequence to removal.

12 Front body panel - removal and refitting

1 Remove the bonnet lock and cable from the panel, as described in Section 10, and the radiator grille, as described in the previous Section.
2 Detach the air cleaner cold air intake hose from the panel.
3 Undo and remove the three screws each

Fig. 12.1 Bonnet lock and release cable details (Sec 10)

1 Bonnet lock   3 Release lever
2 Release cable

side securing the panel to the body side-members.
4 Release the bonnet stay, lift up the panel and remove it from the car.
5 Refitting is the reverse sequence to removal. Ensure that the lugs on the radiator and cooling fan cowl are correctly located in the body panel as it is fitted.

13 Front wing - removal and refitting

1 Open the bonnet and support it in the raised position.
2 Remove the headlamp and front direction indicator lamp, as described in Chapter 10.
3 Remove the front bumper, as described in Section 32 of this Chapter.
4 Undo the screws and remove the wheel arch liner.
5 Refer to Fig. 12.2 and remove the wing retaining bolts from their locations.
6 Carefully ease the front wing off its mating flanges and remove it from the car.
7 Refitting is the reverse sequence to removal, but use a mastic sealing compound to seal the wing to the body, apply protective coating to the wing under surface, and finish the top surface to match the body colour.

Fig. 12.2 Front wing attachment points (Sec 13)

1 *Wing-to-inner valance attachments*
2 *Wing-to-front pillar attachment*
3 *Wing-to-sill panel attachment*
4 *Wing-to-lower valance attachment*
5 *Wing-to-headlamp surround attachment*
6 *Mastic sealant application area*

14 Boot lid -
removal and refitting

1 Release the retaining clips and plastic rivets securing the hinge covers in position and lift away the covers.
2 Prise off the private lock operating rod retaining clip and slide the rod out of the private lock lever.
3 Undo the three bolts securing the lock mechanism to the boot lid and slide the lock assembly clear of the boot lid.
4 Ease the boot release cable outer sheath out of its support plate and disengage the inner cable end from the lock lever.
5 Disconnect the wiring harness connectors then withdraw the harness and release cable from the boot lid.
6 Using a soft pencil, mark the outline of the hinges on the boot lid.

7 Have an assistant support the boot lid, then undo the hinge retaining bolts and lift the boot lid away (photo).
8 Refitting is the reverse sequence to removal. Align the hinges with the outline marks made during removal. Adjust the hinge position slightly if necessary so that the lid closes easily and is in correct alignment. Further adjustment is possible by slackening the striker plate bolts and repositioning the plate (photo).

15 Boot lock -
removal and refitting

Note: *On vehicles equipped with central locking, further information will be found in Chapter 10.*
1 Prise off the private lock operating rod

14.7 Boot lid hinge retaining bolts

retaining clip and slide the rod out of the private lock lever.
2 Undo the three bolts securing the lock mechanism to the boot lid and slide the lock clear (photo).
3 Ease the boot release cable outer sheath out of its support plate and disengage the inner cable end from the lock lever. Where applicable disconnect the wiring connectors then remove the lock from the boot lid.
4 Refitting is the reverse sequence to removal. If necessary adjust the striker plate position after refitting the lock so that the boot lid shuts and locks without slamming.

16 Boot private lock -
removal and refitting

Note: *On vehicles equipped with central locking, further information will be found in Chapter 10.*
1 Prise off the private lock operating rod retaining clip and slide the rod out of the private lock lever.
2 Undo the large nut securing the private lock to the lock retainer (photo). Withdraw the private lock, washer and lock retainer from the boot lid.
3 Refitting is the reverse sequence to removal.

14.8 Boot lock striker plate and retaining bolts

15.2 Boot lock retaining bolts (arrowed)

16.2 Boot private lock retaining nut (arrowed)

12

Fig. 12.3 Boot lock and release cable details (Secs 15. 16 and 17)

1 Private lock retaining nut
2 Lock retainer
3 Washer
4 Private lock barrel
5 Operating rod and clips
6 Boot lock
7 Release lever
8 Release cable
9 Striker plate

17 Boot release cable and lever - removal and refitting

1 Refer to Section 14 and carry out the operations described in paragraphs 1 to 5.
2 Refer to Section 30 and remove the rear seat cushion.
3 Undo the front seat belt lower anchorage attachment and remove the sill interior trim panels.
4 Undo the driver's seat outer rail retaining bolts and withdraw the oddments tray.
5 Undo the screw securing the release lever shield to the body and remove the shield.
6 Undo the two release lever bracket retaining screws, remove the bracket assembly and withdraw the cable.

7 Refitting is the reverse sequence to removal.

18 Windscreen - removal and refitting

All Montego models are equipped with a flush-glazed, laminated windscreen, secured to the bodyshell by direct bonding. Due to this method of retention, special tools and equipment are required to remove and refit the screen, and this task is definitely beyond the scope of the home mechanic. If it is necessary to have the windscreen removed, this job should be left to a suitably equipped specialist or BL dealer.

20.1A Undo the door bin retaining screws . . .

19 Rear window and rear quarter windows - removal and refitting

The rear windows, like the windscreen, also feature direct bonding retention and their removal and refitting should be entrusted to a BL dealer.

20 Front door inner trim panel - removal and refitting

Base and L models

1 Undo the screws securing the door bin to the door, ease the bin away at the bottom and release the upper tags from the armrest (photos).
2 Undo the two armrest retaining screws and remove the armrest from the door (photo).
3 Prise out the finisher cap then undo the window regulator handle retaining screw (photos). Lift off the handle.
4 Prise out the finisher cap and undo the internal door release lever surround retaining screw (photos). Slide the surround off the lever.
5 Starting at the lower rear corner, release the trim panel retaining buttons by carefully

20.1 B . . . and disengage the upper tags from the armrest

20.2 Undo the armrest retaining screws

20.3A Prise out the finisher cap . . .

20.3B . . . then remove the regulator handle retaining screw

20.4A Prise out the finisher cap . . .

20.4B . . . and undo the door release lever surround retaining screw

levering between the panel and door with a screwdriver or suitable flat bar (photo).

6 Undo and remove the screws securing the upper trim capping to the door, lift the rear of the capping over the lock button and lift off.

7 To gain access to the door components, carefully peel back the polythene condensation barrier as necessary (photo).

8 Refitting is the reverse sequence to removal.

HL models

9 Prise out the finisher cap then undo the window regulator handle retaining screw. Lift off the handle.

10 Prise out the finisher cap and undo the internal door release lever surround retaining screw. Slide the surround off the lever.

11 Undo the three screws securing the trim panel to the door; one located in the well of the door pull, and two at the bottom of the door bin.

12 Using a screwdriver or suitable flat bar, carefully lever between the panel and door at the front and rear sides to release the panel retaining buttons.

13 Pull out the bottom edge and lift the panel upwards over the lock button. Disconnect the speaker wiring and any additional wiring then remove the panel.

14 To gain access to the door components, carefully peel back the polythene condensation barrier as necessary.

15 Refitting is the reverse sequence to removal.

20.5 Release the trim panel retaining buttons

20.7 Peel back the polythene sheet to gain access to the door components

21 Front door - removal and refitting

1 Remove the inner trim panel, as described in Section 20.

2 Disconnect the wiring multi-plugs and connectors and, where fitted, at the central locking and electrically-operated window components. Remove the wiring harness from the door.

3 Have an assistant securely support the door then, using a suitable punch, drift out the hinge retaining pins. Withdraw the door from the car.

4 Refitting is the reverse sequence to removal.

22 Front door lock - removal, refitting and adjustment

Note: On vehicles equipped with central locking, further information will be found in Chapter 10.

1 Remove the door inner trim panel, as described in Section 20.

2 Unscrew the interior lock button, temporarily refit the window regulator handle and wind the window fully up.

3 Prise the operating rod out of its retaining bush on the exterior door handle operating lever (photo).

4 Release the retaining clip and withdraw the operating rod from the private lock lever.

Fig. 12.4 Front door inner trim panel removal – HL models (Sec 20)

22.3 Door handle operating rod bush (A) and handle retaining nuts (B)

22.5 Undo the release lever retaining screw (A) and slide the lever rearwards to release it

12

22.7 Door lock retaining screws

5 Undo and remove the screw securing the internal release lever to the door. Release the operating rod from its steady clip and slide the lever rearwards to release it from its location (photo).

6 Undo and remove the screw securing the rear window channel to the door. Release the channel from the felt guide and remove the channel from the door.

7 Undo and remove the three retaining screws (photo) and withdraw the lock assembly, complete with operating rods, from the door aperture. Disconnect the courtesy lamp switch plug.

8 The external handle can also be removed after unscrewing the two nuts and washers.

9 Refitting is the reverse sequence to removal, but adjust the lock striker pin as follows.

10 Check that the latch disc is in the open position then loosen the striker pin nut and position the pin so that the door can be closed easily and is held firmly. Close the door gently, but firmly, when making this adjustment.

11 Tighten the striker pin nut.

23 Front door private lock -
removal and refitting

Note: *On vehicles equipped with central locking, further information will be found in Chapter 10.*

1 Remove the door interior trim panel, as described in Section 20, and wind the window fully up.

2 Release the retaining clip and withdraw the operating rod from the private lock lever.

3 Prise out the retaining ring and withdraw the lock and seating washer from the door.

4 To remove the lock barrel, extract the circlip and remove the spring washer and lock lever. Withdraw the lock barrel from the lock body.

5 Refitting is the reverse sequence to removal.

**Fig. 12.5 Front door lock components
(Secs 22 and 23)**

1 Private lock	4 Lock assembly
2 External handle	5 Internal release
3 Lock button	lever

24 Front door glass and regulator -
removal and refitting

Note: *On vehicles equipped with electrically-operated windows, further information will be found in Chapter 10.*

1 Refer to Section 20 and remove the inner trim panel and, where fitted, the trim capping.

2 Refer to Section 25 and remove the door mirror.

3 Lower the window fully and insert a small block of wood in the base of the door to support the window after removal of the regulator.

4 Undo the three bolts securing the regulator to the door panel. Release the three nylon wheels of the regulator arms from their runners and manipulate the regulator out of the door aperture.

5 Tip the window forward and remove it upwards from the door.

6 Refitting is the reverse sequence to removal.

**Fig. 12.7 Remote control door mirror
attachments (Sec 25)**

1 Cheater panel	3 Retaining plate
internal finisher	4 Adjusting lever
2 Retaining screw	

**Fig. 12.6 Front door glass and regulator
components (Sec 24)**

1 Door window	4 Rear window
2 Lifting channel	channel
3 Window regulator	5 Auxiliary slide

25 Front door mirror -
removal and refitting

1 Open the front door and, if the mirror is of the remotely-controlled type, remove the adjusting lever by moving it rearwards.

2 Carefully prise off the cheater panel internal finisher to provide access to the mirror retaining screws.

3 Undo and remove the three screws, lift off the retaining plate and withdraw the mirror from the door.

4 Refitting is the reverse sequence to removal.

5 The design of the mirror is such that it will give slightly under impact, against spring tension, thus minimising the risk of damage or injury. On remotely-controlled mirrors this will cause the adjusting lever to disengage from

**Fig. 12.8 Mirror adjusting lever
attachments (Sec 25)**

1 Ball plate	3 Mirror head
2 Adjusting lever	

28.5A Press out the locking pin from the bellcrank lever . . .

28.5B . . . then withdraw the bellcrank and pivot

Fig. 12.9 Rear door lock components (Sec 28)

1 Lock button
2 Door exterior handle
3 Lock assembly
4 Internal release lever

the internal mechanism and become inoperative. The lever can be refitted, without removing the mirror, as follows.

6 Open the door and lower the window.
7 Gently move the mirror head toward the front of the car to give a working clearance between the mirror head and the base.
8 With the mirror held in this position, grasp the ball plate with one hand and the ballhead of the adjusting lever with the other. Firmly push the ball-head into the socket on the ball plate until it fully engages. Release the mirror head and check the operation.

26 Rear door inner trim panel - removal and refitting

1 Removal and refitting of the rear inner trim panel is basically the same as that for the front doors, as described in Section 20. The only difference is the retaining screw locations and this will be obvious after inspection.

27 Rear door - removal and refitting

1 If central locking is fitted, remove the inner trim panel, as described in Section 26, and disconnect the wiring harness connectors. Remove the harness from the door.
2 Carefully mark the outline of the door hinges on the pillar using a soft pencil.
3 With the help of an assistant to support the door, undo and remove the bolts securing the upper and lower hinges to the door. Carefully lift away the door.
4 Refitting is the reverse sequence to removal. Align the hinges with the pencil marks made during removal.

28 Rear door lock - removal, refitting and adjustment

Note: *On vehicles equipped with central locking, further information will be found in Chapter 10.*

1 Remove the door inner trim panel and capping, as described in Section 26.
2 Temporarily refit the window regulator handle and wind the window fully up. Unscrew the interior lock button.
3 Prise the operating rod out of its retaining bush on the door exterior handle operating lever.
4 Undo and remove the screw securing the internal release lever to the door. Release the operating rod from its steady clip and slide the lever rearwards to release it from its location.
5 Using a small screwdriver or punch, press out the locking pin from the centre of the bellcrank lever (photo), and withdraw the bellcrank and pivot (photo). Detach the lock operating rod from the bellcrank and from its steady clip.
6 Undo and remove the three screws securing the lock to the door and withdraw the unit, complete with operating rods, from the door aperture. Disconnect the courtesy lamp switch plug.
7 Refitting is the reverse sequence to removal, but adjust the lock striker pin as follows.
8 Check that the latch disc is in the open position, then loosen the striker pin nut and position the pin so that the door can be closed easily, and is held firmly. Close the door gently, but firmly, when making this adjustment.
9 Tighten the striker pin nut.

29 Rear door glass and regulator - removal and refitting

1 Wind the window fully up, and then remove the inner trim panel and capping, as described in Section 26.
2 Undo and remove the two bolts securing the window regulator to the door panel. Support the glass, disengage the regulator arm from the door glass lifting channel, and withdraw the regulator through the door aperture.
3 Lower the glass to the bottom of the door and then remove the rear guide

channel retaining bolt. Release the channel from the glass and remove the felt from the channel.
4 Drill out the rivets securing the cheater panel to the door frame and lift off the panel. Drill an access hole in the bottom of the cheater panel and shake out the rivet debris.
5 Drill out the rivets securing the rear guide channel to the door, withdraw the channel and remove the rivet studs.
6 Carefully lift the glass upwards and out of the door. The lifting channel can now be removed from the glass, if necessary.
7 Refitting is the reverse sequence to removal.

Fig. 12.10 Rear door glass and regulator components (Sec 29)

1 Door window
2 Cheater panel
3 Lifting channel
4 Window regulator
5 Rear guide channel

12

Fig. 12.11 Exploded view of the rear seat components (Sec 30)

1 Cushion clips
2 Squab latches
3 Squab centre hinge bracket
4 Hinge bracket retaining screw
5 Squab extension

30 Seats -
removal and refitting

Front seat

1 Adjust the seat for access to the seat rail retaining bolts and undo the Torx type retaining bolts. Withdraw the seat from the car.

Fig. 12.12 Front seat belts and mountings (Sec 31)

1 Flexible stalk
2 Upper mounting
3 Adjustment slide knob
4 Adjustment slide
5 Belt guide
6 Inertia reel
7 Bottom mounting

2 Refitting is the reverse sequence to removal; apply thread locking fluid to the bolt threads.

Rear seat

3 Push down on the base of the rear seat cushion to release the two retaining clips and remove the cushion.
4 Release the rear seat squab latches from inside the luggage compartment and fold down the squabs.
5 Undo the squab centre hinge bracket retaining screws and lift out the squabs.
6 Undo the bolt securing the seat squab extension lower edge to the wheel arch.
7 Slide the squab extension up and remove it from the car.
8 Refitting the squab extensions, seat guards and cushion is the reverse sequence to removal.

31 Seat belts -
removal and refitting

Caution: If the vehicle has been involved in an accident in which structural damage was sustained, all the seat belt components must be renewed.

1 Move the front seats fully forward, ease the door seal from around the central door pillar, and remove the interior trim covering the seat belt mechanism.
2 Prise off the trim capping from the top mounting. Undo and remove the top, bottom and inertia reel mounting bolts, noting the position of the spacers and washers, and remove the assembly from the car.
3 Press out the belt guide from the interior trim and remove the belt from the trim.
4 Pull off the trim cover then undo and remove the bolt securing the flexible stalk to the floor. Note the position of the washers and spacer, and remove the stalk.
5 Refitting is the reverse sequence to removal, *but ensure that the mounting bolts are tightened to the specified torque.*

32 Bumpers -
removal and refitting

Front bumper

1 Refer to Chapter 10 and remove the battery.
2 Undo the two bolts each side securing the bumper front support brackets to the body.
3 Undo the nuts and remove the washers and spacers securing the bumper and brackets to the front wings.
4 Detach the wheel arch liners from the bumpers and carefully withdraw the bumper from the front of the car.
5 Refitting is the reverse sequence to removal.

Rear bumper

6 Disconnect the battery negative terminal then remove the number plate lamps and

Fig. 12.13 Front bumper components (Sec 32)

1 Bumper moulding 2 Bumper to front wing bracket 3 Bumper front support bracket components

Fig. 12.14 Rear bumper components (Sec 32)

1 Bumper moulding
2 Bumper-to-rear valance
   support bracket
3 Wheel arch liner
4 Bumper support bracket

Fig. 12.15 Sunroof panel attachments (Sec 33)

1 Trim panel front clip
2 Deflector slide
3 Trim panel clip and tensioning spring
4 Trim panel
5 Deflector slide retaining screws
6 Tilt arm front retaining screw
7 Tilt arm rear retaining screw
8 Tilt arm adjustment screw

detach the bulb holders. If necessary refer to Chapter 10.

7 Undo the two bolts each side, accessible from inside the luggage compartment, securing the bumper support brackets to the body.

8 Undo the two screws each side and remove the rear wheel arch liners.

9 Undo the nut securing each bumper front bracket to the rear valance then carefully withdraw the bumper from the car.

10 Refitting is the reverse sequence to removal.

33 Sunroof - removal and refitting

Sunroof panel

1 Open the trailing edge of the sunroof panel, ease each end of the panel liner down and release the trim panel clips from the legs on the liner frame.

2 Close the sunroof and disengage the liner front clips from the deflector slides. Move the liner back between the panels and detach the panel liner tensioning springs.

3 Undo and remove the four screws on each side securing the sunroof panel to the slide and tilt mechanism. *Do not remove the tilt adjustment screws.*

4 Lift out the sunroof panel and, if required, remove the weatherstrip and trim panel clips.

5 If removed, refit the weatherstrip and trim panel clips, locate the sunroof panel in position and loosely secure.

6 Close the sunroof and check its alignment. Tighten the four securing screws in sequence and adjust the tilt arm as necessary.

7 Refit the tensioning springs, open the trailing edge of the sunroof and pull the liner forward, ensuring that the clips on the liner frame engage with the deflector slides.

8 Engage the trim panel clips on the legs of the liner frame and close the sunroof.

Sunroof liner

9 Remove the sunroof panel, as previously described, and then remove the two deflector slides.

10 Slide the liner forward, disengage it from the frame and lift it upwards and out.

11 To refit the liner, locate it on the frame with the slides under the spigots. Slide the liner rearwards, refit the deflector slides and then refit the sunroof panel.

Sunroof frame

12 Remove the sunroof panel, sunroof liner and the wind deflector, as previously described.

13 Remove the operating handle.

14 Release the aperture trim along the front edge and ease away the headliner. Undo and remove the two screws securing the winder mechanism to the frame and front bracket. Take care to protect the roof panel in front of the aperture.

15 Undo and remove the remaining screws securing the frame to the mounting assembly, move the frame forwards and lift it out, taking

Fig. 12.16 Sunroof frame attachments (Sec 33)

1 Wind deflector retaining screws
2 Frame retaining screws
3 Winder-to-front bracket retaining screws
4 Guide pin and rear support bracket

care to avoid scratching the surrounding paintwork.

16 To refit the frame, position it in the aperture and engage the guide pins in the rear support brackets. Refit the retaining screws loosely, locate the wind deflector and tighten all the retaining screws.

17 Refit the sunroof liner and sunroof panel.

34 Centre console - removal and refitting

1 Move both front seats fully forwards and undo the two console rear fixing screws.

2 Move the seats fully rearwards, prise out the seat belt stalk access panel and then unbolt and remove the stalks.

3 Remove both the front seat backrest control handles.

4 Remove the oddments tray from the front of the console to expose the console front fixing screws. Extract the screws.

34.4 Centre console front retaining screws (arrowed)

12

1 Glovebox lid
2 Glovebox
3 Glovebox supports
4 Outer vent
5 Side window demist escutcheon
6 Facia panel
7 Heater duct
8 Lower stiffening rail
9 Instrument panel carrier
10 Parcel shelf
11 Radio and centre vent
   panel housing
12 Oddments tray

Fig. 12.17 Exploded view of the facia and component parts (Sec 35)

5 Prise out the panel, forward of the handbrake lever.

6 On manual transmission models, lift the console upwards - the gear lever and gaiter will remain secured by a retaining plate and screws.

7 On automatic transmission models, move the console to the rear and then lift it upwards over the handbrake and the selector lever. The selector lever, index plate and bulbholder will remain attached to the floor.

8 Refitting is a reversal of removal, tighten the seat belt stalk bolts to the specified torque.

35 Facia panel - removal and refitting

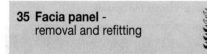

Note: *Removal of the facia is considerably involved, entailing extensive dismantling and the disconnection of many wiring harness plugs and connectors. Read through the entire Section before starting, and familiarize yourself with the procedure by referring to the illustration. Identify all electrical connections with a label before removal and, if necessary, make notes during dismantling.*

1 Disconnect the battery negative terminal.

2 Remove the steering column, as described in Chapter 11.

3 Remove the instrument panel, radio and facia switches, as described in Chapter 10.

4 From within the glovebox, release the two turnbuckles using a coin and lower the control unit panel from the glovebox roof. Disconnect the wiring multi-plugs and remove the panel.

5 Remove the courtesy lamp switch and disconnect its wiring plug.

6 Prise off the switch blanking plate on the right-hand side of the heater control knobs.

7 Undo the screw located behind the blanking plate.

8 Centralize the heater control knobs and ease the control panel, complete with knobs, off the facia. Disconnect the wiring multi-plugs and remove the control panel.

9 Release the cigarette lighter panel from the facia, disconnect the cigarette lighter wiring plug and, where fitted, the balance control wiring plug. Remove the panel.

10 Remove the fusebox cover from the right-hand side of the facia.

11 Prise off the trim caps from the two retaining screws at each end of the facia. Undo the four screws.

12 Undo the facia centre retaining screw situated at the base of the facia panel.

13 Pull the facia rearwards and disconnect any remaining wiring multi-plugs or connectors. Remove the facia from the car.

14 Refitting is a straightforward reverse of the removal sequence.

36 Heater - adjustments

1 The only adjustment possible is that of the heater flap linkage and is carried out as follows, with reference to Fig. 12.18.

2 Disconnect the battery negative terminal then remove the instrument panel, as described in Chapter 10.

3 Slacken the flap link rod trunnion screw situated behind the heater blend control lever.

4 Position the blend control in the fully raised position and move the heater flap lever as far as it will go towards the vehicle interior. Hold the linkage and control in this position and tighten the trunnion screw.

5 Check that the blend control lever moves freely from the fully raised to fully lowered position.

6 Refit the instrument panel and reconnect the battery.

37 Heater - removal and refitting

1 Drain the cooling system, as described in Chapter 2, and then remove the facia, as described in Section 35 of this Chapter.

Fig. 12.18 Heater control and adjustment details (Sec 36)

1 Flap link rod	3 Vacuum switch	5 Upper vacuum actuator
2 Flap link rod trunnion screw	4 Heater flap lever	6 tower vacuum actuator

7 Vacuum switch solenoid

Fig. 12.19 Heater assembly attachment details (Sec 37)

1 Heater base retaining bolt	2 Demister duct	3 Side vent hose	4 Upper retaining bolts and clamp plate

12

Fig. 12.20 Exploded view of the heater assembly (Sec 38)

1 Heater matrix
2 Demister duct
3 Matrix pipe, bracket and
   flange assembly
4 Bulkhead sealing pad
5 Heater body halves
6 Carrier strap and upper
   support pin
7 Motor cover
8 Motor and blower assembly
9 Demister flap
10 Blender flaps
11 Control panel and levers
12 Air inlet port

2 From within the engine compartment slacken the clips and disconnect the two heater hoses at the outlets adjacent to the engine compartment bulkhead.

3 Disconnect the heater vacuum supply hose from the T-piece connector in the engine main vacuum line.

4 Undo the two screws securing the ventilator duct at the base of the heater.

5 Detach the windscreen demister ducts and the side vent hoses from the heater casing.

6 Disconnect the heater blower motor wiring multi-plug.

7 Undo the bolt securing the base of the heater to the support bracket and the two bolts and clamp plate securing the top of the heater to the facia rail.

8 Detach the heater drain hose from the engine compartment bulkhead, withdraw the heater and remove it from inside the car.

9 Refitting is the reverse sequence to removal. Refill the cooling system, as described in Chapter 2, after installation.

38 Heater -
dismantling and reassembly

1 With the heater removed from the car, remove the drain hose then release the retaining spring clips and remove the heater upper support pins and carrier strap.

2 Remove the side vent elbows.

3 Remove the Rokut rivets securing the heater control panel, remove the flap link rod from the trunnion then move the control levers and panel to one side.

4 Undo the screws securing the matrix pipe bracket, pipe support clip and matrix flange. Lift out the matrix and pipes. Undo the retaining screws and remove the pipes and gasket from the matrix.

5 Undo the eight screws and two clips securing the heater motor terminal cover. Lift off the cover and disconnect the motor wiring harness plugs. Remove the harness clips.

6 Undo the two screws and washers securing the demist flaps.

7 Drill out the pop rivet adjacent to the heater lower mounting. Remove the sealing tape from inside the heater control panel aperture.

8 Release the spring retaining clips and separate the two halves of the heater body. Withdraw the resistor unit and place the wiring harness to one side. Remove the two plastic hinge bushes from the flaps.

9 Using a flat screwdriver inserted between the heater body and the rear of the blower motor casing, carefully ease out the motor.

10 With the heater dismantled, inspect the matrix for signs of leaks and, if any are apparent, renew the matrix. If the matrix appears serviceable, brush off any accumulation of dirt or debris from the fins and then reverse flush the core. Inspect the remaining heater components for any signs of damage or distortion and renew as necessary.

11 Reassembly is the reverse sequence to dismantling, but adjust the heater flap linkage, as described in Section 36, on completion.

Chapter 13 Supplement:
Revisions and information on later models

Contents

13

Degrees of difficulty

| Easy, suitable for novice with little experience | | Fairly easy, suitable for beginner with some experience | | Fairly difficult, suitable for competent DIY mechanic | | Difficult, suitable for experienced DIY mechanic | | Very difficult, suitable for expert DIY or professional | 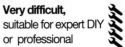 |

1 Introduction

Since its introduction in 1984, the Montego has undergone a number of mechanical and cosmetic changes. These include the availability of an Estate version in October 1984, and the introduction of a new five-speed gearbox in October 1988.

This Supplement deals with the servicing and overhaul procedures which differ from those described in the first twelve Chapters of this manual. The procedures in this Chapter are either applicable to later models only, or they have been revised by the vehicle manufacturer for all models.

In order to use this Supplement to its best advantage, it is suggested that it is referred to before the main Chapters of the manual, in order to ensure that any relevant information is understood and absorbed into the procedures described in Chapters 1 to 12.

2 Specifications

The Specifications given below are a revision of, or are additional to, those given at the beginning of the first twelve Chapters.

Engine – 1.3 litre

Cylinder block (1988-on)

Note: *From 1988, the main bearing bores are colour-coded (see text)*

Main bearing bores:

Red	2.1466 to 2.1470 in (54.52 to 54.53 mm)
Green	2.1462 to 2.1466 in (54.51 to 54.52 mm)
Yellow	2.1458 to 2.1462in (54.50 to54.51 mm)

Crankshaft

Note: *From 1988, the main journal diameters are colour-coded (see text)*

Main journal diameter:

With no colour code	2.0012 to 2.0017 in (50.83 to 50.84mm)
Red	2.0005 to 2.0009 in (50.81 to 50.82mm)
Green	2.0009 to 2.0013 in (50.82 to 50.83mm)
Yellow	2.0013 to 2.0017 in (50.83 to 50.84mm)
Main bearing running clearance	0.0007 to 0.0023 in (0.018 to 0.058mm)
Crankshaft endfloat	0.002 to 0.0023 in (0.018 to 0.058 mm)
Crankshaft endfloat	0.002 to 0.003 in (0.051 to 0.076 mm)
Thrustwasher oversize	0.003 and 0.030 in (0.076 and 0.76 mm)

Valves (1988-on)

Valve seat angle	45° 30'

Head diameter (leaded fuel engines):

Inlet	1.389 to 1.409 in (35.28 to 35.79 mm)
Exhaust	1.150 to 1.160 in (29.21 to 29.46 mm)

Head diameter (unleaded fuel engines):

Inlet	1.307 to 1.312 in (33.20 to 33.32 mm)
Exhaust	1.151 to 1.156 in (29.24 to 29.36 mm)

Stem diameter:

Inlet	0.2790 to 0.2797 in (7.087 to 7.104mm)
Exhaust	0.2788 to 0.2793 in (7.082 to 7.094mm)

Clearance in guide:

Inlet	0.0015 to 0.0027 in (0.038 to 0.069 mm)
Exhaust	0.002 to 0.003 in (0.051 to 0.076 mm)
Valve clearances	0.012 in (0.30 mm)

Lubrication system (1988-on)

Oil pump:

Outer rotor endfloat	0.005 in (0.13 mm)
Inner rotor endfloat	0.005 in (0.13 mm)
Outer rotor-to-body clearance	0.010 in (0.25 mm)

Engine – 1.6 litre

Compression ratio

1989-on, engine number prefix 16HE33 and 34	9.4 : 1
1989-on, engine number prefix 16HE60, 61,62,63,64, 65 and 66	9.2 : 1
1989-on, engine number prefix 16HD86 and 16HD91	9.6 : 1

Crankshaft (1989-on)

Crankpin journal diameter	1.8748 to 1.8756 in (47.62 to 47.64 mm)
Endfloat	0.004 to 0.007 in (0.10 to 0.18 mm)
Thrustwashers available	0.089 to 0.092 in (2.26 to 2.34 mm) in increments of 0.001 in (0.025 mm)

Cylinder head (1989-on)

Maximum face distortion	0.008 in (0.20 mm)

Cylinder block (1989-on)

Maximum face distortion	0.004 in (0.01 mm)

Torque wrench settings

	lbf ft	Nm
Engine mountings:		
5/16 UNF	18	24
3/8 UNF	30	41

Cooling system (all models)

Test pressure (maximum)

Test pressure (maximum)	11 to 15 lbf/in^2 (0.8 to 1.0 bar)

13

Fuel system – 1.3 litre, 1984-on

Carburettor

Fast idle speed .... 1000 to 1200 rpm

Fuel octane rating

12H type engine .... 97 RON leaded

Fuel system – 1.6 litre, 1984-on

Carburettor

Engine number prefix 16HE33 and 16HE34. and 16HE60 to 16HE66
inclusive (as for 16H except for the following):

    Type .... SU HIF 44E with electronic idle speed control and cold drive enrichment

Engine number prefix 16HE33 and 16HE34, and 16HE60 to 16HE66
inclusive (as for 16H except for the following):

    Identification:

        Manual gearbox .... FZX 1517
        Automatic transmission .... FZX 1518
    Base idle speed .... 550 to 650 rpm
    Throttle position speed .... 725 to 775 rpm
    ECU-controlled speed .... 750 rpm

Engine number prefix 16HD86 and 16H D91 (as for 16H E33 except for
the following):

    Base idle speed .... 650 rpm
    Throttle position speed .... 750 rpm
    ECU-controlled speed .... 750 rpm

Fuel octane rating

1.6 litre without catalytic converter:

    16H and 16D .... 97 RON leaded
    16HE33, 34, 60, 61, 62,63, 64,65,66 .... 97 RON leaded, or 95 RON unleaded (minimum)

1.6 litre with catalytic converter:

    16HE60, 61, 64 and 65 .... 95 RON unleaded only (minimum)

Ignition system – 1.3 litre, 1984-on

Ignition coil

Type .... GCL 138 or 143
Primary resistance at 20°C (68°F) .... 0.71 to 0.81 ohms

Distributor

Make/type .... Lucas 59DM4 or 65DM4

Ignition system – 1.6 litre, 1984-on

Ignition coil

Type .... GCL 139 or 143
Primary resistance at 20°C (68°F) .... 0.71 to 0.81 ohms

Programmed ignition system

Electronic control unit type:

    Engine number prefix:

        16H .... Lucas AB17-84185 or 84740
        16HE33 and 16HE44 .... AUU 1644
        16HE60 to 66 inclusive .... AU U 1644 or MEQ 100003
        16H D 86 and 16HD91 .... AUU 1526

Crankshaft sensor .... Lucas 84229

Ignition timing

1989-on 16HE33,16HE34,16HD86 and 16HD91
(vacuum pipe connected) .... 13° to 27° BTDC @ 1500 rpm max with throttle switch closed

1989-on 16HE60,16HE61,16HE62,16HE63,16HE64,16HE65 and
16HE66:

    Vacuum pipe connected .... 13° to 27° BTDC @ 1000 rpm max with throttle switch closed
    Vacuum pipe disconnected .... 4° to 18° BTDC @ 1000 rpm max with throttle switch closed

1990-on 16HE60,16HE61,16HE64 and 16HE65:

    Vacuum pipe connected .... 20° BTDC @ 1000 rpm max with throttle switch closed
    Vacuum pipe disconnected .... 11° BTDC @ 1000 rpm max with throttle switch closed

Ignition timing (at 1000 rpm)
Vacuum hose connected .... 13 to 27° BTDC
Vacuum hose disconnected .... 4° to 18° BTDC

Clutch – 1.6 litre, five-speed, 1989-on
General
Type .... Single dry plate operated by self-adjusting cable
Clutch disc diameter .... 8.46 in (215 mm)

Manual gearbox – 1.6 litre, five-speed, 1989 on
General
Type .... Five forward speeds, all synchromesh, and reverse. Final drive integral with main gearbox
Type code .... T5 AR

Lubrication
Lubricant type/specification* .... Multigrade engine oil, viscosity SAE 10W/40
Lubricant capacity .... 3.9 pints (2.2 litres)
*Note: Austin Rover specify a 10W/40 oil to meet warranty requirements for models produced after August 1983.

Gearbox ratios
1st .... 3.250 : 1
2nd .... 1.894 : 1
3rd .... 1.222 : 1
4th .... 0.906 : 1
5th .... 0.714 : 1
Reverse .... 3.000 : 1
Final drive ratio .... 4.062 : 1

Gearbox overhaul data
Mainshaft:
  Endfloat .... 0.005 to 0.008 in (0.13 to 0.20 mm)
  Adjustment .... Selective circlips
Countershaft:
  1st gear endfloat .... 0.001 to 0.003 in (0.03 to 0.08 mm)
  Adjustment .... Selective thrust washer
  2nd gear endfloat .... 0.001 to 0.003 in (0.03 to 0.08 mm)
  Adjustment .... Selective collar
  Minimum baulk ring-to-gear clearance .... 0.016 in (0.41 mm)
  Maximum reverse idler gear-to-shaft clearance ..... 0.005 in (0.13 mm)
  Maximum selector fork-to-synchro sleeve clearance .. 0.04 in (1.00 mm)
  Maximum reverse gear fork-to-gear clearance .... 0.028 in (0.71 mm)
  Minimum end cover seal diameter .... 1.97 in (50.0 mm)
Differential:
  Endfloat .... 0.006 in (0.15 mm)
  Adjustment .... Selective circlips

Torque wrench settings

	lbf ft	Nm
Bellhousing to engine adaptor plate	66	90
Gearbox steady rod bolt	6	8
Gear lever to gearchange rod	18	25
Remote control housing to underbody	18	25
Oil filter plug	33	45
Oil drain plug	30	40
Countershaft access plug	52	70
Reversing lamp switch	18	25
Reverse idler shaft retaining bolt	49	67
Gearcase to bellhousing bolts	20	27
Speedometer pinion retaining bolt	8	11
Clutch release fork to operating lever bolt	21	29
Countershaft retaining nut	81	110
Reverse gear fork bracket bolts	10	14
Gearchange holder and interlock retaining bolts:		
M8 bolts	21	29
M6 bolts	9	13
Gearchange shaft detent plug	16	22

13

Driveshafts – 1.6 litre, 1989-on

Type	Unequal length solid steel, splined to inner and outer constant velocity joints

Lubrication

Overhaul only – see text

Lubricant type:

Outer constant velocity joint	Molycote grease VN2461/C, or equivalent
Inner constant velocity joint	Mobil 525 grease, or equivalent
Hub bearing water shield	Duckhams Admax, or equivalent

Quantity:

Outer constant velocity joint	90 cc
Inner constant velocity joint	190 to 205 cc

Torque wrench settings	**lbf ft**	**Nm**
Driveshaft retaining nut:		
Castellated nut	140	190
Staked nut	150	203
Roadwheel nuts	53	72
Swivel hub to strut nuts	66	90
Tie-rod outer balljoint to steering arm	22	30

Electrical system

Starter motor

Type and application:

Lucas M79	1.3 models and 1.6 models with manual transmission
Lucas M78R	1.6 models with automatic transmission
Minimum brush length	0.15 in (3.81 mm)
Commutator minimum diameter	1.134 in (28.8 mm)

Suspension and steering

Steering geometry

Camber angle:

1986 to 1988	0°8' positive to 0°34' negative
1988-on:	
Strut type A*	0°6' positive to 0°36' negative
Strut type B*	0°9' positive to 0°51 ' positive
Castor angle (1988-on)	0°7' positive 1°07' positive
Steering axis inclination (1989-on):	
Strut type A*	12 to 13°
Strut type B*	12°03' to 13°03'
Toe setting (1988-on)	Parallel ± 0°8'
Steering angles (at kerb weight):	
Inner wheel	36°59'
Outer wheel	34°05'

For A and B, see text

Power steering

Steering wheel turns lock to lock	2.94
Pump drivebelt deflection	0.25 to 0.50 in (7 to 12 mm)
Fluid type/specification	Dexron IID type ATF
Power steering fluid reservoir capacity	0.9 pints (0.5 litres)

Roadwheels – 1.6 litre, 1989-on

Wheel size:

Base model	5J x 13
Other models	5 1/2J x 14

Tyres – 1.6 litre, 1989-on

Tyre size:

Base model	165 SR 13
Other models	185/65 TR 14

Torque wrench settings	**lbf ft**	**Nm**
Power steering		
Flexible hose to pump union	20	27
Flexible hose to rack unions	11	15
Reservoir-to-pump bracket bolts	18	24
Pipe to pipe adaptor	18	24

Weights (kerb) – 1989-on

Saloons
1.6	2190 lb (995 kg)
1.6L	2270 lb (1030 kg)
1.6SL	2310 lb (1050 kg)
1.6L automatic	2310 lb (1050 kg)
1.6SL automatic	2355 lb (1070 kg)

Estates
1.6	2345 lb (1065 kg)
1.6L	2400 lb (1090 kg)
1.6SL	2445 lb (1110 kg)
1.6L automatic	2445 lb (1110 kg)
1.6SL automatic	2485 lb (1130 kg)

3 Engine

Engine and gearbox (1.6 litre, 1989-on) – removal and refitting

1 From 1989, 1.6 litre models are fitted with a Honda-derived five-speed gearbox.
2 The removal and refitting of the engine and gearbox assembly is basically as described in Chapter 1, noting the different mountings described in this Section.
3 The procedure for removal of the gearbox on its own is given in Section 9 of this Supplement.

Oil filter (1.6 engine)

4 In order to prevent cold start rattle, caused by the engine oil draining back to the sump when the vehicle is standing, it is imperative that the later type of oil filter, incorporating an anti-drain valve, is always fitted at time of renewal. The correct oil filter to use is either Unipart GFE 180 or the Champion equivalent (see Chapter 1 Specifications).

Oil filler pipe emulsification

5 If oil emulsification ('salad cream' type consistency) is evident within the engine oil filler pipe, particularly in cold weather, it can be eliminated in the following way.
6 Remove the air cleaner element and then drill a 0.37 in (9.5 mm) hole through the

casing, as shown at 'A' in Fig. 13.1, to accept a grommet.
7 Remove the oil filler pipe. Drill a 0.20 in (5.0 mm) hole and braze a 1.0 inch (25.0 mm) length of brake hydraulic pipe into the filler tube, as shown in Fig. 13.2.
8 Connect a 16.5 in (420.0 mm) length of flexible tubing between the newly fitted grommet and the oil filler pipe brazed stub. The flexible tubing must protrude into the air cleaner by 5.0 mm and slope downward throughout its length.
9 Start the engine, bring it to normal operating temperature, and check and adjust the idle speed and mixture settings.
10 If slight emulsification still occurs, the oil filler pipe and separator should be insulated. A special lagging kit is available.

Fig. 13.2 Oil filler drilling position – dimensions in mm (Sec 3)

A Pipe stub position   C Tubing
B Section A – A   D Oil filler pipe

Fig. 13.1 Air cleaner drilling position (A) (Sec 3)

Engine modifications for operation on unleaded fuel

11 Fuel octane ratings are given in the Specifications section of this Chapter. Certain 1.6 litre models without catalytic converters may be run on either unleaded or leaded fuel, but models fitted with a catalytic converter **must only** use unleaded fuel, otherwise the converter will be damaged.
12 Note that some engine types are capable of conversion to operate on unleaded fuel (95 RON octane minimum). This conversion must be entrusted to a Rover dealer and where this has been made, the letter 'U' will be stamped between the end of the engine number prefix and the serial number. Where doubt exists regarding the fuel type to use, consult a Rover dealer.
13 The valve seats on engines capable of using unleaded fuel have different angles and are specially hardened. Because of this, they cannot be re-worked using conventional machine tools.

Piston rings (1.6 models) – gap setting

14 It should be noted that, on later models, the second compression ring is stepped.
15 When fitting the oil control ring, fit the lower rail with its gap towards the flywheel, and the upper rail with its gap towards the timing belt. The expander should have its gap away from the thrust side of the piston (away from the dipstick side).

Flywheel retaining bolts – renewal

16 If the flywheel is removed during overhaul, always use new bolts at reassembly. Before fitting the bolts, clean away all trace of old thread-locking material from the threaded holes in the crankshaft. A suitable tap is recommended for this job.

Crankshaft main bearings (1.3 litre, 1988-on) – colour codes

17 As from 1988, all 1.3 litre engines are fitted with selective main bearings, the size being identified by a colour code – red, green or yellow.
18 The main bearing bores, crankshaft main

13

bearing journals, main bearing caps and replacement bearings are all either marked with appropriate coloured dye, or stamped with the letters R, G or Y.

Engine overhaul with power-assisted steering

19 On vehicles fitted with optional power-assisted steering, the steering pump drivebelt must be removed before carrying out any of the following operations.
Renewal of the camshaft front oil seal
Tappet adjustment
Timing belt renewal
20 The steering pump must be unbolted and moved to one side before any of the following operations can be carried out.
Cylinder head – removal and refitting
Engine/transmission – removal and refitting
Engine right-hand mounting – renewal
21 The steering hydraulic pipelines must be unclipped before the engine sump pan can be removed.
22 Refer to Section 13 for details of power-assisted steering system.

4 Engine mountings

Revised removal and dismantling (1.3 models)

1 The following procedure should be substituted for that described for the right-hand mounting in Chapter 1, Section 29. See also Fig. 1.7.
2 Unbolt the coolant expansion tank and move it to one side.
3 Raise the right-hand front roadwheel and support the car securely on stands.
4 Remove the access panel from the right-hand wing valance.
5 Take the weight of the engine/transmission using a hoist or a jack and block of wood as an insulator.
6 Slacken the right-hand mounting through-bolt and remove the bolts which hold the mounting bracket to the engine bracket. Take off the restraint bracket.
7 Unscrew the bolts which hold the support

strap to the wing valance, lower the engine slightly and remove the mounting assembly. Take off the valance bracket plate.
8 The mounting can be dismantled once the through-bolt is unscrewed. This bolt can be very tight, and may require the application of heat and the use of a long knuckle bar.
9 Apply thread-locking fluid to clean threads of the bolts which hold the mounting bracket to the engine bracket, and the support strap to the body bracket.
10 Locate the mounting so that the spacer is offset towards the top, then place the reinforced buffer plate on one side and engage the top locating hole on the mounting. Place the support strap over the mounting, and enter a new through-bolt from the buffer plate side.
11 Attach the assembly to the combined mounting bracket and fixed buffer plate, but do not tighten at this stage.
12 Place the mounting assembly on the valance bracket and fit the support strap, but do not tighten the bolts.
13 Raise the engine/transmission slightly and locate the engine bracket, mounting bracket and restraint bracket. Tighten the mounting bracket bolts to the specified torque (Fig. 13.3).
14 Tighten the mounting through-bolt to the specified torque.
15 Move the support strap and align the mounting rubber as shown in Fig. 1.7 (inset).
16 Tighten the support strap bolts to torque and check that the mounting is parallel to the buffer plates.
17 Fit the access panel, remove the engine/transmission hoist or jack and lower the vehicle to the floor.

Identification and torque tightening fixings

18 In order to clarify the mounting bolt and nut torque wrench settings, refer to Figs. 13.3 and 13.4.
19 All other mounting nuts and bolts should be tightened as given in the Specifications for this Supplement.

Modified front mounting (1.6 models)

20 As from 1985 the front mounting (snubber) is of different design and the removal and refitting procedure is as described in the following paragraphs. Refer to 'A', Fig. 13.4.
21 Disconnect the battery.
22 Slacken the front mounting through-bolt.
23 Unscrew the bolts, nuts and washers which secure the mounting bracket to the body.
24 Unscrew and remove the nuts from the starter motor mounting bolts, detach the wiring harness bracket and remove the mounting bracket.
25 Remove the mounting through-bolt.
26 Refitting is a reversal of removal, tighten all nuts and bolts to the specified torque.

Removal and refitting (1.6 models, 1989-on)

27 The engine mountings on 1.6 litre models from 1989-on have been modified, to accept the Honda-derived five-speed gearbox.
28 Removal and refitting of the mountings is basically as described in Chapter 1, and Section 9 of this Supplement. Use the torque wrench settings given in this Supplement when tightening the mountings.

Fig. 13.3 Engine mounting nuts and bolts torque wrench settings – 1.3 models (Sec 4)

1	18 lbf ft (24 Nm)	5	66 lbf ft (89 Nm)
2	30 lbf ft (41 Nm)	6	60 lbf ft (81 Nm)
3	33 lbf ft (45 Nm)	7	45 lbf ft (61 Nm)
4	37 lbf ft (50 Nm)	8	90 lbf ft (122 Nm)

Fig. 13.4 Engine mounting nuts and bolts torque wrench settings – 1.6 litre models, 1985-on (Sec 4)

A	Front mounting	2A	33 lbf ft (45 Nm)
1	18 lbf ft (25 Nm)	3	33 lbf ft (45 Nm)
2	30 lbf ft (41 Nm)	4	60 lbf ft (81 Nm)

Fig. 13.5 Engine mountings nuts and bolts torque wrench settings – 1.6 litre models, 1989-on (Sec 4)

1a	25 lbf ft (33 Nm)	3	33 lbf ft (45 Nm)
2	30 lbf ft (41 Nm)	5	60 lbf ft (81 Nm)
2b	33 lbf h (45 Nm)		

6.1A Removing the air cleaner top cover

6.1B Cold air intake tube attachment at the front body panel

6.1C Disconnecting the cold air intake tube at the air cleaner

5 Cooling system

Cooling system – pressure testing

1 When using pressure test equipment to check the cooling system for leaks, it is important that the recommended test pressure is not exceeded (see Specifications).

6 Fuel and exhaust systems

Air cleaner and element (1.6 models, 1989 on) – removal and refitting

1 The procedure is similar to that described in Chapter 3, Section 4, but the assembly is slightly different and is shown in Fig. 13.6 (photos).

2 To remove the air cleaner from the engine the HT lead and clutch cable must first be released from the cleaner housing.

3 Note also that one of the housing retaining bolts also secures the thermostat housing. Before removing this bolt, remove the cap from the expansion tank to release any pressure in the cooling system, and refit the bolt after the air cleaner housing is removed to minimise coolant loss.

4 Removal and testing of the thermac unit is as described in Chapter 3 (photos).

1 Air cleaner assembly
2 Filter element
3 Mounting bracket
4 Thermac unit
5 Bolt
6 Intake tube elbow
7 Retaining clip
8 Cold air intake tube
9 Intake tube adaptor
10 Rubber seal
11 Hot air intake tube
12 Hot air box
13 Bolt
14 Plenum chamber intake tube
15 Plenum chamber
16 Gasket
17 Screw
18 Washer
19 Support bracket
20 Nut
21 Spring washer
22 Thermac switch
23 Grommet
24 Seal
25 Large diameter vacuum hose
26 Small diameter vacuum hose
27 T-piece connector
28 Vacuum hose inlet manifold to T-piece

Fig. 13.6 Exploded view of the air cleaner assembly and associated components (Sec 6)

6.1D Air cleaner removed showing vacuum assembly (B) and attachment bracket (A)

6.4A Connecting a vacuum tube to the thermac unit

6.4B Refitting the thermac unit to the plenum chamber

13

Fig. 13.7 Showing single and twin-turret fuel pumps and respective spacer blocks (Sec 6)

A – Spacer block with large cut-out   *B – Spacer block with small cut-out*

Fig. 13.8 SU carburettor with progressive throttle cam (Sec 6)

1 Piston damper oil level	5 Fast idle adjusting screw	A Lost motion clearance
2 Idle speed adjusting screw	6 Fast idle pushrod	B Fast idle rod clearance
3 Progressive throttle cam	7 Mixture adjusting screw	C Throttle lever and linkage
4 Throttle lever screw	8 Lost motion adjusting tag	

Fig. 13.9 ERIC component location diagram – 1.6 models, 1989-on (Sec 6)

1 ECU	sensor	8 Engine multi-function unit
2 Ambient air temperature	4 Crankshaft sensor	9 4-way harness connector
sensor – located behind	5 Knock sensor	10 13-way harness connector
horns	6 Carburettor	11 Engine tuning and
3 Coolant temperature	7 Ignition coil	diagnostic connector

5 When refitting the thermac unit hoses to the connector on the plenum chamber, the connections are as follows:
Large diameter hose –
  thermac switch to thermac unit
Small diameter hose –
  thermac switch to manifold vacuum hose
T-piece connector

Fuel pump spacer block (1.3 litre, all models)

6 It is imperative when fitting a replacement fuel pump to all A-series engines that the correct spacer block is fitted between the pump and cylinder block.

7 Early, single-turret type pumps have a spacer with a large cut-out; later, twin-turret, types have a smaller cut-out (see Fig. 13.7).

8 The spacer block with the large cut-out must not be fitted to a later twin-turret pump because the block will not retain the lever pivot pin, which may come adrift and fall into the engine.

SU carburettor – adjustments

9 Certain later models are fitted with a carburettor which incorporates a progressive throttle cam (Fig. 13.8). When carrying out the adjustments described in Chapter 3, Section 12, the lost motion clearance should be set by bending the tag (8).

Electronically Regulated Ignition and Carburation system (ERIC), (1.6 models, 1989-on) – general description

10 The Electronically Regulated Ignition and Carburation system (ERIC) is a complete engine management system, which meets a very high standard of emission control. Using a single Electronic Control Unit (ECU), which effectively combines the fuel ECU and Ignition ECU modules used in the programmed systems of earlier models, ERIC controls and synchronises all fuel and ignition requirements of the engine. The ECU receives its information from the same source as the earlier systems, and acts on the carburettor and ignition system in the same manner. For the purposes of this Supplement, the fuelling aspects of the system are dealt with in this Section and the ignition aspects in Section 7.

ERIC system – component location, removal and refitting

11 The layout of the ERIC system components and their location is shown in Fig. 13.9.

12 The removal and refitting of the components is as described in Chapters 3 and 4.

ERIC system tuning, adjustment and fault finding

13 The accurate tuning, adjustment and fault diagnosis of the ERIC system requires the use of special test equipment which is likely to be only available to Austin Rover dealers.

Fig. 13.10 Electronically Regulated Ignition and Carburation system (ERIC) wiring diagram – 1.6 models, 1989-on (Sec 6)

1 ECU
2 Carburettor
3 Stepper motor
4 Ignition coil
5 Distributor cap
6 Main relay
7 Manifold heater
8 Manifold heater relay

9 Electric fuel pump (not on 1.6)
10 Fuse No 17 in fusebox
11 Fuel cut-off switch (inertia)
12 Fuel pump relay (not on 1.6)
13 Engine tuning and diagnostic socket
14 Temperature gauge
15 Camshaft sensor

16 Throttle pedal switch
17 Ambient air temperature sensor
18 Coolant thermistor
19 Inlet air temperature sensor (not on 1.6)
20 Knock sensor
21 Fuse No 1 in fusebox

22 Ignition switch
23 Ignition relay
24 Fusible link
25 Battery
26 Automatic transmission inhibitor switch
27 Starter relay
28 Manifold vacuum tube

13

Fig. 13.11 Exploded view of the SU HIF 44E carburettor (Sec 6)

1 Piston damper
2 Spring ring – piston
3 Suction chamber
4 Piston
5 Piston spring
6 Needle retaining screw
7 Needle bias spring
8 Jet needle
9 Needle guide
10 Idle speed adjustment screw
11 Adjusting screw seal
12 Mixture adjustment screw

13 Throttle return screw
14 Throttle spindle seal
15 Throttle disc
16 Throttle spindle
17 Carburettor body
18 Mounting bracket
19 Mixture control stepper motor
20 Fast idle push-rod
21 Jet bearing
22 Jet bearing nut
23 Jet assembler

24 Float needle seat
25 Float needle
26 Bi-metal jet lever
27 Float
28 Jet retaining screw
29 Float chamber cover seal
30 Float chamber cover
31 Throttle cam and return spring
32 Throttle position screw
33 Lost motion link and return spring
34 Fast idle lever

Fig. 13.12 Throttle position speed adjustment on the SU HIF 44E carburettor (Sec 6)

Fig. 13.13 Lost motion clearance adjustment on the SU HIF 44E carburettor (Sec 6)

A – adjustment tag
B – clearance = 0.140 to 0.160 in (3.5 to 4.0 mm)

14 For this reason there is no alternative but to take the vehicle to an Austin Rover dealer for tuning, adjustment and fault diagnosis, and subsequent rectification.

15 The ERIC system is equipped with a diagnostic and tuning socket connector into which the special test equipment can be connected for speedy testing and fault diagnosis. The ECU is equipped with a memory interface in which are stored intermittent faults which can be read off on the test equipment, so simplifying the test procedure and pin-pointing faults.

Carburettor (SU HIF 44E) – overhaul, tuning and adjustment

16 The HF 44E carburettor fitted to 1.6 litre models with the ERIC system is basically the same as the HIF 44 carburettor described in Chapter 3, and can be overhauled using the same procedure, bearing in mind the following differences.

17 There is no fuel shut-off valve.

18 The throttle linkage is slightly different, and the lost motion clearance is adjusted by bending the tag on the throttle lever as described later.

19 Without the special tuning and diagnostic equipment mentioned earlier the carburettor cannot be adjusted accurately. Approximate settings can be obtained following the procedure given in Chapter 3, Section 12, noting the following.

20 Base idle is set to the specified speed using the idle speed adjustment screw, and the CO content is set using the mixture screw (both these screws are as shown in Fig. 3.5 in Chapter 3).

21 Throttle position speed is adjusted on the fast idle adjustment screw.

22 Lost motion clearance is adjusted by bending the tag on the fast idle lever, and must be set to the specified clearance shown in Fig. 13.13.

Fuel octane rating

23 Refer to the Specifications section and Section 4, paragraphs 11 to 13, of this Chapter for details.

Catalytic converter – general

24 Some models are fitted with a catalytic converter in the exhaust system, the function of which is to minimise the pollutants passing through the exhaust system. An 'open-loop' converter system is used, thus there is no information feedback to the fuel and ignition systems via a sensor in the exhaust as on 'closed-loop' systems.

25 The catalytic converter is connected to the exhaust downpipe at its front end and to the exhaust intermediate section at the rear. It has an integral ceramic and precious metals filter to reduce the harmful exhaust emissions and operates at very high temperatures. The catalytic converter is a fragile device which can be easily damaged. With this in mind, it is imperative that the following precautionary observations be noted and adhered to whenever working on, or in the vicinity of, the catalytic converter in order to ensure its efficiency and maximise service life.

Catalytic converter – precautions

26 The catalytic converter is a reliable and simple device which needs no maintenance in itself, but there are some facts of which an owner should be aware if the converter is to function properly for its full service life.

(a) DO NOT use leaded petrol in a car equipped with a catalytic converter – the lead will coat the precious metals, reducing their converting efficiency and will eventually destroy the converter.

(b) Always keep the ignition and fuel systems well-maintained in accordance with the manufacturer's schedule – particularly, ensure that the air cleaner filter element and the spark plugs are renewed at the correct interval – if the intake air/fuel mixture is allowed to become too rich due to neglect, the unburned surplus will enter and burn in the catalytic converter, overheating the element and eventually destroying the converter.

(c) If the engine develops a misfire, do not drive the car at all (or at least as little as possible) until the fault is cured – the misfire will allow unburned fuel to enter the converter, which will result in its overheating, as noted above.

(d) DO NOT push- or tow-start the car – this will soak the catalytic converter in unburned fuel, causing it to overheat when the engine does start – see (b) above.

(e) DO NOT switch off the ignition at high engine speeds – if the ignition is switched off at anything above idle speed, unburned fuel will enter the (very hot) catalytic converter, with the possible risk of its igniting on the element and damaging the converter.

(f) DO NOT use fuel or engine oil additives – these may contain substances harmful to the catalytic converter.

(g) DO NOT continue to use the car if the engine burns oil to the extent of leaving a visible trail of blue smoke – the unburned carbon deposits will clog the converter passages and reduce its efficiency; in severe cases the element will overheat.

(h) Remember that the catalytic converter operates at very high temperatures – hence the heat shields on the car's underbody and the casing will become hot enough to ignite combustible materials which brush against it. DO NOT, therefore, park the car in dry undergrowth, over long grass or piles of dead leaves.

(i) Remember that the catalytic converter is FRAGILE – do not strike it with tools during servicing work, take great care when working on the exhaust system,

Fig. 13.14 Fuel evaporative loss system (EVAP) layout (Sec 6)

1 Fuel tank breather	7 Pressure regulator	13 Fuel feed pipe
2 Fuel filler pipe	8 Injectors	14 2-way valve
3 Fuel pump	9 Charcoal canister	15 Fuel tank to vapour
4 Fuel feed pipe	10 Purge valve	separation tank pipes
5 Fuel tank	11 Fuel filter	16 Fuel filler cap
6 Fuel return pipe	12 Fuel tank vent pipe	17 Separation tank

ensure that the converter is well clear of any jacks or gear used to raise the car and do not drive the car over rough ground road humps, etc, in such a way as to 'ground' the exhaust system.

(j) In some cases, particularly when the car is new and/or is used for stop/start driving, a sulphurous smell (like that of rotten eggs) may be noticed from the exhaust. This is common to many catalytic converter-equipped cars and seems to be due to the small amount of sulphur found in some petrols reacting with hydrogen in the exhaust to produce hydrogen sulphide (H_2S) gas; while this gas is toxic, it is not produced in sufficient amounts to be a problem. Once the car has covered a few thousand miles the problem should disappear – in the meanwhile a change of driving style or of the brand of petrol used may effect a solution.

(k) The catalytic converter, used on a well-maintained and well driven car, should last for between 50 000 and 100 000 miles from this point on, careful checks should be made at all specified service intervals of the CO level to ensure that the converter is still operating efficiently – if the converter is no longer effective it must be renewed.

(l) Do not overfill the engine oil level. Excess oil may enter the exhaust system, cause the catalytic converter to be clogged and excess HC emissions will result as it is being burnt off.

(m) Do not apply an exhaust sealant to any of the system joints forward of the catalytic converter. Any excess sealant compressed into the system when tightening the joints may be transferred into the converter.

Fuel evaporative loss control system (EVAP) – general

27 A fuel evaporative loss system is fitted to 1.6 litre models from November 1988 on. The function of the system is to prevent the fuel vapours that are produced in the fuel tank when the engine is turned off escaping to the atmosphere. This is achieved by transferring the vaporised fuel to a charcoal canister. When the engine is restarted, the stored fuel vapour is transferred from the canister to the induction system and burnt off in the normal combustion process. A schematic diagram of the system is shown in Fig. 13.14.

28 The charcoal canister (located under the right-hand front wing), contains charcoal granules which absorb and store the fuel system vapours. A purge valve, mounted in the engine compartment (at the rear of the

Fig. 13.15 Charcoal canister and connections (Sec 6)

1 Mounting bracket	4 Charcoal canister
2 Vapour pipe	5 Clamp
3 Purge pipe	6 Drain pipe

13

Fig. 13.16 Purge valve connections (Sec 6)

1 Mounting bracket   4 Hose connector
  securing bolts   5 O-ring
2 Mounting bracket   6 Circlip
3 Purge control   7 Vacuum pipe
  valve   8 Wiring multi-plug

Fig. 13.17 2-way valve and connections
(Sec 6)

1 2-way valve
2 Hoses (note fitted positions before
  disconnecting)

Fig. 13.18 Vapour separation tank and
connections (Sec 6)

1 Separation tank   3 Retaining screw
2 Hoses

right-hand headlamp), prevents purging between the charcoal canister and the throttle body under certain operating conditions which would otherwise effect the operation of the engine and/or catalytic converter (where applicable).

29 The vapours pass from the fuel tank to a separation tank, mounted under the right-hand rear wing which collects fuel vapour, separates the fuel from it and passes the remaining vapour to the charcoal canister via a 2-way valve located under the separation tank. The valve opens under pressure (approx 0.4 lbf/in^2) to enable the fuel vapour to pass from the separation tank to the charcoal canister. At the same time, the valve also opens the fuel tank to atmosphere to relieve the depression in the fuel tank. The liquid fuel collected in the separation tank is passed back into the main fuel tank.

Fuel evaporative loss control system (EVAP) components – removal and refitting

Charcoal canister

30 Loosen off (but do not remove at this stage) the right-hand front roadwheel then raise and support the front of the vehicle on axle stands. With the vehicle securely supported, remove the roadwheel.
31 Where applicable, undo the retaining screws and remove the front spoiler.
32 Release the retaining studs and detach the wheel arch liner from the leading edge on the underside of the right-hand front wing.
33 Undo the mounting bracket retaining screw and nuts, then lower the canister plate. Loosen off the securing clip and detach the drain pipe from the canister. Compress the vapour and purge pipe hose clips, lower the canister and detach the hoses from their connectors at the top.
34 Refit in the reverse order of removal.

Ensure that the hoses are in good condition and are securely connected.

Purge valve

35 Undo the bolts securing the valve mounting bracket, then move the bracket to enable the multi-plug to be detached.
36 Disconnect the vacuum pipe from the purge valve, then detach the hose connector circlip and remove the connector. The purge valve can now be slid free from its bracket and removed.
37 Refit in the reverse order of removal. Renew the O-ring when fitting it to the hose connector, smear it with clean engine oil to ease assembly. Ensure that all connections are cleanly and securely made.

2-way valve

38 Loosen off (but do not remove at this stage) the right-hand rear roadwheel, then raise and support the rear of the vehicle on axle stands. With the vehicle securely supported, remove the roadwheel.
39 Unscrew and remove the 2-way valve retaining screw. Note the fitted positions of the hoses, compress their retaining clips and detach the hoses from the valve. Remove the valve.
40 Refit in the reverse order of removal. Ensure that the hoses are correctly secured to the valve prior to refitting it into position.

Vapour separation tank

41 Loosen off (but do not remove at this stage) the right-hand rear roadwheel, then raise and support the rear of the vehicle on axle stands. With the vehicle securely supported, remove the roadwheel.
42 Unscrew and remove the separation tank retaining screws. Note the fitted positions of the hoses, compress their retaining clips and detach them from the tank. Remove the tank.
43 Refit in the reverse order of removal. Ensure that the hoses are correctly and securely connected to the separation tank prior to refitting it into position.

7 Ignition system

Distributor (1.3 models) – removal, overhaul and refitting

⚠ Warning: The amplifier unit in the distributor contains beryllia and must not be opened.

1 The type 65DM4 distributor fitted to later models is removed as described for the type 59DM4 in Chapter 4, except that a spacer is fitted between the distributor mounting pedestal and the engine.
2 Commence overhaul by removing the rotor arm.
3 Extract the fixing screws and remove the amplifier module, its gasket and connector block. Do not attempt to open the amplifier.
4 Extract the retaining screws and separate the upper and lower bodies.
5 Lift the clamp ring and the pick-up winding from the upper body.
6 Extract the vacuum unit fixing screw.
7 Extract the circlip, remove the thrustwasher and withdraw the stator pack from the vacuum link and then remove the vacuum unit.
8 Support the drive dog and drive out the pin. Remove the dog and thrustwasher.
9 Pull the driveshaft from the lower body and remove the spacer. Do not attempt to remove the reluctor from the shaft.
10 Clean and examine all components and renew as necessary. Reassembly is a reversal of dismantling.
11 As reassembly progresses, lightly oil the bushes, pivots and bearing surfaces.
12 When fitting the amplifier, smear its mounting face with heat conductive silicone paste available from your dealer or auto-electrical engineer.
13 If a new mainshaft is being fitted, fit the rotor arm to the original shaft and use it as a

Fig. 13.19 Exploded view of the 65 DM4 distributor (Sec 7)

1 Distributor cap, brush and spring
2 Rotor arm
3 Upper body
4 Vacuum unit
5 Stator pack, thrust washers and circlip
6 Pick-up winding assembly
7 Clamp ring
8 Reluctor, centrifugal advance and shaft
9 Internal thrust washer
10 Lower body
11 O-ring seal
12 External thrust washer and drive dog
13 Connector and gasket
14 Amplifier module

Fig. 13.20 Distributor rotor arm-to-drive dog pin offset (Sec 7)

guide for drilling the 0.13 in (3.20 mm) hole for the drive dog (see Fig. 13.20).

14 Fit a new O-ring and, if fitted, the spacer, and apply a drop of oil to the shaft centre bearing lubrication hole.

15 To refit the distributor, first check that No 1 piston is still at TDC.

16 Hold the distributor over its mounting hole so that the vacuum unit is pointing towards No 1 spark plug and the amplifier is at the 4 o'clock position.

17 Insert the distributor and turn the rotor arm slightly to engage the drive dog torque with the coupling.

18 Align the distributor body-to-engine reference marks and clamp the distributor.

19 Refit the cap and connect all leads, the multi-plug and vacuum hose.

20 Check the ignition timing dynamically using a stroboscope, as described in Chapter 4, Section 5.

Rotor arm securing screw seizure – programmed ignition

21 Seizure of the rotor arm securing screw is due to thread-locking compound remaining in the threads of the hole in the camshaft after the screw is removed.

22 Whenever the rotor arm is removed, the threads in the camshaft must be cleaned out using an M6 tap and die.

23 Apply thread-locking compound in the threads of the securing screw on refitting.

Spark plugs

24 It is recommended that when renewing the spark plugs, the copper-cored type is used, as given in the Specifications.

Ignition warning lamp circuitry

25 The ignition warning lamp live feed is connected to the instrument supply line through a fused circuit controlled by the ignition switch.

26 Should the instrument supply fuse blow, with consequent loss of instrument readings, it should be realised that the ignition (charge) warning lamp will also be extinguished and there will not be any alternator output at low engine speeds. Failure of the ignition warning lamp bulb will also affect alternator output.

Fig. 13.21 Fitted position of spacer (arrowed) on 65 DM4 distributor (Sec 7)

27 On later models, a resistor is connected in parallel with the ignition warning lamp to prevent lack of charge.

Ignition switch/steering column lock (1986 on)

28 The ignition switch used on later models incorporates a safety feature which prevents the starter being energised while the engine is running.

29 The starter cannot be energised twice consecutively unless the key has been turned to position 1 between starting attempts.

Electronically Regulated Ignition and Carburation system (ERIC) – general description

30 As described in Section 6 of this Supplement, the Electronically Regulated Ignition and Carburation system (ERIC) combines the functions of the fuel and ignition systems into one system.

31 Reference should be made to Section 6 for details of the system and to Chapter 4, Part 2 for details of the ignition components of the system, which are the same as used on the earlier programmed ignition system.

8 Clutch

Clutch cable adjustment (all models) – checking

1 Whenever the clutch cable is disturbed for any reason the following adjustment check must be carried out.

2 Using moderate hand pressure, push the clutch lever on the bellhousing downward (in the opposite direction to its normal travel) through its full stroke. When released, the lever should return to its original position.

3 Press the adjuster body into its abutment on the engine bulkhead with one hand, and with the other, pull the outer cable away from

Fig. 13.22 Ignition switch positions (Sec 7)

I   Steering unlocked, radio, blower and windscreen wiper can be operated
II   Ignition on, all electrical circuits operational
III Starter motor operates

13

Fig. 13.23 Exploded view of the clutch and flywheel assembly on 1.6 models with five-speed gearbox, 1989-on (Sec 8)

1 Reluctor ring teeth
2 Flywheel
3 Locking plate
4 Clutch disc
5 Clutch cover assembly
6 Release bearing
7 Release fork
8 Release bearing retaining spring wire
9 Operating lever
10 Operating lever seal
11 Cable retaining clip
12 Cable seating plate
13 Rubber pad
14 Clutch cable

the bulkhead until resistance is felt, holding the outer cable at a point just behind the spring.

4 Release both parts of the cable.

5 This should ensure the self-adjusting mechanism is correctly set. If the adjuster fails to operate correctly, refer to the fault diagnosis (Section 8) of Chapter 5.

Clutch pedal freeplay (all models)

6 The ratchet and spring self-adjusting mechanism which compensates for clutch friction wear operates in steps. The pedal freeplay will therefore diminish between steps and increase again when the next step on the ratchet mechanism is reached.

7 The pedal freeplay can be considered normal if at all times it is between a minimum of 0.47 in (12.0 mm) and a maximum of 1.1 in (28.0 mm).

Clutch (1.6 five-speed, 1989-on) – general description

8 The clutch fitted to 1989-on 1.6 litre models with five-speed gearbox is of conventional diaphragm spring type, operated by self-adjusting cable.

The clutch components comprise a steel cover assembly, clutch disc or driven plate, release bearing and release mechanism. The cover assembly which is bolted and dowelled to the rear face of the flywheel contains the pressure plate and diaphragm spring.

The clutch disc is free to slide along the gearbox input shaft splines and is held in position between the flywheel and pressure plate by the pressure of the diaphragm spring.

Friction material is riveted to the clutch disc, which has a spring-cushioned hub to absorb transmission shocks and to help ensure a smooth take-up of the drive.

Depressing the clutch pedal moves the clutch release lever on the gearbox by means of the clutch cable. This movement is transmitted to the release bearing which moves inwards against the fingers of the diaphragm spring. The spring is sandwiched between two annular rings which act as fulcrum points. As the release bearing pushes the spring fingers in, the outer circumference pivots out, so moving the pressure plate away from the flywheel and releasing its grip on the clutch disc.

When the pedal is released, the diaphragm spring forces the pressure plate into contact with the friction linings of the clutch disc. This disc is now firmly sandwiched between the pressure plate and the flywheel, this transmitting engine power to the gearbox.

Adjustment of the clutch to compensate for wear of the clutch disc friction linings is automatically taken up by the self-adjusting mechanism incorporated in the cable.

Clutch cable (1.6 five-speed, 1989-on) – removal and refitting

9 The procedure is as described in Chapter 5, Section 2.

Clutch assembly (1.6 five-speed, 1989-on) – removal, inspection and refitting

10 Remove the gearbox as described in Section 9.

11 In a diagonal sequence, half a turn at a time, slacken the bolts securing the clutch cover assembly to the flywheel.

12 When all the bolts are slack, remove them and then ease the cover assembly off the locating dowels. Collect the clutch disc which will drop out when the cover assembly is removed.

13 With the clutch assembly removed, clean off all traces of asbestos dust using a dry cloth. This is best done outside or in a well ventilated area; *asbestos dust is harmful, and must not be inhaled.*

14 Examine the linings of the clutch disc for wear and loose rivets, and the disc for rim distortion, cracks, broken torsion springs and worn splines. The surface of the friction linings may be highly glazed, but, as long as the friction material pattern can be clearly seen, this is satisfactory. If there is any sign of oil contamination, indicated by a continuous, or patchy, shiny black discoloration, the disc must be renewed and the source of the contamination traced and rectified. This will be either a leaking crankshaft oil seal or gearbox mainshaft oil seal – or both. Renewal procedures are given in Chapter 1, Section 27 for the engine, whilst for the gearbox refer to Chapter 6, Section 17 (or section 9 of this Chapter for later models fitted with the Honda gearbox). The disc must also be renewed if the lining thickness has worn down to, or just above, the level of the rivet heads.

15 Check the machined faces of the flywheel and pressure plate. If either is grooved, or heavily scored, renewal is necessary. The pressure plate must also be renewed if any cracks are apparent, or if the diaphragm spring is damaged or its pressure suspect.

16 With the gearbox removed it is advisable to check the condition of the release bearing, as described in the following sub-section.

17 To refit the clutch assembly, plate the clutch disc in position with the raised portion of the spring housing facing away from the flywheel. The words FLYWHEEL SIDE will also usually be found on the other side of the disc that faces the flywheel.

18 Hold the disc in place and refit the cover assembly loosely on the dowels (photo). Refit the retaining bolts and tighten them finger tight so that the clutch disc is gripped, but can still be moved.

8.18 Refitting the clutch disc and cover

19 The clutch disc must now be centralised so that when the engine and gearbox are mated, the gearbox input shaft splines will pass through the splines in the centre of the hub.

20 Centralisation can be carried out quite easily by inserting a round bar or long screwdriver through the hole in the centre of the clutch disc, so that the end of the bar rests in the hole in the centre of the crankshaft. Moving the bar sideways or up and down will move the clutch disc in whichever direction is necessary to achieve centralisation. With the bar removed, view the clutch disc hub in relation to the hole in the end of the crankshaft and the circle created by the ends of the diaphragm spring fingers (photo). When the hub appears exactly in the centre, all is correct. Alternatively, if a clutch aligning tool can be obtained this will eliminate all the guesswork, obviating the need for visual alignment.

21 Tighten the cover retaining bolts gradually, in a diagonal sequence to the specified torque wrench setting.

22 The gearbox can now be refitted as described in Section 9.

Clutch release bearing (1.6 five-speed, 1989-on) – removal inspection and refitting

23 Remove the gearbox as described in Section 9.

24 Slip the retaining spring wires ends out of the slots on the bearing body then slide the bearing off the gearbox input shaft (photo).

25 Check the bearing for smoothness of operation and renew it if there is any roughness or harshness as the bearing is spun.

26 Refitting is the reverse sequence of removal, but ensure that the retaining spring wire ends are located behind the release fork.

9 Manual gearbox

Gearbox – general

1 1.3 models and early 1.6 models are fitted with Volkswagen four and five-speed transmission units.

2 From 1989, a Honda-designed, Austin Rover-built unit is fitted to all 1.6 models with five-speed transmission.

Gearchange linkage (four-speed and pre-1989 five-speed) – lubrication

3 It is important that the linkage is regularly lubricated in the following way to maintain smooth and easy gear selection.

4 Raise the front of the vehicle and support it securely on stands, or place it over an inspection pit.

8.20 Centralise the disc so that the clutch disc hub is in line with the hole in the crankshaft and the circle formed by the diaphragm spring fingers

5 Disconnect the selector rod from the gear lever and rod lever, and withdraw the selector rod from its bush.

6 Fill the bush cavities with special grease (consult your dealer); also smear the bush contact area on the selector rod with the same lubricant.

7 Slide the selector rod through the bush and connect the selector rod to the lever.

8 Smear the gear lever shouldered bolt with the special grease and connect the rod to the gear lever. Tighten the shouldered bolt nut.

9 Apply the special grease to all other pivot points, except the balljoints which are self-lubricating.

10 Peel back the flexible boot from the gearbox selector shaft, smear the shaft with general purpose grease and refit the boot.

11 Check the gear lever adjustment (described in Chapter 6, Section 24).

12 It may also be found that on early models the spring clips which secure each end of the rod at the pivot points (item 4 in Fig. 13.24)

Fig. 13.24 Gearchange linkage lubrication points (Sec 9)

1 Selector rod	4 Pivot
2 Bush	5 Selector rod lever
3 Ball	6 Ball-stud

8.24 Slip off the retaining wire ends and withdraw the release bearing

are broken. Modified clips are available from Austin Rover dealers which overcome this problem.

Differential drive flange oil seal (four-speed and pre-1989 five-speed) – renewal

13 A leaking oil seal can be renewed without the need to remove the transmission from the vehicle.

14 Remove the driveshaft from the appropriate side as described in Section 10, and prise the plug from the drive flange.

15 A compressor will now be required to compress the spring at the back of the drive flange, so that the flange dished washer and retaining circlip can be extracted.

16 Although a special tool (18G 1389) is available for the purpose, a simple alternative tool can be made, similar to the one shown in Fig. 13.25. This is bolted to the drive flange using two 75 x 8.0 mm bolts.

Fig. 13.25 Tool for compressing drive flange spring on four-speed and pre-1989 five-speed models (Sec 9)

1 Bolts (75 x 8.0 mm)	4 Circlip
	5 Dished washer
2 Centre screw	6 Drive flange
3 Tool bridge piece	7 Pinion shaft

13

Fig 13.26 Gearbox filler plug location (arrowed) (Sec 9)

17 Once the drive flange has been removed, prise out the defective oil seal.

18 Apply grease to the lips of the new seal and drive it squarely into place.

19 Push (do not tap) the drive flange into position, and use the special tool to compress the centre spring. Fit the dished washer and the circlip, remove the tool and fit the plug to the drive flange.

20 Refit the driveshaft and check for oil leaks.

Gearbox (1.6 five-speed, 1989-on) – general description

21 The gearbox is of Honda design and is equipped with five forward and one reverse gear. Synchromesh gear engagement is used on all forward gears.

The mainshaft and countershaft carry the constant mesh gear cluster assemblies and are supported on ball and roller bearings. The short input end of the mainshaft eliminates the need for additional support from a crankshaft spigot bearing.

The synchromesh gear engagement is by spring rings which act against baulk rings under the movement of the synchroniser sleeves. Gear selection is by means of a floor mounted lever connected by a remote control housing and gear change rod to the gear change shaft in the gearbox. Gear change shaft movement is transmitted to the selector forks via the gear change holder and interlock assembly.

The final drive (differential) unit is integral

Fig 13.27 Gearbox drain plug location (arrowed) (Sec 9)

with the main gearbox and is located between the bellhousing and gearcase. The gearbox and final drive components both share the same lubricating oil.

Gearbox (1.6 five-speed, 1989-on) – maintenance and inspection

22 Maintenance and inspection of the gearbox is as described in Chapter 6, Section 2.

Gearbox (1.6 five-speed, 1989-on) – overhaul (general)

23 Dismantling, overhaul and reassembly of the gearbox is reasonably straightforward and can be carried out without recourse to the manufacturer's special tools. It should be noted however that any repair or overhaul work on the final drive differential must be limited to the renewal of the carrier support bearings. Owing to the complicated nature of this unit and the costs involved, the advice of an Austin Rover dealer should be sought if further repair is necessary.

24 Before starting any work on the gearbox, clean the exterior of the casings using paraffin or a suitable solvent. Dry the unit with a lint-free rag. Make sure than an uncluttered working area is available with some small containers and trays handy to store the various parts. Label everything as it is removed.

25 Before starting reassembly, all the components must be spotlessly clean and

should be lubricated with the recommended grade of gear oil during reassembly.

Gearbox (1.6 five-speed, 1989-on) – removal and refitting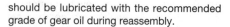

26 Remove the bonnet as described in Chapter 12, Section 8.

27 Disconnect the battery negative terminal (Chapter 10, Section 4).

28 Remove the air cleaner element as described in Section 6 of this Supplement.

29 Remove the starter motor with reference to Chapter 10, Section 10, noting that the starter retaining bolts also secure the manifold support tube and fuel overflow pipe bracket.

30 Disconnect the speedometer cable as described in Chapter 10, Section 40, noting that the cable is secured by a clip, not a bolt as on previous models.

31 Disconnect the reversing light switch at the connector in the lead, not at the switch terminals.

32 Disconnect the crankshaft TDC sensor as described in Chapter 4, Section 13.

33 Disconnect the clutch cable (Chapter 5, Section 2).

34 Raise the vehicle onto axle stands, sufficiently high to enable the gearbox to be manoeuvred out from underneath it.

35 Remove both front wheels.

36 Remove the access plate from the left-hand wheel well.

37 Position a suitable container underneath the gearbox, unscrew the drain plug and drain the oil from the gearbox (see Fig 13.27). When the oil is drained, refit the drain plug.

38 Remove the crankshaft sensor noting the spacer under the flange.

39 Remove the top suspension strut-to-hub bolt and loosen the lower bolt (refer to Chapter 11, Section 3).

40 Refer to Section 10 of this Supplement and lever the inboard end of the left-hand driveshaft from the differential.

41 Being extremely careful not to strain the brake hose, tilt the hub downwards at the same time pulling it outward, and manoeuvre the inboard end of the driveshaft upwards, securing it out of the way.

42 Repeat this operation on the right-hand driveshaft.

9044A Remove the clip from the selector rod roll pin

9.44B Tap out the pin

9.44C Disconnect the selector rod

9.45 Remove the bolt from the gearbox steady rod

9.46A Rear engine mounting bracket bolts seen through the holes in the subframe

9.46B Removing the threaded plate from on top of the subframe

43 Support the engine on a jack, inserting a block of wood between the jack head and the engine, and being careful not to obstruct the gearbox-to-engine reinforcing plate.

44 Remove the clip from the selector rod roll pin, tap out the pin and disconnect the selector rod (photos).

45 Remove the bolt from the gearbox steady rod, noting which way the dished washer fits, and disconnect the steady rod (photo).

46 Remove the rear engine mounting bracket. Access to the bracket-to-sub-frame bolts is gained through the holes in the sub-frame. Note the threaded plate on top of the sub-frame (photos).

47 Remove the engine front mounting (photo).

48 Arrange a suitable sling and lifting gear over the engine bay, attach the sling to the gearbox and just begin to take the weight. The arrangement we used is shown in the photographs (photos).

49 Remove all the gearbox-to-adaptor plate bolts. The gearbox-to-engine reinforcing plate will have to be removed to reach the lower bolts (photo).

50 Remove the left-hand engine mounting, noting the earth lead under one of the bolts. On some models the lead may be under an end-case bolt.

51 Gently taking some weight on the sling, separate the gearbox from the engine, pulling the clutch shaft clear, then carefully lower the gearbox to the ground, twisting it as

necessary to clear obstructions (photo)

52 Release the lifting gear from the gearbox and manoeuvre it from under the vehicle.

53 Refitting the gearbox is a reversal of the removal procedure, bearing in mind the following points.

(a) Tighten all bolts to the specified torque, but do not fully tighten the engine mounting bolts until all the mountings are in place and have been centralised

(b) Refill the gearbox with the specified lubricant.

(c) Lubricate the selector gear rods with a lithium-based grease before refitting.

(d) Carry out the clutch cable adjustment check detailed in Section 8 after refitting the clutch cable.

9.46C Removing the mounting bolts

9.47 Engine front mounting

9.48A Lifting gear arrangement seen from above

9.48B Close-up of the lifting gear

9.49 Removing the engine reinforcing plate bolts

9.51 Lowering the gearbox to the ground

13

Note: *If oil leakage from the bell-housing-to-gearcase joint in the area of the rear engine mounting is evident, the probable cause is the rear mounting bolts pulling the casing apart. Shims are available from Austin Rover dealers to insert between the mounting and the gearcase to prevent this happening, but no more than three shims should be used. If more shims than this are required, the mounting bracket must be renewed.*

Fig. 13.28 Position of rear engine mounting shim on 1.6 five-speed models (Sec 9)

Fig. 13.29 Exploded view of gear lever on 1989-on five speed models (Sec 9)

1	Spacer	6	O-ring
2	O-rings	7	Gear lever seat
3	Bushes	8	Retaining ring
4	Sealing washers	9	Circlip
5	Dust cover		

9.55 Gear lever-to-gearchange remote control retaining bolt

Gear lever and remote control housing (1.6 five-speed, 1989-on) – removal and refitting

Gear lever

54 Jack up the front of the car and support it on axle stands.

55 From under the car undo the nut and withdraw the bolt securing the gear lever to the gearchange remote control rod (photo).

56 From inside the car unscrew the gear lever knob then remove the gaiter and rubber boot.

57 Remove the retaining circlip and withdraw the gear lever from the remote control housing.

Fig. 13.30 Exploded view of 1989-on five-speed gearbox (Sec 9)

1 Clutch release bearing, fork and retaining spring wire
2 Clutch operating lever
3 Clutch operating lever oil seal
4 Differential oil seal
5 Bellhousing
6 Speedometer pinion assembly
7 Locating dowel
8 Gearchange shaft oil seal
9 Rubber boot
10 Gearchange shaft
11 Final drive support bearing
12 Final drivegear
13 Roll pin
14 Final drive casing
15 Differential sun and planet gear components
16 Final drive support bearing
17 Differential end float circlip shim
18 Differential oil seal
19 Oil guide plate
20 Countershaft roller bearing
21 Countershaft
22 Thrustwasher
23 Needle roller bearing
24 1st gear
25 Baulk ring
26 Spring ring
27 1st/2nd synchro hub

28 1st/2nd synchro sleeve
29 Spring ring
30 Baulk ring
31 Distance collar
32 Needle roller bearing
33 2nd gear
34 3rd gear
35 4th gear
36 5th gear
37 Countershaft ball bearing
38 Tongued washer
39 Retaining nut
40 Circlip
41 Mainshaft oil seal
42 Mainshaft ball bearing
43 Mainshaft
44 Needle roller bearing
45 3rd gear
46 Baulk ring
47 Spring ring
48 3rd/4th synchro hub
49 3rd/4th synchro sleeve
50 Spring ring
51 Baulk ring
52 4th gear
53 Needle roller bearing
54 Distance collar
55 Needle roller bearing
56 5th gear
57 Baulk ring
58 Spring ring
59 5th gear synchro hub

60 5th gear synchro sleeve
61 Mainshaft ball bearing
62 Selective circlips
63 Belleville washer
64 Oil guide plate
65 Reversing lamp switch
66 Gearcase
67 Gearbox breather
68 Reverse idler shaft retaining bolt
69 Gearbox breather bracket
70 Roll pin
71 Reverse idler shaft
72 Reverse idler gear
73 Gearchange arm
74 Magnet
75 Detent ball
76 Detent spring
77 Detent plug
78 Reverse gear fork and bracket
79 Gearchange holder and interlock assembly
80 1st/2nd gear selector fork
81 1st/2nd gear selector shaft
82 Roll pin
83 5th/reverse gear selector
84 5th/reverse gear selector shaft
85 3rd/4th gear selector fork
86 5th gear selector fork
87 Thrust washers

9.66 Remote control housing bracket retaining bolts (arrowed)

58 Release the sealing washers, extract the bushes and slide out the spacer complete with O-ring seals located at the base of the gear lever. Examine the components for wear.
59 Inspect the O-rings and gear lever seat in the remote control housing for signs of wear or damage.
60 Renew any worn or damaged parts then reassemble and refit the gear lever using the reverse sequence to removal.

Remote control housing

61 Remove the gear lever as described above.
62 From under the front of the car, remove the spring clip to expose the gearchange rod to gearbox, gearchange shaft retaining roll pin.
63 Using a suitable punch, drive out the roll pin and slide the gearchange rod rearwards off the shaft. Remove the rod from under the car.
64 Undo and remove the small bolt in the centre of the gearbox steady rod, at the gearbox end of the remote control housing.
65 Remove the dished washer, slide off the steady rod and remove the flat washer. Note that the lip on the inner washer faces the steady rod rubber bush.
66 At the remote control housing end, undo the two bolts securing the mounting bracket to the vehicle floor and withdraw the remote control assembly from under the car (photo).
67 Refitting is the reverse sequence of removal.

10 Driveshafts

Driveshafts (1.3 and 1.6, pre-1989) – revised removal procedure

1 While the vehicle is standing on its wheels, firmly engage the handbrake and put the transmission in gear, or in the P position if automatic transmission is fitted.
2 Prise off the wheel trim and extract the driveshaft nut retaining split pin. Using a suitable socket and bar, slacken the nut, but do not remove it at this stage.

3 Slacken the wheel nuts, jack up the front of the car and support it on axle stands. Remove the roadwheel and return the transmission to neutral. Remove the driveshaft nut and washer.
4 From underneath the car, make an alignment mark between the inner constant velocity joint flange and the differential drive flange, as an aid to reassembly. On vehicles equipped with automatic transmission, the left-hand driveshaft must be withdrawn from the drive flange before the alignment marks can be made.
5 Remove the protective caps over the inner joint retaining bolts and using an Allen key of the appropriate size, unscrew and remove the bolts.
6 The procedure now varies slightly depending on whether the left-hand or right-hand driveshaft is being removed.

Left-hand driveshaft

7 On vehicles with manual transmission, ease the inner constant velocity joint away from the differential drive flange and lower the inner end of the shaft. Withdraw the outer constant velocity joint from the wheel hub, lower the driveshaft to the ground and remove it from under the car. Withdraw the bearing water shield from the outer joint.
8 On vehicles with automatic transmission, undo and remove the nuts and washers, then withdraw the two bolts securing the suspension strut to the upper part of the swivel hub. Separate the swivel hub from the strut, ease the inner constant velocity joint away from the differential drive flange and withdraw the outer constant velocity joint from the wheel hub. Remove the driveshaft from under the car and slide the bearing water shield off the outer joint.

Right-hand driveshaft

9 On vehicles with manual transmission, extract the retaining clip and flat washer from the gearchange linkage pivot point directly above the inner constant velocity joint.

Release the linkage from its pivot location and place it to one side.
10 Compress the inboard joint and ease it from the drive flange, then raise the inboard end of the shaft and rest it on the drive flange.
11 Withdraw the outer constant velocity joint from the wheel hub and remove the driveshaft from under the wheel arch. Withdraw the bearing water shield from the outer joint.
12 On vehicles with automatic transmission, the removal operations are as described for manual transmission vehicles, but of course ignore all reference to the gearchange control linkage.

Driveshafts (1.3 and 1.6, pre-1989) – revised refitting procedure

13 When refitting a driveshaft-to-hub securing nut, the following procedure should be used instead of that described in Chapter 8, Section 3, paragraph 13(c).
14 Tighten the inboard joint retaining bolts to the specified torque. On automatic transmission models, tighten the swivel hub retaining nuts on the left-hand driveshaft to the specified torque.
15 Where a castellated type nut is used, have an assistant apply the footbrake and tighten the nut to a torque of 140 lbf ft (190 Nm). If the split pin hole is aligned, fit a new split pin and bend over its ends.
16 If the hole is not aligned, slowly tighten the nut as necessary to a maximum torque of 160 lbf ft (215 Nm) until alignment is achieved.
17 If the split pin hole is still not in alignment, unscrew the nut and fit a thrustwasher of alternative thickness from the three sizes available.
0.240 in (6.10 mm) thick – silver
0.244 in (6.20 mm) thick – green
0.248 in (6.30 mm) thick – dark grey
18 Again tighten to the specified torque and fit a new split pin. Where a staked type nut is fitted, always use a new nut and stake it into the shaft groove.

Fig. 13.31 Sectional view of 1.6 litre 1989-on driveshaft components (Sec 10)

1 Outer constant velocity joint	3 Damper	A = 15.0 to 15.3 in
2 Right-hand driveshaft	4 Inner constant velocity joint	(381.0 to 388.6mm)
	5 Left-hand driveshaft	

10.21 Remove the driveshaft retaining nut and recover the thrustwasher

10.25 Suspension strut-to-swivel hub retaining nuts

10.26 Remove the outer constant velocity joint from the hub

Driveshafts (manual gearbox from 1989) – general description

19 The driveshafts fitted to 1989-on 1.6 litre models with the Honda-derived five-speed gearbox are different to those fitted to earlier models, being of unequal length, solid steel construction, splined to the inner and outer constant velocity joints. Note that the driveshafts fitted to automatic transmission models remain as described in Chapter 8, and earlier in this Section.

Driveshafts (manual gearbox from 1989) – removal and refitting

20 While the vehicle is standing on its wheels, firmly apply the handbrake and put the transmission in gear.
21 Remove the wheel trim and extract the driveshaft retaining nut split pin. If a staked retaining nut is fitted, refer to paragraphs 41 to 43 for its removal and refitting details. Using a suitable socket and bar, undo and remove the driveshaft nut. Recover the thrustwasher (photo).
22 Slacken the wheel nuts, jack up the front of the car and support it on axle stands. Remove the roadwheel and return the gearlever to neutral.
23 Place a suitable container beneath the gearbox drain plug (see Section 9), undo the plug and allow the oil to drain. Refit the plug after draining.
24 Undo and remove the nut securing the tie-rod outer balljoint to the swivel hub steering arm. Release the balljoint from the steering arm using a balljoint separator tool.

25 Undo and remove the nuts and washers then withdraw the two bolts securing the suspension strut to the swivel hub (photo).
26 Pull the upper part of the swivel hub outwards as far as possible without placing undue strain on the flexible brake hose. Push the driveshaft inwards and manoeuvre the outer constant velocity joint from the hub (photo).
27 Using a suitable flat bar or large screwdriver, lever between the inner constant velocity joint and differential housing to release the joint from the differential sun gear.
28 Withdraw the inner joint fully from the differential then remove the driveshaft assembly from under the wheel arch. Recover the plastic bearing water shield from the end of the outer constant velocity joint (photo).
29 To refit the driveshaft, place it in position under the car and enter the inner joint splines into the differential sun gear. Push the driveshaft firmly inward to engage the internal spring ring on the sun gear with the groove in the inner joint splines (photo).
30 Position the bearing water shield on the flange of the outer joint and fill the water shield groove with the specified grease.
31 Pull the swivel hub out at the top and enter the outer constant velocity joint into the hub. Refit the thrustwasher and driveshaft retaining nut and use the nut to draw the joint fully into place.
32 Refit the swivel hub to the suspension strut and secure with the two bolts, washers and nuts tightened to the specified torque.
33 Refit the steering tie-rod outer balljoint to the swivel hub arm. Screw on the nut and tighten it to the specified torque.

34 Refit the roadwheel then lower the car to the ground.
35 With the car standing on its wheels, tighten the wheel nuts to the specified torque, then have an assistant firmly depress the footbrake.
36 Tighten the driveshaft retaining nut to the torque wrench setting given in the Specifications at the beginning of this Supplement.
37 If the split pin hole in the constant velocity joint is aligned with one of the castellations in the nut, fit a new split pin and secure by bending over its ends.
38 If the split pin hole does not align with one of the castellations in the nut, continue tightening until it does, but only up to a maximum torque of 158 lbf ft (215 Nm). If the hole is still not aligned, remove the nut and thrustwasher and fit a new thrustwasher of different thickness from the following range

Silver   0.240 in (6.1 mm)
Green   0.244 in (6.2 mm)
Dark grey   0.248 in (6.3 mm)

39 Using the new thrustwasher, repeat the tightening procedure until the split pin can be inserted.
40 Refit the wheel trim, and refill the gearbox with the specified grade of oil with reference to the Specifications.

Driveshafts retained by staked retaining nut

41 The procedure described in Chapter 8, Section 3 is unchanged except for the following.
42 Before undoing the nut, tap up the staking to release it from the driveshaft joint groove. Discard the old nut.
43 When refitting, tighten the new nut to the torque wrench setting given in the Specifications, then tap its flange into the driveshaft joint groove using a punch.

Constant velocity joints (manual gearbox from 1989) – removal, inspection and refitting

44 The procedure is as described in Sections 4 and 5 of Chapter 8. If on dismantling, the inner constant velocity joint is found to be damaged or badly worn, it must be renewed together with the shaft as a complete unit.

Constant velocity joint rubber boots (manual gearbox from 1989) – renewal

45 Remove the driveshaft from the car as described in earlier paragraphs.

10.28 Withdraw the driveshaft assembly and recover the bearing water shield (A)

10.29 Enter the inner joint splines into the differential sun gear

10.44A Constant velocity joint retaining circlip (arrowed) fitted to driveshaft groove

10.44B Fitting the outer constant velocity joint to the driveshaft

10.54A Fit the inner joint rubber boot . . .

Outer joint rubber boot

46 Remove the outer constant velocity joint from the driveshaft as described in Chapter 8, Section 5. Renewal of the rubber boot is also covered in Chapter 8, Section 5 as it is an integral part of the outer joint removal and refitting procedures.

Inner joint rubber boot

47 Remove the outer constant velocity joint and rubber boot as described in Chapter 8, Section 5.
48 If working on the right-hand driveshaft, mark the position of the damper on the shaft then release the retaining clip and slide off the damper.
49 Release the rubber retaining ring on the small end of the inner joint boot and slide the ring off the driveshaft.
50 Release the retaining clip, slip the boot off the inner joint and withdraw it from the driveshaft.
51 Clean out as much of the grease in the inner constant velocity joint as possible using a wooden spatula and old rags. As the joint cannot be dismantled it is advisable not to clean it using paraffin or solvents.
52 Examine the bearing tracks in the joint outer member for signs of scoring, wear ridges or evidence of lack of lubrication. Also examine the three bearing caps in the same way and check for evidence of excessive play between the roller bearing caps and their tracks in the outer member.
53 If any of the above checks indicate wear in the joint it will be necessary to renew the

driveshaft and inner joint as an assembly; they are not available separately. If the joint is in a satisfactory condition obtain a repair kit consisting of the new rubber boot, retaining clips and the specified grease.
54 Slide the new rubber boot onto the driveshaft followed by the rubber retaining ring. Position the small end of the boot in the driveshaft groove then slip the rubber ring over it to secure it in place (photos).
55 Fold back the boot and pack the constant velocity joint with the specified quantity of the grease supplied in the kit (photo). Work the grease well into the joint while moving it from side to side. Fill the boot with any excess.
56 Position the large end of the boot over the joint outer member so that it locates squarely in the groove.
57 Position the retaining clip over the boot

and engage one of the slots in the clip end over the small tag. Make sure the clip is as tight as possible and, if necessary, use a screwdriver to ease the slot over the tag (photo).
58 Fully tighten the clip by squeezing the raised portion with pincers (photo).
59 Refit the damper to the driveshaft (where applicable) and position it against the marks made on the shaft during removal. If a new driveshaft has been fitted or if the marks have been lost, use the setting dimension given in Fig. 13.31.
60 Secure the damper in position with the retaining clip as described in paragraphs 57 and 58 (photo).
61 Refit the outer constant velocity joint and rubber boot as described in Chapter 8, Section 5, then refit the driveshaft as described in Chapter 8, Section 3.

10.54B . . . and secure its small end with the rubber retaining ring

10.55 Pack the joint with the special grease

10.57 Use a screwdriver to stretch the retaining clip slot over the tag

10.58 Tighten the clip fully by squeezing the raised portion

10.60 Secure the damper in place with the retaining clip

13

11 Braking system

Front brake disc checking – general

1 To avoid the possibility of brake judder being caused by a disc which is wearing unevenly, the front brake disc run-out should be checked whenever a disc is removed.
2 Before refitting the disc, check the thickness using a micrometer at four equidistant points around the disc, and at 0.4 in (10.0 mm) in from the outer edge. If the thickness is outside the tolerance given in the Chapter 9 Specifications the disc must be renewed. Under no circumstances may the disc be refaced or machined in any way whilst removed from the vehicle. It may be possible to surface grind the disc in situ on the hub (not removed from it), but this is a task for a Rover dealer or suitably-equipped automotive engineer.
3 With the disc in place, use a dial test indicator to check the run-out with the probe positioned 0.25 in (6.3 mm) in from the outer edge. Slowly rotate the disc and check that the runout does not exceed the figure given in the Chapter 9 Specifications. If it does, remove the disc, turn it through 180°, refit and check the run-out again. Ensure that complete cleanliness of the disc and drive flange mating faces is maintained, and check that there are no burrs or irregularities on the surface which may affect the readings.
4 If the run-out still exceeds the specified figure, remove the disc and check the drive flange run-out. If this is excessive, renew the drive flange. If the flange run-out is satisfactory, renew the disc.
5 It should be noted that new replacement brake discs sometimes have a protective coating applied to combat corrosion during storage. Where this is the case, it is normal for the manufacturer to specify a suitable solvent with which to clean the lining contact faces of a replacement disc prior to fitting it.
6 Harsh braking during the running-in period of new discs will cause the coating to wear

unevenly, leading to noise, judder and overheating of brake pads.
7 During the running-in period therefore, it is recommended that harsh braking is avoided, as far as possible.

Rear brake drum – inspection

8 Whenever a brake drum is removed, take the opportunity to inspect it for cracks or grooving caused by the shoes.
9 If these conditions are evident, renew the drum; do not have the drum ground or machined as the original diameter of the drum must not be increased.

Brake fluid level indicator – malfunction

10 Overfilling of the brake master cylinder reservoir or inversion of the filler cap during servicing can lead to contamination of the low level warning switch contacts giving rise to illumination of the warning light even when the reservoir is full.
11 If this problem should occur, thoroughly clean the outside of the cap and reservoir using lint-free cloth.
12 Disconnect the switch leads, unscrew the cap, keeping it the right way up and allowing any excess fluid to drain back into the reservoir.
13 Using a piece of cloth to prevent drips, transfer the cap to a clean bench.
14 Prise off the plastic cap and remove the screwed cap.
15 Invert the cap, allowing the float to drop and uncover the switch contacts, which should be cleaned using lint-free cloth.
16 Reassemble the cap, and refit to the reservoir in reverse order of removal.

Brake fluid – approved type

17 Brake hydraulic fluid to DOT 4 specification is now the specified brake system fluid. Austin Rover state that fluid to DOT 3 must no longer be used for topping up the fluid level.
18 DOT 4 has a higher boiling point than DOT 3, although it is completely compatible with, and can be used to top up systems containing DOT 3 fluid.

Handbrake cable seal – displacement

19 The seal on each handbrake cable where the exposed portion of the inner cable enters the outer cable (see Fig. 13.32) is fitted to prevent dirt and water ingress.
20 During routine servicing operations and when a new cable is fitted, ensure that the seal is correctly fitted. The handbrake must be released (after chocking the wheels) while the check is carried out.
21 It is also possible for the cable to rattle against the sides of the hole in the bracket through which it passes. A rubber sleeve is available for fitting to prevent this problem.

12 Electrical system

Battery positive lead – routing

1 In order to eliminate the possibility of chafing, it is important that the battery positive lead is routed above the air cleaner hose, and not underneath it.

Starter motor (later models)

2 Later models are equipped with different types of pre-engaged starter motors (see Specifications). Removal, overhaul and refitting procedures follow.

Starter motor (Lucas type M78R) – removal and refitting

3 Remove the air intake trunking and disconnect the intake air temperature sensor multi-plug.
4 Disconnect the breather hose from the diverter valve (if fitted).
5 Unbolt the air cleaner bracket from the transmission casing, and move the air cleaner enough to gain access to the outlet trunking. Release the clip, remove the trunking and the air cleaner.
6 Disconnect the battery and the leads from the starter solenoid.

Fig. 13.32 Location and correct positioning of the handbrake cable seal (Sec 11)

Fig. 13.33 Handbrake cable and body bracket (Sec 11)

1 Bracket hole

Fig. 13.34 Battery positive lead mounting on 1.6 models (Sec 12)

Fig. 13.35 Starter solenoid (Sec 12)

1 *Battery (BAT) terminal*	3 *Solenoid (50) terminal*
2 *Starter (STA) terminal*	4 *Retaining screws*
	5 *Solenoid*
	6 *Solenoid plunger*

7 Unscrew the starter motor mounting bolts and withdraw the unit from the vehicle. The starter bolts also secure the snubber bracket.
8 Refitting is a reversal of removal; tighten the bolts to the specified torque.

Starter motor (Lucas type M78R) – overhaul

9 With the starter motor removed from the vehicle, clean away external dirt and grease.
10 Disconnect the lead from the solenoid 'STA' terminal, extract the solenoid fixing screws and withdraw the solenoid. At the same time, disengage the solenoid plunger from the engaging lever.
11 Extract the screws and remove the nuts which hold the commutator end bracket. Withdraw the bracket from the yoke.
12 Remove the grommet from the yoke and ease the brush box off the commutator.
13 Remove the brush springs and unclip and remove the earth brushes.
14 Remove the insulation plate and withdraw the brushes complete with bus bar.
15 If the brushes are worn below their specified length, renew them and make sure that they slide freely in their holders.
16 Remove the sun and planet gears and push out the drive and bearing bracket assembly from the drive end bracket.
17 Tap the thrust collar towards the pinion to expose the jump ring, which should be prised from its groove and removed.
18 Remove the collar and drive assembly from the armature shaft.
19 Clean the commutator with a fuel-moistened cloth. If it is badly discoloured polish it with fine glasspaper. Do not undercut the insulators between the segments.
20 This will normally be the limit of economical overhaul. Where the commutator is found to be deeply grooved or the armature shaft bushes are worn, then it is recommended that a new or factory-reconditioned starter is obtained.

Fig. 13.36 Exploded view of type M78R starter (Sec 12)

1 *Solenoid and plunger*	9 *Drive assembly*	17 *Commutator end bracket*
2 *Commutator components*	10 *Drive end bracket bush*	18 *Drive end bracket (automatic transmission)*
3 *Brushes*	11 *Intermediate bracket bush*	19 *Oil seal (automatic transmission)*
4 *Brush springs*	12 *Commutator end bracket bush*	
5 *Armature*	13 *Drive end bracket*	20 *Drive end bracket bush (automatic transmission)*
6 *Jump ring and thrust collar*	14 *Through-bolt*	21 *Drive assembly (automatic transmission)*
7 *Pivot and grommet*	15 *Intermediate bracket*	
8 *Driveshaft, bearing bracket and gears*	16 *Field coil yoke*	

21 Check the drive pinion assembly for wear or damage; also check that the pinion rotates in one direction only, independently of the clutch body.
22 Apply grease to the drive assembly pivot and lever, and fit the drive assembly and the thrust collar to the armature shaft.
23 Fit the jump ring into its groove and tap the thrust collar over the ring.
24 Insert the driveshaft into the drive end bracket bush.
25 Fit the planet and sun gears.
26 Locate the through-bolts, the intermediate bracket and yoke on the drive end bracket.
27 Fit the bus bar to the brush box then locate the brushes and the insulation plate. Insert the earth brushes and fit the clips.
28 Offer the assembly over the commutator and fit the brush springs.
29 Slide the armature and brush box inside the field coils and fit the yoke grommet.
30 Align the commutator end bracket and fit it into the yoke.
31 Engage the solenoid plunger with the engagement lever, fit the solenoid mounting screws then connect the lead to the 'STA' terminal.

Starter motor (Lucas type M79) – removal and refitting

32 The operations are similar to those described earlier for the type M78R, but refer to Chapter 3 for details of the air cleaner trunking and attachments used on 1.3 models. Note also that the engine mounting snubber bracket is held by the starter motor bolts only on 1.6 models.

Starter motor (Lucas type M79) – overhaul

33 Carry out the operations described earlier in paragraphs 9 and 10.
34 Remove the sealing cup and gasket from the commutator end bracket.
35 Extract the circlip and washers from the armature shaft.
36 Note the end bracket to yoke alignment marks, remove the retaining screws and carefully withdraw the end bracket from the yoke.
37 Remove the brush springs and withdraw the earth bushes, then lift the brush box from the commutator.
38 Remove the insulation plate and withdraw the positive brushes with bus bar.

13

Fig. 13.37 Exploded view of type M79 starter (Sec 12)

1 Solenoid and plunger
2 Commutator and bracket
   components
3 Brushes
4 Brush springs
5 Pivot and packing piece
6 Armature
7 Jump ring and thrust collar
8 Drive assembly
9 Field coils and yoke
10 Drive end bracket bush
11 Commutator end bracket
   bush
12 Drive end bracket
13 Insulation plate
14 Commutator end bracket
15 Circlip and washers
16 Sealing cap and gasket

39 If the brushes are worn below their specified length, renew them and make sure that they slide freely in their holders.
40 Remove the pivot and grommet from the drive end bracket.
41 Extract the screws and remove the yoke.
42 Withdraw the armature from the drive end bracket.
43 Tap the thrust collar towards the pinion to expose the jump ring, then prise the ring from its groove and remove it together with the collar and drive assembly.

44 Carry out the operations described in paragraphs 19 to 24 of this Section.
45 Locate the yoke on the drive end bracket and fit the retaining screws.
46 Place the bus bar on the brush box and fit the brushes and the insulation plate. Insert the earth brushes and fit the clips.
47 Offer the assembly over the commutator and fit the brush springs.
48 Slide the commutator end bracket over the brush springs and engage the grommet. Align the reference marks and fit the screws.

Fig. 13.38 Location of relays on 1986 and later models (Sec 12)

1 Ignition
2 Headlamp
3 Auxiliary ignition 2
4 Starter solenoid
5 Auxiliary ignition 1
6 Heated rear screen
7 Carburettor
   manifold heater
8 Interior lamp
9 Windscreen wiper
10 Rear screen wiper
11 Windscreen wiper
   delay unit
F Flasher unit

49 Fit the washers and circlip to the armature shaft, then fit the gasket and sealing cup.
50 Engage the solenoid plunger with the engagement lever and secure it with the screws. Make sure that the 'STA' terminal is adjacent to the starter motor. Fit the lead to the 'STA' terminal.

Fuses, relays and control units – later models

1986 to 1988 models

51 For these models, some of the relays and control units are relocated in a compartment below the steering column, the cover being secured by two turn buckles (Fig. 13.38).

Fuses
1 Engine
2 RH side, tail and number plate lamps
3 Instruments
4 Cigar lighter
5 RH headlamp main beam
6 Electric mirrors
7 Sunroof
8 Dim-dip system
9 Stop-lamps, reversing lamps, indicators
10 Rear foglamps
11 Heated rear screen
12 Interior lamp, luggage compartment lamp, central door locking
13 Cooling fan
14 Heater blower motor
15 Windscreen wiper/washer
16 Tailgate wiper
17 Electric fuel pump
18 LH headlamp main beam
19 Horn, hazard warning lights
20 Electric front windows
21 Turbo carburettor cooling fan
22 Radio/cassette player
23 Spare
24 RH headlamp dip beam
25 LH headlamp dip beam
26 LH side, tail and number plate lamps

Relays
1 Courtesy lamp delay/lights-on alarm
2 Heated rear window timer
3 Headlamp
4 Ignition
5 Auxiliary cooling fan motor
6 Flasher relay
7 Dim-dip control

Fig. 13.39 Fuses and relays in fusebox, 1989-on models fuse rating is by colour code – refer to Chapter 10 Specifications

12.63 Pull the multi-plug from the switch

12.64 Depress the clips on the side of the switch and withdraw the switch

52 In addition, the electronic control unit (ECU) for the fuel system is located behind the panel in the roof of the glovebox.

53 The ignition ECU is mounted on the left-hand valance within the engine compartment, and the fuel cut-off inertia switch, if fitted, is positioned behind and to the right of the radio aperture.

1989-on models

54 In addition to those relays mounted in the fusebox (see Fig. 13.39), the following relays and control units are also used.

55 The ERIC fuel and ignition ECU is mounted on the left-hand valance of the engine compartment.

56 The multi-function unit is also mounted on the left-hand valance of the engine compartment.

57 The electric window lift control unit is located behind a panel in the roof of the glovebox.

58 A delay unit, mounted on the fusebox in the glovebox, allows the electric windows, sunroof and radiator cooling fan to be operated for approximately 45 seconds after the ignition has been switched off.

 Warning: In the case of the cooling fan which is switched on by the thermal switch, it means that the fan can cut in and start running even when the ignition is switched off, so great care must be taken when working on a hot engine which has just been switched off.

59 A timer unit, also mounted in the fuse box, controls the operation of the heated rear screen, limiting its use to ten minutes.

Fig. 13.40 Rear view of the three-gauge instrument panel (Sec 12)

1 Printed circuit
2 Speedometer securing screws
3 Fuel and temperature gauge securing screws
4 Warning light cluster
5 No-charge warning light bulb
6 Shroud retaining screws
7 Shroud retaining clips

Heater fuse (all models, 1987-on) – higher rating

60 Internal modifications to the heater have resulted in the blower motor drawing more current and overloading the existing fuse, which can blow.

61 If this happens repeatedly, with no evidence of malfunction within the heater circuits, renew the existing 15 amp fuse with one of 20 amp rating. The fuse label should be amended accordingly for future reference.

Instrument panel switches (1989-on) – removal and refitting

62 Remove the screws from and tilt forward the instrument panel as described in later paragraphs.

63 Pull off the multi-plug from the switch (photo).

64 Depress the clips on the side of the switch and withdraw the switch from the instrument panel (photo).

65 The switch illumination bulb is housed in the multi-plug connector, and is a push fit in the holder.

66 To refit the switch, reconnect its wiring, then push the switch into the instrument panel until it is felt to clip securely into position.

Instrument panel (1989-on) – removal and refitting

67 Although of different design to earlier models, the procedure for removing the instrument panel is as described in Chapter 10, Section 19.

68 There are two types of panel in use, one with three gauges and one with four. A view of the rear of each panel appears in Figs. 13.40 and 13.41.

Fig. 13.41 Rear view of the four gauge instrument panel (Sec 12)

1 Printed circuit
2 Speedometer securing screws
3 Tachometer, fuel and temperature gauge securing screws
4 Warning light cluster
5 No-charge warning light bulb
6 Panel illumination light bulb
7 Shroud retaining screws
8 Shroud retaining clips

13

12.74 View of the rear of the digital clock with bezel withdrawn

Fig. 13.42 Dim-dip headlamp system resistor (Sec 12)

1 Resistor   2 Mounting nut   3 Multi-plug

12.79 Bulb positions in rear lamp cluster

1 Indicator light   4 Side/parking light
2 Reversing light   5 Stop/tail light
3 Foglight

69 Note also that progressively from 1988, instrument panels manufactured by Nippon Seiki are being used in place of those produced by Lucas.
70 The complete panels are fully interchangeable, but individual instruments are not.
71 The manufacturer's name is clearly marked on the rear of the panels, and to identify them when they are in the fitted position Nippon Seiki types have seven-digit odometers and round trip reset buttons, while Lucas have six-digit odometers and rectangular reset buttons.

Digital clock (1989-on) – removal and refitting

72 Remove the instrument panel bezel as described in the previous sub-Section.
73 Disconnect the clock multi-plug.
74 Remove the clock retaining screws and withdraw the clock (photo).
75 Refit in reverse order.

Dim-dip headlamp system

76 In order to comply with current regulations, all post-October 1986 models are fitted with a headlamp dim-dip system.
77 The system used a relay-controlled resistor circuit, which is incorporated in a control unit mounted at the front of the vehicle, to the rear of the left-hand headlamp.
78 When the parking lamps are illuminated and the ignition is switched on, the headlamps come on automatically at one-sixth of their normal (dipped beam) power. This system prevents the vehicle being driven with only the parking lamps illuminated.

Rear lamp cluster (Saloon models, 1989-on)

Bulb renewal

79 The procedure is as described in Chapter 10, Section 25. The bulb positions are detailed in the accompanying photograph (photo).

Lens renewal

80 The lens is secured to the rear panel by four nuts, accessible after taking down the carpeting in the luggage compartment (photo).
81 Refit in reverse order, ensuring the foam seal is in good condition.

Rear lamp cluster bulbs (Estate models) – renewal

82 Remove the rear storage box cover, then undo the retaining screws and lift out the stowage box (photo).
83 Reach into the aperture and withdraw the relevant bulbholder by turning it anti-clockwise (photo).
84 Press and turn the bulb to remove it from the holder.
85 Refitting is the reverse sequence to removal.

Number plate lamp bulb (Estate models) – renewal

86 Undo the two lens retaining screws and withdraw the lens and bulb (photos).
87 Withdraw the bulb from the contacts.
88 Refitting is the reverse sequence to removal.

12.80 Rear lens unit securing nuts (arrowed)

12.82 Removing the rear stowage box

12.83 Removing a rear lamp cluster bulb

12.86A Rear number plate lamp

12.86B Rear number plate lamp bulb

12.90 Removing the side repeater lamp from the wing

12.91 Pulling the lens unit from the bulb holder

12.97 Removing a bulb from the heater control panel

Side repeater lamp – bulb renewal

89 Later models have side repeater lamps fitted to the front wings.

90 To renew a bulb, push the unit rearwards, then pull it out from the wing panel (photo).

91 Pull the lens unit from the bulbholder to gain access to the bulb, which is a push fit in the holder (photo).

Glovebox lamp – bulb renewal

92 Open the lid of the glovebox and gently prise the lamp from its location. Use a small screwdriver to prise the bulb end cap out of its retaining clips.

Courtesy lamp switches and interior lamps

93 Courtesy lamp switches are incorporated in the door pillars and at the tailgate body flange, or at the door locks, according to model type and year.

94 The lamp-mounted switch has three positions: on, off and door switch controlled.

95 A delay relay is fitted into the front door switch circuit to keep the interior light on for a short period after closing the door.

Heater control panel illumination bulb (1989-on) – renewal

96 Remove the heater control panel as described in Section 14.

97 The bulbs are a bayonet fix in the holder (photo).

98 Refit the panel in reverse order of removal.

Windscreen wiper arms – setting position

99 Operate the wipers and switch them off by means of the wiper switch, not the ignition key. Remove the wiper arms if they require adjustment.

100 When refitting the wiper arms to their spindles, position the arms so that they contact the intake moulding on the finisher below the windscreen. After tightening the retaining nut, lift the arm and locate it against the upper face of the stop peg.

101 Operate the wipers with a wet windscreen and check that they park with the arms contacting the stop pegs.

Tailgate wiper arm and blade (Estate models) – removal and refitting

102 To remove the wiper blade, lift the arm away from the window, release the spring retaining catch and separate the blade from the wiper arm (photo).

103 Insert the new blade into the arm, making sure that the spring retainer catch is correctly engaged.

104 To remove the wiper arm, spring back the hinged cover and withdraw the washer jet from the spindle (photo).

105 Unscrew the retaining nut, then carefully prise the arm off the spindle.

106 Before refitting the arm, switch on the ignition, then turn the wiper on and off, allowing the motor to return to the 'Park' position. Switch off the ignition.

12.102 Removing wiper blade from arm

Fig. 13.43 Windscreen wiper arm setting diagram (Sec 12)

1 Arm setting point – driver's side
2 Arm setting point – passenger's side
3 Parked position against stop pegs

A Right-hand steering
B Left-hand steering

12.104 Removing tailgate washer jet

13

**Fig. 13.44 Tailgate wiper – Estate models
(Sec 12)**

1 Wiper motor   4 Washer jet
2 Grommet   5 Wiring connector
3 Wiper arm

107 Refit the arm to the spindle with the blade positioned just below the lower heater element in the window.
108 Refit and tighten the retaining nut, then refit the washer jet so that the jets are positioned on either side of the arm.
109 Close the hinged cover.

Tailgate wiper motor (Estate models) – removal and refitting

110 Remove the tailgate wiper arm and blade, as described previously.
111 Open the tailgate and release the interior trim moulding by prising out the retaining buttons (photo). Some of these will probably break during removal, so new buttons should be obtained before refitting.
112 Release the trim from the upper retaining tags (photo), disconnect the speaker leads (where fitted) and remove the trim.

Fig. 13.45 Wiring diagram – automatic rear wipe modification (Sec 12)

B   Relay (30/51 – common   271 Washer pump   For colour code, refer to the
    terminal, 85 relay feed)   342 Wiper switch   first page of wiring diagrams
19 Fusebox   343 Washer switch   at the end of the manual
270 Wiper motor   483 Programmed wash/wipe
                                      unit

113 Disconnect the wiring multi-plug and tailgate washer hose at the wiper motor.
114 Undo the wiper mounting bracket retaining bolts and the self-tapping screw from the support plate (photo). Withdraw the motor and mounting bracket from the tailgate.
115 With the assembly on the bench undo the bolts and separate the wiper motor from the mounting bracket.
116 Refitting is the reverse sequence to removal.

Automatic rear wipe in reverse gear (Estate models) – modification

117 Automatic rear wipe when reverse gear is selected can be obtained by fitting a standard

4-pin relay into the reversing light circuit, joining together the red/light green wires (see Fig. 13.45).
118 This will provide intermittent wipe when reverse is selected, irrespective of the position of the facia panel rear wipe switch.
119 By connecting the common terminal of the relay to the light green wire of the facia rear wipe switch (dotted line in Fig. 13.45), continuous rear wipe can be obtained whenever reverse is selected.
120 In both cases, the relay feed should be connected to the reversing light circuit.

Continuous rear wipe (Estate models) – modification

121 The provision of continuous rear wipe

**12.111 Prising out a trim moulding
retaining button**

**12.112 Tailgate trim moulding upper
retaining tag**

**12.114 Tailgate wiper motor showing
washer tube**

can be obtained by fitting an off/off switch to connect the two red/light green wires (pin numbers 1 and 8) on the rear wiper programme unit.

122 The connections are shown by the dotted line in Fig. 13.46, the switch being marked 'A'.

123 With the switch in the open position, normal programmed wipe with delay is available.

124 With the switch closed, continuous wipe is available whenever the facia panel rear wipe switch is operated.

Horns

125 As from February 1986, twin horns are fitted as standard to all models.

Electric window lift control unit and switches

1986 to 1988 models

126 The control unit and switches are located in a housing on the facia panel.

127 Removal and refitting is as described for the electronic radio/cassette player fitted to some models, described later in this Section.

1989-on models

128 The control unit is located behind a panel in the roof of the glovebox.

129 The switches are located in the centre console.

Central door lock switch/solenoid – modified fitting procedure

130 More precise fitting instructions are required to ensure correct operation of the central door lock unit than are contained in Chapter 10, Section 46.

131 Locate the assembly in the door so that the front fixing screw is located in the upper half of its slot and the control unit pushed towards the front of the vehicle as far as it will go. Tighten the screw.

132 Tighten the rear fixing screw, again with it within the upper half of its slot.

Fig. 13.46 Wiring diagram – continuous rear wipe modification (Sec 12)

A	Switch	342 Wiper switch	For colour code, refer to the
19	Fusebox	343 Washer switch	first page of wiring diagrams
270	Wiper motor	483 Programmed wash/wipe	at the end of the manual
271	Washer pump	unit	

Tailgate lock solenoid (Estate models) – removal and refitting

133 To remove the tailgate lock solenoid on models equipped with central locking, open the tailgate and remove the interior trim moulding with reference to previous paragraphs 111 and 112.

134 Disconnect the operating rod from the cylinder lock lever.

135 Undo the nut securing the solenoid mounting plate to the lock barrel.

136 Disconnect the wiring multi-plug and position the mounting plate in the left-hand aperture. Undo the retaining screws and withdraw the solenoid from behind the mounting plate.

137 Refitting is the reverse sequence to removal.

Fig. 13.47 Electric window lift control unit on 1986-88 models (Sec 12)

1 Switch
2 Escutcheon
3 Multi-plug
4 Printed circuit board
5 Housing
6 Escutcheon plate retainers
7 Printed circuit board retainers

Fig. 13.48 Door lock solenoid (Sec 12)

A Front fixing screw
B Rear fixing screw
C Forward setting of unit

13

Fig. 13.49 Soft iron wire (arrowed) wrapped around groove of motor casing (Sec 12)

Boot/tailgate central door locking solenoid (all models) – failure to operate

138 Should the boot/tailgate central door locking solenoid fail to operate, this may be due to 'bounce-back' off the mechanism and can be corrected as follows:

139 Remove the boot/tailgate central locking solenoid and motor assembly as described in Chapter 10, Section 10, Section 47 for the boot, and in this Section for the tailgate.

140 Ensure the slots through which the nylon plunger, which carries the lock bolt, slides are free from manufacturing butts.

141 Using soft iron wire, wrap one turn around the groove of the motor casing as shown in Fig. 13.49, twisting the ends of the wire together using flat-nosed pliers, until **slight** resistance of the plunger is felt.

142 Cut off any surplus wire, and ensure that the remaining wire end cannot foul any part of the lock mechanism.

143 Refit the lock solenoid and motor assembly.

Electrically operated rear view mirror 🔧

144 Later top of the range models have electrically operated and demisted exterior rear view mirrors. The heating elements are automatically energised as soon as the ignition is switched on.

145 Removal is similar to the procedure described in Section 14 for the manually operated type, except that the wiring harness must be disconnected as the mirror is withdrawn.

146 If the glass is to be removed, operate the control switch until the top of the glass is tilted as far as possible into the casing.

147 Insert a forked tool into the gap at the centre of the lower edge of the glass and release the glass retainers.

Fig. 13.50 Electrically operated rear view mirror control (Sec 12)

1 Left-hand mirror selector position
2 Right-hand mirror selector position

148 Again operate the control switch until the bottom of the glass is tilted as far as possible into the casing. Release the glass upper retainers.

149 Disconnect the wiring connectors and withdraw the glass.

150 Before refitting the glass, centralise the control switch (ignition on) and connect the wiring. Check that the insulated connector is uppermost.

151 Align the pegs on the retaining ring, and then press the mirror glass firmly and evenly to engage the retaining clips. It is recommended that protective gloves are used during this work.

Radio/cassette player – removal and refitting

152 In addition to the plate retaining design described in Chapter 10, Section 41, some in-car entertainment units may be retained by clips.

153 To remove this type of unit, remove the knobs, bezels and finisher, and then press the centre of the exposed clips inwards and withdraw the unit, with masking plate. Disconnect the wiring plugs and leads. Refitting is a reversal of removal.

Radio/cassette player (electronic tune type) – removal and refitting 🔧

⚠️ **Warning: Before removing an electronic radio/cassette player, ensure the security code (if so equipped) is de-activated.**

154 Using a small screwdriver, prise the blanking plates from each side of the unit.

155 Bend a piece of welding rod of stiff wire to form two U-shaped tools and insert them into the two holes at each end of the unit panel.

156 Push the tools fully in and incline them outwards to compress the retaining clips, then pull the radio/cassette unit from the console using the tools as handles. Pull smoothly and gently to avoid disconnecting the tools.

157 Disconnect the wiring plugs and leads.

Fig. 13.51 Electronic tune radio/cassette player removal (Sec 12)

1 Blanking plate
2 Radio/cassette player
3 Removal tools
4 Retaining clip

158 To refit, simply press the unit into position until the clips are heard to engage.

Cassette holder – removal 🔧

159 The cassette holder, which is located below the radio/ cassette player, can be removed after the facia panel has first been withdrawn as described in Chapter 12, Section 35.

160 Should a cassette tray fail to open when pushed in, it may be possible to release it using one of the following methods.

161 Insert a thin blade along the upper edge of the tray and attempt to ease the tray downwards.

162 If the tray still fails to release, eject the tray which is operating correctly, pinch its sides and withdraw it.

163 Locate the holes at the back of the cassette holder which service the jammed tray, and press upwards. At the same time depress the release pad to free the catch. Withdraw the tray.

164 Failure to engage the tray guides on their rails will cause jamming of a tray.

Fig. 13.52 Wiring harness – body, fuel contents unit and trailer (Sec 12)

1 Main harness connectors
2 Handbrake switch and rear cigar lighter
3 Fuel tank sender unit
4 Heated rear screen connectors
5 Rear lamps
6 Rear number plate lamps
7 Trailer connector

Fig. 13.53 Wiring harness – electric windows, and central door locking (Sec 12)

1 Connectors
2 Connectors
3 Front speakers
4 Window motors
5 'One touch' window lift unit
6 Electric window switch
7 Central door lock solenoid
8 Relay
9 Boot harness
10 Boot lamp switch
11 Boot lamp

Fig. 13.54 Wiring harness – facia panel (Sec 12)

1 Instruments
2 Rear foglamps, heated rear screen, panel rheostat
3 Clock
4 Cigar lighter, front-to-rear speaker fader
5 Glovebox switch

Fig. 13.55 Wiring harness – engine, heater, radio (Sec 12)

1 Radio connector
2 Main harness connectors
3 Rear speakers
4 Heated harness
5 Demister solenoid
6 Heater blower switch
7 Ignition ECU
8 Ignition coil
9 Speed transducer (1.6)
10 Starter motor
11 Crankshaft sensor (1.6)
12 Knock sensor (1.6)
13 Alternator
14 Stepper motor and fuel cut-off valve
15 Coolant sensor

Radio aerial (windscreen pillar mounted) – removal and refitting

165 Carefully prise up the cover trim at the base of the aerial and undo the baseplate retaining screws. Note the screening braid location on one of the screws.
166 From inside the car, disconnect the aerial lead at the rear of the radio and withdraw the lead from the console and facia.
167 Tie a length of string to the end of the aerial lead as an aid to refitting, and withdraw the aerial and lead upwards and out of the windscreen pillar.
168 Refitting is the reverse sequence to removal. Use the string to pull the aerial lead down the pillar and through behind the facia.

Wiring harness – 1986-on

169 Typical wiring harness layouts are shown in 13.52 to 13.57.

Earthing points – 1986-on

170 It is very important that the vehicle earthing points are kept rust and corrosion free, and the fixing which secures the various circuit earth wires at each of the five locations is kept tight.

13

Fig. 13.56 Wiring harness – engine, steering column, battery, fuses (Sec 12)

1 Main harness
2 Ignition/starter switch connector
3 Steering column switch harness
4 Fusebox and relays
5 Fuel ECU wiper control unit, interior lamp
6 Stop-lamp switch
7 Wiper motor connectors
8 Brake fluid level switch, manifold heater
9 Washer pump
10 Battery lead with fusible links
11 Horn connectors
12 Front lamp connectors
13 Coolant fan connectors
14 Air temperature sensor
15 Oil pressure switch
16 Courtesy lamp harness
17 Disc pad wear sensor

Fig. 13.57 Wiring harness – tailgate (Sec 12)

1 Main harness junction
2 Lamp header
3 Right-hand light cluster
4 Tailgate harness junction
5 Heated rear window
6 Right-hand number plate lamp
7 Central door locking switch
8 Left-hand number plate lamp
9 Central door locking motor
10 Wiper motor
11 Luggage compartment lamp
12 Tailgate speaker harness junction
13 Heated rear window
14 Left-hand light cluster
15 Rear earthing point
16 Left-hand speaker
17 Right-hand speaker

Fig. 13.58 Earthing points on 1986 and later models (Sec 12)

1 Front right-hand inner wing
2 Front left-hand inner wing
3 Bulkhead, top left behind facia panel
4 Rear left-hand wing behind trim panel
5 Rear right-hand wing behind trim panel

13 Suspension and steering

Front suspension – knocking

1 If a loud knock from the front suspension results when a front wheel goes sharply to the full rebound position, the noise can be minimised by fitting modified replacement cup and washer assemblies to the upper end of the suspension strut (see Fig. 11.1, Chapter 11).

2 These components are available from Austin Rover parts dealers.

Camber angle (later models)

3 Later models have had the front suspension camber angle changed from negative to positive by moving the suspension strut lower fixing bolt hole inward by 0.04 in (1.0 mm). On earlier models with negative camber, the bolt holes were in line.

4 This modification does not alter the servicing procedures given in Chapter 11, but for the purposes of the Specifications in this Supplement, the camber angle is grouped under the heading 'strut, type B', to avoid confusion.

Front hub bearings (one-piece type) – description and renewal

5 One-piece front hub bearings were introduced on later models. Early versions of the one-piece bearings used ball-bearings, while later versions use taper-roller bearings, and are the preferred type, although both types are fully interchangeable.

6 Note that neither type of one-piece bearing is interchangeable with the early two-piece bearings. The hub bearing (driveshaft) nut torque wrench setting given in the Specifi-

cations section of Chapter 11 remains the same for all types.

7 Apply the handbrake and remove the front roadwheel.

8 Have an assistant apply the footbrake hard. Unscrew the driveshaft-to-hub nut.

9 Un bolt the brake caliper and tie it up out of the way. There is no need to disconnect the hydraulic hose.

10 Remove the two screws which secure the brake disc to the hub flange. Remove the disc.

11 Extract the screws and remove both halves of the disc shield.

12 Unscrew the nut from the tie-rod end balljoint taper pin, and using a suitable splitter tool disconnect the balljoint from the steering arm.

13 Unscrew and remove the two bolts which hold the base of the suspension strut to the hub carrier.

14 Unscrew the nut from the suspension track control arm balljoint, and using a lever prise the arm downwards to separate the arm from the hub carrier.

15 Remove the hub carrier assembly.

16 A press will now be required to press the drive flange from the hub. Alternatively, a long bolt and nut with distance pieces can be used to draw it out, but on no account attempt to hammer it out. The bearing inner track and ballrace (outer section) will come away with the drive flange, and can be removed with a puller.

17 Extract the two circlips and press the bearing from the hub. Never attempt to re-use the old bearing.

18 Press the bearing into the hub until it contacts the circlip, then fit the second circlip.

19 Support the bearing inner track and press the drive flange into the hub.

20 Refitting the hub carrier is a reversal of removal, but observe the following points.

21 Tighten all nuts and bolts to the specified torque.

22 Fit a new driveshaft nut, tighten to the specified torque and stake the nut into the driveshaft groove.

23 Once the brake caliper has been refitted, apply the footbrake hard two or three times.

Wheel trims (1989-on) – removal and refitting

24 The wheel trims fitted to 1989-on models can be difficult to remove and refit, due to their more positive fit tolerance. The following procedure should be used.

25 To remove a wheel trim, insert the special tool supplied with the vehicle between the trim and the wheel rim, and using a twisting action lever the trim outwards.

26 Repeat the operation in several positions around the rim until the trim is released.

27 To refit the trim, position the wheel with the inflation valve at its lowest point.

28 Offer the trim to the wheel, with the large cut-out over the valve stem, and apply equal pressure to both sides of the wheel trim.

29 Apply pressure to the top of the trim until the trim is fully engaged with the wheel.

Steering wheel (1989-on, all models) – removal and refitting

30 The procedure is as described in Chapter 11, Section 16, but the steering wheel is secured in place by a bolt, and not a nut.

31 Note also the bolt has a different torque wrench setting (see Specifications).

Steering column (1989-on, all models) – removal and refitting

32 The procedure is as described in Chapter 11, Section 17 with the following differences.

33 After lifting out the inner columns, the top and bottom bushes must be tapped out from the outer column using a suitable drift.

Fig. 13.59 Sectional view of front hub with one-piece bearing (Sec 13)

1 Hub nut	5 Bearing
2 Brake disc	6 Hub
3 Drive flange	7 Driveshaft
4 Circlip	

Fig. 13.60 Removal and refitting of later type wheel trims (Sec 13)

13

Fig. 13.61 Power steering fluid reservoir dipstick (Sec 13)

34 Note also that there is a spacer under the top bush.
35 When fitting new bushes, apply Loctite 424 to their outer surfaces, and note that the chamfered edge of the bushes faces towards the centre of the outer column.

Power-assisted steering – description and maintenance

36 As from 1985, power-assisted steering became optionally available on 1.6 litre models.
37 Check the fluid level only when the system is cold and the engine switched off.
38 Wipe the filler cap clean and then unscrew and remove it.
39 Clean the dipstick with non-fluffy cloth or tissue, then refit the cap. Remove the cap once more and check that the fluid mark is between the MIN and MAX marks on the dipstick.
40 Top up if necessary with the specified fluid to the MAX mark.
41 The tension of the power steering pump drivebelt must be checked regularly. The belt

Fig. 13.62 Power steering pump fixings (Sec 13)

1 Camshaft belt upper cover bolt
2 Pump mounting bolt
3 Adjuster bolt (belt tension)

should deflect by 0.5 in (12.5 mm) when moderate thumb pressure is applied to the belt mid-way along its longest run.
42 To adjust the belt tension, first release the fuel pump inlet hose and the expansion tank hose from their clips.
43 Remove the timing belt upper cover.
44 Loosen the high pressure hydraulic pipeline nut and the pump adjustment and mounting bolts.
45 Pull the pump away from the engine by gripping the mounting bracket to apply tension to the belt. Tighten the bolts when the correct tension is achieved. Do not attempt to tension the belt by levering on the reservoir.
46 On completion, tighten the hydraulic pipeline and bleed the system as described later.
47 To renew the belt, follow the same procedure, but push the pump in towards the engine as far as it will go in order to slip the belt from the pulleys.

Power-assisted steering pump – removal and refitting

48 Disconnect the cooling system expansion tank hose and fuel pump inlet hose from their clips and remove the timing belt upper cover.
49 Remove the pump drivebelt.
50 Place a container under the pump and then disconnect the pressure hose union from the pump. Seal the hose and the pump.
51 Remove the pump mounting and adjustment bolts and nuts, and disconnect the return hose from the reservoir pipe. Seal the hose and pipe.
52 Remove the pump and mounting bracket.
53 Unbolt and remove the pulley.
54 Mark the relationship of the pump to its mounting bracket for reference purposes when refitting, and separate the pump and bracket.
55 A faulty pump should be renewed, not overhauled.
56 Refitting is a reversal of removal, but note the following points.
57 The pump pressure hose should be set at 30° towards the right-hand side of the vehicle.
58 Apply thread locking fluid to the threads of the mounting bracket bolts.
59 Tension the drivebelt, and bleed the system, as described elsewhere in this Section.

Power-assisted steering gear – removal and refitting

60 Disconnect the battery.
61 Unscrew and remove the coupling pinch-bolt from the bottom of the steering column shaft.
62 Slacken the front roadwheel nuts, raise the front of the vehicle and remove the roadwheels.
63 Unscrew the tie-rod end balljoint nuts and, using a suitable balljoint splitter tool, disconnect the tie-rod end balljoints from the steering arms.
64 Remove the suspension crossmember support bracket from the driver's side.
65 Disconnect the fluid hoses from the rack pipe. Lockwashers may be fitted, in which case bend their tabs flat. Anticipate the loss of some fluid.
66 Unscrew the steering rack mounting bolts and manoeuvre the rack assembly out from under the front wheel arch on the driver's side.
67 Worn or faulty power steering gear should be renewed, not overhauled, due to the need for special tools and the difficulty of obtaining individual spare parts.
68 Refitting is a reversal of removal, but observe the following points.
69 With the front roadwheels and steering wheel in the straight-ahead position, turn the rack pinion until the tie-rod end balljoints will just drop into the eyes of the steering arms when the rack housing is correctly located for

Fig. 13.63 Power steering pump components (Sec 13)

1 Drivebelt
2 Pulley
3 Mounting bracket
4 Pressure pipe
5 Banjo type union
6 Seals
7 Return pipe and hose
8 Pump

bolting into position. When this situation is achieved, the pinion should be aligned with the steering shaft coupling so that the pinion groove and coupling holes are also in line to accept the pinch-bolt.

70 Tighten all nuts and bolts to the specified torque, except the crossmember support bracket, which should be tightened after the vehicle is lowered to the floor.

71 Bleed the system as described in the following paragraphs.

Power-assisted steering – bleeding

72 The system will require bleeding if the system hoses or pipe lines have been uncoupled and reconnected or new components fitted.

73 Make sure that the fluid reservoir is topped up to the MAX mark. Start the engine and turn the steering slowly several times from lock to lock.

74 Top up the fluid as necessary and repeat.

75 Make a final check of the fluid level when the system has stood inoperative for several hours and is cold.

Manual steering gear – centralising

76 On models built from 1986, the rack centralising hole (Chapter 11, Section 22, paragraph 13) is no longer incorporated.

77 When refitting this later rack and pinion steering gear, refer to paragraph 69 of this Section for details of rack centralising method.

Front wheel alignment – special precautions

78 It is very important that, when checking and adjusting the front wheel alignment (toe), as described in Chapter 11, Section 24, the following special conditions are observed.

79 If a measuring gauge is being used, then the vehicle must have been pushed in a forward direction for at least three metres with the front roadwheels in the straight-ahead position before carrying out any checks.

80 If scuff plates are being used, then the rear roadwheels must be standing on packing pieces of a thickness equivalent to that of the scuff plates.

81 Make sure that the front and rear trim heights are as specified on both sides of the vehicle. If necessary, load or jack one side of the vehicle to achieve similar trim heights on both sides.

Rear axle – modification

82 From VIN 168414, the pivot bushes in the rear axle trailing arms are fitted the other way round, with the flange shoulder towards the outside. When renewing pivot bushes, ensure that they are fitted accordingly (refer to item 2, Fig. 11.2).

Self-levelling rear suspension – description and testing

83 This is optionally available on most models in the Montego range. The system reacts to vehicle loading and automatically maintains the specified vehicle trim heights.

84 The self-levelling units are sealed struts fitted in place of the normal rear suspension units. A pump in the damper operates under the action of the suspension to raise the rear of the car until normal trim height is regained. On an undulating road, this process will be carried out within one mile. When the additional load is removed, the suspension remains at the correct level.

85 To test the operation of the self-levelling struts, measure and record the rear suspension trim height on each side with the vehicle at kerb weight. The trim height is the distance from the centre of the hub to the lower edge of the wheel arch. Compare the figures obtained with those given in the Specifications of Chapter 11.

86 Evenly load the rear of the car with 440 to 550 lbs (200 to 250 kg).

87 Drive the car over undulating roads for at least 3 miles (5 km), then stop the car and measure the rear trim heights again with the driver remaining in his seat. The readings obtained should be within 0.4 in (10.0 mm) of the readings obtained previously. Both sides of the car should have risen by equal amounts and should retain their position after the car

has stopped. A unit that is low, does not hold its position, or shows signs of excessive oil leakage must be renewed.

88 Removal and refitting of the self-levelling struts is the same as for conventional rear suspension units, and reference should be made to Chapter 11, Sections 13 and 14. Note that, on Estate models; access to the upper mounting is gained after removing the panel from the middle of the luggage compartment side trim.

14 Bodywork

Radiator grille (1989-on) – removal and refitting

1 Open the bonnet.

2 Remove the screws securing the upper edge of the grille to the cross panel (photo).

3 Lift the grille upward to disengage the clips at each lower, outer end, and withdraw the grille panel (photo).

4 Refit in reverse order, ensuring that the lower clips are in full engagement.

Front door trim panel (all models, 1989-on) – removal and refitting

5 Prise out the door speaker grille and undo the four screws under it (photos).

6 Remove the screws from the door bin then

14.2 Remove the screws securing the upper edge of the grille to the cross panel

14.3 Lift the grille upward to disengage the clips

14.5A Prise out the speaker grille . . .

14.5B . . . and undo the four door trim screws

13

14.6A Remove the screws from the door bin . . .

14.6B . . . then lift off the door bin and panel

14.7A Prise out the plastic cover . . .

14.7B . . . remove the screw . . .

14.7C . . . and lift off the escutcheon plate

lift off the combined door bin and speaker trim panel (photos).

7 Prise out the plastic cover from the interior release handle escutcheon plate screw, remove the screw and lift off the escutcheon plate (photos).

8 Prise out the plastic cover from the window winder handle, remove the nut and lift off the handle and backing plate (photos). This operation is not applicable where electric windows are fitted.

9 Remove the screws from, and lift off, the armrest (photo).

10 Carefully, using a flat-bladed tool and starting from the lower edge, prise out the plastic 'screws' securing the trim panel to the door, then lift off the panel (photo).

11 Refit in reverse order.

14.8A Prise out the plastic cover . . .

14.8B . . . remove the nut . . .

14.8C . . . lift off the handle . . .

14.8D . . . and backing plate

14.9 Remove the screws from the armrest

14.10 Remove the trim panel

14.14A Remove the screws securing the capping to the door . . .

14.14B . . . and lift off the capping upward

14.19 Remove the two self-tapping screws under the number plate

Front door capping strip (1989-on) – removal and refitting

12 Remove the door trim panel as described earlier.
13 Where fitted, prise out and disconnect the door 'tweeter' speaker.
14 Remove the screws securing the capping to the door, and lift off the capping upwards to disengage the seal (photos).
15 Refit in reverse order.

Rear door trim panel (1989-on) – removal and refitting

16 The procedure is as described for the front doors, but there is no speaker grille.

Rear door capping strip (1989-on) – removal and refitting

17 The procedure is as described for the front doors, but there is no 'tweeter' speaker.

Applique panel (Saloon models, 1989-on) – removal and refitting

18 Prise off the rear number plate which is secured by double-sided tape.
19 Remove the two self-tapping screws under the number plate (photo).
20 Open the boot lid and remove the nuts from the threaded spigots at each end of the applique panel, inside the double skin (photo).

21 Withdraw the applique panel (photo).
22 Refitting is a reversal of removal, but use new double-sided tape, which is available from your dealer. (The use of normal double-sided tape, such as would be used for carpets, is not recommended, and would result in the number plate dropping off).

Headling (Saloon models, 1989-on) – removal and refitting

23 The procedure is similar to that described for Estate models, except that the front seats must be moved fully rearwards and reclined, and the headlining lowered from the front to release the rear end from the plastic trim strip.
24 Manoeuvre the headlining from the vehicle through one of the front doors.

Headling (Estate models) – removal and refitting

25 Disconnect the battery.
26 If fitted, fold down the rear-facing seats, then remove the head restraints from the remaining seats.
27 Release the door seal from the front 'A' pillars.
28 Remove the sunvisors and their brackets, the interior and load space lamps, and the front and rear grab handles.
29 Carefully release the plastic screws and buttons securing the headlining to the roof panel and the rear quarter.
30 Remove the rear edge clips then lower the

lining and carefully manoeuvre it out of the open tailgate.
31 Refit in reverse order.

Integral roof rack (Estate models) – removal and refitting

32 Remove the headlining as described earlier.
33 Depress the spring-loaded clips at the ends of the roof rack cross-rails and remove the cross-rails.
34 Remove the side-rail securing nuts and carefully ease the side rails and gaskets from the roof. Clean all sealant from the holes in the roof and the side-rail posts.
Caution: It is essential that correct and accurate refitting of the roof rack is achieved to prevent the cross-rails becoming detached in use, to avoid water leaks and prevent damage to the roof.
35 Apply sealant (Expandite SR 51 or equivalent) to the base of each rack post, then use an adhesive (Dunlop S 758 or equivalent) to stick new gaskets to the posts.

14.20 Remove the nuts from the threaded spigots

14.21 Withdraw the applique panel

Fig 13.64 Headlining and associated components (Sec 14)

1 Headlining
2 Fixing plug
3 Coat hook
4 Support button
5 Edge clip
6 Sunvisors and fixings
7 Grab handle

13

A Support bracket to roof panel
    i)   Front = 0.50 + 0.06 in (12.5 ± 1.5 mm)
    ii) Centre = 0.60 + 0.06 in (15.2 ± 1.5mm)
    iii) Rear = 0.44 + 0.06in (11.2 ± 1.5mm)
B Distance between upper rails
    = 32.84 ± 0.16 in (830.0 ± 4.0 mm)
C Distance between lower rails
    = 35.43 ± 0.16in (900 ± 4.0 mm)

Fig. 13.65 Integral roof rack fittings and dimensions (Sec 14)

1 Post and side rails
2 Gasket
3 Sealant
4 Mounting bracket
5 Spring-loaded button
6 Locating pins
7 Side rail retaining nut
8 Height adjustment screw
9 Support bracket nuts
10 Tack welds

36 Apply sealant around each roof panel hole.

37 Check the distance between the roof panel and each support bracket measuring at the centre-line of each hole. Dimensions are given in Fig. 13.65.

38 To adjust the brackets, loosen the bracket securing nuts and move the bracket up or down as necessary, tightening the nuts on completion.

39 Fit the side-rail assemblies to the roof, then fit and tighten the securing nuts only finger-tight.

40 Measure the distance between the inside faces of the rails which must be as shown in Fig. 13.65.

41 Adjust as necessary, then tighten the securing nuts to 16 lbf ft (22 Nm).

42 If the correct dimension cannot be obtained it may be necessary to grind down the track welds on the front edge of the front and centre brackets, loosen the nuts and reset the bracket positions. Tighten and tack-weld the nuts on completion.

43 Check for water leaks before refitting the headlining, which is a reverse of removal.

Front seats – loose backrest

44 On some high-mileage 1989-on models, the backrest-to-seat squab bolts may loosen and allow excess play between the backrest and the seat squab.

45 This problem can be overcome by fitting hexagon-headed bolts in place of the Torx type bolts (available from Austin Rover dealers) and tightening them to a torque of 29 to 40 lbf ft (40 to 50 Nm).

Door seals – inadequate retention

46 If the door seals tend to come adrift from the top of the door frame, they can be stuck more firmly in position by using double-sided tape, available from Austin Rover dealers.

Centre console (1989-on) – removal and refitting

47 Disconnect the battery.

48 Remove the gear lever knob on manual transmission models.

49 Prise out the panel at the rear of the console and remove the console retaining screws under it.

50 Prise out the handbrake cover panel and remove the remaining screws securing the console to the floorpan.

51 Lift the console slightly and disconnect the plugs to the window lift switches, and the gear selector illumination bulb on automatic transmission models.

52 Lift out the console.

53 Refit in reverse order.

Facia (1989-on) – removal and refitting

54 The procedure is basically as described in Chapter 12, Section 35.

14.58 Grab handle retaining screw and cover

55 Refer to the relevant Sections of this Supplement for removal of the radio and heater controls, which differ from earlier models.

Tailgate (Estate models) – removal and refitting

56 Open the tailgate and release the interior trim moulding by prising out the retaining buttons. Use two screwdrivers or a forked tool for this operation, but note that the buttons are easily broken and some new ones will probably be needed.

57 Release the trim from the upper retaining tags, disconnect the speaker leads (where fitted) and remove the trim.

58 Spring back the plastic covers over the grab handles, undo the retaining screws and remove the handles from the headlining (photo).

59 Peel back the rubber weatherstrip around the upper edge of the tailgate aperture, then release the clips securing the headlining (photo).

60 Unscrew the headlining retaining buttons

14.59 Removing a headlining retaining clip

Fig. 13.67 Tailgate lift assister fitting diagram (Sec 14)

All dimensions In mm

Fig. 13.66 Facia panel on 1989-on models (Sec 14)

1 Glovebox lid	5 Side window demister escutcheon	9 Instrument carrier
2 Glovebox	6 Facia panel	10 Radio and centre vent housing
3 Glovebox supports	7 Cross duct	11 Coin tray
4 Outer vent	8 Lower stiffening rail	12 Fusebox cover

as necessary (photo), and lower the headlining sufficiently to gain access to the tailgate hinge retaining nuts.

61 Disconnect the wiring multi-plugs and cable ties at all the tailgate electrical components. Tape the multi-plugs to the wiring harness, then tie drawstrings to each harness end. Similarly, disconnect the washer hose and tie a drawstring to its end.

62 Release the grommets in the tailgate and pull the wiring and washer hose out of the tailgate until the drawstrings emerge. Untie the strings, but leave them in place.

63 Have an assistant support the tailgate, then release the support strut upper balljoints, prising off the retaining clips with a screwdriver.

64 Mark the hinge outlines on the body, then reach through the lowered headlining and undo the hinge retaining nuts. Remove the tailgate from the car.

65 Refitting is the reverse sequence to removal. Use the drawstrings to pull the wiring and washer hose through into the tailgate. Adjust the position of the hinges to achieve correct alignment and ease of closure.

Tailgate support struts (Estate models) – removal and refitting

66 Support the tailgate in the open position and prise out the strut upper and lower balljoint retaining clips using a screwdriver (photos).

67 Withdraw the support strut from the car.

68 Refitting is the reverse sequence to removal.

Tailgate lift assisters (Estate models) – fitting

69 Should the tailgate open only as far as the safety catch when the remote release control is operated, a pair of lift assisters (available from your dealer) may be fitted in the following way.

70 Drill a hole as shown in Fig. 13.67 on each side of the luggage area. The diameter of the holes is critical.

71 De-burr the edges of the holes, and paint.

72 Apply underbody protective wax to the assemblies and the edges of the holes.

73 Fit the assisters, screwing them to their minimum length before closing the tailgate for the first time. Unscrew each assister half a turn and check the lift of the tailgate. Unscrew the assisters in half-turn increments until the tailgate operation is satisfactory.

14.60 Removing a headlining retaining button

14.66A Tailgate strut upper balljoint

14.66B Tailgate strut lower balljoint

13

Fig. 13.68 Tailgate lock and support strut components (Sec 14)

1 Strut
2 Lock cylinder
3 Operating rod
4 Latch
5 Striker
6 Remote release lever
7 Remote release cable

Tailgate lock (Estate models) – removal and refitting

74 Remove the tailgate interior trim moulding, as described in paragraphs 56 and 57 of this Section.
75 Release the retaining clip and disconnect the operating rod from the lock lever.
76 Undo the two retaining bolts and remove the lock from the tailgate (photo).
77 Refitting is the reverse sequence to removal. If necessary, adjust the striker plate position after refitting the lock, so that the tailgate shuts and locks without slamming.

Tailgate lock cylinder (Estate models) – removal and refitting

78 Remove the tailgate interior trim moulding, as described in paragraphs 56 and 57 of this Section.
79 Release the retaining clip and disconnect the operating rod from the cylinder lock lever (photo).
80 Undo the retaining nuts, remove the lock lever and withdraw the lock cylinder from the number plate lamp housing.
81 Refitting is the reverse sequence to removal.

Tailgate release cable and lever (Estate models) – removal and refitting

82 Fold back the rear seat cushion and the luggage compartment carpet.

14.76 Tailgate lock and retaining bolts

83 Remove the front and rear sill carpet retainers on the driver's side.
84 Slacken all the driver's seat retaining bolts and remove the bolts from the runner nearest the door.
85 Remove the oddments tray.
86 Undo the release lever retaining screws, lift up the trim moulding and disconnect the release cable. Remove the release lever from the car.
87 Fold back the side of the front and rear carpets, disconnect the cable from the retaining clips and pull the cable into the luggage compartment.
88 Undo the screws and withdraw the tailgate aperture lower trim moulding (photo).
89 Undo the striker plate retaining bolts (photo). Lift up the striker plate and disconnect the cable from the release lever. Withdraw the cable from the car.
90 Refitting is the reverse sequence to removal, but adjust the striker plate position so that the tailgate shuts and locks without slamming.

Rear bumper (Estate models) – removal and refitting

91 Undo the rear wheel arch liner retaining screws and remove the wheel arch liners.
92 Undo the nut securing each bumper support bracket to the rear valance.
93 From inside the car, fold the rear panel of the luggage compartment floor and remove the floor covering.

14.88 Removing tailgate aperture lower trim moulding

14.79 Tailgate lock, lock lever and fixing nuts

94 Undo the two bolts securing each bumper rear support bracket to the body. Lift away the rear bumper assembly.
95 Refitting is the reverse sequence to removal.

Rear seat (Estate models) – removal and refitting

96 With the rear doors open, fold the cushion or cushions forward, undo the retaining screws and withdraw the seat cushion(s).
97 Remove the outer hinge bracket covers, release the seat squab retaining latches and lower the squab. Undo the outer bracket retaining screws.
98 If a one-piece squab is fitted, remove the squab. If a split squab is fitted, undo the retaining screw and extract the clip securing the centre pivots. Withdraw the relevant squab.
99 Refitting is the reverse sequence to removal.

Luggage area side trim moulding (Estate models) – removal and refitting

100 If fitted, fold the rear facing seat, fold the rear seat cushion, lower the squab and remove the squab release handle.
101 Detach the rear door weatherstrip seal from along the side trim moulding.
102 Open the tailgate, and remove the guide plate and the three screws securing the

14.89 Tailgate lock striker

14.102 Tailgate lower trim mouldings and weatherseal

tailgate aperture lower trim moulding on the side being worked on (photo).

103 Undo the upper and lower rear seat belt mounting bolts, and detach the guide escutcheon from the side moulding.

104 Undo the upper and lower rear facing seat belt mounting bolts, detach the guide escutcheon from the side moulding and release the seat belt support strut at its bottom end.

105 Release the fastener securing the moulding to the rear of the wheel arch. Using a forked tool or suitable alternative, carefully release the four clips securing each end of the panel.

106 Pull the sill edge retaining clips from the body brackets and lift the moulding to clear the four bottom edge retainers from the body slots.

107 Disengage the support strut, pass the seat belt webbing through the side trim moulding and remove the moulding.

108 Refitting is the reverse sequence to removal.

Rear seat belts (Saloon models) – removal and refitting

Outer belt

109 Remove the rear seat cushion.

110 Undo the seat belt lower mounting and rear squab extension retaining bolt.

111 Push the squab extension upwards and remove it from the car.

112 Extract the seat belt upper guide bracket plastic cover, then undo the bolt and remove the guide and spacers.

113 Release the door weatherstrip seal from the rear body pillar and remove the finisher trim.

114 Release the parcel shelf trim extension plastic retaining clip and withdraw the extension.

115 Detach the shelf trim finisher from the seat belt, and remove the shelf trim extension by sliding it along the belt.

116 From within the boot, fold back the front of the boot carpet, undo the seat belt locking buckle anchorage bolts, and remove the locking buckle.

Fig. 13.69 Rear seat belt anchorage points – Saloon (Sec 14)

1 Plastic cap	5 Shouldered distance
2 Lower mounting bolt	piece
3 Plain washer	6 Spacer
4 Anti-rattle washer	7 Upper mounting bolt

8 Locking buckle bolt
9 Centre belt bolt
10 Retaining washer (transit)

117 Refitting is the reverse sequence to removal.

Centre belt

118 Remove the rear seat cushion, then, from inside the boot, fold back the front of the boot carpet.

119 Undo the seat belt centre belt anchorage bolts and remove the belts from the car.

120 Refitting is the reverse sequence to removal.

Rear seat belts (Estate models) – removal and refitting

121 Remove the luggage area side trim moulding, as described earlier in this Section.

122 Remove the seat belt guide bracket plastic cover, then undo the retaining bolt and withdraw the belt guide and spacers.

123 Release the belt guide escutcheon from the side moulding, open the escutcheon and slide out the webbing. Pass the belt through the side moulding.

124 Undo the reel retaining bolt and remove the belt assembly.

125 Undo the seat belt locking buckle retaining bolt and remove the locking buckle. Note the position of the rear facing seat belt where these are fitted.

126 Refitting is the reverse sequence to removal.

127 To remove the centre belt, fold the rear facing seat (if fitted) and the rear seat, and remove the backrest(s) as necessary.

128 Undo the locking buckle and anchor

bracket retaining bolts, and remove the complete centre seat belt.

129 Refitting is the reverse sequence to removal.

Rear facing seat belts (Estate models) – removal and refitting

130 Fold the rear seat and the rear facing seat, then remove the rear seat backrest.

131 Remove the upper guide bracket plastic cover, then undo the retaining bolt.

132 Remove the plastic cover, then undo the lower anchorage retaining bolt.

133 Release the belt guide escutcheon from the side moulding, open the escutcheon and slide it off the belt.

134 Remove the relevant grab handle and the rearmost headlining retaining buttons.

135 Release the tailgate weatherstrip seal from the upper edge of the aperture, then extract the headlining retaining clips.

136 Undo the bolt at the top of the support strut, then support the headlining by refitting the retaining clips.

137 Remove the luggage area side trim moulding, as described earlier in this Section.

138 Undo the seat belt support strut lower retaining bolt and the belt reel retaining bolt from inside the side panel.

139 Pass the seat belt through the side moulding and remove the belt assembly.

140 Undo the locking buckle anchorage bolt and remove the locking buckle.

141 Refitting is a reversal of removal.

Fig. 13.71 Remote control door mirror
(Sec 14)

1 Escutcheon panel   4 Control lever
2 Screw   plastic cover
3 Retaining plate

Fig. 13.70 Rear-facing seat belt mountings – Estate (Sec 14)

1 Locking buckle bolt   4 Inertia reel bolt   7 Anti-rattle washer
2 Upper mounting bolt   5 Plastic cap   8 Shouldered distance piece
3 Lower mounting bolt   6 Plain washer   9 Spacer

Remote control door mirror – removal, refitting and glass renewal

142 Remove the door trim panel, as described in Chapter 12.
143 Slide the plastic cover from the mirror control lever.
144 Remove the internal escutcheon panel and extract the exposed mirror fixing screws.
145 Remove the retaining plate and take off the mirror assembly.
146 Refitting is a reversal of removal.
147 If the mirror glass is to be renewed, this can be done without the need to remove the mirror from the door.
148 Wear a protective glove and push the

outboard end of the mirror towards the front of the car, until the mirror casing begins to move away from the glass. Insert the fingers between the glass and the casing and prise the glass gently. When the gap is wide enough, insert a thin screwdriver to release the socket from the pivot ball.
149 Disconnect the tension spring and remove the glass.
150 To fit the glass, first apply silicone grease to the socket, then fit the glass to the retaining arm and connect the spring.
151 Gently apply even pressure to push the glass into position, engaging the socket with the ball.

Fuel filler flap remote control lever and cable – removal and refitting

152 On Saloon models, remove the rear seat cushion and peel back the carpet from the

right-hand side of the luggage compartment.
153 On Estate models, fold the rear seat and peel back the luggage area floor covering. Where fitted, erect the rear facing seats and remove the right-hand side trim from the luggage area.
154 Remove the sill carpet retainers from the driver's side.
155 Slacken the driver's seat belt bolts and then remove the bolts from the outboard seat runner.
156 Remove the oddments tray.
157 Extract the fuel flap release lever fixing screws, raise the moulding and disconnect the release lever from the cable.
158 Peel back the carpets to free the cable by releasing the retaining clips. Withdraw the cable into the boot (Saloon) or luggage area (Estate).
159 Open the fuel filler flap, release the retaining clip and then pull the cable from the rear of the wheel arch into the boot or luggage area.
160 Refitting is a reversal of removal.

Asymmetrical split rear seat

161 On later Estates, the rear seat is split 60/40 in order that, by folding the sections independently, load carrying area is provided while still retaining rear passenger

Fig. 13.72 Door mirror attachment (Sec 14)

1 Mirror arm   4 Glass
2 Ball   5 Tension spring
3 Socket

Fig. 13.73 Remote control fuel filler lid (Sec 14)

Fig. 13.74 Asymmetrical split rear seat – Estate (Sec 14)

2   Seat loops
A   Maximum load area

B   Luggage plus two
    passengers

C   Luggage plus one
    passenger

accommodation. Removal operations are similar to those described in paragraphs 96 to 99 of this Section.

Rear facing child seats

162 Optionally available on Estate models, the seats should be regarded as being for occasional use only. They must only be used with the forward facing rear seat erected and locked. Seat belts must always be used. The seats are not suitable for adults.

Spare wheel and tools (Estate models)

163 The spare wheel and tools are located below the luggage compartment floor. Access is obtained by raising the floor or seat backrest if rear facing seats are fitted.

164 The tools are located in a plastic moulding within the spare wheel.

Grab handles – removal and refitting

165 To remove a grab handle from the headlining above the door opening, flip back the end covers with a small screwdriver to expose the fixing screws. Remove the screws and the handle.
166 Refitting is a reversal of removal.

Plastic components

167 With the use of more and more plastic body components by the vehicle manufacturers (eg bumpers, spoilers, and in some cases major body panels), rectification of more serious damage to such items has become a matter of either entrusting repair work to a specialist in this field, or renewing complete components. Repair of such damage by the DIY owner is not really feasible, owing to the cost of the equipment and materials required for effecting such repairs. The basic technique involves making a groove along the line of the crack in the plastic, using a rotary burr in a power drill. The damaged part is then welded back together, using a hot-air gun to heat up and fuse a plastic filler rod into the groove. Any excess plastic is then removed, and the area rubbed down to a smooth finish. It is important that a filler rod of the correct plastic is used, as body components can be made of a variety of different types (eg polycarbonate, ABS, polypropylene).

168 Damage of a less serious nature (abrasions, minor cracks etc) can be repaired by the DIY owner using a two-part epoxy filler repair material. Once mixed in equal proportions, this is used in similar fashion to the bodywork filler used on metal panels. The filler is usually cured in twenty to thirty minutes, ready for sanding and painting.

169 If the owner is renewing a complete component himself, or if he has repaired it with epoxy filler, he will be left with the problem of finding a suitable paint for finishing which is compatible with the type of plastic used. At one time, the use of a universal paint was not possible, owing to the complex range of plastics encountered in body component applications. Standard paints, generally speaking, will not bond to plastic or rubber satisfactorily. However, it is now possible to obtain a plastic body parts finishing kit which consists of a pre-primer treatment, a primer and coloured top coat. Full instructions are normally supplied with a kit, but basically, the method of use is to first apply the pre-primer to the component concerned, and allow it to dry for up to 30 minutes. Then the primer is applied, and left to dry for about an hour before finally applying the special-coloured top coat. The result is a correctly-coloured component, where the paint will flex with the plastic or rubber, a property that standard paint does not normally possess.

Tilt/slide sunroof components (1987 and later models) – removal and refitting

Glass panel and seal

170 Open the panel to the halfway position, then release the screws which secure the side shield and rear drain channel to the glass panel.
171 Slide the cover, drain channel, and the visor into the recess above the headlining.
172 Close the glass panel then tilt the rear edge.
173 Extract the screws which hold the glass panel to the side arms.
174 Lift off the glass panel and remove the seal.
175 When refitting, first push the seal onto

Fig. 13.75 Spare wheel and tools – Estate (Sec 14)

1   Clamp
2   Wheel trim tool
3   Wheel brace

4   Jack handle
5   Plastic container
6   Jack

7   Carpet
8   Strap (wheel withdrawal)

13

Fig. 13.76 Components of the tilt/slide sunroof (Sec 14)

1 Side arm	9 Rear guide and cable	17 Cable guide and run-out
2 Glass panel	10 Pilot guide	tubes
3 Rear drain channel	11 Guide rail	18 Rear tray seal
4 Side shield	12 Tray seal	19 Tray
5 Slide rail	13 Drivegear	20 Front bracket and
6 Visor	14 Escutcheon	mounting plate
7 Wind deflector	15 Operating handle	21 Relay
8 Deflector lifting arm	16 Bezel	22 Electric motor/gearbox
		drive assembly

Fig. 13.77 Alignment of side arm and lifting arm (Sec 14)

1 Side arm	3 Pilot plate
2 Lifting arm	

the glass panel with the rubber surface facing inwards. Cut the seal to form a butt joint.

176 Set the operating mechanism in the closed position and locate the glass panel on the side arms. Fit the screws, align the panel with the roof and then tighten the screws.

177 Open and close the panel and then check that in the closed position, the front edge is flush with, or up to 0.04 in (1.0 mm) below, the level of the roof. The rear edge should be within the same tolerance above the level of the roof.

178 Open the panel to the halfway position,

locate the side shield and rear drain channel and fit the fixing screws.

Sunroof visor

179 Remove the glass panel as previously described.

180 Remove the pilot plates and side arms.

181 Remove the slide and collect the flat washer from under the front of each side rail.

182 Disengage the rear guides from their channels and allow them to hang in the roof aperture.

183 Press the wind deflector downwards,

then slide the cover and rear chain channel forwards and out through the roof.

184 Slide the visor forwards and out through the roof aperture, taking care not to damage the guides.

185 Refitting is a reversal of removal; remember to fit the flat washer under each side rail.

Sunroof drivegear (manually operated type)

186 Remove the glass panel as previously described, then set the operating mechanism in the closed position.

187 Check that the handle is in the freeplay position, and then remove the handle bezel and escutcheon.

188 Remove the finisher from around the sunroof aperture, and remove both windscreen sunvisors and clips.

189 Remove the grab handle from the passenger side headlining, and the stud from the driver's side.

190 Release and pull down the front edge of the headlining and extract the screws which hold the operating handle.

191 Extract the fixing screw and withdraw the drivegear.

192 To refit, position the side arm assembly so that the hole in the lifting lever and the triangular cut-out in the side arm are aligned with the slot in the pilot plate, as shown in Fig. 13.77.

193 Carry out the alignment on the opposite side.

194 Smear the drivegear with silicone grease and engage the cables. Fit and tighten the mounting screw.

195 Fit the operating handle, secure the headlining and fit the grab handle and visors.

196 Fit the finisher, handle escutcheon and bezel, and the glass panel.

Sunroof drivegear (electrically operated type)

197 Remove the glass panel as previously described.

198 Check that the sunroof mechanism is switched off in the closed position. If there is any doubt about closure, use the emergency hand crank, which is stored in the glovebox.

199 Open the cover, release the switch panel,

disconnect the switch leads and remove the switch panel.

200 Release and pull away the headlining.

201 Extract the screw and release the relay from the motor bracket (Fig. 13.78).

202 Remove the mounting screws and withdraw the motor/gearbox drive assembly, noting that the gear timing hole is adjacent to the terminals when the mechanism is in the roof-closed mode.

203 Commence refitting by aligning the guides to the pilot plates, using 5.0 mm diameter pins to retain the alignment.

204 Lubricate the motor drivegears.

205 Support the motor, connect the multi-plug and switch on the ignition. Actuate the roof switch to bring the gear timing hole to the position shown in Fig. 13.78. Switch off the ignition.

206 Align the gearbox slides and engage the drive cables, then fit the motor/gearbox drive assembly. Withdraw the temporary pins.

207 Refit the headlining, switch panel and glass panel.

Rear guide and cable assemblies

208 Remove the glass panel as previously described.

209 Set the operating mechanism in the closed position.

210 Remove the drivegear (manual) or motor/gearbox (electrically operated).

211 Extract the screws and remove the pilot plates and front slide rails.

212 Remove both side arm assemblies and withdraw the cable and rear guides.

213 Before refitting, inject grease into the cable guide tubes and insert the cables.

214 Locate the rear guides, fit the side arm assemblies, front slide rails and pilot plates.

215 Align the side arms as described in paragraph 192.

216 Fit the drivegear or motor/gearbox according to type. Refit the glass panel.

Sunroof – complete

217 Remove the glass panel as previously described.

Manually operated type

218 Remove the handle bezel, escutcheon and the handle itself.

Electrically operated type

219 Open the cover and release the switch panel. Disconnect the switch and relay and take off the switch panel.

All models

220 Disconnect the drain tubes from the sunroof tray.

221 Locate a block of wood above the front bracket and drill out the two pop-rivets.

222 Fully recline the two front seats and then extract all the screws which hold the sunroof tray to the roof.

223 Lower the tray and withdraw it through the front passenger door. Discard the tray seal.

224 Refitting is a reversal of removal but

Fig. 13.78 Sunroof drive motor (Sec 14)

1 Emergency hand crank
2 Hand crank drive
3 Switch panel
4 Motor mounting screws
5 Relay
6 Gearwheel timing hole

before starting, fit a strip of 20.0 x 20.0 mm compriband seal (available from your dealer) around the edge of the sunroof tray.

Non-vacuum type heater – general

225 Later models are equipped with a modified type of heater unit, whereby the air intake and temperature flaps are operated by cables instead of the vacuum actuators used previously.

226 Apart from the cable locations shown in Fig. 13.79 and the cable adjustment procedure contained in the following paragraphs, the heater is the same in construction and layout as the earlier type. All operations contained in Chapter 12 are still

applicable, but note the cable locations and attachments when carrying out the work.

Non-vacuum type heater control linkage – adjustment

Air distribution lever

227 Raise the control lever fully and slacken the pinch-bolt which holds the control link rod to the flap lever trunnion.

228 Hold the control lever fully up and the flap lever fully down and tighten the pinch-bolt.

Temperature control lever

229 Disconnect the battery and remove the facia panel, as described in Chapter 12.

Fig. 13.79 Heater (non-vacuum type) flap linkage adjustment diagram (Sec 14)

1 Link rod (temperature control)
2 Pinch-bolt and trunnion
3 Link rod (air distribution)
4 Pinch-bolt and trunnion

13

Fig. 13.80 Heater controls on 1989-on models (Sec 14)

1 Air distribution control
2 Blower motor switch
3 Air temperature control
4 Air distribution flap lever
5 Air inlet flap lever and pinch-bolt
6 Matrix air outlet flap lever

14.244 Pull off the control knobs

14.245 Prise the cover panel forward . . .

14.246A Remove the screws securing the backpanel . . .

14.246B . . . and drop the back panel forward

230 Raise the control lever fully and slacken the pinch-bolt which holds the link rod to the trunnion on the lower flap lever which is adjacent to the facia.

231 Hold the control lever fully up and the flap lever towards the vehicle interior and tighten the pinch-bolt.

232 Refit the facia and connect the battery.

Heater (1989-on) – general description

233 The heater on 1989-on models is basically the same as the non-vacuum type fitted to earlier models, but has rotary controls as opposed to levers.

Heater control cables (1989-on) – removal and refitting

234 Disconnect the battery.

235 Remove the centre console and fascia as described.

236 Remove the heater control cover as described in paragraphs 243 to 246.

237 Remove the outer cable clips from the control panel.

238 Release the cable operating racks from the control panel, then disconnect the cables from the racks.

239 Remove the cable clips from the heater casing, disconnect the cables from the flap levers and withdraw the cables.

240 Disconnect the blower motor switch multi-plug and withdraw the control panel.

241 Refitting is a reversal of removal, fully closing the heater flaps before locating the control cables in the racks, which must also be in the fully closed position before fitting the cables to them.

242 Adjust the heater flap by loosening the lever pinch-bolt and pushing the air intake flap lever fully rearwards. Push the matrix air outlet flap lever rearwards and tighten the pinch-bolt.

Heater control panel (1989-on) – removal and refitting

243 Disconnect the battery.

244 Pull off the control knobs (photo).

245 Prise the cover panel forward (photo).

246 Remove the screws securing the back panel to the facia panel, and drop the back panel forwards (photos).

247 Disconnect the lead and withdraw the panel.

248 Refit in reverse order.

Symbols used in the wiring diagrams

1 Component earthed by its lead
2 Component earthed by its fixing
3 If fitted
4 Line connector
5 Sealed joint
6 Printed circuit connector
7 Printed circuit

Connections to other circuits

A Headlamp wash
B Radio/cassette
C Electric windows
D Central locking

Colour code

P	Purple	B	Black
R	Red	G	Green
S	Slate	K	Pink
U	Blue	LG	Light green
W	White	N	Brown
Y	Yellow	O	Orange

When two colour code letters are shown together, the first denotes the main wire colour and the second denotes the tracer colour

Key to main wiring diagram (all models) up to 1986

No	Component	Grid ref.	No	Component	Grid ref.	No	Component	Grid ref.
1	Alternator	A1	44	Ignition/no charge warning lamp	A3	247	Glovebox illumination switch	B3
3	Battery	A1	45	Headlamp flash switch	B1	256	Brake warning blocking diode	A4
4	Starter motor solenoid	A1	46	Coolant temperature gauge	A4	265	Ambient temperature sensor	C1
5	Starter motor	A1	47	Water temperature transducer	C1	267	Headlamp washer motor	B1
6	Lighting switch – main	B1	49	Reverse lamp switch	C4	286	Rear foglamp switch	A2
7	Headlamp dip switch	B1	50	Reverse lamps	B4	287	Rear foglamp warning lamp	A2
8	Headlamp dip beam	B3	56	Clock	A2	288	Rear foglamp(s)	B4
9	Headlamp main beam	B3	57	Cigar lighter	B2	294	Fuel cut-off solenoid	C2
10	Main beam warning lamp	A4	65	Luggage area lamp switch	B3	297	Brake failure warning lamp	A4
11	RH sidelamp	B3	66	Luggage area lamp	B3	308	Direction indicator/hazard flasher unit	C2
12	LH sidelamp	B3	75	Automatic gearbox starter inhibitor switch	A1	325	Brake pad wear warning lamp	A4
14	Panel illumination lamps	A4	76	Automatic gearbox selector indicator lamp	B4	326	Brake pad wear sensor	A4
15	Number plate illumination lamps	B4	77	Windscreen washer motor	B1	347	Electronic control unit – fuel management	C2
16	Stop-lamps	B4	82	Switch illumination lamp(s)	A2	355	Throttle switch	C1
17	RH tail lamp	B4	95	Tachometer	A4	359	Stepper motor	C2
18	Stop-lamp switch	B4	115	Heated rear screen switch	C2	367	Trailer indicator warning light	A3
19	Fusebox	A2,B2	116	Heated rear screen	C2	368	Spare warning lamp	A4
20	Interior lamps	B3	118	Windscreen washer/wiper switch	B3	381	Knock sensor	B 1
21	Interior lamp door switches	C3	150	Heated rear screen warning lamp	A2	382	Crankshaft sensor	C1
22	LH tail lamp	B4	152	Hazard warning lamp	B1	386	One-touch control – window lift	C2
23	Horns	B1	153	Hazard warning switch	B1	389	Column switch illumination	B3
24	Horn push	B1	165	Handbrake warning lamp switch	B4	393	Programmed ignition electronic control unit	C1
26	Direction indicator switch	B1	166	Handbrake warning lamp	A4	398	Manifold heater relay	B1
27	Direction indicator warning lamp(s)	A4	174	Starter solenoid relay	A1	399	Manifold heater	B1
28	RH front direction indicator lamp	B3	178	Radiator cooling fan thermostat	C2	400	Temperature switch	B1
29	LH front direction indicator lamp	B3	179	Radiator cooling fan motor	C2	401	Interior lamp delay unit	C3
30	RH rear direction indicator lamp	B4	182	Brake fluid level switch	B4	402	Windscreen wipe/wash programmed control	B3
31	LH rear direction indicator lamp	B4	208	Cigar lighter illumination lamp	B3	403	Auxiliary ignition relay	A1
32	Heater/fresh air motor switch	B3	210	Panel illumination lamp rheostat/resistor	A3	410	Centre console illumination	B2
33	Heater/fresh air motor	B3	211	Heater control illumination	B2	413	Fusible link	A1
34	Fuel level gauge	A4	231	Headlamp relay	B1	415	Fuel level LED	A4
35	Fuel level gauge tank unit	B1	232	Sidelamp warning lamp	A4	416	Coolant temperature LED	A4
37	Windscreen wiper motor	B3	240	Heated rear screen relay	A2	426	Heater vacuum solenoid	C3
38	Ignition/starter switch	B1	242	Two way interior lamp switch	B3	427	Heater vacuum solenoid switch	C3
39	Ignition coil	A1	246	Glovebox illumination lamp	B3			
40	Distributor	B1						
42	Oil pressure switch	A4						
43	Oil pressure warning lamp	A4						

14

Main wiring diagram (all models) up to 1986

Main wiring diagram (all models) up to 1986 (continued)

Supplementary wiring diagram – wash/wipe with flick wipe circuit (up to 1986)

19	Fusebox	118	Combined windscreen wipe/wash switch
36	Windscreen wiper switch and flick wipe	402	Windscreen wiper programmed control
37	Windscreen wiper motor	A	Switch connector – wipe/wash and flick wipe only
77	Screen washer pump		
78	Screen washer switch		

Supplementary wiring diagram – direction indicator and lighting switch circuit (up to 1986)

3	Battery	24	Horn push switch	38	Ignition switch
6	Lighting switch – main	26	Direction indicator switch	45	Headlamp flasher switch
7	Headlamp dip switch	28	RH front direction indicator lamp	152	Hazard warning light
8	Headlamp dip beam	29	LH front direction indicator lamp	153	Hazard warning switch
9	Headlamp main beam	30	RH rear direction indicator lamp	231	Headlamps relay
11	RH sidelamp	31	LH rear direction indicator lamp	308	Flasher unit
12	LH sidelamp			389	Column switch lamp – fibre optic
17	RH tail lamp			A	Switch connectors
19	Fusebox				
22	LH tail lamp				
23	Horn				

Supplementary wiring diagram – electric front window circuit (up to 1986)

19   Fusebox
216 Window lift switch – driver's
218 Window lift switch – passenger's
220 Window lift motor
221 Window lift relay

386 One-touch window lift unit
A   Multi-plug connections – one-touch unit
B   Switch connections- LH steering

Supplementary wiring diagram – wash/wipe with variable intermittent delay circuit (up to 1986)

19   Fusebox
36   Windscreen wiper switch and flick wipe
37   Windscreen wiper motor
77   Screen washer pump
78   Screen washer switch with intermittent wiper control

118 Combined windscreen wipe/wash and intermittent wiper switch
402 Windscreen wipe/wash programmed control
A   Switch connectors – wipe/wash and intermittent wipe only

14

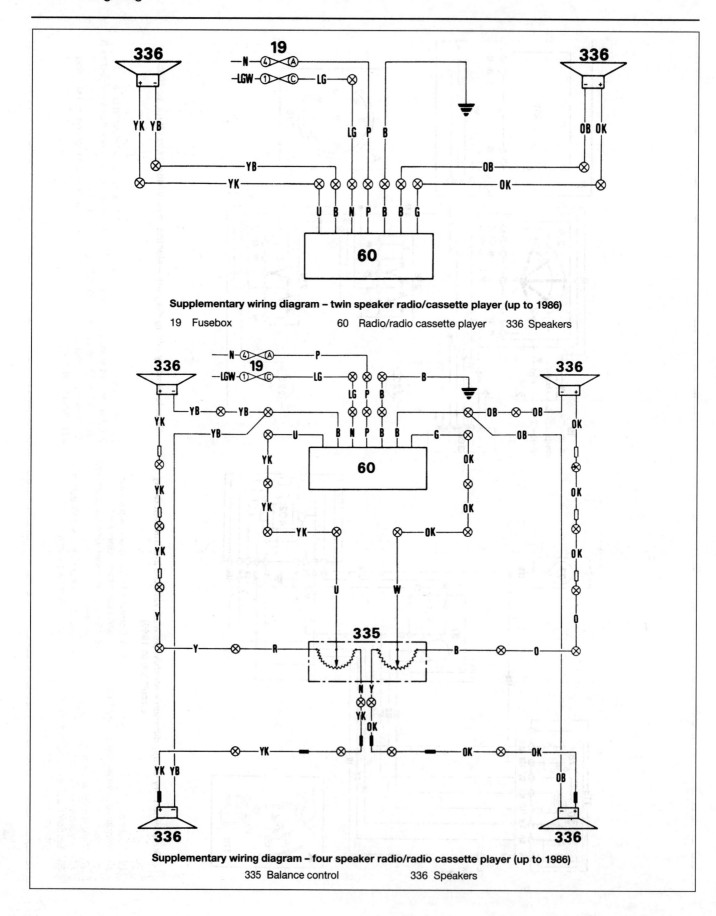

Supplementary wiring diagram – twin speaker radio/cassette player (up to 1986)

19 Fusebox   60 Radio/radio cassette player   336 Speakers

Supplementary wiring diagram – four speaker radio/radio cassette player (up to 1986)

335 Balance control   336 Speakers

**Supplementary wiring diagram – central door locking circuit
(up to 1986)**

19 Fusebox	345 Driver's door lock control
344 Door lock solenoid	unit

**Supplementary wiring diagram – headlamp washer circuit
(up to 1986)**

3 Battery	267 Headlamp washer pump
6 Lighting switch	313 Headlamp washer relay
19 Fusebox	402 Programme control unit –
77 Windscreen washer pump	wash/wipe
118 Windscreen wiper/washer switch	

Supplementary wiring diagram – breakerless ignition circuit (1.3 models)

38 Ignition switch   39 Ignition coil   40 Distributor   365 Ignition amplifier

14

Main wiring diagram – 1.3 models with automatic choke (1986 on)

Main wiring diagram – 1.3 models with automatic choke (1986 on) (continued)

Key to main wiring diagram – 1.3 models with automatic choke (1986 on)

No	Description	Grid reference	No	Description	Grid reference	No	Description	Grid reference
1	Alternator	A1	37	Windscreen wiper motor	B3	231	Headlamp relay	B1
3	Battery	A1	38	Ignition/starter switch	A1	232	Parking lamp warning lamp	A3
4	Starter motor solenoid	A1	39	Ignition coil	A1	246	Glovebox illumination lamp	B2
5	Starter motor	A1	40	Distributor	A1	247	Glovebox illumination switch	B3
6	Lighting switch – main	B1	42	Oil pressure switch	A4	256	Brake warning blocking diode	A4
7	Headlamp dip switch	B 1	43	Oil pressure warning lamp	A4	265	Ambient air temperature sensor	C1
8	Headlamp dip beam	B3	44	Ignition/no charge warning lamp	A3	286	Fog rearguard lamp switch	A3
9	Headlamp main beam	B3	45	Headlamp flash switch	B1	287	Fog rearguard warning lamp	A3
10	Main beam warning lamp	A3	46	Coolant temperature gauge	A4	288	Fog rearguard lamp(s)	B4
11	RH parking lamp	B3	47	Coolant temperature thermistor	C1	294	Fuel cut-off solenoid	C3
12	LH parking lamp	B3	49	Reverse lamp switch	C3	297	Brake failure warning lamp	A4
14	Panel illumination lamps	A4	50	Reverse lamps	B4	300	Ignition switch relay	B1
15	Number plate illumination lamps	B4	56	Clock	A2	308	Direction indicator/hazard flasher unit	C2
16	Stop-lamps	B4	57	Cigar lighter	B2	325	Brake pad wear warning lamp	A4
17	RH tail lamp	B4	65	Luggage area lamp switch	B4	326	Brake pad wear sensor	A4
18	Stop-lamp switch	B3	66	Luggage area lamp	B4	347	ECU – fuel management	C2
19	Fusebox	A2, B2	77	Windscreen washer motor	B3	355	Accelerator pedal switch	C1
20	Interior lamps	C4	82	Switch illumination lamp(s)	A3	359	Stepper motor	C2
21	Interior lamp door switches	C4	110	Side repeater flashers	B3	367	Trailer indicator warning light	A3
22	LH tail lamp	B4	115	Heated rear screen switch	A3	368	Spare warning lamp	A4
23	Horns	B1	116	Heated rear screen	A2	389	Column switch illumination	B2
24	Horn push	B1	118	Windscreen washer/wiper switch	B3	402	Windscreen wipe/wash programmed control	B3
26	Direction indicator switch	B1	150	Heated rear screen warning lamp	A3	403	Auxiliary ignition relay	A2
27	Direction indicator warning lamp(s)	A3	152	Hazard warning lamp	B1	410	Centre console illumination	B2
28	RH front direction indicator lamp	B3	153	Hazard warning switch	B1	413	Fusible link	Al
29	LH front direction indicator lamp	B3	165	Handbrake warning lamp switch	B4	415	Fuel level LED	A3
30	RH rear direction indicator lamp	B4	166	Handbrake warning lamp	A4	416	Coolant temperature LED	A3
31	LH rear direction indicator lamp	B4	178	Radiator cooling fan thermostat	C2	488	Heated rear screen timer and relay	A2
32	Heater/fresh air motor switch	C3	179	Radiator cooling fan motor	C3		**Supplementary diagram connections**	
33	Heater/fresh air motor	C3	182	Brake fluid level switch	B4	A	Radio cassette player	C1
34	Fuel level gauge	A4	208	Cigar lighter illumination lamp	B2			
35	Fuel level gauge tank unit	A3	211	Heater control illumination	C3			

Key to main wiring diagram – 1.3 models with manual choke (1986 on)

No	Description	Grid reference	No	Description	Grid reference	No	Description	Grid reference
1	Alternator	A1	35	Fuel level gauge tank unit	A3	212	Choke control warning light switch	A4
3	Battery	A1	37	Windscreen wiper motor	B3	213	Choke control warning light	A4
4	Starter motor solenoid	A1	38	Ignition/starter switch	A1	231	Headlamp relay	B1
5	Starter motor	A1	39	Ignition coil	A1	232	Parking lamp warning lamp	A3
6	Lighting switch – main	B1	40	Distributor	A1	246	Glovebox illumination lamp	B2
7	Headlamp dip switch	B1	42	Oil pressure switch	A4	247	Glovebox illumination switch	B3
8	Headlamp dip beam	B3	43	Oil pressure warning iamp	A4	256	Brake warning blocking diode	A4
9	Headlamp main beam	B3	44	Ignition/no charge warning lamp	A3	286	Fog rearguard lamp switch	A3
10	Main beam warning lamp	A3	45	Headlamp flash switch	B1	287	Fog rearguard warning lamp	A3
11	RH parking lamp	B3	46	Coolant temperature gauge	A4	288	Fog rearguard lamp(s)	B4
12	LH parking lamp	B3	47	Coolant temperature thermistor	A3	297	Brake failure warning lamp	A4
14	Panel illumination lamps	A4	49	Reverse lamp switch	C3	300	ignition switch relay	B1
15	Number plate illumination lamps	B4	50	Reverse lamps	B4	308	Direction indicator/hazard flasher unit	C2
16	Stop-lamps	B4	56	Clock	A2	325	Brake pad wear warning lamp	A4
17	RH tail lamp	B4	65	Luggage area lamp switch	C4	326	Brake pad wear sensor	A4
18	Stop-lamp switch	C3	66	Luggage area lamp	C4	367	Trailer indicator warning light	A3
19	Fusebox	A2, B2	77	Windscreen washer motor	B3	368	Spare warning light	A4
20	Interior lamps	C4	82	Switch illumination lamp(s)	A3	389	Column switch illumination	B3
21	Interior lamp door switches	C4	110	Side repeater flashers	B3	402	Windscreen wipe/wash programmed control	B3
22	LH tail lamp	B4	115	Heated rear screen switch	A3	403	Auxiliary ignition relay	A1
23	Horns	B1	116	Heated rear screen	A2	410	Centre control illumination	B2
24	Horn push	B1	118	Windscreen washer/wiper switch	B3	413	Fusible link	AI
26	Direction indicator switch	B1	150	Heated rear screen warning lamp	A3	415	Fuel level LED	A3
27	Direction indicator warning lamp(s)	A3	152	Hazard warning lamp	B1	416	Coolant temperature LED	A3
28	RH front direction indicator lamp	B3	153	Hazard warning switch	B1	488	Heated rear screen timer and relay	A2
29	LH front direction indicator lamp	B3	165	Handbrake warning lamp switch	B4			
30	RH rear direction indicator lamp	B4	166	Handbrake warning lamp	A4		**Supplementary diagram connections**	
31	LH rear direction indicator lamp	B4	178	Radiator cooling fan thermostat	C2	A	Radio cassette player	C1
32	Heater/fresh air motor switch	C3	179	Radiator cooling fan motor	C3			
33	Heater/fresh air motor	C3	182	Brake fluid level switch	B4			
34	Fuel level gauge	A4	211	Heater control illumination	C3			

14

Main wiring diagram – 1.3 models with manual choke (1986 on)

Main wiring diagram – 1.3 models with manual choke (1986 on) (continued)

14

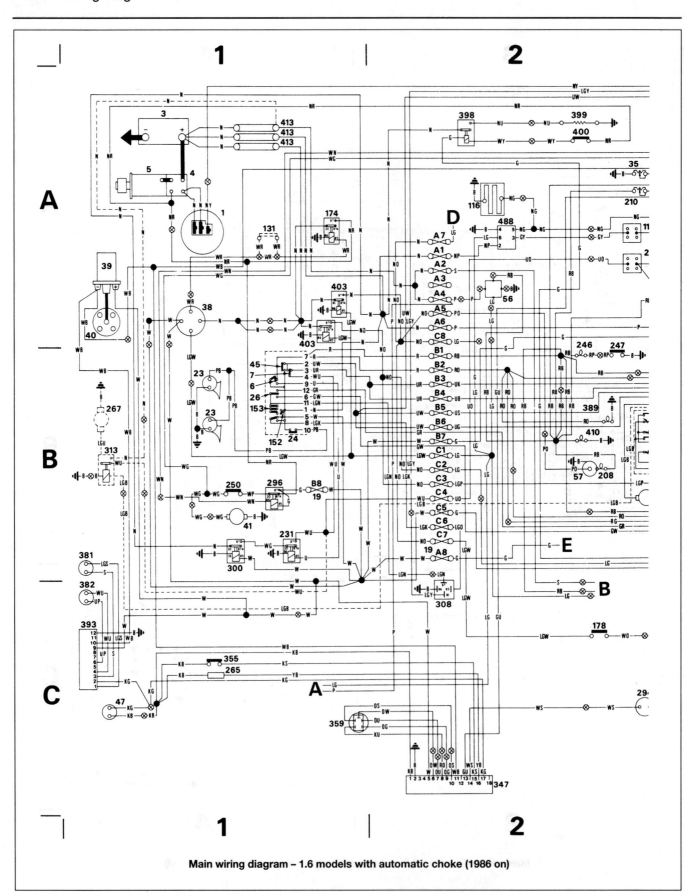

Main wiring diagram – 1.6 models with automatic choke (1986 on)

Main wiring diagram – 1.6 models with automatic choke (1986 on) (continued)

14

Key to main wiring diagram – 1.6 models with automatic choke (1986 on)

No	Description	Grid reference	No	Description	Grid reference	No	Description	Grid reference
1	Alternator	A1	45	Headlamp flash switch	B1	287	Fog rearguard warning lamp	A2
3	Battery	A1	46	Coolant temperature gauge	A4	288	Fog rearguard lamp(s)	B4
4	Starter motor solenoid	A1	47	Coolant temperature thermistor	C1	294	Fuel cut-off solenoid	C2
5	Starter motor	A1	49	Reverse lamp switch	B3	296	Fuel pump relay	B1
6	Lighting switch – main	B1	50	Reverse lamps	B4	297	Brake failure warning lamp	A4
7	Headlamp dip switch	B1	56	Clock	A2	300	ignition switch relay	B1
8	Headlamp dip beam	B3	57	Cigar lighter	B2	308	Direction indicator/hazard flasher unit	C2
9	Headlamp main beam	B3	65	Luggage area lamp switch	C4	313	Headlamp wash relay	B1
10	Main beam warning lamp	A3	66	Luggage area lamp	C4	325	Brake pad wear warning lamp	A4
11	RH parking lamp	B3	77	Windscreen washer motor	B2	326	Brake pad wear sensor	A4
12	LH parking lamp	B3	82	Switch illumination lamp(s)	A3	339	Automatic gearbox quadrant illumination	C4
14	Panel illumination lamps	A4	95	Tachometer	A3	347	ECU – fuel management	C2
15	Number plate illumination lamps	B4	110	Side repeater flashers	B3	355	Accelerator pedal switch	C1
16	Stop-lamps	B4	115	Heated rear screen switch	A2	359	Stepper motor	C1
17	RH tail lamp	B4	116	Heated rear screen	A2	367	Trailer indicator warning light	A3
18	Stop-lamp switch	B3	118	Windscreen washer/wiper switch	B3	368	Spare warning lamp	A4
19	Fusebox	A2, B1, B2	131	Combined automatic gearbox inhibitor and reverse light switch	A1, B3	381	Knock sensor	B1
20	Interior lamps	C4	150	Heated rear screen warning lamp	A3	382	Crankshaft sensor	C1
21	Interior iamp door switches	C4	152	Hazard warning lamp	B1	389	Column switch illumination	B2
22	LH tail lamp	B4	153	Hazard warning switch	B1	393	ECU – Programmed ignition	C1
23	Horns	B1	165	Handbrake warning lamp switch	B4	398	Manifold heater relay	A2
24	Horn push	B1	166	Handbrake warning lamp	A4	399	Manifold heater	A2
26	Direction indicator switch	B1	174	Starter solenoid relay	A1	400	Temperature switch	A2
27	Direction indicator warning lamp(s)	A3	178	Radiator cooling fan thermostat	C2	401	Interior lamp delay unit	B4
28	RH front direction indicator lamp	B3	179	Radiator cooling fan motor	C3	402	Windscreen wipe/wash programmed control	B3
29	LH front direction indicator lamp	B3	182	Brake fluid level switch	B4	403	Auxiliary ignition relay	A1
30	RH rear direction indicator lamp	B4	208	Cigar lighter illumination lamp	B2	410	Centre console illumination	B2
31	LH rear direction indicator lamp	B4	210	Panel illumination lamp rheostat/resistor	A2	413	Fusible link	A1
32	Heater/fresh air motor switch	C3	211	Heater control illumination	C3	415	Fuel level LED	A3
33	Heater/fresh air motor	C3	231	Headlamp relay	B1	416	Coolant temperature LED	A3
34	Fuel level gauge	A4	232	Parking lamp warning lamp	A3	488	Heated rear screen timer and reiay	A2
35	Fuel level gauge tank unit	A2	246	Glovebox illumination lamp	A2	**Supplementary diagram connections**		
37	Windscreen wiper motor	B3	247	Glovebox illumination switch	A2	A	Radio cassette player	C1
38	Ignition/starter switch	A1	250	inertia switch	B1	B	Electric windows	C2
39	ignition coil	A1	256	Brake warning blocking diode	A4	C	Central locking	B4
40	Distributor	A1	265	Ambient air temperature sensor	C1	D	Rear washer/wipe	A2
41	Fuel pump	B1	267	Headlamp washer motor	B1	E	Electric mirror	B2
42b	Oil pressure switch – 1.6	A4	286	Fog rearguard lamp switch	A3			
43	Oil pressure warning lamp	A4						
44	ignition/no charge warning lamp	A3						

Key to main wiring diagram – 1.6 models with manual choke (1986 on)

No	Description	Grid reference
1	Alternator	A1
3	Battery	A1
4	Starter motor solenoid	A1
5	Starter motor	A1
6	Lighting switch – main	B1
7	Headlamp dip switch	81
8	Headlamp dip beam	B3
9	Headlamp main beam	B3
10	Main beam warning lamp	A3
11	RH parking lamp	B3
12	LH parking lamp	B3
14	Panel illumination lamps	A4
15	Number plate illumination lamps	B4
16	Stop-lamps	B4
17	RH tail lamp	B4
18	Stop-lamp switch	B3
19	Fusebox	A2, B1, B2
20	Interior lamps	C4
21	Interior lamp door switches	C4
22	LH tail lamp	B4
23	Horns	B1
24	Horn push	B1
26	Direction indicator switch	B1
27	Direction indicator warning lamp(s)	A3, A4
28	RH front direction indicator lamp	B3
29	LH front direction indicator lamp	B3
30	RH rear direction indicator lamp	B4
31	LH rear direction indicator lamp	B4
32	Heater/fresh air motor switch	C3
33	Heater/fresh air motor	C3
34	Fuel level gauge	A4
35	Fuel level gauge tank unit	A3
37	Windscreen wiper motor	B3
38	Ignition/starter switch	A1
39	Ignition coil	A1
40	Distributor	A1
41	Fuel pump	B1

No	Description	Grid reference
42	Oil pressure switch	A4
43	Oil pressure warning lamp	A4
44	Ignition/no charge warning lamp	A3
45	Headlamp flash switch	B1
46	Coolant temperature gauge	A4
47	Coolant temperature thermistor	C1
49	Reverse lamp switch	C3
50	Reverse lamps	B4
56	Clock	A2
57	Cigar lighter	B2
65	Luggage area lamp switch	C4
66	Luggage area lamp	C4
77	Windscreen washer motor	B3
82	Switch illumination lamp(s)	A3
110	Side repeater flashers	B3
115	Heated rear screen switch	A3
116	Heated rear screen	A2
118	Windscreen washer/wiper switch	B3
131	Combined automatic gearbox inhibitor and reverse light switch	C4
150	Heated rear screen warning lamp	A3
152	Hazard warning lamp	B1
153	Hazard warning switch	B1
165	Handbrake warning lamp switch	B4
166	Handbrake warning lamp	A4
174	Starter solenoid relay	A1
178	Radiator cooling fan thermostat	C2
179	Radiator cooling fan motor	C3
182	Brake fluid level switch	B4
208	Cigar lighter illumination lamp	B3
211	Heater control illumination	C3
212	Choke control warning light switch	A4
213	Choke control warning light	A4
231	Headlamp relay	B1
232	Side lamp warning lamp	A3
246	Glovebox illumination lamp	B2
247	Glovebox illumination switch	B3
250	Inertia switch	B1

No	Description	Grid reference
256	Brake warning blocking diode	A4
267	Headlamp washer motor	B1
286	Fog rearguard lamp switch	A3
287	Fog rearguard warning lamp	A3
288	Fog rearguard lamp(s)	B4
296	Fuel pump relay	B1
297	Brake failure warning lamp	A4
300	Ignition switch relay	B1
308	Direction indicator/hazard flasher unit	C2
313	Headlamp wash relay	B1
325	Brake pad wear warning lamp	A4
326	Brake pad wear sensor	A4
339	Automatic gearbox quadrant illumination	C4
367	Trailer indicator warning light	A3
368	Spare warning lamp	A4
381	Knock sensor	B1
382	Crankshaft sensor	C1
389	Column switch illumination	B3
393	ECU – programmed ignition	C1
398	Manifold heater relay	A2
399	Manifold heater	A3
400	Temperature switch	A3
402	Windscreen wipe/wash Iprogrammed control	B3
403	Auxiliary ignition relay	A1
410	Centre console illumination	B2
413	Fusible link	A1
415	Fuel level LED	A3
416	Coolant temperature LED	A3
488	Heated rear screen relay and timer	A2

Supplementary diagram connections

A	Radio cassette player	C1
B	Electric windows	C3
C	Central locking	B4
D	Rear washer/wiper	A2

14

Main wiring diagram – 1.6 models with manual choke (1986 on)

Main wiring diagram – 1.6 models with manual choke (1986 on)

14

Supplementary wiring diagram – central door locking (1986 on)

19 Fusebox   344 Door lock motor   345 Driver's door lock control unit

Supplementary wiring diagram – electric front window circuit (1986 on)

9 Fusebox   220 Window motors   489 Two-window lift control unit

Supplementary wiring diagram – electric door mirrors (1986 on)

19 Fusebox	430 Mirror switch	Y Horizontal movement motor
429 Mirrors	X Vertical movement motor	

Supplementary wiring diagram – manual tune radio/cassette player with four speakers (1986 on)

19 Fusebox
60 Radio/cassette player
335 Balance control
336 Speakers
A Connectors on Estate version only

14

Supplementary wiring diagram – manual tune radio with two speakers (1986 on)

19 Fusebox
60 Radio
336 Speakers

Supplementary wiring diagram – rear wash/wipe (1986 on)

19 Fusebox
270 Wiper motor
271 Washer pump

342 Wiper switch
343 Washer switch
483 Programmed wash/wipe unit

Supplementary wiring diagram – headlamp dim-dip lighting system

3	Battery	9	Headlamp main beam	45	Headlamp flasher switch	413	Fusible link
6	Main lighting switch	19	Fusebox	152	Hazard warning lamp	493	Dim-dip resistor
7	Headlamp dip switch	24	Horn push	153	Hazard warning switch	494	Dim-dip unit
8	Headlamp dip beam	26	Direction indicator switch	231	Headlamp relay		

Supplementary wiring diagram – electronic tune radio/cassette player with four speakers (1986 on)

60 Radio/cassette player
336 Speakers
A Connectors on Estate version only

14

Supplementary wiring diagram – electric sunroof circuit

19	Fusebox	525	Switch	A	Open	C	Tilt
463	Motor	574	Changeover relay	B	Close		

Supplementary wiring diagram – programmed ignition circuit (1.6 models)

3	Battery	47	Coolant temperature thermistor	355	Throttle switch	393	Programmed ignition ECU
19	Fusebox			359	Stepper motor	413	Fusible link
38	Ignition switch	265	Ambient temperature sensor	381	Knock sensor	A	To tachometer
39	Ignition coil	294	Fuel cut-off solenoid	382	Crankshaft sensor and reluctor disc	B	To coolant temperature gauge
40	Distributor cap	347	Fuel ECU				

Power distribution - All models

Main wiring diagram – 1.6 litre models 1989-on

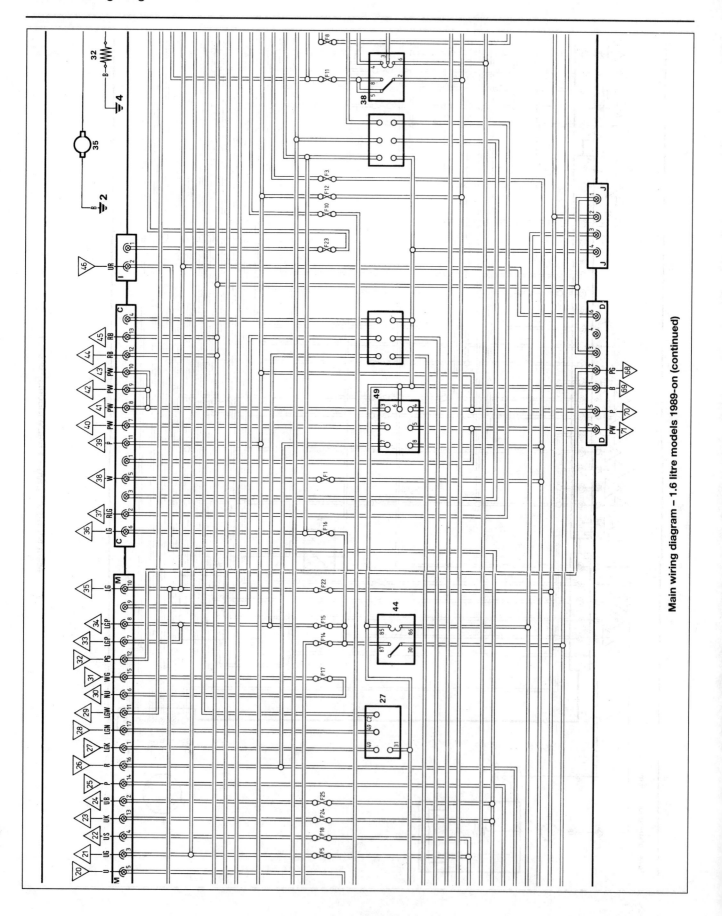

Main wiring diagram – 1.6 litre models 1989-on (continued)

Main wiring diagram – 1.6 litre models 1989-on (continued)

14

Key to main wiring diagram – 1.6 litre models 1989-on

No	Description	No	Description	No	Description
1	Battery	27	Flasher relay	46	Rear screen wiper switch (Estate only)
11	Fuse box	31	Heated rear screen switch	47	Rear screen wash switch (Estate only)
18	Heater or fresh air motor switch(es) or rheostat(s)	32	Heated rear screen element	49	Interior lamp delay unit
		35	Radiator cooling fan motor	51	Fusible links
19	Heater motor	36	Heater control illumination	55	Facia lamp header
21	Ignition/start switch	37	Head lamp relay	56	Facia earth header
24	Foglamp switch	38	Heated rear screen timer	68	Dim-dip resistor
25	Clock	44	Ignition switch relay	69	Dim-dip unit
26	Cigar lighter	45	Auxiliary circuits relay		

Connections to other circuits

No	Description	No	Description	No	Description
1	Exterior lamps/wipers	22	Exterior lamps/wipers	45	Exterior lamps/wipers
2	Exterior lamps/wipers	23	Exterior lamps/wipers	49	All window lift circuits
3	Exterior lamps/wipers	24	Exterior lamps/wipers	50	All window lift circuits
4	Exterior lamps/wipers	25	Power distribution – Dim-dip resistor	53	Exterior lamps/wipers
5	Engine	26	Exterior lamps/wipers	54	Instruments
6	Exterior lamps/wipers	27	Exterior lamps/wipers	55	Instruments
7	Radio/cassette	28	Exterior lamps/wipers	56	instruments
8	Exterior lamps/wipers	29	Exterior lamps/wipers	57	Instruments
9	Exterior lamps/wipers	32	All window lift circuits	58	Mirrors
10	Exterior lamps/wipers	33	Exterior lamps/wipers	59	Instruments
11	Mirrors	34	Exterior lamps/wipers	60	Mirrors
12	Exterior lamps/wipers	35	Radio/cassette	61	4 door window lift
13	Exterior lamps/wipers	36	Exterior lamps/wipers – Estate only	63	Exterior lamps/wipers
14	Exterior lamps/wipers	37	Exterior lamps/wipers – Estate only	65	Engine
15	Mirrors	38	Engine	66	Exterior lamps/wipers
16	Exterior lamps/wipers	39	Radio/cassette	67	Instruments
17	Central door locking	40	Interior lamps	68	All window lift circuits
18	Exterior lamps/wipers	41	Interior lamps	69	Interior lamp circuit
19	All window lift circuits	42	Interior lamps	70	Interior lamp circuit
20	Exterior lamps/wipers	43	Interior lamps	71	Interior lamp circuit
21	Exterior lamps/wipers	44	All window lift circuits		

Colour code

B	Black	K	Pink	N	Brown	P	Purple	S	Slate	W	White
G	Green	LG	Light green	O	Orange	R	Red	U	Blue	Y	Yellow

Fusible link	▭
Fuse	⊸◦⊸
Diode	▸┤
Sealed joint	┬
Input connection	◁
Output connection	▷
Earth point	⊪

Symbols used in circuit diagrams

Earth point locations – 1989-on

No	Description	No	Description
1	Front RH inner wing	4	Rear LH wing behind trim panel
2	Front LH inner wing	5	Battery negative terminal
3	Top LH bulkhead behind facia panel		

Key to wiring diagram for exterior lamps/wipers – Estate, 1989-on

No	Description	No	Description	No	Description
2	Main lighting switch	20	Windscreen wiper motor	53	Rear lamp header
3	Headlamp dip switch	22	Headlamp flash switch	54	Fusebox header
4	Dip beam	23	Reverse lamp switch	57	LH flasher
5	Main beam	28	Automatic transmission selector	58	RH flasher
6	Sidelamp – RH		indicator lamp	63	Load space lamp
7	Sidelamp – LH	29	Windscreen washer pump	64	Latch switch
8	Number plate illumination lamp(s)	30	Windscreen washer switch	65	Rear screen washer motor
9	Tail lamp – RH	33	Hazard warning lamp	66	Wash/wipe switch
10	Stop-lamp switch	34	Hazard warning switch	67	Column switch
12	Tail lamp – LH	39	Glovebox illumination lamp	75	Reverse lamp switch-gearbox (all
13	Horn(s)	40	Glovebox illumination switch		models except 1.6 automatic)
14	Horn push	41	Rear screen wiper motor	186	LH headlamp
15	Direction indicator switch	43	Windscreen wiper delay unit	187	RH headlamp
16	RH front direction indicator lamp	48	Radiator cooling fan switch		
17	LH front direction indicator lamp	52	Passenger header		

Connections to other circuits – as Saloon

Key to wiring diagram for exterior lamp/wipers – Saloon, 1989-on

No	Description	No	Description	No	Description
2	Main lighting switch	23	Reverse lamp switch in centre console	66	Wash/wipe switch
3	Headlamp dip switch		(1.6 automatic only)	67	Column switch
4	Dip beam	28	Automatic transmission selector	70	Boot lamp
5	Main beam		indicator lamp	71	Boot lamp switch
6	Sidelamp – RH	29	Windscreen washer pump	75	Reversing lamp switch (gearbox) – all
7	Sidelamp – LH	30	Windscreen washer switch		models except 1.6 automatic
8	Number plate illumination lamp(s)	33	Hazard warning lamp	186	LH headlamp
9	Tail lamp – RH	34	Hazard warning switch	187	RH headlamp
10	Stop-lamp switch	39	Glovebox illumination lamp		**Connections to other circuits**
12	Tail lamp – LH	40	Glovebox illumination switch	1 to 71	Power distribution circuit
13	Horn(s)	43	Windscreen wiper delay unit	72	Instruments
14	Horn push	48	Radiator fan switch	73	Radio/cassette
15	Direction indicator switch	52	Passenger header	74	Mirrors
16	RH front indicator lamp	53	Rear lamp header	75	Instruments
17	LH front indicator lamp	54	Fusebox header	80	Central door locking
20	Windscreen wiper motor	57	LH repeater lamp	81	Mirrors
22	Headlamp flash switch	58	RH repeater lamp	83,85,87 and 88	Engine

14

Exterior lamps/wipers – Estate

Wiring diagram for exterior lamps/wipers – Estate, 1989-on

Wiring diagram for exterior lamps/wipers – Estate, 1989-on (continued)

14

Wiring diagram for exterior lamp/wipers – Saloon, 1989-on

Wiring diagram for exterior lamp/wipers – Saloon, 1989-on (continued)

14

Wiring diagram for engine circuit – 1.6 models, 1 989-on

Wiring diagram for engine circuit – 1.6 models, 1 989-on (continued)

14

Key to wiring diagram for engine circuit – 1.6 models, 1 989-on

No	Description	No	Description	No	Description
1	Battery	86	Knock sensor	108	Ambient thermistor
11	Fusebox	87	Crankshaft sensor	109	Throttle pedal switch
21	Ignition switch	97	Fuel pump relay	110	Diagnostic socket
51	Fusible links	98	Main relay	111	Stepper motor
54	Fusebox header	99	P.T.C. relay	112	Fuel cut-off solenoid
80	Alternator	104	Multi-function unit	113	Manifold heater
81	Starter motor/solenoid	105	Inhibitor switch	194	Knock sensor screen
82	Starter relay	106	E.R.I.C ECU	195	Crank sensor screen
83	Ignition coil	107	Coolant thermistor		

Connections to other circuits

No	Description
89	Instruments
91	Instruments
92	Instruments

Key to wiring diagram for instrument pack – 1.6 models, 1989-on

No	Description	No	Description	No	Description
11	Fusebox	120	Oil pressure warning lamp	128	Panel illumination
102	Fuel sensor	121	Brake system warning lamp	129	Side lamp warning light
114	Oil pressure switch	122	Choke warning lamp	130	Main beam warning lamp
115	Brake fluid level switch	123	Tachometer	131	LH indicator warning lamp
116	Handbrake switch	124	Temperature gauge	132	RH indicator warning lamp
117	Pad wear sensor	125	Fuel gauge	133	Trailer warning lamp
118	Choke switch	126	Low fuel warning lamp	134	Instrument illumination rheostat
119	Ignition warning lamp	127	High temperature warning L.E.D.	135	Instrument pack

Connections to other circuits

No	Description	No	Description	No	Description
1 to 71	Base circuit	86	Exterior lamps/wipers	91	Engine
72	Exterior lamps/wipers	89	Engine	96	Engine
75	Exterior lamps/wipers				

Wiring diagram for instrument pack – 1.6 models, 1989-on

Wiring diagram for radio/cassette player, 1989-on

No	Description
11	Fusebox
173	Radio/cassette
174	Front/right speaker
175	Front/left speaker

No	Description
176	Aerial
177	Rear/right speaker
178	Rear/left speaker
179	Tweeter

Connections to other circuits

No	Description
73	Power distribution circuit

Wiring diagram for electric front windows, 1989-on

No	Description
11	Fuse box
76	RH front window lift motor
77	LH front window lift motor

No	Description
78	LH front window switch
79	RH front window switch
156	Control unit

Connection to other circuits

No	Description
32	Interior lamps/sunroof

Wiring diagram for central door locking, 1989-on

No	Description	No	Description	No	Description	No	Description
11	Fusebox	137	Central door locking	167	Driver's door control unit	170	Passenger door motor
64	Tailgate lock switch		header	168	Tailgate lock motor (Estate)	171	RH rear motor
	(Estate)			169	LH rear motor		

Connections to other circuits

No	Description
80	Exterior lamps/wipers

14

Wiring diagram – interior lamps/sunroof, 1989-on

No	Description	No	Description	No	Description	No	Description
A	Without sunroof	60	LH door switch	150	RH interior lamp	156	Two door window lift control unit
B	With mechanical sunroof	61	RH rear door switch	151	LH interior lamp	157	Four door window lift control unit
C	With electric sunroof	62	LH rear door switch	152	Sunroof switch		
11	Fusebox	148	Interior lamp unit	153	Sunroof unit	196	Changeover relay
59	RH door switch	149	Front interior lamp	154	Sunroof motor		

This is a guide to getting your vehicle through the MOT test. Obviously it will not be possible to examine the vehicle to the same standard as the professional MOT tester. However, working through the following checks will enable you to identify any problem areas before submitting the vehicle for the test.

Where a testable component is in borderline condition, the tester has discretion in deciding whether to pass or fail it. The basis of such discretion is whether the tester would be happy for a close relative or friend to use the vehicle with the component in that condition. If the vehicle presented is clean and evidently well cared for, the tester may be more inclined to pass a borderline component than if the vehicle is scruffy and apparently neglected.

It has only been possible to summarise the test requirements here, based on the regulations in force at the time of printing. Test standards are becoming increasingly stringent, although there are some exemptions for older vehicles. For full details obtain a copy of the Haynes publication Pass the MOT! (available from stockists of Haynes manuals).

An assistant will be needed to help carry out some of these checks.

The checks have been sub-divided into four categories, as follows:

1 Checks carried out **FROM THE DRIVER'S SEAT**

2 Checks carried out **WITH THE VEHICLE ON THE GROUND**

3 Checks carried out **WITH THE VEHICLE RAISED AND THE WHEELS FREE TO TURN**

4 Checks carried out on **YOUR VEHICLE'S EXHAUST EMISSION SYSTEM**

---

1 Checks carried out **FROM THE DRIVER'S SEAT**

Handbrake

☐ Test the operation of the handbrake. Excessive travel (too many clicks) indicates incorrect brake or cable adjustment.

☐ Check that the handbrake cannot be released by tapping the lever sideways. Check the security of the lever mountings.

Footbrake

☐ Depress the brake pedal and check that it does not creep down to the floor, indicating a master cylinder fault. Release the pedal, wait a few seconds, then depress it again. If the pedal travels nearly to the floor before firm resistance is felt, brake adjustment or repair is necessary. If the pedal feels spongy, there is air in the hydraulic system which must be removed by bleeding.

• ☐ Check that the brake pedal is secure and in good condition. Check also for signs of fluid leaks on the pedal, floor or carpets, which would indicate failed seals in the brake master cylinder.

☐ Check the servo unit (when applicable) by operating the brake pedal several times, then keeping the pedal depressed and starting the engine. As the engine starts, the pedal will move down slightly. If not, the vacuum hose or the servo itself may be faulty.

Steering wheel and column

☐ Examine the steering wheel for fractures or looseness of the hub, spokes or rim.

☐ Move the steering wheel from side to side and then up and down. Check that the steering wheel is not loose on the column, indicating wear or a loose retaining nut. Continue moving the steering wheel as before, but also turn it slightly from left to right.

☐ Check that the steering wheel is not loose on the column, and that there is no abnormal

movement of the steering wheel, indicating wear in the column support bearings or couplings.

Windscreen and mirrors

☐ The windscreen must be free of cracks or other significant damage within the driver's field of view. (Small stone chips are acceptable.) Rear view mirrors must be secure, intact, and capable of being adjusted.

290mm

Seat belts and seats

Note: *The following checks are applicable to all seat belts, front and rear.*

☐ Examine the webbing of all the belts (including rear belts if fitted) for cuts, serious fraying or deterioration. Fasten and unfasten each belt to check the buckles. If applicable, check the retracting mechanism. Check the security of all seat belt mountings accessible from inside the vehicle.

☐ The front seats themselves must be securely attached and the backrests must lock in the upright position.

Doors

☐ Both front doors must be able to be opened and closed from outside and inside, and must latch securely when closed.

2 Checks carried out WITH THE VEHICLE ON THE GROUND

Vehicle identification

☐ Number plates must be in good condition, secure and legible, with letters and numbers correctly spaced – spacing at (A) should be twice that at (B).

☐ The VIN plate and/or homologation plate must be legible.

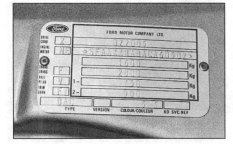

Electrical equipment

☐ Switch on the ignition and check the operation of the horn.

☐ Check the windscreen washers and wipers, examining the wiper blades; renew damaged or perished blades. Also check the operation of the stop-lights.

☐ Check the operation of the sidelights and number plate lights. The lenses and reflectors must be secure, clean and undamaged.

☐ Check the operation and alignment of the headlights. The headlight reflectors must not be tarnished and the lenses must be undamaged.

☐ Switch on the ignition and check the operation of the direction indicators (including the instrument panel tell-tale) and the hazard warning lights. Operation of the sidelights and stop-lights must not affect the indicators - if it does, the cause is usually a bad earth at the rear light cluster.

☐ Check the operation of the rear foglight(s), including the warning light on the instrument panel or in the switch.

Footbrake

☐ Examine the master cylinder, brake pipes and servo unit for leaks, loose mountings, corrosion or other damage.

☐ The fluid reservoir must be secure and the fluid level must be between the upper (**A**) and lower (**B**) markings.

☐ Inspect both front brake flexible hoses for cracks or deterioration of the rubber. Turn the steering from lock to lock, and ensure that the hoses do not contact the wheel, tyre, or any part of the steering or suspension mechanism. With the brake pedal firmly depressed, check the hoses for bulges or leaks under pressure.

Steering and suspension

☐ Have your assistant turn the steering wheel from side to side slightly, up to the point where the steering gear just begins to transmit this movement to the roadwheels. Check for excessive free play between the steering wheel and the steering gear, indicating wear or insecurity of the steering column joints, the column-to-steering gear coupling, or the steering gear itself.

☐ Have your assistant turn the steering wheel more vigorously in each direction, so that the roadwheels just begin to turn. As this is done, examine all the steering joints, linkages, fittings and attachments. Renew any component that shows signs of wear or damage. On vehicles with power steering, check the security and condition of the steering pump, drivebelt and hoses.

☐ Check that the vehicle is standing level, and at approximately the correct ride height.

Shock absorbers

☐ Depress each corner of the vehicle in turn, then release it. The vehicle should rise and then settle in its normal position. If the vehicle continues to rise and fall, the shock absorber is defective. A shock absorber which has seized will also cause the vehicle to fail.

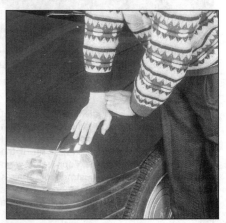

Exhaust system

☐ Start the engine. With your assistant holding a rag over the tailpipe, check the entire system for leaks. Repair or renew leaking sections.

3 Checks carried out **WITH THE VEHICLE RAISED AND THE WHEELS FREE TO TURN**

Jack up the front and rear of the vehicle, and securely support it on axle stands. Position the stands clear of the suspension assemblies. Ensure that the wheels are clear of the ground and that the steering can be turned from lock to lock.

Steering mechanism

☐ Have your assistant turn the steering from lock to lock. Check that the steering turns smoothly, and that no part of the steering mechanism, including a wheel or tyre, fouls any brake hose or pipe or any part of the body structure.

☐ Examine the steering rack rubber gaiters for damage or insecurity of the retaining clips. If power steering is fitted, check for signs of damage or leakage of the fluid hoses, pipes or connections. Also check for excessive stiffness or binding of the steering, a missing split pin or locking device, or severe corrosion of the body structure within 30 cm of any steering component attachment point.

Front and rear suspension and wheel bearings

☐ Starting at the front right-hand side, grasp the roadwheel at the 3 o'clock and 9 o'clock positions and shake it vigorously. Check for free play or insecurity at the wheel bearings, suspension balljoints, or suspension mountings, pivots and attachments.

☐ Now grasp the wheel at the 12 o'clock and 6 o'clock positions and repeat the previous inspection. Spin the wheel, and check for roughness or tightness of the front wheel bearing.

☐ If excess free play is suspected at a component pivot point, this can be confirmed by using a large screwdriver or similar tool and levering between the mounting and the component attachment. This will confirm whether the wear is in the pivot bush, its retaining bolt, or in the mounting itself (the bolt holes can often become elongated).

☐ Carry out all the above checks at the other front wheel, and then at both rear wheels.

Springs and shock absorbers

☐ Examine the suspension struts (when applicable) for serious fluid leakage, corrosion, or damage to the casing. Also check the security of the mounting points.

☐ If coil springs are fitted, check that the spring ends locate in their seats, and that the spring is not corroded, cracked or broken.

☐ If leaf springs are fitted, check that all leaves are intact, that the axle is securely attached to each spring, and that there is no deterioration of the spring eye mountings, bushes, and shackles.

☐ The same general checks apply to vehicles fitted with other suspension types, such as torsion bars, hydraulic displacer units, etc. Ensure that all mountings and attachments are secure, that there are no signs of excessive wear, corrosion or damage, and (on hydraulic types) that there are no fluid leaks or damaged pipes.

☐ Inspect the shock absorbers for signs of serious fluid leakage. Check for wear of the mounting bushes or attachments, or damage to the body of the unit.

Driveshafts (fwd vehicles only)

☐ Rotate each front wheel in turn and inspect the constant velocity joint gaiters for splits or damage. Also check that each driveshaft is straight and undamaged.

Braking system

☐ If possible without dismantling, check brake pad wear and disc condition. Ensure that the friction lining material has not worn excessively, (A) and that the discs are not fractured, pitted, scored or badly worn (B).

☐ Examine all the rigid brake pipes underneath the vehicle, and the flexible hose(s) at the rear. Look for corrosion, chafing or insecurity of the pipes, and for signs of bulging under pressure, chafing, splits or deterioration of the flexible hoses.

☐ Look for signs of fluid leaks at the brake calipers or on the brake backplates. Repair or renew leaking components.

☐ Slowly spin each wheel, while your assistant depresses and releases the footbrake. Ensure that each brake is operating and does not bind when the pedal is released.

□ Examine the handbrake mechanism, checking for frayed or broken cables, excessive corrosion, or wear or insecurity of the linkage. Check that the mechanism works on each relevant wheel, and releases fully, without binding.

□ It is not possible to test brake efficiency without special equipment, but a road test can be carried out later to check that the vehicle pulls up in a straight line.

Fuel and exhaust systems

□ Inspect the fuel tank (including the filler cap), fuel pipes, hoses and unions. All components must be secure and free from leaks.

□ Examine the exhaust system over its entire length, checking for any damaged, broken or missing mountings, security of the retaining clamps and rust or corrosion.

Wheels and tyres

□ Examine the sidewalls and tread area of each tyre in turn. Check for cuts, tears, lumps, bulges, separation of the tread, and exposure of the ply or cord due to wear or damage. Check that the tyre bead is correctly seated on the wheel rim, that the valve is sound and

properly seated, and that the wheel is not distorted or damaged.

□ Check that the tyres are of the correct size for the vehicle, that they are of the same size and type on each axle, and that the pressures are correct.

□ Check the tyre tread depth. The legal minimum at the time of writing is 1.6 mm over at least three-quarters of the tread width. Abnormal tread wear may indicate incorrect front wheel alignment.

Body corrosion

□ Check the condition of the entire vehicle structure for signs of corrosion in load-bearing areas. (These include chassis box sections, side sills, cross-members, pillars, and all suspension, steering, braking system and seat belt mountings and anchorages.) Any corrosion which has seriously reduced the thickness of a load-bearing area is likely to cause the vehicle to fail. In this case professional repairs are likely to be needed.

□ Damage or corrosion which causes sharp or otherwise dangerous edges to be exposed will also cause the vehicle to fail.

4 Checks carried out on YOUR VEHICLE'S EXHAUST EMISSION SYSTEM

Petrol models

□ Have the engine at normal operating temperature, and make sure that it is in good tune (ignition system in good order, air filter element clean, etc).

□ Before any measurements are carried out, raise the engine speed to around 2500 rpm, and hold it at this speed for 20 seconds. Allow

the engine speed to return to idle, and watch for smoke emissions from the exhaust tailpipe. If the idle speed is obviously much too high, or if dense blue or clearly-visible black smoke comes from the tailpipe for more than 5 seconds, the vehicle will fail. As a rule of thumb, blue smoke signifies oil being burnt (engine wear) while black smoke signifies unburnt fuel (dirty air cleaner element, or other carburettor or fuel system fault).

□ An exhaust gas analyser capable of measuring carbon monoxide (CO) and hydrocarbons (HC) is now needed. If such an instrument cannot be hired or borrowed, a local garage may agree to perform the check for a small fee.

CO emissions (mixture)

□ At the time of writing, the maximum CO level at idle is 3.5% for vehicles first used after August 1986 and 4.5% for older vehicles. From January 1996 a much tighter limit (around 0.5%) applies to catalyst-equipped vehicles first used from August 1992. If the CO level cannot be reduced far enough to pass the test (and the fuel and ignition systems are otherwise in good condition) then the carburettor is badly worn, or there is some problem in the fuel injection system or catalytic converter (as applicable).

HC emissions

□ With the CO emissions within limits, HC emissions must be no more than 1200 ppm (parts per million). If the vehicle fails this test at idle, it can be re-tested at around 2000 rpm; if the HC level is then 1200 ppm or less, this counts as a pass.

□ Excessive HC emissions can be caused by oil being burnt, but they are more likely to be due to unburnt fuel.

Diesel models

□ The only emission test applicable to Diesel engines is the measuring of exhaust smoke density. The test involves accelerating the engine several times to its maximum unloaded speed.

Note: *It is of the utmost importance that the engine timing belt is in good condition before the test is carried out.*

□ Excessive smoke can be caused by a dirty air cleaner element. Otherwise, professional advice may be needed to find the cause.

Introduction

A selection of good tools is a fundamental requirement for anyone contemplating the maintenance and repair of a motor vehicle. For the owner who does not possess any, their purchase will prove a considerable expense, offsetting some of the savings made by doing-it-yourself. However, provided that the tools purchased meet the relevant national safety standards and are of good quality, they will last for many years and prove an extremely worthwhile investment.

To help the average owner to decide which tools are needed to carry out the various tasks detailed in this manual, we have compiled three lists of tools under the following headings: *Maintenance and minor repair*, *Repair and overhaul*, and *Special*. Newcomers to practical mechanics should start off with the *Maintenance and minor repair* tool kit, and confine themselves to the simpler jobs around the vehicle. Then, as confidence and experience grow, more difficult tasks can be undertaken, with extra tools being purchased as, and when, they are needed. In this way, a *Maintenance and minor repair* tool kit can be built up into a *Repair and overhaul* tool kit over a considerable period of time, without any major cash outlays. The experienced do-it-yourselfer will have a tool kit good enough for most repair and overhaul procedures, and will add tools from the *Special* category when it is felt that the expense is justified by the amount of use to which these tools will be put.

Maintenance and minor repair tool kit

The tools given in this list should be considered as a minimum requirement if routine maintenance, servicing and minor repair operations are to be undertaken. We recommend the purchase of combination spanners (ring one end, open-ended the other); although more expensive than open-ended ones, they do give the advantages of both types of spanner.

☐ *Combination spanners: 10, 11, 12, 13, 14 mm, 7/16, 1/2, 9/16, 5/8, 3/4, 7/8 and 15/16 in AF*
☐ *Adjustable spanner - 35 mm jaw (approx)*
☐ *Gearbox drain plug key*
☐ *Set of feeler gauges*
☐ *Spark plug spanner (with rubber insert)*
☐ *Spark plug gap adjustment tool*
☐ *Brake bleed nipple spanner*

☐ *Screwdrivers: Flat blade and cross blade – approx 100 mm long x 6 mm dia*
☐ *Combination pliers*
☐ *Hacksaw (junior)*
☐ *Tyre pump*
☐ *Tyre pressure gauge*
☐ *Oil can*
☐ *Oil filter removal tool*
☐ *Fine emery cloth*
☐ *Wire brush (small)*
☐ *Funnel (medium size)*

Repair and overhaul tool kit

These tools are virtually essential for anyone undertaking any major repairs to a motor vehicle, and are additional to those given in the *Maintenance and minor repair* list. Included in this list is a comprehensive set of sockets. Although these are expensive, they will be found invaluable as they are so versatile - particularly if various drives are included in the set. We recommend the half-inch square-drive type, as this can be used with most proprietary torque wrenches. If you cannot afford a socket set, even bought piecemeal, then inexpensive tubular box spanners are a useful alternative.

The tools in this list will occasionally need to be supplemented by tools from the *Special* list:

☐ *Sockets (or box spanners) to cover range in previous list*
☐ *Reversible ratchet drive (for use with sockets)* **(see illustration)**
☐ *Extension piece, 250 mm (for use with sockets)*
☐ *Universal joint (for use with sockets)*
☐ *Torque wrench (for use with sockets)*
☐ *Self-locking grips*
☐ *Ball pein hammer*
☐ *Soft-faced mallet (plastic/aluminium or rubber)*
☐ *Screwdrivers:*
  Flat blade - long & sturdy, short (chubby), and narrow (electrician's) types
  Cross blade - Long & sturdy, and short (chubby) types
☐ *Pliers:*
  Long-nosed
  Side cutters (electrician's)
  Circlip (internal and external)
☐ *Cold chisel - 25 mm*
☐ *Scriber*
☐ *Scraper*

☐ *Centre-punch*
☐ *Pin punch*
☐ *Hacksaw*
☐ *Brake hose clamp*
☐ *Brake bleeding kit*
☐ *Selection of twist drills*
☐ *Steel rule/straight-edge*
☐ *Allen keys*
☐ *Selection of files*
☐ *Wire brush*
☐ *Axle stands*
☐ *Jack (strong trolley or hydraulic type)*
☐ *Light with extension lead*

Special tools

The tools in this list are those which are not used regularly, are expensive to buy, or which need to be used in accordance with their manufacturers' instructions. Unless relatively difficult mechanical jobs are undertaken frequently, it will not be economic to buy many of these tools. Where this is the case, you could consider clubbing together with friends (or joining a motorists' club) to make a joint purchase, or borrowing the tools against a deposit from a local garage or tool hire specialist. It is worth noting that many of the larger DIY superstores now carry a large range of special tools for hire at modest rates.

The following list contains only those tools and instruments freely available to the public, and not those special tools produced by the vehicle manufacturer specifically for its dealer network. You will find occasional references to these manufacturers' special tools in the text of this manual. Generally, an alternative method of doing the job without the vehicle manufacturers' special tool is given. However, sometimes there is no alternative to using them. Where this is the case and the relevant tool cannot be bought or borrowed, you will have to entrust the work to a franchised garage.

☐ *Valve spring compressor* **(see illustration)**
☐ *Valve grinding tool*
☐ *Piston ring compressor* **(see illustration)**
☐ *Piston ring removal/installation tool* **(see illustration)**
☐ *Cylinder bore hone* **(see illustration)**
☐ *Balljoint separator*
☐ *Coil spring compressors (where applicable)*
☐ *Two/three-legged hub and bearing puller* **(see illustration)**

Sockets and reversible ratchet drive

Valve spring compressor

Piston ring compressor

Piston ring removal/installation tool

Cylinder bore hone

Three-legged hub and bearing puller

Micrometer set

Vernier calipers

Dial test indicator and magnetic stand

Compression testing gauge

Clutch plate alignment set

Brake shoe steady spring cup removal tool

- ☐ Impact screwdriver
- ☐ Micrometer and/or vernier calipers **(see illustrations)**
- ☐ Dial gauge **(see illustration)**
- ☐ Universal electrical multi-meter
- ☐ Cylinder compression gauge **(see illustration)**
- ☐ Clutch plate alignment set **(see illustration)**
- ☐ Brake shoe steady spring cup removal tool **(see illustration)**
- ☐ Bush and bearing removal/installation set **(see illustration)**
- ☐ Stud extractors **(see illustration)**
- ☐ Tap and die set **(see illustration)**
- ☐ Lifting tackle
- ☐ Trolley jack

Buying tools

For practically all tools, a tool factor is the best source, since he will have a very comprehensive range compared with the average garage or accessory shop. Having said that, accessory shops often offer excellent quality tools at discount prices, so it pays to shop around.

Remember, you don't have to buy the most expensive items on the shelf, but it is always advisable to steer clear of the very cheap tools. There are plenty of good tools around at reasonable prices, but always aim to purchase items which meet the relevant national safety standards. If in doubt, ask the proprietor or manager of the shop for advice before making a purchase.

Care and maintenance of tools

Having purchased a reasonable tool kit, it is necessary to keep the tools in a clean and serviceable condition. After use, always wipe off any dirt, grease and metal particles using a clean, dry cloth, before putting the tools away. Never leave them lying around after they have been used. A simple tool rack on the garage or workshop wall for items such as screwdrivers and pliers is a good idea. Store all normal spanners and sockets in a metal box. Any measuring instruments, gauges, meters, etc, must be carefully stored where they cannot be damaged or become rusty.

Take a little care when tools are used. Hammer heads inevitably become marked, and screwdrivers lose the keen edge on their blades from time to time. A little timely attention with emery cloth or a file will soon restore items like this to a good serviceable finish.

Working facilities

Not to be forgotten when discussing tools is the workshop itself. If anything more than routine maintenance is to be carried out, some form of suitable working area becomes essential.

It is appreciated that many an owner-mechanic is forced by circumstances to remove an engine or similar item without the benefit of a garage or workshop. Having done this, any repairs should always be done under the cover of a roof.

Wherever possible, any dismantling should be done on a clean, flat workbench or table at a suitable working height.

Any workbench needs a vice; one with a jaw opening of 100 mm is suitable for most jobs. As mentioned previously, some clean dry storage space is also required for tools, as well as for any lubricants, cleaning fluids, touch-up paints and so on, which become necessary.

Another item which may be required, and which has a much more general usage, is an electric drill with a chuck capacity of at least 8 mm. This, together with a good range of twist drills, is virtually essential for fitting accessories.

Last, but not least, always keep a supply of old newspapers and clean, lint-free rags available, and try to keep any working area as clean as possible.

Bush and bearing removal/installation set

Stud extractor set

Tap and die set

Whenever servicing, repair or overhaul work is carried out on the car or its components, observe the following procedures and instructions. This will assist in carrying out the operation efficiently and to a professional standard of workmanship.

Joint mating faces and gaskets

When separating components at their mating faces, never insert screwdrivers or similar implements into the joint between the faces in order to prise them apart. This can cause severe damage which results in oil leaks, coolant leaks, etc upon reassembly. Separation is usually achieved by tapping along the joint with a soft-faced hammer in order to break the seal. However, note that this method may not be suitable where dowels are used for component location.

Where a gasket is used between the mating faces of two components, a new one must be fitted on reassembly; fit it dry unless otherwise stated in the repair procedure. Make sure that the mating faces are clean and dry, with all traces of old gasket removed. When cleaning a joint face, use a tool which is unlikely to score or damage the face, and remove any burrs or nicks with an oilstone or fine file.

Make sure that tapped holes are cleaned with a pipe cleaner, and keep them free of jointing compound, if this is being used, unless specifically instructed otherwise.

Ensure that all orifices, channels or pipes are clear, and blow through them, preferably using compressed air.

Oil seals

Oil seals can be removed by levering them out with a wide flat-bladed screwdriver or similar implement. Alternatively, a number of self-tapping screws may be screwed into the seal, and these used as a purchase for pliers or some similar device in order to pull the seal free.

Whenever an oil seal is removed from its working location, either individually or as part of an assembly, it should be renewed.

The very fine sealing lip of the seal is easily damaged, and will not seal if the surface it contacts is not completely clean and free from scratches, nicks or grooves. If the original sealing surface of the component cannot be restored, and the manufacturer has not made provision for slight relocation of the seal relative to the sealing surface, the component should be renewed.

Protect the lips of the seal from any surface which may damage them in the course of fitting. Use tape or a conical sleeve where possible. Lubricate the seal lips with oil before fitting and, on dual-lipped seals, fill the space between the lips with grease.

Unless otherwise stated, oil seals must be fitted with their sealing lips toward the lubricant to be sealed.

Use a tubular drift or block of wood of the appropriate size to install the seal and, if the seal housing is shouldered, drive the seal down to the shoulder. If the seal housing is unshouldered, the seal should be fitted with its face flush with the housing top face (unless otherwise instructed).

Screw threads and fastenings

Seized nuts, bolts and screws are quite a common occurrence where corrosion has set in, and the use of penetrating oil or releasing fluid will often overcome this problem if the offending item is soaked for a while before attempting to release it. The use of an impact driver may also provide a means of releasing such stubborn fastening devices, when used in conjunction with the appropriate screwdriver bit or socket. If none of these methods works, it may be necessary to resort to the careful application of heat, or the use of a hacksaw or nut splitter device.

Studs are usually removed by locking two nuts together on the threaded part, and then using a spanner on the lower nut to unscrew the stud. Studs or bolts which have broken off below the surface of the component in which they are mounted can sometimes be removed using a stud extractor. Always ensure that a blind tapped hole is completely free from oil, grease, water or other fluid before installing the bolt or stud. Failure to do this could cause the housing to crack due to the hydraulic action of the bolt or stud as it is screwed in.

When tightening a castellated nut to accept a split pin, tighten the nut to the specified torque, where applicable, and then tighten further to the next split pin hole. Never slacken the nut to align the split pin hole, unless stated in the repair procedure.

When checking or retightening a nut or bolt to a specified torque setting, slacken the nut or bolt by a quarter of a turn, and then retighten to the specified setting. However, this should not be attempted where angular tightening has been used.

For some screw fastenings, notably cylinder head bolts or nuts, torque wrench settings are no longer specified for the latter stages of tightening, "angle-tightening" being called up instead. Typically, a fairly low torque wrench setting will be applied to the bolts/nuts in the correct sequence, followed by one or more stages of tightening through specified angles.

Locknuts, locktabs and washers

Any fastening which will rotate against a component or housing during tightening should always have a washer between it and the relevant component or housing.

Spring or split washers should always be renewed when they are used to lock a critical component such as a big-end bearing retaining bolt or nut. Locktabs which are folded over to retain a nut or bolt should always be renewed.

Self-locking nuts can be re-used in non-critical areas, providing resistance can be felt when the locking portion passes over the bolt or stud thread. However, it should be noted that self-locking stiffnuts tend to lose their effectiveness after long periods of use, and should then be renewed as a matter of course.

Split pins must always be replaced with new ones of the correct size for the hole.

When thread-locking compound is found on the threads of a fastener which is to be re-used, it should be cleaned off with a wire brush and solvent, and fresh compound applied on reassembly.

Special tools

Some repair procedures in this manual entail the use of special tools such as a press, two or three-legged pullers, spring compressors, etc. Wherever possible, suitable readily-available alternatives to the manufacturer's special tools are described, and are shown in use. In some instances, where no alternative is possible, it has been necessary to resort to the use of a manufacturer's tool, and this has been done for reasons of safety as well as the efficient completion of the repair operation. Unless you are highly-skilled and have a thorough understanding of the procedures described, never attempt to bypass the use of any special tool when the procedure described specifies its use. Not only is there a very great risk of personal injury, but expensive damage could be caused to the components involved.

Environmental considerations

When disposing of used engine oil, brake fluid, antifreeze, etc, give due consideration to any detrimental environmental effects. Do not, for instance, pour any of the above liquids down drains into the general sewage system, or onto the ground to soak away. Many local council refuse tips provide a facility for waste oil disposal, as do some garages. If none of these facilities are available, consult your local Environmental Health Department, or the National Rivers Authority, for further advice.

With the universal tightening-up of legislation regarding the emission of environmentally-harmful substances from motor vehicles, most vehicles have tamperproof devices fitted to the main adjustment points of the fuel system. These devices are primarily designed to prevent unqualified persons from adjusting the fuel/air mixture, with the chance of a consequent increase in toxic emissions. If such devices are found during servicing or overhaul, they should, wherever possible, be renewed or refitted in accordance with the manufacturer's requirements or current legislation.

OIL CARE
FOLLOW THE CODE

OIL BANK LINE
0800 66 33 66

Note: It is antisocial and illegal to dump oil down the drain. To find the location of your local oil recycling bank, call this number free.

Buying spare parts

Spare parts are available from many sources, for example: BL garages, other garages and accessory shops, and motor factors. Our advice regarding spare part sources is as follows:

Officially appointed BL garages – This is the best source of parts which are peculiar to your car and are not generally available (eg complete cylinder heads, internal gearbox components, badges, interior trim, etc). It is also the only place at which you should buy parts if your vehicle is still under warranty – non-BL components may invalidate the warranty. To be sure of obtaining the correct parts it will always be necessary to give the storeman your car's vehicle identification number, and if possible, to take the 'old' part along for positive identification. Many parts are available under a factory exchange scheme - any parts returned should always be clean. It obviously makes good sense to go straight to the specialists on your car for this type of part for they are best equipped to supply you.

Other dealers and accessory shops – These are often very good places to buy materials and components needed for the maintenance of your car (eg oil filters, spark plugs, bulbs, drivebelts, oils and grease, touch-up paint, filler paste, etc). They also sell general accessories, usually have convenient opening hours, charge lower prices and can often be found not far from home.

Motor factors – Good factors will stock all of the more important components which wear out relatively quickly (eg clutch components, pistons, valves, exhaust systems, brake pipes/seals and pads, etc). Motor factors will often provide new or reconditioned components on a part exchange basis – this can save a considerable amount of money.

Vehicle identification numbers

Modifications are a continuing and unpublicised process in vehicle manufacture, quite apart from major model changes. Spare parts manuals and lists are compiled upon a numerical basis, the individual vehicle numbers being essential to correct identification of the component required.

When ordering spare parts, always give as much information as possible. Quote the car model, year of manufacture, body and engine numbers as appropriate.

The vehicle identification number is stamped on a plate attached to the front body panel, or to the left-hand front door pillar. The number is repeated on the right-hand front strut turret.

The engine number is stamped on a plate attached to the cylinder block below No 1 spark plug.

The gearbox number is stamped on the bottom face of the gearbox casing.

The automatic transmission number is stamped on the top face of the final drive housing.

The body number plate is located on the right-hand side of the spare wheel well.

Fault Finding

Introduction

The vehicle owner who does his or her own maintenance according to the recommended schedules should not have to use this section of the manual very often. Modern component reliability is such that, provided those items subject to wear or deterioration are inspected or renewed at the specified intervals, sudden failure is comparatively rare. Faults do not usually just happen as a result of sudden failure, but develop over a period of time. Major mechanical failures in particular are usually preceded by characteristic symptoms over hundreds or even thousands of miles. Those components which do occasionally fail without warning are often small and easily carried in the vehicle.

With any fault finding, the first step is to decide where to begin investigations. Sometimes this is obvious, but on other occasions a little detective work will be necessary. The owner who makes half a dozen haphazard adjustments or replacements may be successful in curing a fault (or its symptoms), but he will be none the wiser if the fault recurs and he may well have spent more time and money than was necessary. A calm and logical approach will be found to be more satisfactory in the long run. Always take into account any warning signs or abnormalities that may have been noticed in the period preceding the fault – power loss, high or low gauge readings, unusual noises or smells, etc – and remember that failure of components such as fuses or spark plugs may only be pointers to some underlying fault.

The pages which follow here are intended to help in cases of failure to start or breakdown on the road. There is also a Fault Diagnosis Section at the end of each Chapter which should be consulted if the preliminary checks prove unfruitful. Whatever the fault, certain basic principles apply. These are as follows:

Verify the fault. This is simply a matter of being sure that you know what the symptoms are before starting work. This is particularly important if you are investigating a fault for someone else who may not have described it very accurately.

Don't overlook the obvious. For example, if the vehicle won't start, is there petrol in the tank? (Don't take anyone else's word on this particular point, and don't trust the fuel gauge either!) If an electrical fault is indicated, look for loose or broken wires before digging out the test gear.

Cure the disease, not the symptom. Substituting a flat battery with a fully charged one will get you off the hard shoulder, but if the underlying cause is not attended to,the new battery will go the same way. Similarly, changing oil-fouled spark plugs for a new set will get you moving again, but remember that the reason for the fouling (if it wasn't simply an incorrect grade of plug) will have to be established and corrected.

Don't take anything for granted. Particularly, don't forget that a 'new' component may itself be defective (especially if it's been rattling round in the boot for months), and don't leave components out of a fault diagnosis sequence just because they are new or recently fitted. When you do finally diagnose a difficult fault, you'll probably realise that all the evidence was there from the start.

Electrical faults

Electrical faults can be more puzzling than straightforward mechanical failures, but they are no less susceptible to logical analysis if the basic principles of operation are understood. Vehicle electrical wiring exists in extremely unfavourable conditions – heat, vibration and chemical attack and the first things to look for are loose or corroded connections and broken or chafed wires, especially where the wires pass through holes in the bodywork or are subject to vibration.

All metal-bodied vehicles in current production have one pole of the battery 'earthed', ie connected to the vehicle bodywork, and in nearly all modern vehicles it is the negative (–) terminal. The various electrical components – motors, bulb holders, etc – are also connected to earth, either by means of a lead or directly by their mountings. Electric current flows through the component and then back to the battery via the bodywork. If the component mounting is loose or corroded, or if a good path back to the battery is not available, the circuit will be incomplete and malfunction will result. The engine and/or gearbox are also earthed by means of flexible metal straps to the body or subframe; if these straps are loose or missing, starter motor, generator and ignition trouble may result.

Assuming the earth return to be satisfactory, electrical faults will be due either to component malfunction or to defects in the current supply. Individual components are dealt with in Chapter 10. If supply wires are broken or cracked internally this results in an open-circuit, and the easiest way to check for this is to bypass the suspect wire temporarily with a length of wire having a crocodile clip or suitable connector at each end. Alternatively, a 12V test lamp can be used to verify the presence of supply voltage at various points along the wire and the break can be thus isolated.

If a bare portion of a live wire touches the bodywork or other earthed metal part, the electricity will take the low-resistance path thus formed back to the battery: this is known as a short-circuit. Hopefully a short-circuit will blow a fuse, but otherwise it may cause burning of the insulation (and possibly further short-circuits) or even a fire. This is why it is inadvisable to bypass persistently blowing fuses with silver foil or wire.

Spares and tool kit

Most vehicles are supplied only with sufficient tools for wheel changing; the *Maintenance and minor repair* tool kit detailed in *Tools and working facilities*, with the addition of a hammer, is probably sufficient for those repairs that most motorists would consider attempting at the roadside. In addition a few items which can be fitted without too much trouble in the event of a breakdown should be carried. Experience and available space will modify the list below, but the following may save having to call on professional assistance:

- [ ] *Spark plugs, clean and correctly gapped*
- [ ] *HT lead and plug cap – long enough to reach the plug furthest from the distributor*
- [ ] *Distributor rotor*
- [ ] *Drivebelt(s) — emergency type may suffice*
- [ ] *Spare fuses*
- [ ] *Set of principal light bulbs*
- [ ] *Tin of radiator sealer and hose bandage*
- [ ] *Exhaust bandage*
- [ ] *Roll of insulating tape*
- [ ] *Length of soft iron wire*
- [ ] *Length of electrical flex*
- [ ] *Torch or inspection lamp (can double as test lamp)*
- [ ] *Battery jump leads*

- [ ] *Tow-rope*
- [ ] *Ignition waterproofing aerosol*
- [ ] *Litre of engine oil*
- [ ] *Sealed can of hydraulic fluid*
- [ ] *Emergency windscreen*
- [ ] *Wormdrive clips*
- [ ] *Tube of filler paste*

If spare fuel is carried, a can designed for the purpose should be used to minimise risks of leakage and collision damage. A first aid kit and a warning triangle, whilst not at present compulsory in the UK, are obviously sensible items to carry in addition to the above. When touring abroad it may be advisable to carry additional spares which, even if you cannot fit them yourself, could save having to wait while parts are obtained. The items below may be worth considering:

- [ ] *Clutch and throttle cables*
- [ ] *Cylinder head gasket*
- [ ] *Alternator brushes*
- [ ] *Tyre valve core*

One of the motoring organisations will be able to advise on availability of fuel, etc, in foreign countries.

Engine will not start

Engine fails to turn when starter operated

- [ ] Flat battery (recharge use jump leads or push start)
- [ ] Battery terminals loose or corroded
- [ ] Battery earth to body defective
- [ ] Engine earth strap loose or broken
- [ ] Starter motor (or solenoid) wiring loose or broken
- [ ] Ignition/starter switch faulty
- [ ] Major mechanical failure (seizure)
- [ ] Starter or solenoid internal fault (see Chapter 10)

Starter motor turns engine slowly

- [ ] Partially discharged battery (recharge, use jump leads, or push start)
- [ ] Battery terminals loose or corroded

- [ ] Battery earth to body defective
- [ ] Engine earth strap loose
- [ ] Starter motor (or solenoid) wiring loose
- [ ] Starter motor internal fault (see Chapter 10)

Starter motor spins without turning engine

- [ ] Flywheel gear teeth damaged or worn
- [ ] Starter motor mounting bolts loose

Engine turns normally but fails to start

- [ ] Damp or dirty HT leads and distributor cap (crank engine and check for spark)
- [ ] No fuel in tank (check for delivery)
- [ ] Fouled or incorrectly gapped spark plugs (remove, clean and regap)
- [ ] Other ignition system fault (see Chapter 4)
- [ ] Other fuel system fault (see Chapter 3)

A simple test lamp is useful for checking electrical faults

Carrying a few spares may save you a long walk!

- [ ] Poor compression (see Chapter 1)
- [ ] Major mechanical failure (eg camshaft drive)

Engine fires but will not run

- [ ] Air leaks at carburettor or inlet manifold
- [ ] Fuel starvation (see Chapter 3)
- [ ] Ignition fault (see Chapter 4)

Engine cuts out and will not restart

Engine cuts out suddenly – ignition fault

- [ ] Loose or disconnected LT wires
- [ ] Wet HT leads or distributor cap (after traversing water splash)
- [ ] Coil failure (check for spark)
- [ ] Other ignition fault (see Chapter 4)

Engine misfires before cutting out – fuel fault

- [ ] Fuel tank empty
- [ ] Fuel pump defective or filter blocked (check for delivery)
- [ ] Fuel tank filler vent blocked (suction will be evident on releasing cap)
- [ ] Carburettor needle valve sticking

Crank engine and check for spark. Note use of insulated tool

- [ ] Carburettor jets blocked (fuel contaminated)
- [ ] Other fuel system fault (see Chapter 3)

Engine cuts out – other causes

- [ ] Serious overheating
- [ ] Major mechanical failure (eg camshaft drive)

Engine overheats

Ignition (no-charge) warning light illuminated

- [ ] Slack or broken drivebelt — retension or renew (Chapter 10)

Ignition warning light not illuminated

- [ ] Coolant loss due to internal or external leakage (see Chapter 2)
- [ ] Thermostat defective
- [ ] Low oil level
- [ ] Brakes binding
- [ ] Radiator clogged externally or internally
- [ ] Engine waterways clogged
- [ ] Ignition timing incorrect or automatic advance malfunctioning
- [ ] Mixture too weak

Note: *Do not add cold water to an overheated engine or damage may result*

Low engine oil pressure

Note: *Low oil pressure in a high-mileage engine at tickover is not necessarily a cause for concern. Sudden pressure loss at speed is far more significant. In any event check the gauge or warning light sender before condemning the engine.*

Gauge reads low or warning light illuminated with engine running

- [ ] Oil level low or incorrect grade
- [ ] Defective gauge or sender unit
- [ ] Wire to sender unit earthed
- [ ] Engine overheating
- [ ] Oil filter clogged or bypass valve defective
- [ ] Oil pressure relief valve defective
- [ ] Oil pick-up strainer clogged
- [ ] Oil pump worn or mountings loose
- [ ] Worn main or big-end bearings

Engine noises

Pre-ignition (pinking) on acceleration

- [ ] Incorrect grade of fuel
- [ ] Ignition timing incorrect
- [ ] Distributor faulty or worn
- [ ] Worn or maladjusted carburettor
- [ ] Excessive carbon build-up in engine

Whistling or wheezing noises

- [ ] Leaking vacuum hose
- [ ] Leaking carburettor or manifold gasket
- [ ] Blowing head gasket

Tapping or rattling

- [ ] Incorrect valve clearances
- [ ] Worn valve gear
- [ ] Worn timing chain or belt
- [ ] Broken piston ring (ticking noise)

Knocking or thumping

- [ ] Unintentional mechanical contact (eg fan blades)
- [ ] Worn drivebelt
- [ ] Peripheral component fault (generator, water pump, etc)
- [ ] Worn big-end bearings (regular heavy knocking, perhaps less under load)
- [ ] Worn main bearings (rumbling and knocking, perhaps worsening under load)
- [ ] Piston slap (most noticeable when cold)

Length (distance)

Inches (in)	x 25.4	= Millimetres (mm)	x 0.0394	=	Inches (in)
Feet (ft)	x 0.305	= Metres (m)	x 3.281	=	Feet (ft)
Miles	x 1.609	= Kilometres (km)	x 0.621	=	Miles

Volume (capacity)

Cubic inches (cu in; in³)	x 16.387	= Cubic centimetres (cc; cm³)	x 0.061	=	Cubic inches (cu in; in³)
Imperial pints (Imp pt)	x 0.568	= Litres (l)	x 1.76	=	Imperial pints (Imp pt)
Imperial quarts (Imp qt)	x 1.137	= Litres (l)	x 0.88	=	Imperial quarts (Imp qt)
Imperial quarts (Imp qt)	x 1.201	= US quarts (US qt)	x 0.833	=	Imperial quarts (Imp qt)
US quarts (US qt)	x 0.946	= Litres (l)	x 1.057	=	US quarts (US qt)
Imperial gallons (Imp gal)	x 4.546	= Litres (l)	x 0.22	=	Imperial gallons (Imp gal)
Imperial gallons (Imp gal)	x 1.201	= US gallons (US gal)	x 0.833	=	Imperial gallons (Imp gal)
US gallons (US gal)	x 3.785	= Litres (l)	x 0.264	=	US gallons (US gal)

Mass (weight)

Ounces (oz)	x 28.35	= Grams (g)	x 0.035	=	Ounces (oz)
Pounds (lb)	x 0.454	= Kilograms (kg)	x 2.205	=	Pounds (lb)

Force

Ounces-force (ozf; oz)	x 0.278	= Newtons (N)	x 3.6	=	Ounces-force (ozf; oz)
Pounds-force (lbf; lb)	x 4.448	= Newtons (N)	x 0.225	=	Pounds-force (lbf; lb)
Newtons (N)	x 0.1	= Kilograms-force (kgf; kg)	x 9.81	=	Newtons (N)

Pressure

Pounds-force per square inch (psi; lbf/in²; lb/in²)	x 0.070	= Kilograms-force per square centimetre (kgf/cm²; kg/cm²)	x 14.223	=	Pounds-force per square inch (psi; lbf/in²; lb/in²)
Pounds-force per square inch (psi; lbf/in²; lb/in²)	x 0.068	= Atmospheres (atm)	x 14.696	=	Pounds-force per square inch (psi; lbf/in²; lb/in²)
Pounds-force per square inch (psi; lbf/in²; lb/in²)	x 0.069	= Bars	x 14.5	=	Pounds-force per square inch (psi; lbf/in²; lb/in²)
Pounds-force per square inch (psi; lbf/in²; lb/in²)	x 6.895	= Kilopascals (kPa)	x 0.145	=	Pounds-force per square inch (psi; lbf/in²; lb/in²)
Kilopascals (kPa)	x 0.01	= Kilograms-force per square centimetre (kgf/cm²; kg/cm²)	x 98.1	=	Kilopascals (kPa)
Millibar (mbar)	x 100	= Pascals (Pa)	x 0.01	=	Millibar (mbar)
Millibar (mbar)	x 0.0145	= Pounds-force per square inch (psi; lbf/in²; lb/in²)	x 68.947	=	Millibar (mbar)
Millibar (mbar)	x 0.75	= Millimetres of mercury (mmHg)	x 1.333	=	Millibar (mbar)
Millibar (mbar)	x 0.401	= Inches of water (inH₂O)	x 2.491	=	Millibar (mbar)
Millimetres of mercury (mmHg)	x 0.535	= Inches of water (inH₂O)	x 1.868	=	Millimetres of mercury (mmHg)
Inches of water (inH₂O)	x 0.036	= Pounds-force per square inch (psi; lbf/in²; lb/in²)	x 27.68	=	Inches of water (inH₂O)

Torque (moment of force)

Pounds-force inches (lbf in; lb in)	x 1.152	= Kilograms-force centimetre (kgf cm; kg cm)	x 0.868	=	Pounds-force inches (lbf in; lb in)
Pounds-force inches (lbf in; lb in)	x 0.113	= Newton metres (Nm)	x 8.85	=	Pounds-force inches (lbf in; lb in)
Pounds-force inches (lbf in; lb in)	x 0.083	= Pounds-force feet (lbf ft; lb ft)	x 12	=	Pounds-force inches (lbf in; lb in)
Pounds-force feet (lbf ft; lb ft)	x 0.138	= Kilograms-force metres (kgf m; kg m)	x 7.233	=	Pounds-force feet (lbf ft; lb ft)
Pounds-force feet (lbf ft; lb ft)	x 1.356	= Newton metres (Nm)	x 0.738	=	Pounds-force feet (lbf ft; lb ft)
Newton metres (Nm)	x 0.102	= Kilograms-force metres (kgf m; kg m)	x 9.804	=	Newton metres (Nm)

Power

Horsepower (hp)	x 745.7	= Watts (W)	x 0.0013	=	Horsepower (hp)

Velocity (speed)

Miles per hour (miles/hr; mph)	x 1.609	= Kilometres per hour (km/hr; kph)	x 0.621	=	Miles per hour (miles/hr; mph)

Fuel consumption*

Miles per gallon (mpg)	x 0.354	= Kilometres per litre (km/l)	x 2.825	=	Miles per gallon (mpg)

Temperature

Degrees Fahrenheit = (°C x 1.8) + 32   Degrees Celsius (Degrees Centigrade; °C) = (°F - 32) x 0.56

It is common practice to convert from miles per gallon (mpg) to litres/100 kilometres (l/100km), where mpg x l/100 km = 282

A

ABS (Anti-lock brake system) A system, usually electronically controlled, that senses incipient wheel lockup during braking and relieves hydraulic pressure at wheels that are about to skid.

Air bag An inflatable bag hidden in the steering wheel (driver's side) or the dash or glovebox (passenger side). In a head-on collision, the bags inflate, preventing the driver and front passenger from being thrown forward into the steering wheel or windscreen.

Air cleaner A metal or plastic housing, containing a filter element, which removes dust and dirt from the air being drawn into the engine.

Air filter element The actual filter in an air cleaner system, usually manufactured from pleated paper and requiring renewal at regular intervals.

Air filter

Allen key A hexagonal wrench which fits into a recessed hexagonal hole.

Alligator clip A long-nosed spring-loaded metal clip with meshing teeth. Used to make temporary electrical connections.

Alternator A component in the electrical system which converts mechanical energy from a drivebelt into electrical energy to charge the battery and to operate the starting system, ignition system and electrical accessories.

Ampere (amp) A unit of measurement for the flow of electric current. One amp is the amount of current produced by one volt acting through a resistance of one ohm.

Anaerobic sealer A substance used to prevent bolts and screws from loosening. Anaerobic means that it does not require oxygen for activation. The Loctite brand is widely used.

Antifreeze A substance (usually ethylene glycol) mixed with water, and added to a vehicle's cooling system, to prevent freezing of the coolant in winter. Antifreeze also contains chemicals to inhibit corrosion and the formation of rust and other deposits that would tend to clog the radiator and coolant passages and reduce cooling efficiency.

Anti-seize compound A coating that reduces the risk of seizing on fasteners that are subjected to high temperatures, such as exhaust manifold bolts and nuts.

Asbestos A natural fibrous mineral with great heat resistance, commonly used in the composition of brake friction materials.

Asbestos is a health hazard and the dust created by brake systems should never be inhaled or ingested.

Axle A shaft on which a wheel revolves, or which revolves with a wheel. Also, a solid beam that connects the two wheels at one end of the vehicle. An axle which also transmits power to the wheels is known as a live axle.

Axleshaft A single rotating shaft, on either side of the differential, which delivers power from the final drive assembly to the drive wheels. Also called a driveshaft or a halfshaft.

B

Ball bearing An anti-friction bearing consisting of a hardened inner and outer race with hardened steel balls between two races.

Bearing The curved surface on a shaft or in a bore, or the part assembled into either, that permits relative motion between them with minimum wear and friction.

Bearing

Big-end bearing The bearing in the end of the connecting rod that's attached to the crankshaft.

Bleed nipple A valve on a brake wheel cylinder, caliper or other hydraulic component that is opened to purge the hydraulic system of air. Also called a bleed screw.

Brake bleeding Procedure for removing air from lines of a hydraulic brake system.

Brake bleeding

Brake disc The component of a disc brake that rotates with the wheels.

Brake drum The component of a drum brake that rotates with the wheels.

Brake linings The friction material which contacts the brake disc or drum to retard the vehicle's speed. The linings are bonded or riveted to the brake pads or shoes.

Brake pads The replaceable friction pads that pinch the brake disc when the brakes are applied. Brake pads consist of a friction material bonded or riveted to a rigid backing plate.

Brake shoe The crescent-shaped carrier to which the brake linings are mounted and which forces the lining against the rotating drum during braking.

Braking systems For more information on braking systems, consult the *Haynes Automotive Brake Manual*.

Breaker bar A long socket wrench handle providing greater leverage.

Bulkhead The insulated partition between the engine and the passenger compartment.

C

Caliper The non-rotating part of a disc-brake assembly that straddles the disc and carries the brake pads. The caliper also contains the hydraulic components that cause the pads to pinch the disc when the brakes are applied. A caliper is also a measuring tool that can be set to measure inside or outside dimensions of an object.

Camshaft A rotating shaft on which a series of cam lobes operate the valve mechanisms. The camshaft may be driven by gears, by sprockets and chain or by sprockets and a belt.

Canister A container in an evaporative emission control system; contains activated charcoal granules to trap vapours from the fuel system.

Canister

Carburettor A device which mixes fuel with air in the proper proportions to provide a desired power output from a spark ignition internal combustion engine.

Castellated Resembling the parapets along the top of a castle wall. For example, a castellated balljoint stud nut.

Castor In wheel alignment, the backward or forward tilt of the steering axis. Castor is positive when the steering axis is inclined rearward at the top.

Catalytic converter A silencer-like device in the exhaust system which converts certain pollutants in the exhaust gases into less harmful substances.

Catalytic converter

Circlip A ring-shaped clip used to prevent endwise movement of cylindrical parts and shafts. An internal circlip is installed in a groove in a housing; an external circlip fits into a groove on the outside of a cylindrical piece such as a shaft.

Clearance The amount of space between two parts. For example, between a piston and a cylinder, between a bearing and a journal, etc.

Coil spring A spiral of elastic steel found in various sizes throughout a vehicle, for example as a springing medium in the suspension and in the valve train.

Compression Reduction in volume, and increase in pressure and temperature, of a gas, caused by squeezing it into a smaller space.

Compression ratio The relationship between cylinder volume when the piston is at top dead centre and cylinder volume when the piston is at bottom dead centre.

Constant velocity (CV) joint A type of universal joint that cancels out vibrations caused by driving power being transmitted through an angle.

Core plug A disc or cup-shaped metal device inserted in a hole in a casting through which core was removed when the casting was formed. Also known as a freeze plug or expansion plug.

Crankcase The lower part of the engine block in which the crankshaft rotates.

Crankshaft The main rotating member, or shaft, running the length of the crankcase, with offset "throws" to which the connecting rods are attached.

Crankshaft assembly

Crocodile clip See Alligator clip

D

Diagnostic code Code numbers obtained by accessing the diagnostic mode of an engine management computer. This code can be used to determine the area in the system where a malfunction may be located.

Disc brake A brake design incorporating a rotating disc onto which brake pads are squeezed. The resulting friction converts the energy of a moving vehicle into heat.

Double-overhead cam (DOHC) An engine that uses two overhead camshafts, usually one for the intake valves and one for the exhaust valves.

Drivebelt(s) The belt(s) used to drive accessories such as the alternator, water pump, power steering pump, air conditioning compressor, etc. off the crankshaft pulley.

Accessory drivebelts

Driveshaft Any shaft used to transmit motion. Commonly used when referring to the axleshafts on a front wheel drive vehicle.

Drum brake A type of brake using a drum-shaped metal cylinder attached to the inner surface of the wheel. When the brake pedal is pressed, curved brake shoes with friction linings press against the inside of the drum to slow or stop the vehicle.

E

EGR valve A valve used to introduce exhaust gases into the intake air stream.

Electronic control unit (ECU) A computer which controls (for instance) ignition and fuel injection systems, or an anti-lock braking system. For more information refer to the *Haynes Automotive Electrical and Electronic Systems Manual.*

Electronic Fuel Injection (EFI) A computer controlled fuel system that distributes fuel through an injector located in each intake port of the engine.

Emergency brake A braking system, independent of the main hydraulic system, that can be used to slow or stop the vehicle if the primary brakes fail, or to hold the vehicle stationary even though the brake pedal isn't depressed. It usually consists of a hand lever that actuates either front or rear brakes mechanically through a series of cables and linkages. Also known as a handbrake or parking brake.

Endfloat The amount of lengthwise movement between two parts. As applied to a crankshaft, the distance that the crankshaft can move forward and back in the cylinder block.

Engine management system (EMS) A computer controlled system which manages the fuel injection and the ignition systems in an integrated fashion.

Exhaust manifold A part with several passages through which exhaust gases leave the engine combustion chambers and enter the exhaust pipe.

F

Fan clutch A viscous (fluid) drive coupling device which permits variable engine fan speeds in relation to engine speeds.

Feeler blade A thin strip or blade of hardened steel, ground to an exact thickness, used to check or measure clearances between parts.

Feeler blade

Firing order The order in which the engine cylinders fire, or deliver their power strokes, beginning with the number one cylinder.

Flywheel A heavy spinning wheel in which energy is absorbed and stored by means of momentum. On cars, the flywheel is attached to the crankshaft to smooth out firing impulses.

Free play The amount of travel before any action takes place. The "looseness" in a linkage, or an assembly of parts, between the initial application of force and actual movement. For example, the distance the brake pedal moves before the pistons in the master cylinder are actuated.

Fuse An electrical device which protects a circuit against accidental overload. The typical fuse contains a soft piece of metal which is calibrated to melt at a predetermined current flow (expressed as amps) and break the circuit.

Fusible link A circuit protection device consisting of a conductor surrounded by heat-resistant insulation. The conductor is smaller than the wire it protects, so it acts as the weakest link in the circuit. Unlike a blown fuse, a failed fusible link must frequently be cut from the wire for replacement.

G

Gap The distance the spark must travel in jumping from the centre electrode to the side electrode in a spark plug. Also refers to the spacing between the points in a contact breaker assembly in a conventional points-type ignition, or to the distance between the reluctor or rotor and the pickup coil in an electronic ignition.

Adjusting spark plug gap

Gasket Any thin, soft material - usually cork, cardboard, asbestos or soft metal - installed between two metal surfaces to ensure a good seal. For instance, the cylinder head gasket seals the joint between the block and the cylinder head.

Gasket

Gauge An instrument panel display used to monitor engine conditions. A gauge with a movable pointer on a dial or a fixed scale is an analogue gauge. A gauge with a numerical readout is called a digital gauge.

H

Halfshaft A rotating shaft that transmits power from the final drive unit to a drive wheel, usually when referring to a live rear axle.

Harmonic balancer A device designed to reduce torsion or twisting vibration in the crankshaft. May be incorporated in the crankshaft pulley. Also known as a vibration damper.

Hone An abrasive tool for correcting small irregularities or differences in diameter in an engine cylinder, brake cylinder, etc.

Hydraulic tappet A tappet that utilises hydraulic pressure from the engine's lubrication system to maintain zero clearance (constant contact with both camshaft and valve stem). Automatically adjusts to variation in valve stem length. Hydraulic tappets also reduce valve noise.

I

Ignition timing The moment at which the spark plug fires, usually expressed in the number of crankshaft degrees before the piston reaches the top of its stroke.

Inlet manifold A tube or housing with passages through which flows the air-fuel mixture (carburettor vehicles and vehicles with throttle body injection) or air only (port fuel-injected vehicles) to the port openings in the cylinder head.

J

Jump start Starting the engine of a vehicle with a discharged or weak battery by attaching jump leads from the weak battery to a charged or helper battery.

L

Load Sensing Proportioning Valve (LSPV) A brake hydraulic system control valve that works like a proportioning valve, but also takes into consideration the amount of weight carried by the rear axle.

Locknut A nut used to lock an adjustment nut, or other threaded component, in place. For example, a locknut is employed to keep the adjusting nut on the rocker arm in position.

Lockwasher A form of washer designed to prevent an attaching nut from working loose.

M

MacPherson strut A type of front suspension system devised by Earle MacPherson at Ford of England. In its original form, a simple lateral link with the anti-roll bar creates the lower control arm. A long strut - an integral coil spring and shock absorber - is mounted between the body and the steering knuckle. Many modern so-called MacPherson strut systems use a conventional lower A-arm and don't rely on the anti-roll bar for location.

Multimeter An electrical test instrument with the capability to measure voltage, current and resistance.

N

NOx Oxides of Nitrogen. A common toxic pollutant emitted by petrol and diesel engines at higher temperatures.

O

Ohm The unit of electrical resistance. One volt applied to a resistance of one ohm will produce a current of one amp.

Ohmmeter An instrument for measuring electrical resistance.

O-ring A type of sealing ring made of a special rubber-like material; in use, the O-ring is compressed into a groove to provide the sealing action.

Overhead cam (ohc) engine An engine with the camshaft(s) located on top of the cylinder head(s).

Overhead valve (ohv) engine An engine with the valves located in the cylinder head, but with the camshaft located in the engine block.

Oxygen sensor A device installed in the engine exhaust manifold, which senses the oxygen content in the exhaust and converts this information into an electric current. Also called a Lambda sensor.

P

Phillips screw A type of screw head having a cross instead of a slot for a corresponding type of screwdriver.

Plastigage A thin strip of plastic thread, available in different sizes, used for measuring clearances. For example, a strip of Plastigage is laid across a bearing journal. The parts are assembled and dismantled; the width of the crushed strip indicates the clearance between journal and bearing.

Plastigage

Propeller shaft The long hollow tube with universal joints at both ends that carries power from the transmission to the differential on front-engined rear wheel drive vehicles.

Proportioning valve A hydraulic control valve which limits the amount of pressure to the rear brakes during panic stops to prevent wheel lock-up.

R

Rack-and-pinion steering A steering system with a pinion gear on the end of the steering shaft that mates with a rack (think of a geared wheel opened up and laid flat). When the steering wheel is turned, the pinion turns, moving the rack to the left or right. This movement is transmitted through the track rods to the steering arms at the wheels.

Radiator A liquid-to-air heat transfer device designed to reduce the temperature of the coolant in an internal combustion engine cooling system.

Refrigerant Any substance used as a heat transfer agent in an air-conditioning system. R-12 has been the principle refrigerant for many years; recently, however, manufacturers have begun using R-134a, a non-CFC substance that is considered less harmful to the ozone in the upper atmosphere.

Rocker arm A lever arm that rocks on a shaft or pivots on a stud. In an overhead valve engine, the rocker arm converts the upward movement of the pushrod into a downward movement to open a valve.

Rotor In a distributor, the rotating device inside the cap that connects the centre electrode and the outer terminals as it turns, distributing the high voltage from the coil secondary winding to the proper spark plug. Also, that part of an alternator which rotates inside the stator. Also, the rotating assembly of a turbocharger, including the compressor wheel, shaft and turbine wheel.

Runout The amount of wobble (in-and-out movement) of a gear or wheel as it's rotated. The amount a shaft rotates "out-of-true." The out-of-round condition of a rotating part.

S

Sealant A liquid or paste used to prevent leakage at a joint. Sometimes used in conjunction with a gasket.

Sealed beam lamp An older headlight design which integrates the reflector, lens and filaments into a hermetically-sealed one-piece unit. When a filament burns out or the lens cracks, the entire unit is simply replaced.

Serpentine drivebelt A single, long, wide accessory drivebelt that's used on some newer vehicles to drive all the accessories, instead of a series of smaller, shorter belts. Serpentine drivebelts are usually tensioned by an automatic tensioner.

Serpentine drivebelt

Shim Thin spacer, commonly used to adjust the clearance or relative positions between two parts. For example, shims inserted into or under bucket tappets control valve clearances. Clearance is adjusted by changing the thickness of the shim.

Slide hammer A special puller that screws into or hooks onto a component such as a shaft or bearing; a heavy sliding handle on the shaft bottoms against the end of the shaft to knock the component free.

Sprocket A tooth or projection on the periphery of a wheel, shaped to engage with a chain or drivebelt. Commonly used to refer to the sprocket wheel itself.

Starter inhibitor switch On vehicles with an automatic transmission, a switch that prevents starting if the vehicle is not in Neutral or Park.

Strut See MacPherson strut.

T

Tappet A cylindrical component which transmits motion from the cam to the valve stem, either directly or via a pushrod and rocker arm. Also called a cam follower.

Thermostat A heat-controlled valve that regulates the flow of coolant between the cylinder block and the radiator, so maintaining optimum engine operating temperature. A thermostat is also used in some air cleaners in which the temperature is regulated.

Thrust bearing The bearing in the clutch assembly that is moved in to the release levers by clutch pedal action to disengage the clutch. Also referred to as a release bearing.

Timing belt A toothed belt which drives the camshaft. Serious engine damage may result if it breaks in service.

Timing chain A chain which drives the camshaft.

Toe-in The amount the front wheels are closer together at the front than at the rear. On rear wheel drive vehicles, a slight amount of toe-in is usually specified to keep the front wheels running parallel on the road by offsetting other forces that tend to spread the wheels apart.

Toe-out The amount the front wheels are closer together at the rear than at the front. On front wheel drive vehicles, a slight amount of toe-out is usually specified.

Tools For full information on choosing and using tools, refer to the *Haynes Automotive Tools Manual*.

Tracer A stripe of a second colour applied to a wire insulator to distinguish that wire from another one with the same colour insulator.

Tune-up A process of accurate and careful adjustments and parts replacement to obtain the best possible engine performance.

Turbocharger A centrifugal device, driven by exhaust gases, that pressurises the intake air. Normally used to increase the power output from a given engine displacement, but can also be used primarily to reduce exhaust emissions (as on VW's "Umwelt" Diesel engine).

U

Universal joint or U-joint A double-pivoted connection for transmitting power from a driving to a driven shaft through an angle. A U-joint consists of two Y-shaped yokes and a cross-shaped member called the spider.

V

Valve A device through which the flow of liquid, gas, vacuum, or loose material in bulk may be started, stopped, or regulated by a movable part that opens, shuts, or partially obstructs one or more ports or passageways. A valve is also the movable part of such a device.

Valve clearance The clearance between the valve tip (the end of the valve stem) and the rocker arm or tappet. The valve clearance is measured when the valve is closed.

Vernier caliper A precision measuring instrument that measures inside and outside dimensions. Not quite as accurate as a micrometer, but more convenient.

Viscosity The thickness of a liquid or its resistance to flow.

Volt A unit for expressing electrical "pressure" in a circuit. One volt that will produce a current of one ampere through a resistance of one ohm.

W

Welding Various processes used to join metal items by heating the areas to be joined to a molten state and fusing them together. For more information refer to the *Haynes Automotive Welding Manual*.

Wiring diagram A drawing portraying the components and wires in a vehicle's electrical system, using standardised symbols. For more information refer to the *Haynes Automotive Electrical and Electronic Systems Manual*.

Haynes Manuals – The Complete List

Title	Book No.
ALFA ROMEO	
Alfa Romeo Alfasud/Sprint (74 - 88)	0292
Alfa Romeo Alfetta (73 - 87)	0531
AUDI	
Audi 80 (72 - Feb 79)	0207
Audi 80, 90 (79 - Oct 86) & Coupe (81 - Nov 88)	0605
Audi 80, 90 (Oct 86 - 90) & Coupe (Nov 88 - 90)	1491
Audi 100 (Oct 82 - 90) & 200 (Feb 84 - Oct 89)	0907
Audi 100/A6 (May 91 - May 97)	3504
AUSTIN	
Austin/MG Maestro 1.3 & 1.6 (83 - 95)	0922
Austin/MG Metro (80 - May 90)	0718
Austin Montego 1.3 & 1.6 (84 - 94)	1066
Austin/MG Montego 2.0 (84 - 95)	1067
Mini (59 - 69)	0527
Mini (69 - Oct 96)	0646
Austin/Rover 2.0 litre Diesel Engine (86 - 93)	1857
BEDFORD	
Bedford CF (69 - 87)	0163
Bedford Rascal (86 - 93)	3015
BMW	
BMW 316, 320 & 320i (4-cyl) (75 - Feb 83)	0276
BMW 320, 320i, 323i & 325i (6-cyl) (Oct 77 - Sept 87)	0815
BMW 3-Series (Apr 91 - 96)	3210
BMW 3-Series (sohc) (83 - 91)	1948
BMW 520i & 525e (Oct 81 - June 88)	1560
BMW 525, 528 & 528i (73 - Sept 81)	0632
BMW 5-Series (sohc) (81 - 91)	1948
BMW 1500, 1502, 1600, 1602, 2000 & 2002 (59 - 77)	0240
CITROËN	
Citroën 2CV, Ami & Dyane (67 - 90)	0196
Citroën AX Petrol & Diesel (87 - 94)	3014
Citroën BX (83 - 94)	0908
Citroën C15 Van Petrol & Diesel (89 - 98)	3509
Citroën CX (75 - 88)	0528
Citroën Saxo Petrol & Diesel (96 - 98)	3506
Citroën Visa (79 - 88)	0620
Citroën Xantia Petrol & Diesel (93 - 98)	3082
Citroën XM Petrol & Diesel (89 - 98)	3451
Citroën ZX Diesel (91 - 93)	1922
Citroën ZX Petrol (91 - 94)	1881
Citroën 1.7 & 1.9 litre Diesel Engine (84 - 96)	1379
COLT	
Colt 1200, 1250 & 1400 (79 - May 84)	0600
DAIMLER	
Daimler Sovereign (68 - Oct 86)	0242
Daimler Double Six (72 - 88)	0478
FIAT	
Fiat 126 (73 - 87)	0305
Fiat 127 (71 - 83)	0193
Fiat 500 (57 - 73)	0090
Fiat Cinquecento (June 93 - 98)	3501
Fiat Panda (81 - 95)	0793
Fiat Punto (94 - 96)	3251
Fiat Regata (84 - 88)	1167
Fiat Strada (79 - 88)	0479

Title	Book No.
Fiat Tipo (88 - 91)	1625
Fiat Uno (83 - 95)	0923
Fiat X1/9 (74 - 89)	0273
FORD	
Ford Capri II (& III) 1.6 & 2.0 (74 - 87)	0283
Ford Capri II (& III) 2.8 & 3.0 (74 - 87)	1309
Ford Cortina Mk IV (& V) 1.6 & 2.0 (76 - 83)	0343
Ford Escort (75 - Aug 80)	0280
Ford Escort (Sept 80 - Sept 90)	0686
Ford Escort (Sept 90 - 97)	1737
Ford Escort Mk II Mexico, RS 1600 & RS 2000 (75 - 80)	0735
Ford Fiesta (inc. XR2) (76 - Aug 83)	0334
Ford Fiesta (inc. XR2) (Aug 83 - Feb 89)	1030
Ford Fiesta (Feb 89 - Oct 95)	1595
Ford Fiesta Petrol & Diesel (Oct 95 - 97)	3397
Ford Granada (Sept 77 - Feb 85)	0481
Ford Granada (Mar 85 - 94)	1245
Ford Mondeo (93 - 99)	1923
Ford Mondeo Diesel (93 - 96)	3465
Ford Orion (83 - Sept 90)	1009
Ford Orion (Sept 90 - 93)	1737
Ford Sierra 1.3, 1.6, 1.8 & 2.0 (82 - 93)	0903
Ford Sierra 2.3, 2.8 & 2.9 (82 - 91)	0904
Ford Scorpio (Mar 85 - 94)	1245
Ford Transit Petrol (Mk 2) (78 - Jan 86)	0719
Ford Transit Petrol (Mk 3) (Feb 86 - 89)	1468
Ford Transit Diesel (Feb 86 - 95)	3019
Ford 1.6 & 1.8 litre Diesel Engine (84 - 96)	1172
Ford 2.1, 2.3 & 2.5 litre Diesel Engine (77 - 90)	1606
FREIGHT ROVER	
Freight Rover Sherpa (74 - 87)	0463
HILLMAN	
Hillman Avenger (70 - 82)	0037
HONDA	
Honda Accord (76 - Feb 84)	0351
Honda Accord (Feb 84 - Oct 85)	1177
Honda Civic (Feb 84 - Oct 87)	1226
Honda Civic (Nov 91 - 96)	3199
HYUNDAI	
Hyundai Pony (85 - 94)	3398
JAGUAR	
Jaguar E Type (61 - 72)	0140
Jaguar MkI & II, 240 & 340 (55 - 69)	0098
Jaguar XJ6, XJ & Sovereign (68 - Oct 86)	0242
Jaguar XJ6 & Sovereign (Oct 86 - Sept 94)	3261
Jaguar XJ12, XJS & Sovereign (72 - 88)	0478
JEEP	
Jeep Cherokee Petrol (93 - 96)	1943
LADA	
Lada 1200, 1300, 1500 & 1600 (74 - 91)	0413
Lada Samara (87 - 91)	1610
LAND ROVER	
Land Rover 90, 110 & Defender Diesel (83 - 95)	3017
Land Rover Discovery Diesel (89 - 95)	3016
Land Rover Series IIA & III Diesel (58 - 85)	0529
Land Rover Series II, IIA & III Petrol (58 - 85)	0314

Title	Book No.
MAZDA	
Mazda 323 fwd (Mar 81 - Oct 89)	1608
Mazda 323 (Oct 89 - 98)	3455
Mazda 626 fwd (May 83 - Sept 87)	0929
Mazda B-1600, B-1800 & B-2000 Pick-up (72 - 88)	0267
MERCEDES-BENZ	
Mercedes-Benz 190, 190E & 190D Petrol & Diesel (83 - 93)	3450
Mercedes-Benz 200, 240, 300 Diesel (Oct 76 - 85)	1114
Mercedes-Benz 250 & 280 (68 - 72)	0346
Mercedes-Benz 250 & 280 (123 Series) (Oct 76 - 84)	0677
Mercedes-Benz 124 Series (85 - Aug 93)	3253
MG	
MGB (62 - 80)	0111
MG Maestro 1.3 & 1.6 (83 - 95)	0922
MG Metro (80 - May 90)	0718
MG Midget & AH Sprite (58 - 80)	0265
MG Montego 2.0 (84 - 95)	1067
MITSUBISHI	
Mitsubishi 1200, 1250 & 1400 (79 - May 84)	0600
Mitsubishi Shogun & L200 Pick-Ups (83 - 94)	1944
MORRIS	
Morris Ital 1.3 (80 - 84)	0705
Morris Minor 1000 (56 - 71)	0024
NISSAN	
Nissan Bluebird fwd (May 84 - Mar 86)	1223
Nissan Bluebird (T12 & T72) (Mar 86 - 90)	1473
Nissan Cherry (N12) (Sept 82 - 86)	1031
Nissan Micra (K10) (83 - Jan 93)	0931
Nissan Micra (93 - 96)	3254
Nissan Primera (90 - Oct 96)	1851
Nissan Stanza (82 - 86)	0824
Nissan Sunny (B11) (May 82 - Oct 86)	0895
Nissan Sunny (Oct 86 - Mar 91)	1378
Nissan Sunny (Apr 91 - 95)	3219
OPEL	
Opel Ascona & Manta (B Series) (Sept 75 - 88)	0316
Opel Ascona (81 - 88) (Not available in UK see Vauxhall Cavalier 0812)	3215
Opel Astra (Oct 91 - 96) (Not available in UK see Vauxhall Astra 1832)	3156
Opel Calibra (90 - 98) (See Vauxhall/Opel Calibra Book No. 3502)	
Opel Corsa (83 - Mar 93) (Not available in UK see Vauxhall Nova 0909)	3160
Opel Corsa (Mar 93 - 97) (Not available in UK see Vauxhall Corsa 1985)	3159
Opel Frontera Petrol & Diesel (91 - 98) (See Vauxhall/Opel Frontera Book No. 1985)	
Opel Kadett (Nov 79 - Oct 84)	0634
Opel Kadett (Oct 84 - Oct 91) (Not available in UK see Vauxhall Astra & Belmont 1136)	3196
Opel Omega & Senator (86 - 94) (Not available in UK see Vauxhall Carlton & Senator 1469)	3157
Opel Omega Petrol & Diesel (94 - 98) (See Vauxhall/Opel Omega Book No. 3510)	

Title	Book No.
Opel Rekord (Feb 78 - Oct 86)	0543
Opel Vectra (88 - Oct 95) (Not available in UK see Vauxhall Cavalier 1570)	3158
Opel Vectra Petrol & Diesel (95 - 98) (Not available in UK see Vauxhall Vectra 3396)	3523

PEUGEOT

Title	Book No.
Peugeot 106 Petrol & Diesel (91 - June 96)	1882
Peugeot 205 (83 - 95)	0932
Peugeot 305 (78 - 89)	0538
Peugeot 306 Petrol & Diesel (93 - 98)	3073
Peugeot 309 (86 - 93)	1266
Peugeot 405 Petrol (88 - 96)	1559
Peugeot 405 Diesel (88 - 96)	3198
Peugeot 406 Petrol & Diesel (96 - 97)	3394
Peugeot 505 (79 - 89)	0762
Peugeot 1.7/1.8 & 1.9 litre Diesel Engines (82 - 96)	0950
Peugeot 2.0, 2.1, 2.3 & 2.5 litre Diesel Engines (74 - 90)	1607

PORSCHE

Title	Book No.
Porsche 911 (65 - 85)	0264
Porsche 924 & 924 Turbo (76 - 85)	0397

PROTON

Title	Book No.
Proton (89 - 97)	3255

RANGE ROVER

Title	Book No.
Range Rover V8 (70 - Oct 92)	0606

RELIANT

Title	Book No.
Reliant Robin & Kitten (73 - 83)	0436

RENAULT

Title	Book No.
Renault 5 (72 - Feb 85)	0141
Renault 5 (Feb 85 - 96)	1219
Renault 9 & 11 (82 - 89)	0822
Renault 18 (79 - 86)	0598
Renault 19 Petrol (89 - 94)	1646
Renault 19 Diesel (89 - 95)	1946
Renault 21 (86 - 94)	1397
Renault 25 (84 - 92)	1228
Renault Clio Petrol (91 - 93)	1853
Renault Clio Diesel (91 - June 96)	3031
Renault Espace (85 - 96)	3197
Renault Laguna (94 - 96)	3252
Renault Mégane & Scénic Petrol & Diesel (96 - 98)	3395

ROVER

Title	Book No.
Rover 111 & 114 (95 - 96)	1711
Rover 213 & 216 (84 - 89)	1116
Rover 214 & 414 (89 - 96)	1689
Rover 216 & 416 (89 - 96)	1830
Rover 200 Series Petrol & Diesel (95 - 98)	3399
Rover 400 Series Petrol & Diesel (95 - 98)	3453
Rover 618, 620 & 623 (93 - 97)	3257
Rover 820, 825 & 827 (86 - 95)	1380
Rover 3500 (SD1) (76 - 87)	0365
Rover Metro (May 90 - 94)	1711

SAAB

Title	Book No.
Saab 90, 99 & 900 (79 - Oct 93)	0765
Saab 900 (Oct 93 - 98)	3512

Title	Book No.
Saab 9000 (4-cyl) (85 - 95)	1686

SEAT

Title	Book No.
Seat Ibiza & Malaga (85 - 92)	1609

SKODA

Title	Book No.
Skoda Estelle 105, 120, 130 & 136 (77 - 89)	0604
Skoda Favorit (89 - 92)	1801
Skoda Felicia Petrol & Diesel (95 - 98)	3505

SUBARU

Title	Book No.
Subaru 1600 & 1800 (Nov 79 - 90)	0995

SUZUKI

Title	Book No.
Suzuki SJ Series, Samurai & Vitara (82 - 97)	1942
Suzuki Supercarry (86 - Oct 94)	3015

TALBOT

Title	Book No.
Talbot Alpine, Solara, Minx & Rapier (75 - 86)	0337
Talbot Horizon (78 - 86)	0473
Talbot Samba (82 - 86)	0823

TOYOTA

Title	Book No.
Toyota Carina E (May 92 - 97)	3256
Toyota Corolla (fwd) (Sept 83 - Sept 87)	1024
Toyota Corolla (rwd) (80 - 85)	0683
Toyota Corolla (Sept 87 - 92)	1683
Toyota Corolla (Aug 92 - 97)	3259
Toyota Hi-Ace & Hi-Lux (69 - Oct 83)	0304

TRIUMPH

Title	Book No.
Triumph Acclaim (81 - 84)	0792
Triumph GT6 & Vitesse (62 - 74)	0112
Triumph Spitfire (62 - 81)	0113
Triumph Stag (70 - 78)	0441
Triumph TR7 (75 - 82)	0322

VAUXHALL

Title	Book No.
Vauxhall Astra (80 - Oct 84)	0635
Vauxhall Astra & Belmont (Oct 84 - Oct 91)	1136
Vauxhall Astra (Oct 91 - 96)	1832
Vauxhall/Opel Calibra (90 - 98)	3502
Vauxhall Carlton (Oct 78 - Oct 86)	0480
Vauxhall Carlton (Nov 86 - 94)	1469
Vauxhall Cavalier 1600, 1900 & 2000 (75 - July 81)	0315
Vauxhall Cavalier (81 - Oct 88)	0812
Vauxhall Cavalier (Oct 88 - Oct 95)	1570
Vauxhall Chevette (75 - 84)	0285
Vauxhall Corsa (93 - 97)	1985
Vauxhall/Opel Frontera Petrol & Diesel (91 - 98)	3454
Vauxhall Nova (83 - 93)	0909
Vauxhall/Opel Omega Petrol & Diesel (94 - 98)	3510
Vauxhall Rascal (86 - 93)	3015
Vauxhall Senator (Sept 87 - 94)	1469
Vauxhall Vectra Petrol & Diesel (95 - 98)	3396
Vauxhall/Opel 1.5, 1.6 & 1.7 litre Diesel Engines (82 - 96)	1222

VOLKSWAGEN

Title	Book No.
VW Beetle 1200 (54 - 77)	0036
VW Beetle 1300 & 1500 (65 - 75)	0039
VW Beetle 1302 & 1302S (70 - 72)	0110
VW Beetle 1303, 1303S & GT (72 - 75)	0159
VW Golf Mk 1 1.1 & 1.3 (74 - Feb 84)	0716
VW Golf Mk 1 1.5, 1.6 & 1.8 (74 - 85)	0726

Title	Book No.
VW Golf Mk 1 Diesel (78 - Feb 84)	0451
VW Golf Mk 2 (Mar 84 - Feb 92)	1081
VW Golf Mk 3 Petrol & Diesel (Feb 92 - 96)	3097
VW Jetta Mk 1 1.1 & 1.3 (80 - June 84)	0716
VW Jetta Mk 1 1.5, 1.6 & 1.8 (80 - June 84)	0726
VW Jetta Mk 1 Diesel (81 - June 84)	0451
VW Jetta Mk 2 (July 84 - 92)	1081
VW LT vans & light trucks (76 - 87)	0637
VW Passat (Sept 81 - May 88)	0814
VW Passat (May 88 - 96)	3498
VW Polo & Derby (76 - Jan 82)	0335
VW Polo (82 - Oct 90)	0813
VW Polo (Nov 90 - Aug 94)	3245
VW Polo Hatchback (95 - 98)	3500
VW Santana (Sept 82 - 85)	0814
VW Scirocco Mk 1 1.5, 1.6 & 1.8 (74 - 82)	0726
VW Scirocco (82 - 90)	1224
VW Transporter 1600 (68 - 79)	0082
VW Transporter 1700, 1800 & 2000 (72 - 79)	0226
VW Transporter with air-cooled engine (79 - 82)	0638
VW Transporter water-cooled (82 - 90)	3452
VW Vento Petrol & Diesel (Feb 92 - 96)	3097

VOLVO

Title	Book No.
Volvo 142, 144 & 145 (66 - 74)	0129
Volvo 240 Series (74 - 93)	0270
Volvo 262, 264 & 260/265 (75 - 85)	0400
Volvo 340, 343, 345 & 360 (76 - 91)	0715
Volvo 440, 460 & 480 (87 - 92)	1691
Volvo 740 & 760 (82 - 91)	1258
Volvo 850 (92 - 96)	3260
Volvo 940 (90 - 96)	3249

YUGO/ZASTAVA

Title	Book No.
Yugo/Zastava (81 - 90)	1453

TECH BOOKS

Title	Book No.
Automotive Brake Manual	3050
Automotive Carburettor Manual	3288
Automotive Diagnostic Fault Codes Manual	3472
Automotive Diesel Engine Service Guide	3286
Automotive Disc Brake Manual	3542
Automotive Electrical and Electronic Systems Manual	3049
Automotive Engine Management and Fuel Injection Systems Manual	3344
Automotive Gearbox Overhaul Manual	3473
Automotive Service Summaries Manual	3475
Automotive Timing Belt Manual - Ford	3474
Automotive Welding Manual	3053
In-Car Entertainment Manual (3rd Edition)	3363

CAR BOOKS

Title	Book No.
Automotive Fuel Injection Systems	9755
Car Bodywork Repair Manual	9864
Caravan Manual (2nd Edition)	9894
Motorcaravan Manual, The	L7322
Small Engine Repair Manual	1755
SU Carburettors	0299
Weber Carburettors (to 79)	0393

CL07.01/99

Preserving Our Motoring Heritage

< The Model J Duesenberg Derham Tourster. Only eight of these magnificent cars were ever built – this is the only example to be found outside the United States of America

Almost every car you've ever loved, loathed or desired is gathered under one roof at the Haynes Motor Museum. Over 300 immaculately presented cars and motorbikes represent every aspect of our motoring heritage, from elegant reminders of bygone days, such as the superb Model J Duesenberg to curiosities like the bug-eyed BMW Isetta. There are also many old friends and flames. Perhaps you remember the 1959 Ford Popular that you did your courting in? The magnificent 'Red Collection' is a spectacle of classic sports cars including AC, Alfa Romeo, Austin Healey, Ferrari, Lamborghini, Maserati, MG, Riley, Porsche and Triumph.

A Perfect Day Out

Each and every vehicle at the Haynes Motor Museum has played its part in the history and culture of Motoring. Today, they make a wonderful spectacle and a great day out for all the family. Bring the kids, bring Mum and Dad, but above all bring your camera to capture those golden memories for ever. You will also find an impressive array of motoring memorabilia, a comfortable 70 seat video cinema and one of the most extensive transport book shops in Britain. The Pit Stop Cafe serves everything from a cup of tea to wholesome, home-made meals or, if you prefer, you can enjoy the large picnic area nestled in the beautiful rural surroundings of Somerset.

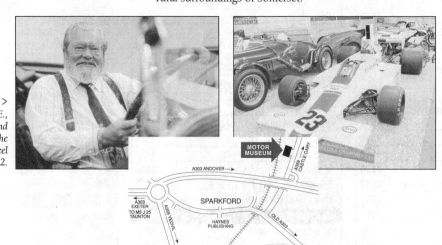

> John Haynes O.B.E., Founder and Chairman of the museum at the wheel of a Haynes Light 12.

< Graham Hill's Lola Cosworth Formula 1 car next to a 1934 Riley Sports.

The Museum is situated on the A359 Yeovil to Frome road at Sparkford, just off the A303 in Somerset. It is about 40 miles south of Bristol, and 25 minutes drive from the M5 intersection at Taunton.
Open 9.30am - 5.30pm (10.00am - 4.00pm Winter) 7 days a week, *except Christmas Day, Boxing Day and New Years Day*
Special rates available for schools, coach parties and outings Charitable Trust No. 292048